The Boxers, China,
and the World

D1598561

The Boxers, China, and the World

Edited by
Robert Bickers and R. G. Tiedemann

ROWMAN & LITTLEFIELD PUBLISHERS, INC.
Lanham • Boulder • New York • Toronto • Plymouth, UK

ROWMAN & LITTLEFIELD PUBLISHERS, INC.

Published in the United States of America
by Rowman & Littlefield Publishers, Inc.
A wholly owned subsidiary of The Rowman & Littlefield Publishing Group, Inc.
4501 Forbes Boulevard, Suite 200, Lanham, Maryland 20706
www.rowmanlittlefield.com

Estover Road, Plymouth PL6 7PY, United Kingdom

British Library Cataloguing in Publication Information Available

Library of Congress Cataloging-in-Publication Data
The Boxers, China, and the world / edited by Robert Bickers and R. G.
Tiedemann.
     p. cm.
  "These papers were prepared for a conference at the School of Oriental and
African Studies, London University, on 22-24 June 2001, on '1900: The Boxers,
China, and the World'."—Acknowledgments.
  Includes bibliographical references and index.
  ISBN-13: 978-0-7425-5394-1 (cloth : alk. paper)
  ISBN-10: 0-7425-5394-9 (cloth : alk. paper)
  ISBN-13: 978-0-7425-5395-8 (pbk. : alk. paper)
  ISBN-10: 0-7425-5395-7 (pbk. : alk. paper)
  1. China—History—Boxer Rebellion, 1899-1901. 2. Imperialism—History—
20th century. I. Bickers, Robert A. II. Tiedemann, R. G., 1941-
  DS771.B69 2007
  951'.035—dc22

                                                              2007002569

Printed in the United States of America

♾ ™ The paper used in this publication meets the minimum requirements of
American National Standard for Information Sciences—Permanence of Paper
for Printed Library Materials, ANSI/NISO Z39.48-1992.

Contents

Figures

Acknowledgments

These papers were prepared for a conference at the School of Oriental and African Studies, London University, on 22–24 June 2001, on "1900: The Boxers, China, and the World." The conference steering group comprised Robert Bickers, Rosemary Seton, Roger Thompson, Gary Tiedemann, Hans van de Ven, and Frances Wood. The selection of papers for publication was initially undertaken by Robert Bickers, Gary Tiedemann, and Hans van de Ven (who also undertook some initial editorial work on some chapters). The conference was generously supported by the Chiang Ching-kuo Foundation for International Scholarly Exchange, the British Academy's conference fund, the Universities' China Committee, and the School of Oriental and African Studies research fund. The organizers wish to express their thanks to these bodies for their support. We also wish to thank the following who presented papers: David Atwill, Timothy Barrett, Cord Eberspächer, Jane Elliott, James Flath, Susanna Hoe, Richard Horowitz, Frank H. H. King, Thoralf Klein, Susanne Kuß, Monika Lehner, Liu Tianlu, Lu Yao, Klaus Mühlhahn, Ian Nish, Régine Thiriez, and Jeffrey N. Wasserstrom, and to Bernd Martin, Susan Naquin, and Naoko Shimazu, who chaired sessions. For their help during the conference we are also grateful to Karen Greening and to Tiina Airaksinen. Robert Bickers would also like to thank the students in his Special Topic unit at the University of Bristol, Origins and Consequences of the Boxer Uprising in China, who have asked so many difficult questions about these events.

Robert Bickers
University of Bristol

R. G. Tiedemann
Centre for the Study of Christianity in China (Oxford)

Introduction

Robert Bickers

In 1900, China chose to take on imperialism by fighting a war with the world on the parched North China Plain. This book explores the causes of the Boxer Uprising and also of what is now known as the Boxer War, examines its particular, and particularly well-known, cruelties, and analyzes its impact on China, on foreign imperialism in China, and on the foreign imagination. The events of 1900 gave the world the "Boxers," the seemingly fanatical, violent xenophobes, who, believing themselves invulnerable to foreign bullets, died in the thousands in front of foreign-made guns. But 1900 also saw the aggressive foreign imperialism of the 1890s given a sharp check, and the Qing rulers of China embarked on a series of shattering reforms thereafter. As Mary C. Wright argued in 1968, 1900 was a watershed year, a "major turning point of modern Chinese history."[1] This book explores the impact of the events of 1900 on Chinese rural communities and on foreign empire building. Mostly overshadowed by the contemporaneous conflict in South Africa, Britain's biggest imperial crisis since the 1857 Sepoy Mutiny in India, the Boxer War was nonetheless an important event in the global, and globalized, history of European imperialism and in the continuing development of Japanese imperialism.

The Boxers have often been represented as a force from China's past, resisting an enforced modernity. They had little by way of opportunity to speak for themselves before their destruction, and speak to us now mostly through their contemporary foreign or indeed Chinese critics.[2] Foreign troops took no prisoners. Boxers attacked railways and telegraph lines, and believed that ritual would help them overcome industrially produced armaments. As a result they too easily found themselves a niche in the belittling of China and Chinese in the foreign imagination.[3] Their state supporters have been portrayed as opportunistic reactionaries. This volume argues instead that the Boxer War was a wholly modern episode and a wholly modern resistance to globalizing power, representing new trends in modern China and in international relations. It was also a series of local episodes, building on local particularities in many of the areas involved. The local, the national, and the international were entwined in the fabric of the Boxer months. We know, for example, that news about events in the treaty ports, and about interactions between foreigners and Chinese more generally, spread more easily and more widely than had previously been thought.[4] And Chinese observers knew what was going on overseas. They worried that their country would share the fate of Poland, which had been carved up by neighboring empires and was seemingly extinct. They watched anticolonial struggles with interest. In December 1899, Sir Robert Hart, the British national who had served as Inspector General of the Imperial Maritime Customs Service since 1861, reported with amusement a conversation with a Chinese employee who was well versed in the details of Britain's South African quagmire: He "knew the names of places—*Ma-fu-king, Kim-ba-li, Lei-teh-ze-ma-teh* [Mafeking, Kimberley, Ladysmith] . . . with numbers engaged, numbers of killed and wounded." Hart then made a serious point about that conflict: "Unless we win and dictate terms, our prestige everywhere will be done for."[5] As with the Boer republics, so would it be with China. The Eight Power "expedition"—the allied invasion of north China in late summer 1900—was the first multinational intervention in the name of "civilization," with the issues and attendant problems that have become all too familiar in the early twenty-first century. This volume also explores issues in the conduct of warfare, of occupation, of the ideologies underpinning intervention and its representation, and the representation of those challenging globalizing power. Understanding the Boxer Uprising and the Boxer War remains a pressing contemporary issue.

In the half-decade prior to 1900, the Qing court had suffered a series of humiliating impositions delivered by the aggressive imperialism of Germany, Russia, France, and Britain.[6] These had built on the mid-century advances of the British and French in particular, but had dramatically changed the treaty port landscape that had developed after the First (1839–1842) and Second (1856–1860) Opium Wars. China's brave new armies had been defeated in the 1894–1895 war with Japan over Korea, a conflict mostly fought in Manchuria, which had had a profound impact on the rest of the country. The 1895 Treaty of Shimonoseki, which ended the war, opened new ports to foreign trade and residence, permitted foreign manufacturing plants to be established in China, stripped Taiwan away from the Qing, and hobbled the state with debts to pay off the indemnity demanded by the victors. The Japanese advance whetted European appetites. The country's Manchu rulers were then boxed in by the new demands for ports, for railway concessions, and for exclusive spheres of influence, which arose as Europe's powers exported their continental competitions to China. Some demands were rebuffed—Italy's claim for an exclusive zone at Sanmen Bay in Fujian in 1899, for example—but overall the "scramble for concessions" saw new sites of European and Japanese imperialism developed in China and new forms of activity commence. Some activist imperialists did indeed assume that the hour of formal domination was drawing near.

The Qing state learned more quickly—and with more success—than usually has been credited to it, how to use the international norms of diplomacy to protect itself, but armed conflict had delivered little for the modernizing state.[7] However, on 21 June 1900 an edict was issued, in the name of the Empress Dowager Cixi, declaring that a state of war existed between the Qing and the foreign powers. The court had chosen to actively ally itself with a mass rising of mostly young, rural men who called themselves "Yihequan," the "Boxers united righteousness," and who are more familiar to us as the "Boxers."[8] Facing first floods and then drought, these men had placed their hopes for salvation in the cleansing power of a bundle of martial arts and spirit possession practices that had emerged in northwest Shandong province between 1898 and 1899. As they understood it, the alien presences in the land and their Chinese compatriots who had turned their backs on their identity by converting to Christianity had knocked the world out of kilter. To restore order and to bring on the rains, the land needed to be purged. In many instances existing local tensions and conflicts between Christian and non-Christian communities and villages—over land, over water, over participation in community life—further fed the flames. Attacks on Christians spiraled into attacks on missionaries and other foreigners.

As the movement spread north from Shandong and into the cities, foreign residents in the capital and in Tianjin began to worry about security. As they had in October 1898, in the aftermath of the empress dowager's coup that terminated the "Hundred Days reform" program, the legations in Beijing called for additional military protection, and foreign troops and marines were moved in from the coast in late May.[9] More were requested on 10 June, but this time, however, the expedition led by British Admiral Sir Edward Seymour had no authority from the court to move inland—in 1898 the Zongli yamen (which handled the Qing's foreign relations) had organized a special train to move in the 120 troops. Seymour's contingent was soon regarded as an invading force and confronted as such by state and popular forces. Tension in Beijing turned to violence as legation guards and armed foreign civilians clashed with Boxers—often only vaguely identified as such—and Qing troops. Foreign residents and thousands of Chinese Christians took refuge in the barricaded confines of the legation quarter and the Beitang, or the Northern Cathedral. The Nantang, or the Southern Cathedral, was attacked and destroyed on 13 June and large numbers of

Christians were killed. As a similar crisis developed at Tianjin, foreign forces seized the Dagu forts on 17 June. The seizure of the forts and the Seymour expedition were regarded as acts of war. Events now spiraled swiftly out of control. The Zongli yamen issued an ultimatum on 19 June requiring the legations to evacuate to the coast. Seymour's force was defeated and had to retreat. The German Minister, Baron von Ketteler, was shot dead in the street on 20 June (and foreign troops and fighters had been shooting Chinese they suspected of being Boxers). States of siege developed in Beijing, Tianjin, and in foreign minds; the court declared on 21 June that a state of war existed and officially recognized the Boxers as a legitimate militia. Violence was then legitimized. The Qing took a gamble in harnessing this mass movement to join its new armies in repulsing the foreign invasion and to drive out the foreign presence once and for all.

In response, an Eight Power allied expeditionary force was assembled. It marched on the capital and extirpated popular and state resistance. It was a short, vicious, bloody war and it changed China irrevocably. By the end of the summer huge parts of the city of Beijing lay in ruins. Tens of thousands of Chinese combatants and civilians were dead. The war was fought in the immediate aftermath of the signing of the 1899 Hague Convention on warfare, which was completely disregarded.[10] Foreign columns spread out into the north Chinese countryside to "punish" "Boxer" cities, towns and villages.[11] The diplomatic quarter of Beijing had undergone a fifty-five-day siege; less well-remembered, because far fewer of the besieged were foreigners, was the parallel siege of Beijing's Northern Cathedral. The foreign quarter in the port city of Tianjin had been besieged for a month; the city of Harbin was cut off from 27 June until Russian forces lifted the siege on 22 July. The court fled to the northwest and foreign troops paraded through the palaces of the Manchus and systematically and greedily looted what they found. To China had come German, Russian, and Japanese troops. Punjabi cavalry from India, Gurkhas from Nepal, U.S. Marines, and African American cavalry, as well as Austro-Hungarian, French, and Italian soldiers were involved. The recently created British-officered Weihaiwei Regiment of Chinese infantry saw action in Tianjin. In Europe, in North America, and in their empires, newspaper readers devoured accounts of the sieges, the battles on the plain, atrocities committed against Christians and missionaries (and then of those committed against the Chinese), and the looting. Before the special correspondents made their way out to the scene and their reports made their way back, old accounts and images were reprinted in illustrated journals and over-hasty obituaries appeared in the British press. Faked newsreel footage of Boxer attacks was filmed in a London suburb. It was the second armed conflict to make it onto cinema screens as it unfolded (the first was the Spanish-American War of 1898).

In the war's aftermath came a war of words. Missionary triumphalism clashed with the sarcastic sallies of Mark Twain, who lampooned the apologias for looting given by American missionary William Scott Ament.[12] British diplomats smothered their deeds with the imperial poetry of Rudyard Kipling, preserving a bullet-pocked "lest we forget" wall in the once-besieged legation for decades after the events, while Cambridge scholar G. Lowes Dickinson, masquerading as "John Chinaman," quietly pricked the vanity of "civilization's" China conquest in his slim anonymous volume, *Letters from John Chinaman* (1901).[13] Failing initially to see through the satire, the three-time U.S. Democratic presidential candidate William Jennings Bryan took the book seriously enough to counter it with some *Letters to a Chinese Official; Being a Western View of Eastern Civilization* (1906), which contained a very tart Western view. Editorials in the Indian vernacular press saw the cause of what they characterized as a popular patriotic movement lying squarely in the aggressive new imperialism of the European powers. The Boxers sharpened debates and polarized opinions the reading world over. As Chris Bayly demonstrates here, its "intertextuality," the ways in which the events found expression across a polyglot range of newspapers and books published by colonizer and colonized, imperialist and anti-imperialist, made it a distinctively global episode and a subject for debate and dissent.

A military struggle continued in China after 1900, culminating in the Russo-Japanese war of 1904–1905 and the defeat of St. Petersburg's forces.[14] Struggles of a different sort began immediately over the meanings of 1900, the origins of the Boxer movement, and the level of official patronage it had received. Qing rule was preserved, however, and all participants eventually accepted that the high tide of aggressive imperialism had passed.[15] The Boxers had, despite themselves, saved China. It only remained, in September 1901, to sign a peace treaty, the Boxer Protocol, which outlined the reparations and restitutions to be made. Apology missions were dispatched, memorials were erected, a two-year prohibition on munitions imports was agreed to, punishments for pro-Boxer officials were itemized, and a staggering sum was extracted from China by way of indemnity and compensation losses.[16] The Boxer Indemnity was to bring its own problems for China, but the Protocol marked off and closed the events of 1899–1900.[17] China could move on.

THE BOXERS IN WORLD HISTORY

We might best start a search for an understanding of the place of the Boxer War in the global history of imperialism by looking at how it was seen by its foreign participants and by its foreign observers. As regards the Britons encamped in the legation quarter in June 1900, what emerges most strikingly is that they were self-conscious actors in an imperial episode. They knew the script and needed no prompting. Parallels with the Sepoy Mutiny of 1857 in India were not only drawn in the aftermath of the uprising and war, as C. A. Bayly shows in this volume, but also as they happened. Besieged Britons performed the Siege of Lucknow garbed in Chinese dress. As they sat and sewed, besieged foreign women in Beijing listened to one of their number read aloud an account of the eighty-seven-day siege that occurred during the Sepoy Mutiny of 1857:

> We had often spoken of this remarkable siege before, wondering as we passed through certain experiences, whether these others had had similar trials or mercies. So now this gave us a chance to compare. As the one read, the others would often interrupt her, renaming the persons or the places of the story, as they seemed familiar—"Why that is Major Conger or Sir Claude [MacDonald, the British Minister at Peking]," or "Call that Tungchou or Ch'ien Men." Never was history so interesting.[18]

Twenty-five-year-old C. C. A. Kirke, a student interpreter (a trainee consul) at the British legation, noted in his diary that his companion Lancelot Giles was on 27 June, the eighth day of the siege, "reading Tennyson's 'Siege of Lucknow,' with appropriate comments."[19] "Ever upon the topmost roof," runs the poem's recurring refrain, the "banner of England blew." Giles's photographs form a key visual record of the episode and he captioned one postsiege photograph of the British legation gate with Tennyson's words.[20] Lucknow had of course an optimistic trajectory, as that siege was relieved. It was better for those in the legation quarter to think of that episode than of Cawnpore (Kanpur), where no Britons survived, but thinking of Cawnpore lay behind the refusal of the legations to evacuate to the coast as demanded by the court on 19 June—those who had accepted safe passage in 1857 had been tricked and slaughtered.[21] If Tennyson supplied a means of conceptualizing the experience of siege, Rudyard Kipling's poem "Recessional" supplied the language through which remembering was structured (and as Bayly shows in this volume, provided one Indian critic—the poet Rabindranath Tagore—with a pungent target). The refrain at the heart of this 1897 poem—"Lest we forget, lest we forget!"—a call for caution, vigilance, and the responsibility of imperial power, prompted by the celebrations for Queen Victoria's jubilee that year, took on a life of its own as a memorializing shorthand. This began almost from the first instance, when British survivors set apart a corner of the bullet-pocked legation compound as a memorial, choosing a site at which "Lest we forget" had been inscribed onto the stone.[22] Ceremony thereafter in the foreign communities in the treaty ports in China focused around "Recessional" even into the 1930s.[23]

James L. Hevia has argued elsewhere that for Protestant missionaries, the bloodletting of the Boxer year and its aftermath served formally to incorporate their China story into the history of Protestant Christianity.[24] Kipling and Tennyson's secular language of empire clearly served the same function. British India had long supplied models of practice and interpretation for the British in China, as well as an empire vocabulary (tiffin, bund), personnel (British Indian Army troops, Sikh policemen for the Chinese treaty ports), and of course opium and finance. British India set a standard and offered a model.[25] The Boxer Uprising was the British China enterprise's Indian "mutiny," and the Legation Siege was their Lucknow. While it was undeniably an event in China and in Chinese history, it was also an event in the history of the British imperial imagination. Events in South Africa in 1900 certainly gripped the attention of Britain's domestic audience more completely, but the China episode garnered a full share of international attention. It was an event in European history, in Austria-Hungary, in France, in Germany, Russia, and, as Chris Bayly and Anand Yang show in their contributions to this volume, it was an event in subaltern histories too. What this discursive predisposition smothered, however, was an understanding of the Boxer conflict as a war between the Qing and foreign imperialism. It became a revolt, rather than a war. It has taken almost a century for English-language scholarship to start to unpick that problem. But either as war or revolt, and more than at any other point in the nineteenth century, China in 1900 was a field of action fully incorporated into a globalizing world.

THE HISTORIOGRAPHY OF THE BOXERS

Most historical work on the events has been located within either the historiography of China or of international imperialism. With his *Boxer Catastrophe* (1955), Chester Tan was the first serious scholar to look at the Boxer conflict after George Nye Steiger in 1927. Steiger had proposed the idea that the Boxers themselves were in origin an official militia, sponsored by the state and its provincial officials, and that their movement did not stem from populist, or sectarian, roots.[26] Tan used newly available Chinese materials to explore the Boxers and also laid out the high politics very clearly. The popular representation of the Boxers dominated understandings of events, however, notably through British journalist Peter Fleming's racy account, *The Siege at Peking* (1959), and the 1963 film of the events, *55 Days at Peking*. In the popular imagination, the Boxer episode focused entirely on the Beijing siege, where it seemed easy enough to distinguish right from wrong and good from bad. The siege also provided a clear narrative structure. The fuzziness offered by the provincial origins of the rising, and its provincial passages, the events at Tianjin and elsewhere in China, and the immediate aftermath of the Eight Power invasion were, not surprisingly, neglected. The clear exception, discussed in this volume by Roger Thompson, was provided by events at Taiyuan, where it was widely believed that foreign missionaries were tricked into capture and then murdered in public at the orders, and in the presence, of the Shanxi governor Yuxian. This narrative too owes something to the 1857 rising in India and accounts of the Cawnpore massacre, as it does to Protestant martyrology.

For retired colonial service official Sir Victor Purcell, who took up a Cambridge University Lectureship in Far Eastern History in 1949 and who published *The Boxer Uprising: A Background Study* in 1963, the pressing issue was an understanding of Chinese nationalism and the need for an accommodation with it. Purcell, who had worked in Chinese affairs in the British Malayan Civil Service from 1921–1946, had been a fierce critic of the British imperial state's handling of Malaya and the Chinese communist insurgency there between 1948–1960. Purcell saw lessons to be learned from 1900 for use in the Malayan crisis and for Chinese nationalism more generally. He also made full use of new documentary and oral history materials collected in the People's Republic of China (PRC) after 1949, collaborating with Jerome Ch'en, who also published materials about the rising.[27] For Purcell, the key research questions lay in understanding when the Boxers turned from an antidynastic to a prodynastic movement and in clarifying the genealogy of a movement he saw as having longer-term roots in the world of Chinese sectarianism. It proved difficult to find any convincing evidence, but Purcell found refuge in the conclusion that "Secret societies are, by definition, secret," and so noted that hard evidence might therefore be hard to find.[28] The premise underlying these approaches, which were widely accepted, is now given short shrift. Purcell was entirely wrong in framing the episode in this way, and he has been largely ignored in the more recent literature on the Boxers. He deserves to be understood, however, as a writer exploring how the world ought to adjust to Chinese nationalism after 1949. Joseph Esherick's 1987 study *The Origins of the Boxer Uprising* was in part an exercise in bringing to bear on Chinese history conceptual innovations in the social sciences; it was also a work still informed by the anti-imperialist politics of the Vietnam War era, notably in its robust hostility toward the foreign missionary enterprise in China. Offering a detailed exploration of the localities from which the Boxers emerged, it analyzed the events and pressures which generated the movement in Shandong.

Esherick's work did not follow the Boxers or their ideas and practices out of the province, however. In *History in Three Keys*, Paul Cohen did explore this question. After all, Esherick's stress on local particularities prompted questions about the ways in which such local developments could find a ready audience in the heterogeneous socioeconomic regions through which the movement spread like wildfire in 1900. Cohen took his analysis as far as was possible, given the evidence, down to the individual lived experience of the Boxer, and in particular to the young men and boys who made the movement and who died as a result. As well as an exploration of the ways in which history can be written and imagined, the volume was also an understated—but nonetheless robust—defense of history against the wilder claims of postmodernism. Up to a point, the Boxers have rarely been studied in the English-language scholarship entirely for their own sake. Nonetheless, both Esherick and Cohen took the Boxers themselves seriously, as seriously in fact, although with more nuance, than researchers in the PRC. So discredited has the topic been for many historians in China and in Taiwan, as a result of the highly politicized attention accorded to it during most of the decades after the establishment of the PRC in 1949, that the young men who acted in 1900 perhaps get less attention then they would otherwise be due.

More recent foreign monographs have returned to high politics and military minutiae or have looked at representations of the events.[29] A scattering of papers over the last few decades by Jerome Ch'en, Mark Elvin, and Bruce Doar, as well as by those represented in this volume, have also thrown new light on discrete issues in the debate.[30] Outside the China field historians of the British empire in particular have examined the balance of power politics that accompanied the growing tensions of the scramble for concessions in the 1890s, the Boxer War, and its aftermath.[31] The recent return to diplomatic history has seen important new work on the high politics of east Asia and northeast Asia at the turn of the century. This volume brings together new work in most of these fields and argues that scholars of modern east Asian history and of the history of imperialism have much to offer each other in understanding the internationalized events of 1900 and, by extension, still much to offer in understanding the course of modern east Asian history.

The first two chapters in this collection offer new perspectives on the Boxers in various localities; most of the existing literature concentrates on the Boxers' origins and on Shandong province, where, as Joseph Esherick argued, "it all began."[32] As has been observed, a comprehensive analysis of the origins of the movement in the specific particularities of northwest Shandong's society does not provide an explanation for why young men elsewhere so eagerly adopted Boxer practices in 1899–1900, nor does it help us understand why local elites encouraged the movement. Henrietta Harrison explores the roots and pattern of violence in Shanxi. Existing narratives saddled Governor Yuxian with a great deal of responsibility for events in the province, but Harrison's analysis of the motivation and force behind mobilization concludes that "the demand for righteousness and the preservation of the moral order was clearly at the heart of the Boxer activities."[33] R. G. Tiedemann also offers a further corrective, moving the portrayal of missionaries away from a sometimes caricatured close alliance of "Bible and [imperialist] flag" before 1900, whereby missionaries allied their interests very closely to those of foreign aggressors, notably the new German presence in Shandong after 1897. Like Harrison, Tiedemann locates Catholic missionaries and their communities in Chinese localities, and he argues instead that it is necessary to remember that Catholic evangelization was a supranational movement, not, for example, in Shandong, a German movement.[34] Catholic communities participated in the violent competition for scarce resources on the North China Plain. Their foreign missionaries provided orthodox social leadership, but also less routine access to influence, technology, and contacts, which often proved crucial during the violence of 1900.

Roger Thompson delves further into the question of Yuxian, the so-called "Butcher of Shansi [Shanxi]." Post-Boxer accounts generated a powerful narrative in which the provincial governor, who had been moved from Shandong in December 1899 in response to foreign diplomatic pressure, reflecting a belief that he had sponsored the early development of the Shandong Boxers, took a cold-blooded revenge. Yuxian, appointed to the Shanxi post in March 1900, is charged with having personally supervised the execution of forty-four foreigners—missionaries and their families—at his official residence in the city of Taiyuan. As an image of "Chinese" cruelty, the Taiyuan massacre has not been bettered.[35] Thompson roots the portrayal of the event in Protestant narrative making, in which nineteenth-century versions of *Foxe's Book of Martyrs* played a crucial structural and understanding role. Its easy acceptance can also be seen as owing something to portrayals of the Cawnpore massacre. He then also explores in detail the panic and hysteria which gripped Taiyuan, as rumors swept the city that armed Catholic bands were about to attack. One key general point both Harrison and Thompson make, and which has also been examined by R. G. Tiedemann, is the role of Catholic fighters, sometimes with foreign priests leading them, in the developing conflict, both in defensive and offensive terms.[36] The Boxers held no monopoly on violence in north China. Thompson also reminds us, crucially, that by the time of the "massacre" China was at war, and that a multinational expedition led by Admiral Seymour was attempting to make what looked like an offensive attack on the imperial capital. Yuxian and his subordinates acted to try and maintain order in Taiyuan and to prepare their province to support resistance against the enemy. Yuxian was certainly in the militant camp, but his actions as governor in Shanxi were rational under the circumstances.

The foreign forces entered Beijing on 14 July 1900, and over the following months "pacified" the city and then, through large-scale punitive expeditions, many of the troubled areas of north China. The court fled to Xi'an, leaving the provincial viceroy Li Hongzhang to lead the negotiation of a peace treaty to resolve the conflict. In the immediate aftermath of the entrance of Punjabi troops through the city's Water Gate, however, the foreign forces ransacked the city thoroughly and mostly shamelessly. Anand Yang's chapter explores the reflections on the Boxer campaign of an Indian Army soldier, Gadhadhar Singh—a soldier's soldier, in Yang's estimation, but also a nuanced critic of events and the horrors he saw. His account contrasts sharply with that of his British commanding officer and the memoir of an elite Indian participant in the campaign.[37] Through Singh's account Yang identifies in China what C. A. Bayly identifies in the vernacular newspaper editorials in India: a nascent sense of pan-Asian sympathy. As do most participants, Singh also touches on loot. The Boxer War was as noteworthy for the looted material that came out of China as the Second Opium War, which culminated in 1860 with the seizure and destruction of the Summer Palace at Beijing. The holdings of many overseas museums clearly have a Boxer War provenance, although as James L. Hevia shows in this volume, it is often a muted one.[38] The contributions of Hevia and Benjamin Middleton explore the structure of systematic looting after the siege of the legations in Beijing and its political aftermath. Hevia outlines the "carnival of loot" that ensued, in which all participated. Anxieties were certainly raised by the issue of looting. Troops had fought their way to Beijing "to exterminate this demon" the "savage and sanguinary" Chinese enemy, "*not imitate him,*" declared the *North China Herald*, but as Hevia shows, these were anxieties more about the racialized boundaries between "civilization" and "barbarism" than the widespread violations of the Hague Conventions that looting represented. Middleton explores the way in which the Japanese Army's high-level involvement in looting was exposed by the press in the winter of 1901–1902. Domestic critics of Japanese imperialism used the affair to castigate the government, and the stain on the army's reputation was long lasting. Here again, debates on civilization and barbarism were also in the fore.

Less controversially, "civilization" and "modernity" were also represented in the work of the Tientsin Provisional Government (TPG), explored here by Lewis Bernstein, which administered the Chinese city for twenty-five months from July 1900 to August 1902. The TPG perpetuated the multinational collaboration that had characterized the Eight Power invasion. The city had been cruelly wasted by the war and restoring order was a key task. As Bernstein shows, and as Ruth Rogaski has further explored, the TPG embarked on an ambitious public hygiene program, physically transforming the city.[39] At Beijing, the quarter housing the foreign legations was declared, in the protocol, "especially reserved for their use and placed under their exclusive control, in which Chinese shall not have the right to reside, and which may be made defensible." The site was physically transformed and also permanently garrisoned with foreign troops.[40] At Tianjin, however, the physical changes were in the destruction of walls and physical boundaries, opening up the city. Neither city was the same after the events of 1900, but the transformations took differing forms.

Bayly and Otte explore the international theme, looking at the reception of the events in India and in the chambers of power in London, and show how intertwined the episode was in European, imperialist, and global anti-imperialist politics, discourse, and imaginations. Hevia's "carnival of loot" contrasts here with what Bayly describes as the "carnival of violence" unleashed by the Boxer Uprising. Information flowed swiftly across the world, through the new technologies which linked up centers and peripheries and joined together, in an increasingly uncentered fashion, the global discourse on the rights and wrongs of the new imperialism and its enemies in China. Where technology failed to get information fast enough, rumor (of the destruction of the legations and the massacre of the foreigners at Beijing), forgery (the London-filmed newsreels) followed, or substitutions were published, as old accounts of older China wars were rushed off the press. For all the frenzy, and for all the violence and activity on the ground, T. G. Otte reminds readers of the high politics and languid administration of empire. This chapter charts the high-level debates within British government about the crisis and reminds us that the subaltern view needs always be placed in context alongside the elite.

While Singh slogged his way to Beijing, the British prime minister, Lord Salisbury, retired to his country house for the summer and with his colleagues worked through the diplomatic maneuvers that have until recently attracted less attention than is necessary. Otte also shows how the Boxer War forced policy makers in Britain to think more globally than they had done and to guard against a repeat in China or elsewhere, which had the potential to cause European conflict.

In his chapter, Paul A. Cohen takes us back to the Boxers themselves. Harrison, Thompson, and Tiedemann all place the Boxers firmly in their local and logical contexts, in their villages and communities with their concerns, tensions, and rivalries. Cohen explicitly engages further with what can help observers in the twenty-first century understand the Boxers. Over one hundred years of misrepresentation obscures the view, and neither Hollywood, nor the Legation Siege, nor the politics of history help such an understanding. A key point here is to remember that the magicoreligious world of the Boxer could find many parallels in that of the Christian, Chinese, or foreign. The Boxers, as this volume shows, had no monopoly on violence, and they had no monopoly on magicoreligious belief. While there has been a public retreat from the mainstream racist caricaturing of Chinese that was commonly held by foreign participants in, and observers of, the Boxer Uprising and War, the Boxers themselves are still too easily sidelined as exotics. It is fitting then to conclude the volume—which aims to normalize our understanding of what happened in China in 1899–1900 as a war and as an uprising, and to outline its globalized impact and context—with an essay which aims to "humanize" the Boxers themselves.

The centenary of the Boxer events was marked by conferences in China and overseas (including the 2001 conference in London for which these papers were prepared), and also by the publication or republication of numerous popular histories.[41] The Vatican canonized 120 martyrs on 1 October 2000; eighty-three of them were casualties of the Boxer violence, Chinese and foreign. The events themselves linger on in overseas memories, though it is the Legation Siege or missionary fates that mostly find an audience there. As James L. Hevia has shown in his work on the Oberlin Arch controversy, finding a balance between remembering the foreign and Chinese, and Christian and non-Christian dead, has not proved easy.[42] Aside from being in what can only be described as a romantic fascination with the events of the siege and as bit part players in the continuing diplomatic imbroglio between the Vatican and the PRC, the Boxers are to all intents and purposes dead. Passersby strolling in the Mall in London are not likely to notice the memorial there to Royal Marine Light Infantry troops who died in China and in South Africa—a monument that accords an equal symbolic weight to the two campaigns. If they were to look closely they would see British troops in the act of killing Chinese soldiers at the siege of Tianjin, a stark but telling image for a London street.

At the start of the twenty-first century, however, understanding the Boxers and fixing their meaning remains a live issue in China. On 11 January 2006, Zhongshan University Professor Yuan Weishi published an article in *Bingdian* (Freezing Point), a weekly supplement to *Zhongguo Qingnian bao* (China Youth Daily), criticizing what he saw as distorted representations in school textbooks of China's nineteenth-century encounter with foreign imperialism.[43] Yuan was clear in his belief that there was much bitter truth to remember and to learn from, but he argued that a rational understanding of the past, and a rational assessment of historical actors, was now necessary to underpin China's successful engagement with the world. School history textbooks were stuck in the past. Hailing the Boxers as patriotic heroes, glossing over their violence, and evading the problems raised by their beliefs would only perpetuate misunderstandings and fuel xenophobia. Barbarity, he argued, was not revolution. Yuan drew a clear parallel with the ongoing controversy in China over Japanese history textbooks, some of which it was argued misrepresented the scale and violence of the twentieth-century Japanese assault on China.[44] Within two weeks *Freezing Point* had been closed down for a period of "re-organization," and a China Youth League Central Propaganda Department announcement strongly criticized what it described as an attempt to "vindicate the criminal acts by the imperialist powers in China," which "seriously distorted historical facts." When the weekly resumed publication on 1 March 2006, it did so with a lead article attacking the premise, details, and conclusions of Yuan's essay.[45] The Boxers, it argued,

> had many flaws, and they were limited by virtue of their class and the era. But it must be pointed out that the overall xenophobic nature of the Boxers contained the ideas of national revolution within the historical limitations of the peasant class, and it is also the primitive model of how the Chinese people can resist the foreign imperialist invasion.

This dispute has parallels with other episodes, where historians in China have moved beyond the bounds of what was politically acceptable as they revisited the history of the nineteenth and twentieth centuries in the post-Mao era.[46] The new Chinese nationalism and the issue of relations with Japan clearly complicate the "rational" assessment of the past that Yuan Weishi and others wish to see normalized.

The Boxers then remain alive in politics, as they do in history. What this volume demonstrates primarily, aside from the continuing richness of the work that is being undertaken on the events in north China in 1899–1900, is the need to normalize our understanding of the place and context of Chinese history. Understanding global history requires an understanding of China's role, but still too often accounts of the history of European and American imperialism and colonialism evade the China question. This event, so obscured by the fog of romance or of politics, and which seems so quintessentially an event in and of China, was clearly nothing of the sort. The Boxer Uprising and the Boxer War were incidents inextricably tied into the world of 1899–1900, of global developments in imperial thought and practice, and in anti-imperial critique. Understanding the Boxer episode helps an understanding of the modern world of 1900, of its technologies, ideologies, and cruelties, and how these came to spark an internationalized conflict in north China villages, towns, and cities, and debate in newspapers, literary reviews, and chancelleries across the globe.

NOTES

1. In her introduction to Mary Clabaugh Wright, ed., *China in Revolution: The First Phase, 1900–1913* (New Haven: Yale University Press, 1968), 3. The single best narrative of the entire episode is Paul A. Cohen, *History in Three Keys: The Boxers as Event, Experience, and Myth* (New York: Columbia University Press, 1997), part 1, "The Boxer Uprising: A Narrative History," 14–56. The most comprehensive series of bibliographies of Chinese and foreign language sources and scholarship on the events of 1899–1900 can be found in Su Weizhi and Liu Tianlu, eds., *Yihetuan yanjiu yibai nian* [A century of Boxer studies] (Jinan: Qilu shushe, 2000).

2. The major exception to the fact that most of what we can find out about the Boxers comes through critical contemporary reporting came through fieldwork projects (principally in 1960 and 1965–1966, with follow-up visits in the 1980s) undertaken by historians from Shandong University, which sought to elicit testimonies from rural survivors of the Boxer era. These materials have received their fullest publication in Lu Yao et al., eds., *Shandong daxue Yihetuan diaocha ziliao huibian* [Collection of Shandong University survey materials on the Boxers], 2 vols. (Jinan: Shandong daxue chubanshe, 2000). On this initiative and its wider context, see also Luke S. K. Kwong, "Oral History in China: A Preliminary Review," *Oral History Review* 20, nos. 1–2 (1992), 23–50. The Boxers are mostly known in China today as the *Yihetuan*, "militia united in righteousness," a term that started to be used in late 1899 as a way of seeking or conferring legitimacy for their actions. For an explanation of the terms see Cohen, *History in Three Keys*, 16–17.

3. Colin Mackerras, *Western Images of China* (Hong Kong: Oxford University Press, 1989); Robert Bickers, *Britain in China: Community, Culture and Colonialism, 1900–49* (Manchester: Manchester University Press, 1999), chapter 2, "China in the British Imagination," 22–66.

4. Henrietta Harrison, "Newspapers and Nationalism in Rural China, 1890–1929," *Past and Present* 166 (2000): 181–204. See also James A. Flath, *The Cult of Happiness: Nianhua, Art, and History in Rural North China* (Seattle: University of Washington Press, 2004).

5. Chen Xiafei and Han Rongfang, eds., *Archives of China's Imperial Maritime Customs: Confidential Correspondence between Robert Hart and James Duncan Campbell, 1874–1907*, volume III (Beijing: Foreign Languages Press, 1990), Hart to J. D. Campbell, 17 December 1899, 450.

6. The most comprehensive surveys at present remain John K. Fairbank, "The Creation of the Treaty System," in *The Cambridge History of China, 10: Late Ch'ing, 1800–1911, Part 1*, ed. John K. Fairbank (Cambridge: Cambridge University Press, 1978), 213–63; and two chapters in John K. Fairbank and Liu Kwang-ching, eds., *The Cambridge History of China, Vol. 11, Late Ch'ing, 1800–1911, Part 2* (Cambridge: Cambridge University Press, 1980): Immanuel C. Y. Hsü, "Late Ch'ing Foreign Relations, 1866–1905," 70–141; Yen-p'ing Hao and Wang Erhmin, "Changing Chinese Views of Western Relations, 1840–95," 142–201.

7. Richard S. Horowitz, "Central Power and State Making: The Zongli Yamen and Self-Strengthening in China" (unpublished PhD diss., Harvard University, 1998); Jennifer Rudolph, "Negotiating Power and Navigating Change in the Qing: The Zongli Yamen, 1861–1901" (unpublished PhD diss., University of Washington, 1999).

8. The key texts for an understanding of the origins of the movement and its trajectory are Joseph W. Esherick, *The Origins of the Boxer Uprising* (Berkeley: University of California Press, 1987), and Cohen, *History in Three Keys*.

9. *Times*, 8 October 1898, 7.

10. Technically the convention did not come into effect until 4 September 1900. China was a signatory, but was not able to ratify until 21 November 1904, and so was technically not a contracting party, and was not accorded the protection of the convention.

11. A good survey is in James L. Hevia, *English Lessons: The Pedagogy of Imperialism in Nineteenth-Century China* (Durham, N.C.: Duke University Press, 2003), 220–29. On the German contribution, see Sabine Dabringhaus, "An Army on Vacation? The German War in China (1900/1901)," in *Anticipating Total War: The German and American Experiences, 1871–1914*, ed. Manfred F. Boemeke, Roger Chickering, and Stig Förster (Cambridge: Cambridge University Press, 1999), 459–76.

12. Mark Twain, "To the Person Sitting in Darkness," *North American Review* 172 (1901): 161–76 and "To My Missionary Critics," *North American Review* 172 (1901): 520–34. See also Gilbert Reid, "The Ethics of Loot," *Forum* 31 (1901): 581–86 and "The Ethics of the Last War," *Forum* 32 (1902): 446–55.

13. G. Lowes Dickinson, *Letters from John Chinaman* (London: R. Brinley Johnson, 1901).

14. On the pre-1904 phase of the Russian presence see George Alexander Lensen, *The Russo-Chinese War* (Tokyo: Sophia University, 1967); on the war itself and its international character and impact, see John W. Steinberg, Bruce W. Menning, David Schimmelpenninck van der Oye, David Wolff, and Shinji Yokote, eds., *The Russo-Japanese War in Global Perspective: World War Zero* (Brill: Leiden, 2005).

15. On post-Boxer reforms see the papers collected as Roger R. Thompson, ed., "The Lessons of Defeat: Transforming the Qing State after the Boxer War," in *Modern Asian Studies* 37, no. 4 (2003): 769–862.

16. On the Protocol and negotiations see John S. Kelly, *A Forgotten Conference: The Negotiations at Peking, 1900–1901* (Geneva: Droz, 1963), and Hevia, *English Lessons*, 242–250.

17. On its history see Frank H. H. King, "The Boxer Indemnity—'Nothing but Bad,'" *Modern Asian Studies* 40, no. 3 (2006): 663–90.

18. Mary Gamewell (1848–1906), an American Methodist missionary, quoted in A. H. Mateer, *Siege Days: Personal Experiences of American Women and Children during the Peking Siege* (New York: F. Ravell & Co., 1903), 377. I owe this reference to Susanna Hoe, *Women at the Siege: Peking 1900* (Oxford: Holo Books, Women's History Press, 2000), 262–63.

19. Kirke papers, diary, 27 June 1900, private collection. The poem is "The Defence of Lucknow," first published in 1879 in *The Nineteenth Century*.

20. Australian National University Library, the Giles-Pickford Photographic Collection, album 2 page 1, photograph 1–2, "British Legation—Main Gate," image 2233396. Giles's diary of the siege was published as *The Siege of the Peking Legations: A Diary*, edited by Leslie R. Marchant (Nedlands: University of Western Australia Press, 1970).

21. "We were all dead against it," wrote Giles in his diary, "having regard to the historical precedent of Cawnpore. Some days later (I know not on what authority) we heard that the Boxers had actually planned to blow up the boats we should have used on the canal." Giles, *The Siege of the Peking Legations*, 120–21. There was no truth in the rumor that Sir Claude MacDonald, the British minister at Peking during the events, had experienced, as a child, the Siege of Lucknow, but it was true that his father had escaped from Neemuch in 1857 and organized an ad hoc antirising unit; Hoe, *Women in the Siege*, 105; Rev. W. Forsyth, *In the Shadows of Cairngorm: Chronicles of the United Parishes of Abernethy and Kincardine* (Inverness: The Northern Coun-

ties Publishing Company Ltd, 1900), chapter XXXII, <www.electricscotland.com/history/cairngorm/32.htm> (12 May 2006).

22. The poem is of course a warning about the threat of the imperialism of the Germans—the "lesser breeds without the law."

23. Bickers, *Britain in China*, 107.

24. James L. Hevia, "Leaving a Brand on China: Missionary Discourse in the Wake of the Boxer Movement," *Modern China* 18, no. 3 (1992): 321.

25. Bickers, *Britain in China*, 76–77, 91–92, 106–8.

26. George Nye Steiger, *China and the Occident: The Origin and Development of the Boxer Movement* (New Haven: Yale University Press, 1927).

27. Purcell's *Memoirs of a Malayan Official* (London: Cassell, 1965) provides an insight into the thinking of a figure who stood awkwardly always a little out of the official mainstream.

28. Victor Purcell, *The Boxer Uprising: A Background Study* (Cambridge: Cambridge University Press, 1963).

29. Lanxin Xiang, *The Origins of the Boxer War: A Multinational Study* (London: Routledge, 2003); Jane Elliott, *Some Did It for Civilisation, Some Did It for Their Countries: A Revised View of the Boxer War* (Hong Kong: Chinese University of Hong Kong Press, 2002).

30. Jerome Ch'en, "The Nature and Characteristics of the Boxer Movement: A Morphological Study," *Bulletin of the School of Oriental Studies* 23, no. 2 (1960): 287–308, and "The Origin of the Boxers," in *Studies in the Social History of China and South East Asia*, ed. Jerome Ch'en and Nicholas Tarling (Cambridge: Cambridge University Press, 1970), 57–84; Mark Elvin, "Mandarins and Millenarians: Reflections on the Boxer Uprising of 1899–1900," *Journal of the Anthropological Society of Oxford* 10, no. 3 (1979): 115–38; Bruce Doar, "The Boxers and Chinese Drama: Questions of Interaction," *Papers on Far Eastern History*, no. 29 (1984): 91–118; R. G. Tiedemann, "Boxers, Christians and the Culture of Violence in North China," *The Journal of Peasant Studies* 25, no. 4 (1998): 150–60; David Schimmelpenninck van der Oye, "Russia's Ambivalent Response to the Boxers," *Cahiers du monde russe* 41, no. 1 (2000): 57–78.

31. T. G. Otte, *The China Question: Great Power Rivalry and British Isolation, 1894–1905* (Oxford: Oxford University Press, 2007).

32. Esherick, *Origins of the Boxer Uprising*, title of chapter 1.

33. See Harrison, this volume.

34. Esherick, *Origins of the Boxer Uprising*, chapter 3, "Imperialism for Christ's Sake," 68–95.

35. Notions of the propensity for "cruelty" of "the Chinese" were integral to many Western presentations of the "Chinese character" and Chinese society. Arthur Smith found a level of cruelty and indifference to suffering "probably not to be matched in any other civilised country": see Arthur H. Smith, *Chinese Characteristics* (Shanghai: printed and published at the "North-China Herald," 1890), 213.

36. Tiedemann, "Boxers, Christians and the Culture of Violence," 150–60.

37. Susanne Hoeber Rudolph and Lloyd I. Rudolph with Mohan Singh Kanota, eds., *Reversing the Gaze: Amar Singh's Diary, A Colonial Subject's Narrative of Imperial India* (New Delhi: Oxford University Press, 2000).

38. For a discussion of one such example, and continuing sensitivities see Robert Bickers, "Boxed Out: How the British Museum Suppressed Discussion of British Looting in China," *The Times Literary Supplement*, no. 5129 (2001): 15.

39. Ruth Rogaski, *Hygienic Modernity: Meanings of Health and Disease in Treaty-Port China* (Berkeley: University of California Press, 2004), 165–224.

40. On the Legation Quarter, see Michael J. Moser and Yeone Wei-chih Moser, *Foreigners within the Gates: The Legations at Peking* (Oxford, Oxford University Press, 1993).

41. Diana Preston, *The Boxer Rebellion: The Dramatic Story of China's War on Foreigners that Shook the World in the Summer of 1900* (New York: Walker, 2000 [British title: *Besieged in Peking: The Story of the 1900 Boxer Rising* (London: Constable, 1999)]); Hoe, *Women at the Siege: Peking 1900*.

42. James L. Hevia, "Monument and Memory: The Oberlin College Boxer Memorial as a Contested Site," in *Dong-Ya Jidujiao zaiquanyi* (Reinterpreting the East Asian Christianity), ed. Tao Feiya and Philip Yuen-Sang Leung (Hong Kong: Centre for the Study of Religion and Chinese Society, Chung Chi College, Chinese University of Hong Kong, 2004), 487–506.

43. Yuan Weishi, "Modernization and History Textbooks," *Bingdian* supplement, *Qingnian bao*, 11 January 2006. The original text and translation, as well as related material, can be found at www.zonaeuropa.com/20060126_1.htm (22 June 2006).

44. On the textbook controversy see Caroline Rose, *Interpreting History in Sino-Japanese Relations* (London: Routledge, 1998); Laura Hein and Mark Selden, eds., *Censoring History: Citizenship and Memory in Japan, Germany, and the United States* (Armonk: M.E. Sharpe, 2000).

45. Zhang Haipeng, "The Main Theme in Modern Chinese History Is Anti-Imperialism/Anti-Feudalism," *Bingdian* supplement, *Qingnian bao*, 1 March 2006. The original text and translation, as well as related material, can be found at www.zonaeuropa.com/20060302_1.htm (22 June 2006).

46. A classic case from 1994 is explored in Robert Bickers and Jeffrey N. Wasserstrom, "Shanghai's 'Chinese and Dogs Not Admitted' Sign: History, Legend and Contemporary Symbol," *The China Quarterly*, no. 142 (1995): 444–66.

1

Village Politics and National Politics

The Boxer Movement in Central Shanxi

Henrietta Harrison

This essay looks at the events of the summer of 1900 and their repercussions in four counties in central Shanxi. Taiyuan, Yuci, Xugou, and Taigu counties lay on the fertile plain of the Fen River to the south of Taiyuan City. The area was a wealthy one: Taigu was a major national trading and banking center, while in Taiyuan County the Jin River irrigation system provided water for rice fields and a variety of local industries. It also saw some of the worst slaughter of the entire uprising. Boxer groups formed armies of several hundred men who attacked Catholic villages, burned churches, and slaughtered the villagers. Why did such terrible violence take place? And why did certain villages become centers of Boxer attack or Catholic resistance? The Boxer movement in Shanxi has often been seen as a result of the transferal of Shandong governor Yuxian to the province in the spring of 1900; the provincial authorities did indeed play an important role, but the movement was also popular, with Boxer groups being widely initiated at a local level. Paul Cohen and Roger Thompson have suggested that the violence grew out of tensions caused by Christianity within villages.[1] Christianity was certainly problematic in Chinese villages, but in central Shanxi most deaths occurred when one village fought against another, rather than within villages. While I agree with earlier scholars' emphasis on both the administrative causes of the uprising and the importance of the village moral order, I argue that we also need to take account of power relationships between villages and communities.

1

CHRISTIANITY IN CENTRAL SHANXI

Catholicism had first arrived in central Shanxi in the seventeenth century. As early as 1705 there were said to be two thousand believers in the Taiyuan city area. Although the number of Catholics dropped during the persecutions of the eighteenth century, Christian families and communities persisted. For many years after the expulsion of the Jesuits there was only a single Cantonese priest in the province, but the number of Catholics continued to grow and the faith was assimilated into local social structures and ideologies in ways which shocked later missionaries.[2] By the end of the nineteenth century, Catholics formed a sizeable minority of the population of central Shanxi: Catholic records for the diocese of Central and North Shanxi give figures of 17,330 Catholic believers, 20 Chinese priests, and 16 foreign priests in 1899.[3] The diocesan compound in Taiyuan with its huge cathedral built in the early 1870s reflected the size and history of the Catholic community. When a British Protestant visited the church in the 1880s, he wrote that the party could hardly believe they were in China as they looked at the gorgeous high altar, shrines, confessionals, pictures of the stations of the cross, and holy water stoops.[4] The Catholics were not always popular with the local population, but there was little history of open antagonism. Cen Chunxuan, who was appointed governor after the uprising, summed up the history of Catholicism in the province in a memorial to the emperor: "I find that in Shanxi province there was already a Catholic church in the provincial capital at the beginning of the dynasty. After the country was opened to trade, large numbers of missionaries came to the province; there were many churches and more and more of the common people joined the religion, but the commoners and Christians lived quietly together and there was never any discord."[5]

As a result of this history, most Catholics in the villages of the central Shanxi plain had been born and brought up in the faith: Of the 533 people killed during the uprising in this area and later recorded by the church as martyrs only eleven were converts.[6] Many communities could tell of a founding ancestor who brought the religion back to his native village. Thus Xugou County Catholics claim that their religion first reached the county in the eighteenth century when a merchant from the Chang family converted while working in Beijing. He then married a woman from Heicheng village, moved to live there, and brought up seven sons, all of them Catholic. Heicheng grew into a base of Catholicism in the county and in 1900 more than thirty members of the Chang lineage were killed there.[7] Foreign missionaries encouraged the growth of these Christian communities, and by 1900 there were one or two entirely Catholic villages in the area and many others in which a large proportion of the population was Catholic. The village of Dongergou, which had a seminary and a Franciscan friary, was well known for its entirely Catholic population. It was said to have been founded by the Catholic Wu family, who were then joined by the Duan family, fleeing from religious persecution in their own nearby village. Finally, the Liu family came as laborers to work on the church and were converted.[8] Passing by Dongergou in 1902, local diarist Liu Dapeng wrote,

> The villagers all follow the foreign religion. The village lies at the foot of the hills, with the church standing on the slope of the hill, surrounded by a wall. There are many buildings within the wall. The site is impressive and the buildings are all in the foreign style.[9]

Another village, Guchengying, was not entirely Catholic but the religion had existed there, too, since the eighteenth century. The first converts were members of the influential Yan lineage, who then caused others to convert, and by 1900 members of the Dong lineage were Catholic as well as members of four other families. The village included a Catholic degree holder and a member of the Dong family who was studying to be a priest and had recently traveled to Europe with Bishop Fogolla.[10] The wealth and power of the Guchengying Catholics is suggested by the amount of property for which they claimed reparations after the uprising: two churches (one in a subsidiary hamlet), 328 *jian* (room units) built of mud brick, and 96 *jian* of more expensive baked brick.[11] Guchengying and Dongergou were not particularly unusual. Eight villages in Taiyuan County alone lost Catholic churches during the uprising.[12]

The first Protestant missionaries to take up residence in Taiyuan did not arrive until the famine of 1877. Their numbers then increased rapidly and they began to establish churches, opium refuges, and medical clinics. Liu Dapeng, visiting Taiyuan City for the provincial examinations in 1894, noticed the English missionaries' church with a tablet above the entrance saying "Save the World Hall."[13] But despite the large numbers of missionaries, Protestant conversions were slow: in 1898 Shanxi had 151 Protestant missionaries and merely 1,513 Chinese church members. When this is compared to the province's 26,961 Catholics and 36 Catholic missionaries, it is obvious that Chinese Protestants were few in relative numbers and that Protestantism was far less integrated into local communities.[14] The general population did not, however, distinguish between Catholics and Protestants: the same term was used for both, and Protestant missionaries commented on the problems they had in distinguishing themselves from the Catholics.[15]

THE SPREAD OF THE VIOLENCE

The Boxer movement began in Shandong and Zhili provinces. Reports of strange new martial arts practices and of the attacks on Christianity that went with them first reached Shanxi in the spring of 1900. Then people heard that the foreign powers had seized Tianjin and that the court had declared war and ordered that Christians should be treated as collaborators. Yuxian, the new governor, had immediately ordered the arrest of foreigners.[16] For the moment, however, boxing in Shanxi was restricted to the gathering of groups of young men to practice. There were rumors that Christians were responding to the growing threat by attempting to poison wells. Sometimes the poison was said to be shaken from a sleeve, sometimes a great green bottle was said to be inverted over the well.[17] Boxer groups began to take precautions against this threat: anyone who stopped at a well to drink would be searched for poison, many wells were guarded day and night, and potions were used to counteract the Christian poisons.[18]

The first killing occurred in the town of Shitie. The victim was not a Christian but had been mistaken for one by a group of Boxers.[19] Shitie was on the main road into the province from Zhili and was always busy with travelers. It had both a large Catholic community and a Protestant mission station. At least some Shandong Boxers appear to have come into the province along this road, which was in any case a standard route for migrants.[20] Since the famine of 1877, which depopulated the province, there had been waves of immigration from Shandong and Zhili. These immigrants were the first to suffer from rising grain prices and were easily involved in violence.[21] Later on in the uprising several cases were recorded in which Shandong or Zhili men acted as mercenaries for Catholic villages.[22] Whether or not Shandong Boxers personally played a major role in introducing boxing, the spread of violent incidents that followed this first murder suggests that the movement at least had come over the passes and reached Shanxi through Shitie. The next two killings were nearby and from there the murders spread south and west. Several of the victims were vagrants, traditional objects of suspicion. In one case, Liu Dapeng reports the killing of a Buddhist monk. Even where the victims were indeed Christians, they, too, were almost always from outside the village.[23] These sporadic murders, fueled by the general panic about poisoning, spread along the roads leading out from Yuci at the end of the Zhili road.

The first major fighting also occurred on this side of the plain when Boxers from Yuci attacked the Catholics of nearby Wangdu village. Boxer violence began in the countryside, although it inevitably interacted with the actions of the provincial government. A crucial part of this process was Yuxian's welcoming of the Shitie Boxer leader Jiang Jinhua, a fifteen-year-old peasant who had formed a Boxer group. His group grew rapidly after the first murder and received permission from the magistrate to train in a neighborhood temple in the county town. Shortly afterward Jiang Jinhua led a group of Boxers into Taiyuan City, wearing a red head cloth and riding a horse through streets packed with wildly excited crowds. Yuxian was said to have come out to welcome him to the provincial government compound. Two days later Jiang Jinhua led three hundred Yuci County Boxers to attack the Catholic stronghold of Wangdu, break through the defenses, and burn the church.[24] The attack on Wangdu was the first of a series of Boxer assaults on Catholic communities. In Sanxian, where there had been a Catholic community since 1760, a large group of Boxers from the town of Beige marched to attack the Catholics who had taken refuge in the church. The resistance was fierce; the men fired guns from the church roof while the women sprinkled holy water on the Boxers (to drive out the spirits that possessed them). The Boxers besieged the church for three days during which time four or five of them were killed and many more injured, including one of their leaders. When the church eventually fell the Boxers slaughtered several hundred Catholics, including many women and children, and burned the church building. The Catholics' houses had already been burned to the ground.[25] These attacks set the pattern for the violence, with large, well-armed groups of Boxers fighting pitched battles against Catholics, also armed and usually besieged in the village church. By the end of the fighting whole lineages had been entirely wiped out.

The timing of these events means that it is not possible to see the causes of the violence solely in terms of Yuxian's transfer from Shandong to Shanxi. The initial murders spread out from the end of the main road over the mountains from Zhili. The subsequent fighting between villages was certainly encouraged by Yuxian's activities, including the execution of all foreigners and his failure to punish those who burned the Catholic cathedral in Taiyuan, but it was not directly caused by these events. It is easy to see why Yuxian was later blamed by the Chinese officials responsible for negotiating the indemnities, for in doing so they could place responsibility for the violence on the shoulders of one man. However, during the uprising Yuxian had been following a popular policy and the movement had a momentum of its own.[26] It is thus necessary, if we are to understand the uprising, to look for its causes within Shanxi society.

THE SOCIAL CAUSES OF VIOLENCE

The current literature suggests two main social causes for the uprising. The first sees the tensions as arising out of disputes over village levies.[27] Since the Qing system of local government did not extend much below the level of the county town, it had long been necessary for villages to raise informal taxes for communal affairs. These were often collected for the primary purpose of paying for an annual temple fair and there had been disputes caused by Catholics refusing to contribute since the eighteenth century.[28] The idea that financial disputes of this kind underlay the increasing hostility

between Catholics and non-Catholics was put forward by Chinese officials
and others in the immediate aftermath of the fighting.[29] In the case of one
village, which saw a massacre of nearly fifty Catholic adults and nineteen
children, a dispute over opera taxes had taken place quite recently, but even
there the Boxers came from outside the village.[30] Another important social
cause is suggested by Paul Cohen, who argues that Christianity had become
a particular threat because of drought.[31] Much of the rhetoric of the Shanxi
Boxers did indeed describe the Christians as threatening the moral order,
angering the gods, and thus causing the drought. This was tied to a strong
belief in the power of Christian magic: Christians were accused of poisoning wells, scattering blood to make people go mad, creating magical armies
out of paper figures, and causing a strange hissing wind to terrify people.[32]
Problems intensified when they refused to take part in community prayers
for rain. Boxers arriving at the Jinci temple complex worshipped in the temple of the god of drought, but on the other hand the much worse drought
of 1877 did not give rise to any particular anti-Christian feeling.[33]

Drought did make it more likely that people would turn to violence. As
the dry weather continued and grain prices rose, farmers feared the loss of
their crops, and laborers in the area's many industries saw the value of their
wages fall and faced unemployment if farmers could no longer afford their
products. There were several straightforward cases of looting of shops during the uprising and some Christian property was presumably looted when
churches and houses were burned.[34] Central Shanxi was certainly not as violent a place as the Shandong heartland of the Boxer movement, but nevertheless literary degrees were thinly spread and military degrees were important sources of status, regularly referred to in the biographies of
members of the local elite. Many of the area's most powerful families traced
their origins to soldiers from the northwest frontier.[35] And the Jin River irrigation system, which was crucial to the distribution of wealth and power
in Taiyuan County, was founded on a myth of intervillage warfare: every
year at Qingming the villagers of Huata went to the source of the river in
the great temple at Jinci to sacrifice to their ancestors who had fought and
won the right of the villages of the north stream of the Jin River to seven-
tenths of its water.[36] This was an area where martial arts and violent behavior could readily be accepted by communities concerned with defending
their interests.

THE TARGETS OF VIOLENCE

Village financial disputes, drought, and the acceptance of violence all
played a part in the rapidly escalating tensions between Christians and their
neighbors. Together with the political decisions of the court in Beijing, re-

flected in Yuxian's shifting and ambiguous policies, they created the conditions for the violence. However, we also need to understand the targets of that violence. Disputes over village levies could, and did on other occasions in other places, lead to beatings and even murder within the village. In the same way, prayers for rain were usually a community matter. In either case we would expect violence to occur between non-Christians and Christians within the context of the village. However, what in fact happened in central Shanxi was that Boxer villages attacked Catholic villages.

The major Boxer attacks emanated from five centers: Qingyuan, Xiaodian, Beige, Yuci, and Nanchengjiao. The first four were sizeable towns located on major roads, but Nanchengjiao was an unimportant village without even a major temple. Its Boxer group drew members from a considerable distance and gathered for military expeditions in the large temple complex at Jinci several miles away, but was always described as belonging to the village.[37] When the prefect was sent to investigate the group he went straight to the village and found the Boxers gathered in the temple.[38] The identification of Boxer groups with villages was common. In one Taigu village, the Boxers were said to have completed their drilling, then gone to the village elders and said "Our drill is finished. We are turned into Boxers. Now whom shall we kill?"[39]

The targets of Boxer violence in this area were also villages. Groups of Boxers from one village attacked Catholics from another. Indeed, in many cases there is evidence that non-Catholic villagers were prepared to help their Catholic neighbors; Catholics who escaped the violence often did so because they had been warned and many women and children were hidden in their neighbors' houses.[40] When the Nanchengjiao Boxers attacked the village of Guchengying, the Boxers accused the village head of pretending to try to kill the Christians but actually firing on the Boxers. He was tied up beside the church and only released the next day when the church was taken and more than a hundred Catholics killed.[41] In Chewang village, the home of a Protestant convert was burned and his daughter-in-law, three children, and a blind servant were killed by Boxers from neighboring towns. Other members of the family were helped to escape by their neighbors. Afterward, the villagers were terrified and the village's leading men agreed to stop Boxer groups practicing in the village, to train a village militia with guns, and to build a wall around the village. Members of the wealthy Chang family provided two thousand silver taels for the construction of the wall and each of the streets of the village contributed labor. The village is also said to have contracted alliances with other villages specifically for defense against the Boxers.[42] Here the Boxers were regarded as a catastrophe against which the villagers were prepared to unite to defend themselves.

After the uprising local people, officials, and foreign negotiators all interpreted what had taken place in terms of intervillage warfare. As Boxer activities were suppressed, Catholic villages began to take revenge on the villages they saw as responsible for the violence. The Catholics of Wufuying, who had fled and thus survived the worst of the violence, marched en masse toward Nanchengjiao and violence was only prevented by the timely arrival of the magistrate.[43] Reparations for the deaths were also extracted from villages. The coffins of the Catholics who had been killed when the church at Guchengying was destroyed were taken to Dongergou for burial. All the nearby villages had to send men to help carry the coffins and certain villages were also required to pay for the funerals. In addition, Nanchengjiao was ordered to pay 800,000 cash to Dongergou.[44] Thus Boxer violence was interpreted as a village responsibility.

The Pattern of the Violence

If both the targets and the perpetrators of Boxer violence were villages, then we need a somewhat different approach to understand it. I argue firstly that the pattern of violence reflected preexisting intervillage power structures and secondly that the violence was possible because the Boxers succeeded in manipulating the ambiguity of the central government's position by laying claim to a status as village militias.

INTERVILLAGE POWER STRUCTURES

The Jin River flowed from a spring at the base of the hills west of Taiyuan County town and irrigated approximately thirty villages, several of which were heavily involved in the uprising. These villages depended on the water to grow profitable cash crops and for industries such as paper making and the manufacture of alum. Since the tenth century the water had been divided at Jinci, the source, into two main streams. It was then regulated by a series of hatches controlled by village hatch keepers, who were subordinate to channel heads appointed from certain dominant villages. The prosperity of any individual was often directly dependent on the position of his village in the irrigation hierarchy. Fights, the stealing of water, the breaking of dykes, and lawsuits between villages were common. Stability and control were provided by religious legitimation: a vast temple complex in honor of the Holy Mother, originally the goddess of the Jin River, had been constructed around the spring at Jinci. Here the channel heads held sacrifices and banquets which were attended by members of their villages, sometimes walking in procession from the village behind a statue of a deity. Records of the legal decisions that determined the exact pattern of the rotations of water to the different villages were inscribed on stone tablets kept in the temple. Once a year the statue of the Holy Mother was brought out of the temple and paraded around several of the villages of the irrigation system to the county town. In addition, every aspect of work on the irrigation system was restricted by rituals and sacrifices that specified when it should take place and who was to be present to observe it.[45] The economic power of the villages that controlled the irrigation system was closely tied to rituals and festivals that centered on Jinci.

It is thus not surprising that the area's Boxers gathered at Jinci. Three great gatherings were held there as the Boxers prepared to march out against the Catholic villages. Liu Dapeng described how the Boxers arrived in small groups with each man carrying a weapon and wearing a red head cloth, belt, and leg bands. When several hundred men were assembled, they formed up into companies and marched off behind two banners bearing the Boxer slogans "Support the Qing and destroy the foreign!" and "Implement the Way on behalf of Heaven!"[46] The importance of Jinci is also suggested by the emphasis put on it by the Italian Catholic priests in their demands for reparations after the uprising was over. They demanded that the town be "practically handed over to them."[47] Their correspondence suggests that what they wanted above all was control of the water.[48] This is also suggested by an observer who commented that the Catholics' intention was to divert the water to the lands of their own people.[49]

The Jin River irrigation system was central to local power relations and it was those relations that determined the targets of Boxer violence. The villages in Taiyuan County that sustained the most damage were Sanxian, Guchengying, and Wangguo.[50] Sanxian and the villages that attacked it all lay outside the Jin River irrigation system. Guchengying and Wangguo, on the other hand, were two of the four most powerful villages in the system and were attacked by Boxers from Nanchengjiao, which also lies within the system. Since the tenth century, Wangguo had controlled vital hatches that either forced the water to flow along the edge of the valley, irrigating distant and drought-prone villages, or allowed it to flow naturally down toward the Fen River. The same balance of power can be seen in the way in which channel head and hatch keeper positions were distributed among the villages and costs of repairs were allocated. The Wangguo channel head controlled a total of thirty-six hatch keepers and the village contributed 6.3 percent of the cost of repairs to the system. The only communities to exceed this proportion of the costs were the county towns, which contributed 13.3 percent, and Guchengying, which contributed a massive 21.9 percent of the cost of repairs. Guchengying also had its own channel head and a large group of nine hatch keepers. (By contrast, Nanchengjiao, though relatively close to the source of the river, had no channel head and only two hatch keepers.) Channel head and hatch keeper positions were usually rotated among the village's landowners: The Wangguo channel head position was filled by the farmers of the village in an annual rotation, while in Guchengying not only was the post filled by all the farmers in turn but each was allowed to hold the post only once in his life.[51] With such arrangements it was inevitable that the villages' Catholic families would play a role in the irrigation system. Wangguo and Guchengying, which were the targets of major Boxer attacks, were villages that not only had Catholic populations but also held prominent positions in intervillage power structures, in this case dictated by the irrigation system.

The Boxers as Village Militias

Boxer attacks on powerful local villages could only go unchecked because of the ambiguity of the Boxers' relationship to the government. From the beginning Yuxian had been eager to make use of the Boxers. In the spring of 1900 he wrote to the central government that he was enrolling them in the army and if the numbers grew larger than those needed for the army he would form militias. As the movement grew he acted accordingly, creating five battalions of Boxer guards based in the Dragon King Temple just outside the main gate of the provincial government buildings. He personally supervised the drilling of these new soldiers with guns and cannon and they were not dispersed until the autumn.[52] This official recognition was strengthened by proclamations that Christians should leave their religion and by rumors such as the one that an announcement had been posted in the Taiyuan City telegraph office which told of the emperor's pleasure with the Boxers after their victory over two foreign warships.[53]

At the local level, Boxer ideals were also morally acceptable to many members of the elite, who hoped, like Yuxian, that foreign invasion could be resisted by calling the people to arms. The belief that the government should take a firmer line against Christian heterodoxy was also widespread among this group. Liu Dapeng argued that the Boxer movement began because the officials had failed to deal with the Christians:

> The court could not execute them and the officials did not dare, so the Boxers executed them. Even those who were not Boxers all also wanted to catch the Christians and kill them. Surely it was their cruelty and selfishness that caused Heaven's awe-inspiring anger of which the Boxers were the tool.[54]

In Taigu County, Ji Lanxi, an upper degree holder and tutor like Liu Dapeng, gathered the Boxers of two villages and formed a county battalion. After the deaths of the American missionaries he had the head of one of them hung at the gate of the village temple.[55] Support, not to mention active leadership, from men like Liu Dapeng and Ji Lanxi inevitably strengthened the claims of Boxer groups to political orthodoxy.

The result of this acceptance of their orthodoxy was that Boxer groups could claim to be official local militias. In Yuci the magistrate was said to have ordered people to provide Jiang Jinhua's group with food and money, as well as spirit money and incense to burn.[56] In Taigu County the Boxers demanded, unsuccessfully, that the magistrate provide them with knives and boots.[57] Boxer groups presented themselves as militias by marching in orderly cohorts under banners that proclaimed their support for the dynasty and forming armies that went considerable distances, sometimes across county boundaries, to attack Catholic villages. An unsuccessful Boxer attack on Liangquan village involved groups from Qixian, Taigu, Yuci, Xugou, and Wenshui counties as well as the nearby district of Qingyuan.[58] The Nanchengjiao Boxers not only attacked Guchengying and Wangguo, but also the village of Liulin, which lay on the far side of the Fen River. Many of the groups, as they marched out, carried a banner announcing that they were the Boxers of such and such a village.[59]

Boxer groups needed a legitimate position as village militias because from the very beginning of the uprising their activities were a threat to the administration of the state. The violence began with murders that should have been investigated by the local authorities but were not. The Boxers knew that their ability to act depended on official recognition and were therefore constantly pressing the authorities to expand that recognition. When this merely meant requests to be allowed to practice in particular temples, or even for a supply of boots, some magistrates might be prepared to comply. Others, aware of the disputes within the government, vacillated, which was taken as a sign of approval or at the very least as a license for the violence to continue. But ultimately several groups demanded recognition that went far beyond what any magistrate could find acceptable. In Taiyuan County the magistrate's troubles began with the murder of a Catholic butcher in Nanchengjiao. When the Boxers had committed murder and no action had been taken against them, it was clear that they were to some extent above the law. Their leader, a laborer who spent the winter pushing carts of coal down from the mountains, took a hundred of his followers to the county town to demand grain. The magistrate dithered but was eventually persuaded to go out to the city gate and formally welcome the Boxer group into the county yamen. In a dramatic reversal of roles the Boxer leader strode into the main hall and sat down in the magistrate's seat. His followers stood to left and right with drawn swords. Terrified, the magistrate and gentry knelt before them. Eventually the Boxers left, taking a large quantity of grain.[60] Similar events took place in Taigu County town where four Boxers marched into the city behaving like officials and commanding all those they met in the streets to kneel.[61] As Boxers pushed the limits of their position as village militias they became an unacceptable threat to local government. Even Yuxian reported that requests for troops were coming in from all around as magistrates tried to deal with the fighting.[62]

CONCLUSION

During the course of the uprising Boxers and magistrates pursued inter-twined but ultimately different visions of the moral order. The Boxers at-tacked villages whose Catholic religion had disturbed the moral order, and which, in their opinion, should have been punished by the government. Magistrates who resisted Boxer activities revealed that the government's pri-mary commitment was not to the moral order, but to the preservation of ex-isting power structures. In this process the deceptions of moral hegemony were laid bare: The morality of the state with its emphasis on individual virtues and state powers was not and had never been the same as the moral order of the villages, which were bound together in relations of power and exploitation by rituals, wealth, and traditions of violence that were alien to the state. The Boxer uprising and its aftermath made these differences obvi-ous. The demand for righteousness and the preservation of the moral order was clearly at the heart of the Boxer activities. However, neither the Boxer groups nor the Catholics they attacked saw righteousness primarily in terms of the individual. Instead, the moral order was understood in terms of the relationships between villages. This reflected the nature of power in the Shanxi countryside, where crucial elements of economic control were held by villages. When righteousness failed and justice was not done, the inter-twined strands that linked the morality of rural institutions with those of the state began to fall apart and villages were freed to become even more powerful and antagonistic players.

NOTES

1. Paul A. Cohen, *History in Three Keys: The Boxers as Event, Experience and Myth* (New York: Columbia University Press, 1997); Roger Thompson, "Twilight of the Gods in the Chinese Countryside: Christians, Confucians, and the Modernizing State, 1861–1911," in Daniel H. Bays, ed., *Christianity in China from the Eighteenth Century to the Present* (Stanford: Stanford University Press, 1996).

2. Fortunato Margiotti, *Il cattolicismo nello Shansi dalle origini al 1738* (Roma: Edi-zioni Sinica Franciscana, 1958), 182, 206, 228–9, 606; Ioannes Ricci, *Vicariatus Taiyuanfu seu Brevis Historia Antiquae Franciscanae Missionis Shansi et Shensi a sua orig-ine ad dies nostros (1700–1928)* (Pekini: Congregationis Missionis, 1929), 25–55.

3. Arnulf Camps and Pat McCloskey, *The Friars Minor in China (1294–1955)* (Rome: General Secretariat for Missionary Evangelization, General Curia, Order of Friars Minor, 1995), 27.

4. A. T. Schofield, ed., *Memorials of R. Harold A. Schofield M.A., M.B. (Oxon.) (Late of the China Inland Mission), First Medical Missionary to Shan-si, China* (London: Hod-der and Stoughton, 1885), 179; Guo Chongxi, "Taiyuan tianzhujiao zhuyao tangkou jianjie" [A brief introduction to the main Catholic churches of Taiyuan] *Taiyuan wenshi ziliao* 15 (1991).

5. Gugong bowuyuan Ming Qing dang'anbu, ed., *Yihetuan dang'an shiliao* [Archival sources on the Boxers] (Beijing: Zhonghua shuju, 1959), 1233.

6. Ioannes Ricci, "Acta Martyrum Sinensium anno 1900 in Provincia *San-si* occisorum historice collecta ex ore Testium singulis in locis ubi Martyres occubere. Relatio ex parte Ordinis Fratrum Minorum," *Acta Ordinis Fratrum Minorum* 30-32.

7. Liu Wenbing, *Xugou xianzhi* [Xugou gazetteer] (Taiyuan: Shanxi renmin chubanshe, 1992), 270, 285.

8. Camps and McCloskey, 26; Guo Chongxi, "Taiyuan tianzhujiao zhuyao tangkou."

9. Liu Dapeng, "Tuixiangzhai riji" [Diary from the study for retreat and contemplation], *Jindaishi ziliao Yihetuan shiliao* [Materials for modern history: Materials on the Boxers] (Beijing: Zhongguo shehui kexue chubanshe, 1982), 819.

10. Guo Chongxi, "Taiyuan tianzhujiao shilue" [A history of Catholicism in Taiyuan] *Taiyuan wenshi ziliao* 17 (1992); Ioannes Ricci, "Acta Martyrum" 30: 281.

11. Zhongyang yanjiuyuan jindaishi yanjiusuo, *Jiaowu jiaoan dang* [Archives of religious affairs and cases] (Taibei: Zhongyang yanjiuyuan jindaishi yanjiusuo, 1981), 7.1: 497-98.

12. Zhongyang yanjiuyuan jindaishi yanjiusuo, 496-98. See also Giovanni Ricci, *Barbarie e Trionfi: ossia le vittime illustri del San-si in Cina nella persecuzione del 1900,* 2nd ed. (Firenze: Associazioni Nazionale per Soccorrere I missionari Cattolici Italiani, 1910), 121, 130.

13. Liu Dapeng, *Tuixiangzhai riji* [Diary of the study for retreat and contemplation] (Taiyuan: Shanxi renmin chubanshe, 1990), 33.

14. E. H. Edwards, *Fire and Sword in Shansi: The Story of the Martyrdom of Foreigners and Chinese Christians* (Edinburgh: Oliphant, Anderson and Ferrier, 1908), 47; Camps and McCloskey, 27.

15. American Board of Commissioners for Foreign Missions (hereafter ABCFM), Shansi Mission, 3/242b, Annual report of T'ai-ku Station for 1899.

16. Liu Dapeng, "Qianyuan suoji" [Notes from the Qian garden], in Qiao Zhiqiang, ed., *Yihetuan zai Shanxi diqu shiliao* [Historical materials concerning the Boxer movement in Shanxi] (Taiyuan: Shanxi renmin chubanshe, 1982), 28, 31-2.

17. ABCFM. Shansi Mission. 3/251. Report of women's work for T'ai-ku for 1899.

18. E. H. Edwards, *Fire and Sword in Shansi,* 55; Liu Dapeng, "Qianyuan suoji," 34-35.

19. Liu Dapeng, "Qianyuan suoji," 43.

20. Zhongyang yanjiuyuan jindaishi yanjiusuo, 498; ABCFM, Alice M. Williams Miscellaneous Papers, 12, Journal of Miss Susan Rowena Bird, 4 July 1900.

21. E. H. Edwards, *Fire and Sword in Shansi,* 52.

22. Shanxi sheng Yuci shizhi bianzuan weiyuanhui, ed., *Yuci shizhi* [Yuci City gazetteer] (Beijing: Zhonghua shuju, 1996), 1057; Liu Dapeng, "Qian yuan suoji," 44, 48; Ricci, "Acta Martyrum," 31: 337.

23. Ricci, "Acta Martyrum," 30: 329, 361; 31: 304; Liu Dapeng, "Qian yuan suoji," 35, 43-45; ABCFM, Alice M. Williams Miscellaneous Papers, 12, Journal of Miss Susan Rowena Bird, 3, 5-6 July 1900, Rowena Bird to her brother, 6, 8, 10 July 1900; Liu Wenbing, *Xugou xianzhi,* 284; Liu Dapeng, *Jinci zhi* [Jinci Gazetteer] (Taiyuan: Shanxi renmin chubanshe, 1986), 1049.

24. Wu Tingluan, "Yuci yihetuan yundong shimo" [The full story of the Yuci Boxers], *Jinzhong shizhi ziliao* 12, no. 1 (1989), 234-39; Shi Rongchang, "Gengzi ganshi

shi" [Poems in response to 1900], *Jindaishi ziliao* [Materials for modern history] 11 (1956); Shanxi sheng Yuci shi bianzuan weiyuanhui, *Yuci shizhi* 1057; Liu Dapeng, "Qian yuan suoji," 31.

25. Margiotti, *Il cattolicismo nello Shansi*, 670; Liu Dapeng, *Jinci zhi*, 1048–9; "Qianyuan suoji," 38.

26. E. H. Edwards, *Fire and Sword in Shansi*, 117.

27. Roger Thompson in this volume.

28. Margiotti, *Il cattolicismo nello Shansi*, 441.

29. Zhongguo diyi lishi dang'anguan, and Fujian shifan daxue lishixi, eds., *Qingmo jiaoan* [Late Qing religious cases] (Beijing: Zhonghua shuju, 1998), 229–30.

30. Ricci, "Acta Martyrum," 31: 185–9.

31. Paul A. Cohen in this volume.

32. Liu Dapeng, "Qianyuan suoji," 34–35.

33. Liu Dapeng, *Jinci zhi*, 1048. For a general survey of the famine see Kathryn Edgerton-Tarpley, *Tears from Iron: Cultural Responses to Famine in Nineteenth-Century China*. Berkeley: University of California Press, 2007.

34. ABCFM, Alice M. Williams Miscellaneous Papers, 12, Journal of Miss Susan Rowena Bird, 9 July 1900.

35. E.g., Qingxu xian difangzhi bianzuan weiyuanhui, ed., *Qingxu xianzhi* [Qingxu County gazetteer] (Taiyuan: Shanxi guji chubanshe, 1999), 110; Guo Yuanchou, Ma Yunjiang, and Guo Sujie, *Xuncha Taiwan yushi Yang Eryou* [Yang Eryou, the censor sent to inspect Taiwan] (Taiyuan: Shanxi renmin chubanshe, 1993), 2–4.

36. Liu Dapeng, *Jinci zhi*, 114.

37. Liu Dapeng, "Qianyuan suoji," 37.

38. Gugong bowuyuan Ming Qing dang'an bu, *Yihetuan dang'an shiliao*, 313.

39. ABCFM, Alice M. Williams Miscellaneous Papers, 12, Rowena Bird to her brother, 11 July 1900.

40. Liu Dapeng, *Jinci zhi*, 1048; Ricci, "Acta Martyrum," 31: 186.

41. Liu Dapeng, "Qianyuan suoji," 38; Ricci, "Acta Martyrum," 32: 191–96.

42. ABCFM, Alice M. Williams Miscellaneous Papers, 12, Journal of Miss Susan Rowena Bird, 18 July 1900; Chang Zanchun, *Changshi jiacheng* [Chang surname family records] (Privately published, [1923]), 1: 12a; Shanxi sheng Yuci shizhi bianzuan weiyuanhui, *Yuci shizhi* 1057–58.

43. Liu Dapeng, "Qianyuan suoji," 71.

44. Liu Dapeng, "Tuixiangzhai riji," 793–95.

45. Liu Dapeng, *Jinci zhi*, 20–21, 189–95, 803–991; Yoshinami Takashi, "*Shinshishi* yorimita Shinsui shi kyo no suiri kangai" [Water utilization and irrigation through the four channels of the Jin River from reading the *Jincizhi*], *Shigaku kenkyu* 170 (1986).

46. Liu Dapeng, *Jinci zhi*, 1048; "Qianyuan suoji," 38.

47. E. H. Edwards, *Fire and Sword in Shansi*, 166.

48. "Diguozhuyi esha Shanxi Yihetuan de zuizheng" [Evidence of the smothering of the Shanxi Boxers by Imperialism], *Shanxi wenshi ziliao* 2–3 (1962).

49. *North China Herald*, 4 September 1901, 442.

50. "Diguozhuyi esha Shanxi Yihetuan de zuizheng."

51. Liu Dapeng, *Jinci zhi*, 777–992; Yoshinami Takashi, "*Shinshishi* yorimita Shinsui shi kyo no suiri kangai."

52. Gugong bowuyuan Ming Qing dang'anbu, *Yihetuan dang'an shiliao*, 181, 563; Shi Rongchang, "Gengzi ganshi shi."

53. Robert Coventry Forsyth, *The China Martyrs of 1900: A Complete Roll of the Christian Heroes Martyred in China in 1900 with Narratives of the Survivors* (London: The Religious Tract Society, 1904), 366; Liu Wenbing, *Xugou xianzhi*, 285.

54. Liu Dapeng, "Qianyuan suoji," 32–33.

55. Taigu xianzhi bianzuan weiyuanhui, *Taigu xianzhi* [Taigu County gazetteer] (Taiyuan: Shanxi renmin chubanshe, 1993), 631; ABCFM, Shansi Mission, 5,450, I. J. Attwood to Judson Smith, T'ai Ku, 16 September 1901.

56. Shanxi sheng Yuci shizhi bianzuan weiyuanhui, *Yuci shizhi*, 1057.

57. ABCFM, Alice M. Williams Miscellaneous Papers, 12, Journal of Miss Susan Rowena Bird, 7 July 1900.

58. Liu Dapeng, *Jinci zhi*, 1048; "Qianyuan suoji," 48.

59. Liu Dapeng, "Qianyuan suoji," 38.

60. Liu Dapeng, *Jinci zhi*, 1049; "Qianyuan suoji," 35–36; Taiyuan shi nanjiaoqu zhi bianzuan weiyuanhui, *Taiyuan shi nanjiaoqu zhi* [Taiyuan City southern suburban district gazetteer] (Beijing: Sanlian shudian, 1994), 956; Gugong bowuyuan Ming Qing dang'anbu, *Yihetuan dang'an shiliao*, 313.

61. ABCFM, Alice M. Williams Miscellaneous Papers, 12, Rowena Bird to her brother, 7 July 1900.

62. Gugong bowuyuan Ming Qing dang'anbu, *Yihetuan dang'an shiliao*, 367.

2

The Church Militant

Armed Conflicts between Christians and Boxers in North China

R. G. Tiedemann

From the beginning of the Christian enterprise in China, Roman Catholic and Protestant missionaries were sent out "to attack the Prince of Darkness in his most impregnable fortress."[1] Although the "military metaphor" usually had only rhetorical meaning, armed conflict between Christians and non-Christians became a reality in north China during the Boxer Uprising. Most readers will be familiar with the fifty-five-day siege and subsequent relief of the foreign legations in Beijing in the summer of 1900, for that story was covered in sensational accounts in the Western press at the time and has since been retold in popular books and motion pictures. Some will also have heard of the second siege in Beijing, namely of the North Cathedral (Beitang), where several Lazarist (or Vincentian) priests, European sisters, and a large number of Chinese Catholics held out until the foreign expeditionary force rescued them.[2] However, less well known is the fact that, notwithstanding the widespread destruction of Christian life and property, Catholics in certain rural communities in various parts of north China were able to successfully resist Boxer attacks during that fateful summer and autumn. This essay considers some of these locations and examines the nature and extent of Christian militancy. In addition to places in what may be termed the original Boxer heartland on the North China Plain,[3] a few examples of Christian community defense in southern Shanxi and Inner Mongolia are also examined, for comparative purposes.

This study of armed conflicts between Christians and Boxers offers an unusual perspective on the interaction of endogenous and exogenous developments in the hinterland of north China. It will be argued that Christian militancy, at least on the North China Plain, should be seen in the context of a long tradition of collective violence in this area. Particular attention

17

will, therefore, be paid to the long-term integration of Catholic communities into this turbulent rural environment. It will, furthermore, be shown that the missionaries were instrumental in organizing Christian self-defense during the Boxer crisis. In this connection, the role of the foreign priests is perhaps best understood as that of leaders of local (Christian) communities, not very different from that of Chinese rural notables. Since they had access to more effective external power, we may ask to what extent Christian militancy was further encouraged by missionary collaboration with foreign secular imperialism, including direct foreign military intervention.

Although this essay is not concerned with the origins of the Boxer movement, it will nevertheless be assumed that the various Boxer incidents were in some ways a departure from the "normal" patterns of mass action incidents on the North China Plain. In other words, it was the outcome of a conjuncture of particular circumstances at the very end of the nineteenth century. It should also be noted that the majority of the Christian casualties during the conflict were sustained not in the original Boxer heartland but in northern Zhili, Shanxi, and Inner Mongolia.

The primary purpose of this essay is, however, to examine Christian community defense against Boxer attacks in areas with a long-lived culture of violence, as well as in areas without such a tradition. Before considering such protective action in the context of the complex interplay of endogenous contradictions, imperialist aggression, and missionary ambitions, it is necessary to briefly outline the history and spatially differentiated development of Christianity in north China.

THE ESTABLISHMENT AND GROWTH
OF CATHOLICISM ON THE NORTH CHINA PLAIN

Although a few Christian communities had been established on the North China Plain in the seventeenth century, it was during Bishop Bernardo Della Chiesa's residence at the important Grand Canal entrepôt of Linqing, hard on the border with Zhili province, that Italian Franciscans were able to establish numerous Catholic congregations in western Shandong and adjacent districts of Zhili (now Hebei province). This early missionary work flourished particularly during the latter part of the Kangxi reign. However, as a consequence of the periodic persecutions during the Yongzheng, Qianlong, and Jiaqing reigns, Christianity was forced to retreat to the administrative and/or geographic peripheries. Rural Catholic communities such as Zhaojiazhuang and Weicun (both in Wei *xian*) and Qingcaohe (Jing *zhou*) on the Zhili side of the border, as well as Shierlizhuang (Wucheng *xian*) on the Shandong side, served as secure refuges for believers and the handful of priests who from time to time were able to minister to the faithful.[4]

When Roman Catholic missionary work was resumed in the 1840s, the newly arrived foreign priests were able to use these surviving congregations as vital bases for their subsequent evangelization work. This new endeavor continued to be overwhelmingly rural in character. Thus Luigi Moccagatta, OFM, the vicar apostolic of Shandong, chose the village of Shierlizhuang as his episcopal residence in the 1840s and 1850s. Across the provincial border, French Jesuits established the episcopal residence of their newly established Vicariate Apostolic of Southeast Zhili at Zhaojiazhuang (Wei *xian*) in 1856 until it was moved to the more secure village of Zhangjiazhuang near Xianxian in the early 1860s.[5]

It is important to note that the above locations are all in the northern half of the North China Plain. There were no surviving congregations in southern Shandong, in the southern appendage of Zhili, or on the entire Huaibei Plain (the southernmost part of the North China Plain), with the sole exception of Luyi in Guide prefecture, Henan. In the past, the turbulent southwestern part of Shandong province had been considered too dangerous for missionary work. It was not until the 1880s and 1890s that the newly established, rather more dynamic, Society of the Divine Word (SVD) appeared on the scene.[6] Under its ambitious vicar apostolic, the Bavarian Johann Baptist Anzer, the vicariate of South Shandong developed into one of the most successful mission fields in China. Furthermore, SVD activities created evangelistic opportunities for French Jesuits across the border in Xuzhou prefecture, Jiangsu. The entire village of Houjiazhuang in Dangshan *xian*, hard on the border with Shandong, was converted in 1890 and became the base for the rapid expansion of Christianity in northernmost Jiangsu in the 1890s.[7]

THE CULTURE OF VIOLENCE ON THE NORTH CHINA PLAIN

The growth of the missionary enterprise during the second half of the nineteenth century was accompanied by persistent anti-Christian protest. In certain parts of China such violence could be part of the growing resistance by the Chinese people to the increasing pressures exerted by the imperialist powers. It can also be argued in some instances that such conflict was a reaction to the disruptive effect of foreign missionary activities on the traditional political and cultural fabric of rural society. Important though these external factors may have been in generating *jiaoan*[8] in some parts of China, this essay asserts that on the North China Plain the most important source of anti-Christian conflict sprang from increasingly intolerable endogenous circumstances.

This densely populated yet highly insecure environment, with progressively deteriorating economic conditions and a paucity of upper gentry, fostered socially disruptive human behavior and encouraged aggressive survival strategies. In this overwhelmingly rural periphery—in both macroregional and administrative terms—one found autonomous collectivities pursuing illicit productive activities beyond the reach of the law and of tax collectors, subversive elements ranging from heterodox sects to seditious secret societies and martial arts specialists, as well as bands of brigands and salt smugglers.[9]

One of these marginal zones of the north China macroregion was Huaibei, an area of chronic rebelliousness studied by Elizabeth Perry.[10] Her multidimensional "ecological" approach establishes the underlying reality of geographically differentiated patterns of organized violence. In her treatment of various types of local militarized collectivities, Perry has established two analytically distinct modes of collective competitive action: a predatory strategy which included feuding, banditry, and salt smuggling, and a protective strategy which included crop-watching, community fortification, and various forms of village and intervillage self-defense. Factional strife was predominantly, but not exclusively, competition for scarce resources of all kinds: gaining or protecting economic resources as well as expanding or preserving political and social prestige among leaders. Perry argues that "under conditions of scarcity, violence against fellow competitors is often a rational strategy. Environments where resources are in short and unpredictable supply may breed conflict as a way of life. Denial of essentials to others is seen as contributing directly to one's own chances for survival."[11]

Indeed, since the mid-nineteenth-century rebellions, and especially so by the late 1890s when predatory activities had become ubiquitous in the border areas, many villages of north China had become fortified. Evidence of this aspect of competitive violence was observed by the British legation official Sydney Francis Mayers when he traveled through the Henan-Shandong-Jiangsu border region in December 1897:

> On leaving Kuei-tê-fu one enters into a sort of no man's land, between the three provinces of Honan, Shantung, and Chiangsu, which is infested with all the outlaws of these three jurisdictions. They are leagued together in an organisation locally known as the "Shih pa t'uan," or 18 bands, and inhabit the walled villages or "chai" along the main road [from Guide to Xuzhou]. They elect a headman and combine together to resist official interference in their affairs. But their combination begins and ends in being "agin the Government," and does not prevent them from constantly waging desperate war against each other. Every 5 miles or so we passed one of their "chai."[12]

Yet it was precisely in these turbulent and disaster-prone backwaters on the North China Plain that the rapid expansion of Christianity occurred. In this culture of violence the missionaries were able to offer much more than spiritual benefits. Here their effective intervention in what essentially were on-going struggles for scarce resources were of crucial importance and brought remarkable results. Their "political" incentives, in particular, were a powerful attraction. Many of those who could not expect help from or were at odds with the dominant elements in these fiercely competitive local systems turned to the church for support. The foreign priests demonstrated their power by winning disputes on behalf of converts and potential converts, exposing false accusations, and preventing exactions by rapacious yamen underlings, excessive landlord exploitation, and sometimes even bandit attacks. Thus "conversion" became part of the repertoire of collective—and to some extent individual—rural survival strategies for a significant minority in a violently competitive environment. In other words, missionaries became effective local protectors, influencing patterns of predatory and parasitic activities.

While the causes of anti-Christian violence in China were many, this essay argues that in certain localities collective violence in response to Christian proselytism more often than not was a continuation of existing patterns of traditional organized conflict, which were merely aggravated by the intrusion of alien influences. The espousal of and violent reaction to Christianity should, therefore, be seen primarily as elements of the existing patterns of competitive violence.[13] In the context of the prevailing *internal* social instability during and after the Sino-Japanese War and China's increasingly precarious *external* situation, missionaries were in a position to offer attractive political and economic inducements to the rural inhabitants. In Xuzhou prefecture, for example, the French Jesuits had gained the reputation of being very powerful as a consequence of their successful settlement of the Big Sword (Dadaohui) affair in 1896. As a result of such determined and successful missionary intervention to alleviate their adherents' misery, local officials had to offer apologies, pay indemnities, and promise to protect the church. As Rosario Renaud has noted, "No power—that of the Emperor excepted—has ever achieved anything like it in Xuzhou [prefecture]."[14]

As we have already indicated, the Christians' approach was not all that different from that of traditional Chinese rural society in general and especially so in the turbulent border area, with its endemic competitive violence and relative weakness of state power. In this area the oppressed looked for new sources of power, hoping to change the status quo in their favor and settle old scores in the process. Consequently, during the years of missionary dominance after the Sino-Japanese War, their interventions substantially altered established patterns of oppression and exploitation in certain localities. The expanding Christian congregations, in turn, took full advantage of their newfound power. Or as a Jesuit priest put it, "It is above all the thirst for justice which drives the poor Chinese to us. But this liberty, or rather liberation from oppression, has gone to the heads of several. From [being] the oppressed they have become oppressors."[15] By enlisting the support of the Church, the weaker groups in local factional struggles thus had a chance to stand up to the dominant and oppressive elements. As another Jesuit priest put it, the "victims of injustice" turned to the missionaries to escape from the clutches of those making a living from litigation and false accusations.[16]

Given the prevailing unsettled conditions on the North China Plain, it is not surprising that Catholics, too, took steps to fortify their major communities. This adaptation to the local environment is perhaps best illustrated by the history of the main Jesuit residence of the Vicariate Apostolic of Southeast Zhili, namely Zhangjiazhuang (just outside Xianxian, some 130 kilometers south of Tianjin). Having witnessed the destructiveness of the so-called "White Lotus Uprising" of 1862–1863 in the Shandong-Zhili border region, the Jesuits decided to fortify their newly established central station to provide protection for the church, residence, seminary, and orphanage as well as for the five to six thousand Christians of Hejian prefecture. At the same time, the Jesuit priest Prosper Leboucq sought—and obtained—permission from the Chinese government and the French legation to proceed with the defensive project. Chonghou, the imperial commissioner for the northern ports, even provided two cannons. A work force of five hundred men—two hundred of whom were non-Christians—began construction in early June 1863. Two French officers who visited the place declared the defenses impregnable, at least as far as possible attacks by "White Lotus" and bandit gangs were concerned. Indeed, Zhangjiazhuang was protected by a moat that was fifteen to twenty feet wide and ten to twelve feet deep. Furthermore, the excavated soil was used to build part of the interior earth wall, which was some twenty-five feet high. In addition, the missionaries had purchased three cannons and cast another eight in 1868 to protect themselves against bandits and rebels. Indeed, the fortification of Zhangjiazhuang was welcomed by Christians and non-Christians alike, since the nearby county seat of Xianxian had been destroyed by Taiping forces in 1853 and thus could not offer protection. Hence the local magistrate and other wealthy non-Christians were willing to supply the mission with the necessary resources to ensure themselves of a place of safety.[17] The fortification of Zhangjiazhuang in the 1860s offers an early example of cooperation between Christians and non-Christians in the face of external threats.

With the significant increase of predatory activities on the North China Plain in the 1890s, the need for protection became even greater. Now all missionaries invariably lived in fortified compounds. The village of Poli (Yanggu *xian*) in Shandong, for instance, possessed excellent defensive structures. Since it had been the first episcopal residence of the newly established Vicariate Apostolic of South Shandong, this station had a rather large church, an extensive missionary residence, orphanages for boys and girls, schools, workshops and agricultural facilities, houses for catechumens, an old people's asylum, and a clinic and dispensary.

> This huge complex is surrounded by high walls, which with their strong corner and flanking towers protect the residence in such a way that a few sentries, deployed on these towers, can hold in check a sizeable number of attackers.— Thus Poli, with its many towers and high walls, looks from a distance like a mighty fortress, like a castle of peace which, surrounded by a modest village and green trees, looks like a romantic [castle] from the Middle Ages, transplanted and adapted to the Chinese landscape.[18]

The protective aspect of mission stations is also well illustrated by the bird's-eye view of the French Jesuit station at Houjiazhuang, Dangshan *xian*, in northern Jiangsu, in Rosario Renaud's history of the Vicariate Apostolic of Suchow [Xuzhou].[19]

Although many walled villages dotted the North China Plain by the end of the nineteenth century, the above accounts indicate that rural mission stations were protected rather more effectively than ordinary settlements. In other words, in the original heartland of the Boxer movement and its precursors, that is, the Plum Flower Boxers and the Big Sword Society, the Catholic missionary enterprise was well adapted to the prevailing culture of violence. At the same time, although the Boxer episode has certain special characteristics, it is nevertheless clear that in the turbulent environment on the North China Plain the conflict between Christians and non-Christians generally was part and parcel of a tradition of violent competition for scarce resources.

BOXER ATTACKS REPULSED

When the Boxers' anti-Christian campaign was at its height in the spring and summer of 1900, thousands of Christians lost their lives and a great deal of property was destroyed all over northern China. Yet significant numbers of Catholics managed to escape to a number of fortified strongpoints in northwestern Shandong, northern Henan, Zhili, Shanxi, and Inner Mongolia. With the exception of Zhujiahe[20] in Jing *zhou*, southeastern Zhili, and one or two strongpoints in Inner Mongolia and Shanxi, the fortified mission stations successfully withstood various Boxer attacks in the summer and autumn of 1900. In the vicariate apostolic of Southeast Zhili alone, fifteen Catholic strongholds emerged (nine in the north and six in the south), "where the assembled Christians, under the direction of their missionaries, have succeeded in defending themselves and generally saved their lives and

their property."[21] In this connection, it should be pointed out that Zhangjiazhuang, Southeast Zhili's central mission station, was not attacked, although two large Boxer contingents were based at the nearby villages of
Zhangjialin and Nanzita. The place was simply too well fortified and defended.

Since the pattern of Catholic protective strategies was more or less the
same across north China, it would be tedious to present an account of each
individual armed encounter between Boxers and Christian communities.
For our purposes, the case of Wei county in southeastern Zhili is most instructive as an example of Catholic militancy. Especially in the village complex of Zhaojiazhuang, Weicun, and Pancun, the Christians and Jesuit missionaries were well prepared for the skirmishes of 1900. When
anti-Christian ferment was beginning to build up in the Shibacun[22] area
during the conflict with Zhao Sanduo's Plum Flower Boxers in the autumn
of 1898, Remi Isoré, the local Jesuit priest, was able to persuade his
congregation at Zhaojiazhuang to organize a Christian self-defense force.[23]
Albert Wetterwald established another armed group at nearby Weicun.
Wetterwald claimed, in fact, that it had been the Christians' conspicuous
defensive preparations which caused their opponents to hesitate and become divided in early November 1898.[24]

During the summer of 1900 the village triangle of Weicun-Pancun-Zhao-
jiazhuang became the center of Christian defense in the Wei district, while
all around smaller Catholic congregations were destroyed.[25] When the
question was raised whether the missionaries should stay or leave, it was decided to defend the larger congregations, with the missionaries staying as
"the moving spirit of the defense." Indeed, Albert Wetterwald assumed overall military command of the three villages. The existing ramparts around
Zhaojiazhuang were strengthened. Pancun fortified its houses into a single
defensive platform. In total, there were three guardhouses where arms and
ammunition were stored and where the fighters would assemble in case of
attack. Each post was flying a flag with a big black cross on it. Weicun had
three hundred to four hundred combatants, the entirely Christian village of
Zhaojiazhuang provided two hundred men, and Pancun fifty men, with
nearby Chenjiazhuang and Zhongguanying also supplying fifty men. They
had all kinds of arms at their disposal: some twenty *taiqiang* (Chinese blun-
derbuss or "jingal," usually operated by two men), as well as about one
hundred old-style Chinese and foreign rifles, fabricated by itinerant arti-
sans. The rest carried swords and spears. Although the missionary referred
to his arsenal as "a real museum," he added that the Christians were rather
better armed than the more numerous Boxers. In addition, the Christian
fighters were wearing white caps with either a red cross or an image of the
Sacred Heart on it.

Wetterwald noted on 7 July that the Christian *shengyuan* degree holder of Pancun had been summoned by the magistrate of Wei *xian* in response to a rumor that the converts wanted to attack the district capital. But it was not until 17 July that a Boxer force suddenly appeared on the flats of Daning, "with flags and trumpets." The Christian militia immediately moved out in battle formation, led by Wetterwald, revolver in hand. After this initial encounter, a force of a thousand Boxers approached once more from the direction of Daning on the following day. But the Catholic force attacked them from three sides, forcing the Boxers to retreat, leaving behind a number of casualties and weapons. According to Wetterwald, Zhao Laozhu (i.e., Zhao Sanduo), was one of the first to flee. "Several of our sharpshooters took aim at him, for he could be very clearly seen, parading on his horse." In this confrontation, sixty-eight Boxers were either killed or wounded.

On 20 July the Boxers commenced a rather more serious attack, with one force advancing from Daning, another from Shaxi, south of Weicun. According to Wetterwald, regular soldiers equipped with Winchesters and Mausers joined in the attack. Nevertheless, the militant priest launched a pincer movement and employed his cannons, whereupon the assailants fled in all directions. Indeed, it was reported that the defeat provoked a dispute between Zhao Sanduo and Qu Xin'gao, another Boxer leader. Qu wanted to leave with his force but in the end was persuaded to stay and launch another attack. However, in a preemptive strike by the Catholics on 22 July, their opponents were dispersed. But the Christian victory came with painful losses: the Boxers had committed atrocities in undefended Zhongguanying and Mazhuang, killing several Christians. Thereafter the Boxer threat subsided in the Weicun area. A Boxer band based at Hezhaozhen (an exclave of Shandong's Qiu district, northeast of Weicun) was forced to leave in early August when the local people refused to feed these "parasites." Wetterwald regretted the fact that a battle did not materialize at this time, "for a resounding victory would have rid us of that rabble" once and for all.[26]

The Wei *xian* episode revealed an additional tendency: The prolonged Boxer presence increasingly alienated ordinary non-Christians who were forced to feed them, as was the case at Daning—the reason why Qu wanted to leave was the lack of food for his men. Since the Christian congregations outside the fortified strongholds had all been looted, the Boxers began to capture small non-Christian landowners and hold them for ransom. Thus it is not surprising that at Zuzhencun the non-Christian militia was prepared to bar the entry of any outside band. Moreover, it remained neutral vis-à-vis the Christians. By the end of July, when the Boxer threat had significantly diminished in Wei county, deputations of local notables were arriving at the Catholic village of Weicun to discuss measures to maintain the peace. Wetterwald noted that this indicated that most "heathens" were not hostile toward the Catholics.

MISSIONARIES AND IMPERIALISM

So far we have stressed endogenous sources as an important factor in the growth of Christianity as well as opposition to it. However, the exogenous elements in this process should not be underestimated. Indeed, as far as the rise of the Boxer movement is concerned, Joseph Esherick has singled out aggressive foreign imperialism as a significant factor.[27] Although we do not fully share his assertions, the growth and relevance of certain exogenous pressures cannot be denied. From the middle of the nineteenth century, missionary work was greatly facilitated by the "unequal treaties" and associated agreements. The Beijing Convention concluded in 1860 with France, in particular, creating the conditions for the significant evangelistic expansion during the last third of the nineteenth century. Nevertheless, it was the existing internal contradictions that afforded the missionaries the opportunity to intervene in local affairs, ostensibly to protect the "religious" interests of their native adherents. Yet without the backing of foreign governments, such intervention would have been far more difficult and far less productive. In other words, although intrusive Christianity had not initiated the long-term deterioration of the rural social order, it could aggravate the trend in significant ways. The very success of missionary interference could thus give rise to new disputes and conflicts between Christians and non-Christians.

The missionaries' power and the Christians' assertiveness derived from their privileged position under the treaties and, perhaps most importantly, the French and (from 1890) German protectorates. In view of the fact that so many *jiaoan* were settled only after foreign diplomatic involvement, it is, therefore, not surprising that the missionary enterprise has long been closely identified with the overall process of imperialist expansion. But this does not necessarily indicate a deliberate collusion between the missionaries and the foreign powers, with the former acting as the tools for spreading the invasion of the foreign aggressors in the nineteenth century. What is clear, though, is that the missionaries' position would have been rather more precarious in the interior without the frequent diplomatic interventions and threats of military action.

As far as the Steyl mission of South Shandong is concerned, its vicar apostolic, Johann Baptist Anzer, is usually singled out for having provoked the upsurge of anti-Christian violence by his aggressive missionary approach and reliance on foreign intervention. He certainly was a controversial and difficult leader. Nevertheless, a careful examination of the available records reveals that before 1900 there was no sustained explicit "political collaboration" between the SVD mission and the German government. It is our contention that the SVD priests were not as such concerned with the furtherance of the narrow political and economic aims of the fatherland in

China. Theirs was essentially a supranational enterprise, and their primary loyalties lay with the Vatican, rather than with Berlin. It would be more accurate to say that, after Germany had wrested from France the protectorate over the German Catholic mission in Shandong in 1890, Anzer opportunely exploited the existing intense Franco-German imperialist rivalries to further the work of the universal church, of the Steyl mission, as well as his own personal ambitions.[28]

This opportunistic approach is well demonstrated by the events at Zhangjiazhuang (also known as Mopan-Zhangjiazhuang, in Juye *xian*, southwestern Shandong), a village that figures so prominently in the story of the proto-Boxer movement. Here, opposition to Catholic conversions began in the mid-1880s and was organized by one Yao Honglie, a military *juren* from nearby Yaojialou. He was the commander (*tuanzong*) of the local militia for some twenty villages, but his influence apparently extended over a much wider area of Caozhou prefecture.[29] It is, however, important to note that such determined and concerted action against the spread of Christianity was often inextricably linked up with a multiplicity of existing internal contradictions and patterns of competitive strife, especially—but by no means exclusively—in southwestern Shandong. Closer examination of the Zhangjiazhuang *jiaoan* of 1884–1886 suggests, for instance, that anti-Christian opposition stemmed from ongoing intracommunal discord. The very fact that so many of the village's neophytes had been members of a folk religious sect is a good indication that the decline of village cohesion was not of recent origin. Community solidarity had been further undermined by a long-standing property dispute over one *mu* of land. It probably was this dispute which prompted some of the villagers to turn to the Steyl missionaries for help.[30] Finally, Yao Honglie's intense and prolonged hostility may, in fact, have been triggered by the conversion to Christianity of one of his brothers.[31]

However, it was the murder of two missionaries more than ten years later, on 1 November 1897, that brought Zhangjiazhuang to the attention of the outside world. The story is well known and need not be retold here. What is important for our purposes is the fact that the settlement of the "Juye affair" brought the Steyl mission substantial benefits and was hailed as "a splendid atonement for the death of two missionaries." The settlement, formulated collectively by the German minister Edmund Heyking, provicar Josef Freinademetz, Bishop Anzer, and Berlin—and forced upon the Chinese—consisted of a payment of 3,000 taels as compensation for stolen or damaged property and the construction of three large "atonement" churches (at 66,000 taels each) in Yanzhou, Caozhou, and Jining (notwithstanding the fact that the Jining cathedral was already under construction and nearing completion), each to have a tablet bearing the inscription "Catholic Church Built by Order of the Emperor" (*chijian tianzhutang*). Of particular importance to this essay is the demand that seven smaller *fortified* residences were to be constructed in various localities in Caozhou prefecture (at a total cost of 24,000 taels), plus the land required therefore made available. The construction of Christian strongholds had been requested by Freinademetz who also wanted the provision of armed escorts for traveling missionaries, because such protective privileges were already being enjoyed by the French Jesuits in neighboring Xuzhou prefecture.[32]

Indeed, nowhere in north China was missionary power displayed more conspicuously than in the French Jesuit missions of southeast Zhili and northern Jiangsu. Especially in the latter area, several important Christian congregations had been established in the 1890s as a result of missionary intervention in long-standing intra- and intercommunal conflict. The feud between the Pang and Liu "clans" of Dangshan *xian*, culminating in the Big Sword incident of 1896, is our most noteworthy example. Given the general insecurity of northern Jiangsu, the foreign priests had constructed several large fortified compounds—usually funded from local indemnity payments— that were protected by permanent military guards provided by the Chinese authorities. When the above-mentioned British official passed the Jesuit mission station of Majing (Xiao *xian*, Xuzhou prefecture, Jiangsu), he observed, "Here is the church militant indeed. The buildings are surrounded by a strong castellated wall, and guarded at the corners by watch-towers, in which guns are mounted and ammunition stored."[33]

In this violently competitive environment, many Christian communities were thus better protected than most non-Christian groups. It is, however, important to keep in mind that in a sociopolitical order consisting of competing vertical power structures, the missionaries—like other local community leaders—used their power and influence to maximize their group's access to and control over resources. Missionaries had, of course, considerably more power and were able to advance their group's causes more effectively. Through their elaborate ecclesiastical networks and links with national government representatives, missionaries were able to bring persistent pressure to bear on the Chinese central government, which, in turn, was compelled to prod local officials into action. Especially in the provincial peripheries, such church-induced state interventions could compromise the long-cherished semiautonomy of local systems.

CONFLICTS IN SOUTH SHANXI

As is well known, Christians and missionaries suffered more in Shanxi than any other province during the Boxer Uprising. Yet here too Chinese Catholics, supported and led by their foreign missionaries, put up determined resistance in selected places. My attention was first drawn to this conflict in the obituary of the vicar apostolic of North Shandong, Ephrem Giesen (1868–1919). It transpired that Giesen had twice been wounded in violent clashes with Boxers in the summer of 1900, while a member of the Dutch Franciscan mission of south Shanxi.[34] The discovery of a rare publication concerning these events prompted me to follow up this story.[35] The account that follows is based on a collection of letters sent during the conflict by Dutch missionaries in southern Shanxi to their bishop, Joannes Hofman, who had fled to the Christian stronghold of Tianjiajing (Lin *xian*) in neighboring Henan province. It should be noted that these reports were written during the Boxer Uprising for internal consumption and thus are more likely to represent the missionaries' actual views at the time. These missionary observations were made in an environment that is rather different from that on the North China Plain. As late as mid-May 1900 all was quiet in the region. Yet in early July much of the mission lay in ruin.[36] However, once the decision had been taken to stand and fight, a pattern emerged that was remarkably similar to the one on the North China Plain. A cluster of fortified strongholds was hastily established in the vicinity of the prefectural city of Lu'an (now Changzhi). Seven Dutch friars assembled at Machang and its satellite village of Gaojiazhuang.[37] The aforementioned Ephrem Giesen was based at Xinzhuang, about one and a half to two hours south of Machang. A third center of resistance, but further to the north of Lu'an, was built at Zhaojialing by Theodorus Leenan and Winfridus Groeneveld. A separate fortified stronghold was based at Hanluoyan near Hongdong, further to the west.

The missionaries immediately took charge of the defensive operations, supervising the construction of earth walls around the respective villages. They authorized the purchase and manufacture of weapons and ammunition, and personally directed military operations against their assailants. Although in this part of north China the rural inhabitants were not known for their bellicosity and did not have a tradition of collective violence, the local Catholics learned very quickly how to use firearms and other weapons.[38] Yet the Christians, outnumbered and not particularly well equipped, managed to hold off and on several occasions defeat their assailants during the prolonged sieges in the summer of 1900. Indeed, none of the Dutch friars was killed. It should also be noted that Catholic missionaries, where they were able to do so,[39] would stay with their converts and provide vital leadership in dangerous times.

INCIDENTS IN INNER MONGOLIA

Inner Mongolia represents yet another contextual setting. Here the older Catholic congregations had come into being as refuges for Christians from the northern provinces during earlier persecutions. During the second half of the nineteenth century these missions had come under the care of mainly Belgian priests of the Congregation of the Immaculate Heart of Mary (CICM or Scheut Fathers), who worked primarily among the Chinese settlers. While it is not my intention to provide a detailed account of the background to and history of the Boxer crisis in Inner Mongolia, I would like to point out certain differences and similarities in the patterns of persecution and self-defense north of the Great Wall, compared to the situation on the North China Plain. The Mongol factor obviously represents a significant difference. It should be noted, for instance, that in western Inner Mongolia the united banners of Otok, Üchin, and Djasak took part in the attacks on (Chinese) Catholics.[40] It is, therefore, not surprising that the combination of "Boxer"[41] elements, regular Chinese troops, and Mongol forces was a powerful threat to the Christian communities. Consequently, the missions north of the Great Wall also suffered heavy losses during the summer of 1900.[42] Nevertheless, as in other parts of north China, certain Christian strongholds managed to hold out against powerful and persistent attacks throughout the prolonged crisis. The Belgian priests had, in fact, begun to fortify a few of their stations in the mid-1890s, in the face of increasing general turbulence in the region.[43] Thus protective measures had been taken at the major Catholic settlement of Xiaoqiaopan (called Klein-Brugge by the Scheut Fathers), western Inner Mongolia, in 1895, as rumors of a new Moslem rebellion in Gansu began to circulate. On 31 July 1900, ten Belgian missionaries and five Italian Franciscans from the Shanxi mission assembled at this strongpoint. The village's defenses proved effective during the prolonged siege by a large anti-Christian force from 9 August to 29 September 1900.[44]

A rather unusual aspect of Christian self-defense in Inner Mongolia at this time was the involvement of Commander of Artillery Arthur Wittamer of the Belgian Army who happened to be in the area as a member of a Belgian exploratory expedition to Gansu. At the height of the Boxer troubles he made his way from Gansu across Inner Mongolia to the important mission station of Xiwanzi near Zhangjiakou (Kalgan). Upon his arrival there in late June 1900, the vicar apostolic of Central Mongolia, Jeroom Van Aertselaer, CICM, appointed him "minister of arms." Wittamer immediately took charge of defensive preparations, organizing the Christians into two regiments, providing military instruction, having trenches dug, and setting up a workshop to produce artillery pieces and gunpowder. According to Wittamer, Xiwanzi was made impregnable with its four hundred rifles and six cannons. In view of these effective defensive preparations, the station was not seriously troubled by the Boxers. Indeed, Wittamer is said to have sought permission to march through Mongolia with four hundred Christians to fight the Boxers. In any event, Bishop Van Aertselaer did not agree.[45]

In view of his military training, Wittamer obviously had the necessary expertise to improve the defensive capabilities of the principal mission station in the vicariate apostolic of Central Mongolia. In the neighboring vicariate apostolic of Eastern Mongolia it was Russian troops who intervened and provided protection of the episcopal residence at Songshuzuizi (known in the missionary literature as Notre-Dame des Pins) and the three thousand Christians who had sought refuge there. This place was already heavily fortified prior to the arrival in mid-October of a small force of Siberian light cavalry and Cossacks, seventy-five men in all.[46] The defensive work in progress comprised a ditch and wall, including ten fortified points, around the village. The station had about two thousand pounds of gunpowder and an equal number of lead balls. The Russian commander Iu. L. Elets immediately set out to integrate the twenty-three foreign missionaries and local Christians into his military command structure. This combined force subsequently launched mop-up campaigns against so-called Boxers and regular Chinese military. Especially after the arrival of Lieutenant General Tserpinskii with a thousand soldiers,[47] the Russians were able not only to maintain peace in the area, but they also apprehended and tried those who were accused of having incited the Boxers against the Christians.[48] The provincial CICM (Louis Van Dyck) thought it odd that the Russians were willing to protect the station, whereas the French unit at nearby Shanhaiguan refused to do so, in spite of the fact that France exercised the religious protectorate over Belgian Catholics in China. He complained that "Christian France is in the hands of Freemasons and Jews!"[49]

FOREIGN MILITARY INVOLVEMENT ON THE NORTH CHINA PLAIN

The Russian military occupied the Songshuzuizi mission station because of its proximity to their main base at Shanhaiguan. But direct foreign military intervention in missionary cases had occurred or had been threatened from time to time ever since the conclusion of the 1858–1860 treaties. However, such intervention usually had taken place in treaty ports on the coast and along the Yangzi River. Nevertheless, as the history of the Vicariate Apostolic of Southeast Zhili indicates, occasionally there were exceptions. The French Jesuits in southeast Zhili had a longstanding relationship with the French authorities in Beijing and Tianjin. The first European military presence in this mission occurred in 1863, but it was not in connection with missionary affairs. When Imperial Commissioner Chonghou was ordered to put down "banditry" in southern Zhili, he asked for a small contingent of British drill instructors at the Dagu Forts to accompany his force. The ensuing campaign against rebels south of Weixian is not directly relevant to our story. What is interesting, however, is the fact that Chong-hou requested the French Jesuit Prosper Leboucq (later known as François-Xavier Leboucq) to act as interpreter to the British soldiers led by Captain A. H. Coney (H.M. 67th Regiment of Foot) and Tianjin Acting Consul John Gibson.[50] It is quite possible that this British foray deep into French mission territory prompted French officials to take greater interest in the affairs of the southeast Zhili vicariate. We have already noted that in the wake of the "White Lotus" unrest of 1863, the Jesuits decided to fortify the episcopal residence at Zhangjiazhuang. Not only was Leboucq sent to Beijing and Tianjin to obtain official Chinese and French approval as well as weapons for this project, during its construction two French military officers visited the mission station and, no doubt, offered valuable advice.

In the spring of 1868, the Tianjin consulate sent Mr. Simon, a former noncommissioned officer in the French infantry, to train the Zhangjiazhuang Christians in the use of some three hundred European rifles which the mission possessed. As Bishop Edouard Dubar put it, "That brave Monsieur does not spare himself; he finds much goodwill and military aptitude among our Christians." Given the expertise the Catholics were able to attract, even the most influential non-Christians were placing their hopes in the Christian defensive operations.[51] Moreover, it is interesting to note that many of the Jesuit lay brothers had spent some time in the French Army and thus had the necessary expertise to organize and drill the local Christians for defensive purposes. Finally, French civil and military officials continued to visit Zhangjiazhuang from time to time in the late nineteenth century.[52]

After the relief of the Beijing legations in August 1900, a number of punitive expeditions were sent into the surrounding countryside to protect Christian communities and collect indemnities from non-Christian inhabitants. For the most part, these post–Boxer Uprising military interventions occurred in Beijing-Tianjin area, far away from the original Boxer heartland, with one exception. In order to hasten local negotiations in the Jesuit mission of southeast Zhili, a French force was sent to Xianxian and used the Zhangjiazhuang episcopal residence as headquarters during their local pacification campaign.[53] As one Jesuit priest observed in a communication to the French minister,

> We have a French post of 2 companies who are rendering great service in the pacification of the area. Thanks to it all the Chinese officers provide themselves with a French flag and all the mandarins are busying themselves for fear of a visit from these soldiers. I have written to General Voyron about it and you can tell him of all the good this outpost has done. Our 200 men are doing more here than 1000 in Tianjin; for the Chinese feel more threatened and more overrun. The eleven magistrates of Hejian prefecture got the notables to send to the [French] soldiers their presents in [the form of] cattle, sheep, etc.

At the same time, the French troops were instrumental in compelling "guilty villages" to indemnify their Christian neighbors. Once local estimates had been established, an initial payment was exacted, supplemented in the poorer areas by compulsory levies or payments from the provincial treasury.[54]

CONCLUSION

This essay has focused on an aspect of the Boxer episode that has hitherto been ignored in the scholarly literature, namely the incidents of armed conflict between Chinese Catholics and Boxers. Such confrontations have been considered in three distinct environments: 1) on the North China Plain with a long tradition of collective violence; 2) in southern Shanxi, an area without such a tradition; and 3) in Inner Mongolia against the background of emerging competition among Chinese settlers as well as between settlers and nomadic Mongols. In each of these areas the Christians' armed response was usually led by foreign missionaries.

Needless to say, on the North China Plain the missionaries' militant approach was in keeping with the long tradition of predatory and protective violence there. Yet as the examples from other parts of north China show, Catholic determination to resist Boxer attacks was not confined to areas of traditional competitive conflict. Although the Christians in northern Zhili, Shanxi, and Inner Mongolia bore the brunt of the Boxer conflagration, here too a number of Catholic communities created strongholds and successfully fought off their adversaries. The common factor that connected Catholic militancy in these diverse ecological zones and social systems was the presence of Catholic priests. Missionaries were not merely the spiritual guides in Christian communities but were expected to exercise effective leadership in their respective local systems. Thus, when the occasion demanded it, priests everywhere, regardless of congregational affiliation or nationality, were instrumental in mobilizing their congregations for protective purposes.

Although the Christians' defensive strategy, including the construction of fortified villages, was not a departure from the traditional pattern of competitive violence on the North China Plain, the missionaries—given their Janus-faced role—had significant advantages over their non-Christian rivals. Their extensive higher-level networks enabled them to share information and acquire superior technology as well as know-how, and occasionally draw on the political power of foreign governments. Thus they had access to resources of all kinds on behalf of their Christian congregations. This contributed to the ability of a number of larger Christian communities to put up an effective resistance and weather the Boxer storm.

At the same time, a changing relationship between Catholic missionaries and secular imperialism can be perceived in the course of the Boxer episode. Initially, foreign priests and their Chinese adherents relied on "unequal" treaties and religious protectorates to operate in the interior. Whereas the relationship between religious and secular imperialism had been at best ambiguous in north China on the eve of the Boxer Uprising, in its immediate aftermath there are clear indications of close collaboration in certain localities. The foreign punitive expeditions in the wake of the uprising obviously represent one of the darkest episodes of Sino-foreign relations in modern times. Yet as has been shown, such direct foreign military intervention was confined to the Beijing-Tianjin region (including Baoding) and the Xiwanzi area north of the Great Wall. Only the French column at Zhangjiazhuang (Xianxian) came close to entering the original Boxer heartland.

In any case, rather than associating Christian militancy exclusively with foreign imperialist aggression, we have located the armed confrontations in the first instance in the culture of violence that was prevalent in the border districts on the North China Plain. It is, therefore, more appropriate to explain the Boxer Uprising in terms of the particular conjuncture from late 1898 of several internal and external developments ("scramble for concessions," accelerated growth of the Christian enterprise, the collapse of the Hundred Days Reforms in September 1898 and the rise of militant-conservatives at the Court, start of a prolonged drought) in an increasingly unstable socioeconomic environment. Since the Boxers emerged in the remote backwaters on the North China Plain, far from the centers of foreign secular imperialism, Paul Cohen's explanation of their origin and spread makes a great deal of sense, namely that the severe drought, "more than any other [factor] . . . accounted for the explosive growth of the Boxer movement." Crucially, it was the powerful anxiety-producing rumors about foreign intentions that triggered the outburst of traditional antiforeignism that had been "there all along in latent form."[55] In the hinterland of north China, the general fear of the "outsider" came to focus on missionaries and their converts as the "other," making them targets in a time of great fear and uncertainty. It was the conjuncture that transformed specific anti-Christian incidents, many of which had their origins in ongoing nonreligious conflict, into the collective action of the Boxer movement. This, in turn, prompted collective resistance by Chinese Catholics and their foreign leaders.

Indeed, it can be argued that the Boxer Uprising was in some ways a short-lived aberration emerging from the special and complex conjuncture of late 1898. It does not fit the "normal" pattern of cooperation and competition that was prevalent in late nineteenth- and early twentieth-century north China. Even during the widespread hostilities in 1900, examples can be found of cooperation between local Christians and non-Christians to repel incursions of so-called "Boxers" from outside the locality.[56] Certainly after 1900 the brief period of intense anti-Christian confrontation generally gave way to greater cooperation. Rural society at large came to appreciate the missionary's role as mediator and protector in all manner of conflicts. In the face of widespread banditry and warlord contests, fortified mission stations became once more safe havens for Christians and non-Christians alike, in north China as well as in Inner Mongolia.[57]

NOTES

1. Rev. H. Humphrey, sermon at the ordination ceremony of the American Board missionary Elijah Coleman Bridgman, Belchertown, 6 October 1829, cited in Michael C. Lazich, *E. C. Bridgman (1801–1861), America's First Missionary to China* (Lewiston, Queenstown, Lampeter: Edwin Mellen Press, 2000), 55.

2. See, for example, Joseph Freri, ed., *The Heart of Pekin: Bishop A. Favier's Diary of the Siege, May–August 1900*, (Boston: Marlier, 1901).

3. In fact, in addition to the Spirit Boxers (*Shenquan*) of northwestern Shandong, I am including here what are sometimes called proto-Boxer groups, namely the Big Sword Society (*Dadaohui*) in the Shandong-Jiangsu border area and the Plum Flower Boxers (*Meihuaquan*) in the Shandong-Zhili border area.

4. Della Chiesa, bishop of the diocese of Beijing, moved his episcopal residence to Linqing in 1701 and died there in 1721. On the early growth of Christianity on the Zhili side of the border, see especially Georges Mensaert, "Les Franciscains au service de la Propagande dans la Province de Pékin, 1705–1785," *Archivum Franciscanum Historicum* 51, nos. 1–2 (January–April 1958): 161–200; 51, no. 3 (July 1958): 273–311. On the late eighteenth-century persecutions, see Bernward H. Willeke, *Imperial Government and Catholic Missions in China during the Years 1784–1785* (St. Bonaventure, N.Y.: Franciscan Institute, 1948).

5. On the early history of the Jesuit mission in southeast Zhili, see [Henri Bernard], *La Compagnie de Jésus: L'Ancien vicariat apostolique du Tchéli sud-est - ses filiales, ses annexes* (Tianjin: Procure de la Mission de Sienhsien, 1940); François-Xavier Leboucq, *Monseigneur Édouard Dubar de la Compagnie de Jésus, évêque de Canathe, et la Mission catholique du Tche-ly-sud-est, en Chine* (Paris: F. Wattelier, 1880); Emile Becker, *Un demi-siècle d'apostolat en Chine. Le Révérend Père Joseph Gonnet de la Compagnie de Jésus*, 2nd ed. (Hejian: Imprimerie de la Mission, 1900).

6. This section is based on J. J. A. M. Kuepers, *China und die katholische Mission in Süd-Shantung 1882–1900: Die Entstehung einer Konfrontation* (Steyl: Drukkerij van het Missiehuis, 1974); Fritz Bornemann, *Johann Baptist Anzer bis zur Ankunft in Shantung 1880* (Rome: Collegium Verbi Divini, 1977); Bornemann, *Der selige P.J. Freinademetz 1852–1909. Ein Steyler China-Missionar. Ein Lebensbild nach zeitgenössischen Quellen* (Bozen: Freinademetz-Haus, 1977); Richard Hartwich, *Steyler Missionare in China, vol. 1: Missionarische Erschliessung Südshantungs 1879–1903* (St. Augustin: Steyler Verlag, 1983); Augustin Henninghaus, *P. Joseph Freinademetz SVD. Sein Leben und Wirken. Zugleich Beiträge zur Geschichte des Mission Süd-Schantung* (Yanzhou: Verlag der Katholischen Mission, 1920). Note that on account of the *Kulturkampf* in

Germany, the Society of the Divine Word (SVD) was established by the German priest Arnold Janssen in the small Dutch village of Steijl near the German border in 1875. Hence the SVD missionaries are also known as Steyl missionaries.

7. On the opening of missionary work in Xuzhou prefecture, see Rosario Renaud, *Süchow. Diocèse de Chine, vol. 1: (1882–1931)* (Montreal: Editions Bellarmin, 1955); [Henri Boucher], *Le Père L. Gain S.J. (1852–1930). Apôtre du Siu-tcheou Fou, Vicariat de Nan-king* (Xujiahui, Shanghai: Imprimerie de l'Orphelinat de T'ou-sè-wè, 1931); Augustin-M. Colombel, *L'Histoire de la Mission du Kiang-nan,* 3 parts in 5 vols. (Shanghai: Imprimerie de l'Orphelinat de T'ou-sè-wè, 1899).

8. The Chinese term *jiaoan* is usually translated as "missionary case." A more appropriate translation would be "religious case."

9. See G. William Skinner, "Social Ecology and the Forces of Repression in North China: A Regional-Systems Framework for Analysis" (paper prepared for the ACLS Workshop on Rebellion and Revolution in North China, Harvard University, 27 July–2 August 1979), 47–48.

10. Elizabeth J. Perry, *Rebels and Revolutionaries in North China* (Stanford: Stanford University Press, 1980).

11. Perry, *Rebels and Revolutionaries,* 3.

12. Sidney Francis Mayers, "Report of a Journey from Peking to Shanghai Overland," in Great Britain, *Foreign Office Papers, Diplomatic and Consular Reports, Miscellaneous Series, No. 466* (1898) (London: Eyre & Spottiswoode, 1898), 13.

13. For a fuller discussion of the spread of and reaction to Christianity in this area on the eve of the Boxer Uprising, see R. G. Tiedemann, "Rural Unrest in North China, 1868–1900: With Particular Reference to South Shandong" (PhD diss., School of Oriental and African Studies, University of London, 1991), chapter 5.

14. Renaud, *Süchow,* 200.

15. J. Twdry, SJ. Lüzhou (Anhui), letter dated 16 December 1898, in *Lettres de Jersey* 18, no. 1 (June 1899): 30.

16. Gain, Xuzhou, June 1897, in Renaud, *Süchow,* 217–18. In Shan *xian* (Shandong) the entire village of Jiazhuang was converted because of a long-standing conflict with neighboring villages. See Bornemann, *Freinademetz,* 180–81. On converts as an integral part of a violent environment, see also Leboucq, 18 January 1870, in *Annales de la Propagation de la Foi* 42 (September 1870): 342–43.

17. Leboucq, *Dubar,* 210–14; Gonnet to Lallemand, n.d., in France, Archives Diplomatiques, Nantes, Beijing Legation Archives, Carton 67, Dossier: Correspondances, Missions Tcheli Sud-East 1863–1890. Note that Marie-Charles-Henri-Albert, comte de Lallemand, was French minister to China from 1866–1868.

18. Josef Kösters, "Puoli einst und jetzt," *Stadt Gottes* 46 (1922–1923): 182. See also the photo of part of the wall on the same page. In the summer of 1900 the Poli mission complex withstood four assaults. Located near the northern boundary of the vicariate of South Shandong—and thus close to the cradle of the Spirit Boxers (*Shenquan*)—it was the only fortified station of the SVD mission to be attacked by what appear to have been Boxers. See Bornemann, *Freinademetz,* 332–39, 677–78.

19. Illustration in Renaud, *Süchow,* between pages 158 and 159.

20. For an account of the destruction of Zhujiahe, see Jean-Paul Wiest, "Catholic Images of the Boxers," *American Asian Review* 9, no. 3 (Fall 1991): 41–66. On Catholic self-defense in northern Zhili, see Jean-Marie Planchet, comp., *Documents*

sur les martyrs de Pékin pendant la persécution des Boxeurs, 2nd ed. (Beijing: Impr. des Lazaristes, 1922–1923). 2 vols. Events in Xuanhua district are covered in vol. 2, 321–448.

21. Emile Becker to the French minister, Xianxian, 25 Nov 1900, in France, Archives Diplomatiques, Nantes, Beijing Legation Archives, Carton 21, Dossier II. Although foreign missionaries generally took control of defensive operations against the Boxers, it should be noted that in a few instances Chinese priests were in charge. Thus the defense of the old Christian village of Qingcaohe, Jing *zhou,* southeast Zhili, was led by the Chinese Jesuit priest Chiu. See P. X. Mertens, *The Yellow River Runs Red: A Story of Modern Chinese Martyrs* (St. Louis, Missouri: B. Herder Book Co., 1939), 45, note 9.

22. Shibacun was a Shandong exclave in Zhili province, bordering on Wei *xian* to the west and south.

23. Remi Isoré, "La chrétienté de Tchao-kia-tchoang sur le pied de guerre (Journal du P. Isoré)," *Chine et Ceylan* 1, no. 2 (April 1899): 107.

24. For details of the 1898 conflict, see Tiedemann, "Rural Unrest in North China," 282–88.

25. This detailed account is based on Albert Wetterwald, "Une armée chrétienne improvisée. Défense de Wei-tsuen. (Extraits du journal du P. A. Wetterwald)," *Études* 38e année, tome 86 (5 March 1901): 663–93; also published in *Chine et Ceylan* 2 (March 1901): 275–314. Note that a second center of resistance was based at Zhangjiazhuang in northern Wei *xian,* under the leadership of Wetterwald's cousin, the ex-major Victor Lomüller. Although Zhangjiazhuang held out in 1900, Lomüller was killed on 26 April 1902, when Jing Tingbin's tax resistance movement joined up with Boxer remnants in southern Zhili. It should also be noted that Wetterwald's brother Paul was in charge of the successful defense of the Christian settlement of Fanjiageda, east of the city of Hejian, in 1900. See Jules Bataille, "Siège de Fan-kia-kata par les Boxeurs (juin—septembre 1900)," *Études* 38e année, tome 87 (20 May 1901): 433–56.

26. The Wei *xian* episode of 1900 is also summarized in Lu Yao, *Yihequan yundong qiyuan tansuo* [A search for the origins of the Boxer movement] (Ji'nan: Shandong daxue chubanshe, 1990), 148–50.

27. Joseph W. Esherick, *The Origins of the Boxer Uprising* (Berkeley: University of California Press, 1987). See especially chapter 3, "Imperialism for Christ's Sake."

28. Although there is as yet no comprehensive account of the imperialist dimension of missionary affairs in Shandong, the issue is too complex to be dealt with here. For further details on the French protectorate in general, see H. M. Cole, "The Origins of the French Protectorate over Catholic Missions in China," *American Journal of International Law* 34, no. 3 (July 1940): 373–491. On the German protectorate, see Karl Josef Rivinius, *Weltlicher Schutz und Mission. Das deutsche Protektorat über die katholische Mission von Süd-Shantung* (Cologne and Vienna: Böhlau Verlag, 1987), chapters 7 and 8. The prevailing view that the overly aggressive missionary approach in southern Shandong gave rise to the Boxer movement is rather simplistic. After all, this part of the North China Plain was only marginally affected by the uprisings in the summer of 1900.

29. See Bornemann, *Freinademetz,* 103–4 and 570, notes 61–70; Kuepers, *China und die katholische Mission,* 31–32, 40; Henninghaus, *Freinademetz,* 176, 182–83;

Hartwich, *Steyler Missionare*, 84–85. Yao Honglie was a military *juren* of 1851. See *Shandong tongzhi* [Gazetteer of Shandong province], repr. of 1915 edition (Shanghai: Commercial Press, 1934–1935), 3161. During the Nian rebellion, he had been a major militia leader in western Shandong. See *Xuxiu Juye xianzhi* [Continuation of the Juye gazetteer], facsimile of the 1921 ed. (Taibei: Chengwen chubanshe, 1967), 261. See also the reminiscences of respondents Yao Langtong and Yao Laicheng, in *Shandong Yihetuan diaocha ziliao xuanbian* [Selected survey materials on the Boxers in Shandong] (Ji'nan: Qi-Lu shushe, 1980), 34. They claim that Yao Honglie's household owned some ten qing (one thousand mu) of land.

30. Tagliabue to Patenôtre, Beijing, 20 July 1885, in France, Archives Diplomatiques, Nantes, Beijing Legation Archives, carton 10; Cogordan to Zongli Yamen, 31 Jan 1886, in France, Archives Diplomatiques, Nantes, Beijing Legation Archives, carton 10; Zhongyang yanjiuyuan jindaishi yanjiusuo, ed., *Jiaowu jiaoan dang* [Files on religious affairs and missionary cases], series IV, vol. 1 (Taibei: Zhongyang yanjiu yuan, Jindai shi yanjiusuo, 1976), #285. Note that at the beginning of 1887 there were 115 Christians in the village, 90 of whom had been baptized. Hartwich, *Steyler Missionare*, 108.

31. *St. Michaels Kalender* (Steyl, 1888): 56; Kuepers, *China und die katholische Mission*, 47. In addition to Yao Honglie, the Juye gazetteer lists another two individuals with the same generational element in their given names, namely Yao Hongjie, likewise a militia leader during the Nian rebellion, and in 1885–1886 and 1893–1894 magistrate of Feng *xian* (Jiangsu); and Yao Hongkui, who was a military *juren* of 1888. *Xuxiu Juye xianzhi*, 214, 246–47; *Feng xianzhi* [Gazetteer of Feng district], 1894 ed., 200; *Shandong tongzhi*, 3168.

32. See Freinademetz's lengthy list of desiderata entitled, "Kurzer Überblick über die Missionsverhältnisse in der Praefectur Z'ao-tschou-fu," n.d., received by the German legation on 5 Dec 1897, Bundesarchiv Berlin Lichterfelde, Deutsche Gesandtschaft Peking (R 9208), vol. 326, fol. 200–202.

33. Mayers, "Report of a Journey," 14.

34. Fidentius van den Borne, "In Memoriam Z. D. H. Mgr. Giesen O.F.M.," *Het Missiewerk* 1 (1919/20), 161–62.

35. The letters and reports were published as *Een blik in Zuid-Chan-Si tijdens de jongste verfolging*, Verslag van eenige Missionarissen aan Mgr. J. Hofman, Vic. Ap. Met toelichtingen (Cuyk a. d. Maas: Jos. J. van Lindert, n.d. [Imprimatur 1901]). I would like to thank Sara Lievens of the Chinese Memorial Library, F. Verbiest Foundation, Leuven, Belgium, for having made a copy of this rare publication for me.

36. *Een Blik*, 19. It is interesting to note that Qiao Zhiqiang, *Yihetuan zai Shanxi diqu shiliao* [Historical documents on the Boxers in the Shanxi region] (Taiyuan: Renmin chubanshe, 1980) does not include any cases from southern Shanxi.

37. Odericus Timmer, Norbertus Janssens, Cassianus Pompe, Gerardus van Elk, Aegidius Broekman, Christopherus van Bussel, Sergius Schuurman.

38. Only the Catholics at Hanluoyan knew how to handle firearms, because of the well-established practice of hunting in this part of Shanxi.

39. It should be noted that the missionaries in Shandong, Protestants as well as Catholics, were ordered by Governor Yuan Shikai to leave the interior. Only two or three managed to stay behind. In other provinces of north China most Catholic missionaries did, in fact, remain with their converts.

40. Joseph Leonard Van Hecken, *Les réductions catholiques du pays des Ordos: une méthode d'apostolat des missionnaires de Scheut* (Schöneck/Beckenried: Administration der Neuen Zeitschrift für Missionswissenschaft, 1957), 20.

41. The term "Boxer" may not always be appropriate in its north China context, but in Inner Mongolia its use is particularly ambiguous.

42. Two thousand Christians and eight CICM missionaries, including the bishop of the Vicariate Apostolic of Southwest Mongolia, Ferdinand Hamer, were killed in the summer of 1900. The fortified mission station of Tiegedan'gou, to the north of Guihuacheng (now Hohhot), Inner Mongolia, also offers a rare example of Protestant missionaries being invited to seek shelter at a fortified Catholic mission station. However, the station was taken by Chinese troops on 22 August and three CICM priests were killed, as well as several Swedish Protestant missionaries and their children, along with a large number of Chinese Catholics.

43. On the rise of Mongolian banditry in reaction to the influx of Chinese settlers, the change of economic conditions, and Catholic missionary land purchases, see Michael Underdown, "Banditry and Revolutionary Movements in Late 19th and Early 20th Century Mongolia," *Mongolian Studies* 6 (1980): 109–16. See also Walther Heissig, "Some New Information on Peasant Revolts and People's Uprisings in Eastern (Inner) Mongolia in the 19th Century (1861–1901): 77–99," in *Analecta Mongolica. Dedicated to the Seventieth Birthday of Professor Owen Lattimore*, ed. Urgunge Onon and John Gombojabe Hangin (Bloomington, Indiana: Mongolia Society, 1972).

44. Bongaerts, 30 September 1900, in *Missions en Chine et au Congo* (1901): 7–8. See also Carlo van Melckebeke, *Service social de l'Église en Mongolie* (Brussels: Éditions de Scheut, [1968]), 65–66. For an illustration of the impressive defensive works of the Xiaoqiaopan complex, admittedly from a slightly later period but providing indications of the earliest fortifications, see the drawing between pages 68 and 69. For a detailed account of the siege, see also Edmond Vereenooghe, *Vervolging in China. Belegering van Klein-Brugge, Ortos, Zuid-West Mongolië. Van 1 Oogst (vooravond van St. Pieter in de banden) tot 29 September 1900* (Brugge: Karel Beyart, 1901).

45. For more details, see Koen De Ridder, "Congo in Gansu (1898–1906): 'Missionary versus Explorer/Exploiter,'" in *Footsteps in Deserted Valleys: Missionary Cases, Strategies and Practice in Qing China*, ed. Koen De Ridder (Louvain: Leuven University Press, 2000), 131, note 81; André Lederer, *La mission du Commandant A. Wittamer en Chine (1898–1901)* (Brussels: Koninklijke Academie voor Overzeese Wetenschapen, 1984), 63–64.

46. See Louis Van Dyck's journal, 26 July 1900, in *Missions en Chine et au Congo* (1901), 17. See also the photo of a section of the high stone wall, on p. 65.

47. Van Dyck, letter dated Shanhaiguan, 19 November 1900, in *Missions en Chine et au Congo* (1901): 11–12.

48. Note the photograph in *Missions en Chine et au Congo* (1901): 65, with the caption "Commander Elets condemning to death a heathen burgomaster," with all present, including the condemned man, looking intently at the camera. Elets later noted that the "tormentor of missionaries" was executed in public and his body left in the offending village to serve as an example. Iu. L. Elets, "La Mongolie Orientale et les Missions belges pendant la révolte de ce pays en 1900," *Bulletin de la Société Royale de Géographie d'Anvers* 27 (1903): 339.

49. Van Dyck, Notre-Dame des Pins (Songshuzuizi), 28 November 1900, in *Missions en Chine et au Congo* (1901): 68. For further details concerning the incorporation of the assembled missionaries into the defense of Songshuzhuizi, see also Elets, "La Mongolie Orientale," 335–55; Elets, *Smert' idet! (Osvobozhdenie Russkim otradom episkopa, 13 sviashchennikov i 3000 khristian Vostochnoi Mongolii v posledniuiu Kitaiskuiu voinu)* [Death marches! (The liberation by a Russian detachment of a bishop, 23 priests and 3000 Christians of Eastern Mongolia in the recent Chinese war)] (Moscow, 1901).

50. See Gibson to Bruce, #6, 21 Feb 1863; #13, 30 Apr 1863; #14 , 4 May 1863, in Great Britain, Foreign Office Archives, Kew: The National Archives, FO 228, Embassy and Consular Archives, vol. 355. Gibson was wounded during the campaign. Leboucq received the "blue button in a gold order" from the Chinese government in recognition of his services during the campaign. See also Leboucq, *Dubar,* 199–206.

51. Dubar to Lallemand, Zhangjiazhuang, 15 May 1868, in France, Archives Diplomatiques, Nantes, Beijing Legation Archives, Carton 67, Dossier: Correspondances, Missions Tcheli Sud-East 1863–1890. See also Leboucq, *Dubar,* 281. Simon was later killed during the "Tianjin Massacre" of 1870.

52. For example, Gaston de Bezaure, the newly arrived student interpreter at the French legation, spent several months at the Jesuit residence in 1871. In late 1899, and against the background of Franco-German rivalry over the religious protectorate, the German SVD priest Rudolf Pieper asked the German legation to ship arms and ammunition to his mission in South Shandong. As Boxer activities intensified in the spring of 1900, the German minister Clemens von Ketteler was no longer opposed. However, the outbreak of the Boxer War prevented the actual shipment of arms. Ketteler to Freinademetz, Beijing, 27 April 1900, Bundesarchiv Berlin Lichterfeld, Deutsche Gesandtschaft Peking (R 9208), vol. 328, fols. 133–134. The preceding correspondence is found on fols. 110–132.

53. See the report (with photographs) in *Chine et Madagascar* 8 (September 1901): 427–28, 439.

54. French legation, Beijing, to Delcassé, #53, 1 May 1902, in France, Archives Diplomatiques, Nantes, Beijing Legation Archives, Carton 21, Dossier II. When the French forces departed in 1901, they left behind a stockpile of weapons. In 1928, when the region was once again in turmoil, the missionaries requested the French legation to replace the stored arms with more modern equipment.

55. Paul A. Cohen, *History in Three Keys: The Boxers as Event, Experience, and Myth* (New York: Columbia University Press, 1997), 95, 94.

56. Note, for example, the joint resistance of Catholics and the original Big Swords of South Shandong when other so-called "Big Swords" intruded from outside the area. See R. G. Tiedemann, "The Big Sword Society and Its Relations with the Boxer Movement, 1895–1900" (unpublished paper presented at the Symposium Commemorating the Centenary of the Boxer Movement, held in Ji'nan, Shandong, China, October 9–12, 2000), 17-18. Aside from the problem of determining what is meant by "Boxers," the relationship between the non-Christian population and the so-called Boxers is a complex issue that deserves further study. Suffice it here to say that in the contest between "Boxers" and Christians, the local non-Christian

population could be pro-Boxer, or more commonly opportunistically neutral, or even anti-Boxer, especially during the later stages of the Boxer movement.

57. On the protective function of mission stations after 1900, see R. G. Tiedemann, "They Also Served! Missionary Interventions in North China, 1900–1945," in *Dong-Ya Jidujiao zaiquanyi (Re-interpreting the East Asian Christianity)*, ed. Tao Feiya and Philip Yuen-Sang Leung (Hong Kong: Centre for the Study of Religion and Society, Chung Chi College, Chinese University of Hong Kong, 2004), 155–94. On the intensification of the Christian village fortification program in Inner Mongolia in the early twentieth century, see for example Van Melckebeke, *Service social de l'Église en Mongolie.*

3

(A) Subaltern('s) Boxers

An Indian Soldier's Account of China and the World in 1900–1901

Anand A. Yang

This chapter casts an unusual perspective on the Boxer Uprising by examining it from the standpoint of Gadhadhar Singh, an Indian soldier who was part of the international expedition of eight nations that lifted the siege of Beijing. It follows him into the thick of the tumultuous events in China in 1900–1901 to delve into four topics: 1) the Boxer Uprising as recounted by this Indian subaltern; 2) his sense of self-identity as shaped by his China experiences; 3) his eyewitness account of the "looting" of China; and 4) his reflections on comparing China and India to one another and both of them to Japan and Europe, a comparative perspective that oriented toward pan-Asianism.

Gadhadhar Singh, a subaltern,[1] "speaks" through a text that he authored entitled *Chin meh Terah Mas* (Thirteen months in China). Parenthetically subtitled *Chin Sangram* (The China War), the book advertises itself on its cover as "a full eyewitness account of the great war in China in 1900–1901 A.D., and a brief history of China and Japan, customs and practices, Chinese religious beliefs, [their] well being, relations with other countries, information regarding military forces and states, and a complete description of famous temples, buildings etc., Boxer uprising, foreign occupation—so on and so forth, generally characteristic descriptions of all knowable and suitable subjects." Published in the north Indian city of Lucknow in 1902, the book identifies its author on the cover as Thakur Gadhadhar Singh, the *thakur* in the name adding the honorific title meaning "lord" or "master" that is generally attached to Rajput elite or to landed gentry—Rajputs are Kshatriya or warrior caste. It also lists the well-known area of Dilkushi, Lucknow, as Singh's address and indicates that the book could be obtained from him. The initial run of this work was one thousand copies.[2]

My interest in this subaltern is not only because Singh's "enunciatory position" is accessible—for the colonial period such opportunities are few and far between (As one subaltern studies historian writes, "Workers or peasants . . . produce goods and services, not documents"[3])—but also because his "voice-consciousness" surfaced in a particularly complex encounter, a "contact zone" in Mary Louise Pratt's terms, "a space in which peoples geographically and historically separated come into contact with each other and establish ongoing relations, usually involving conditions of coercion, radical inequality, and intractable conflict"; in short, a social space "where disparate cultures meet, clash, and grapple with each other, often in highly asymmetrical relations of domination and subordination."[4]

The subaltern who speaks—subaltern not only in the Gramscian sense of an unvoiced and disempowered person but also in the contemporary sense of a junior officer mediating between the upper echelons and the rank and file—is Gadhadhar Singh, and the "contact zone" he was lodged in was the China of 1900, where he had been dispatched as a member of the largely Indian-manned British military force that participated in the international expedition.[5] To his superiors Singh was merely another faceless "Jack Sepoy"; to his fellow French and German soldiers he was a "coolie," a term that these soldiers applied derisively to Indian troops; and to the Chinese he was a *"heigui,"* a black devil.[6]

Singh was a member of the 7th Rajputs, also known as the 7th Duke of Connaught's Own Bengal Infantry. Although his account of his experiences in China is rather prosaically entitled *Thirteen Months in China*, its contents are remarkably compelling: It is a vernacular text written in Hindi by a subaltern, about subaltern experiences, and intended for fellow subalterns and the emerging reading public. As he announces in the preface, his intention is to share the *samachar* (news or information) about the China campaign with others returning from the war, those interested in the story of victorious soldiers, and those interested in learning about China.

This subaltern's voice, furthermore, cuts through and rises above the "noise" of the contemporary colonial discourse. Consider how different is the tone and tenor of his commanding officer, H. B. Vaughan, whose "Account of the Relief of the Peking Legations by an Officer of the British Contingent," ostensibly cobbled together from his diary, was packaged as a book entitled *St. George and the Chinese Dragon*, first published in 1902 and reissued in 2000, presumably as a piece of Raj nostalgia and to commemorate the Boxer centennial.[7] Instructive as well is a comparison of this subaltern's account with that of Amar Singh, a Rajput nobleman who was also part of the international expedition but as a member of an elite corps. His voluminous diaries have been edited by two prominent political scientists as *Reversing the Gaze*; in the words of the dust jacket, it is the writings of "a colonial subject [who] contemplates an imperial other."[8] The latter does indeed dwell on the "other," although not from a subaltern perspective. We also know quite a bit about the general history of this regiment through a detailed account of the 3rd Battalion of this regiment and its 1900–1901 China-specific activities from official dispatches and reports generated during that campaign.[9]

The China that Gadhadhar Singh encountered in 1900—and seemingly construed as such—was a "semicolony," a country under "multiple colonialisms" to use Paul Cohen's term, in which the multiple colonial effect stemmed from its "partial domination not by one but by a plurality of foreign nations" and thus had a "'layered' or 'spliced' character" to it.[10] The formidable presence of this "plurality" was evidenced by the multinational character of the so-called Beijing "relief force" of eight nations. As a member of this force, Singh recounts many occasions when he fought alongside or participated in activities involving men of other nations. At times, he came into direct contact with Americans, Japanese, and Russians, as well as with the local Chinese populace. In some cases, he recalls conversations with specific foreign individuals whom he generally identifies by nationality and occupation but not by name.

As a native of colonial India recruited to fight on behalf of his British masters, Singh had firsthand experience of the workings of colonialism—at home and now abroad as well. Unusual, too, was his involvement in the international expedition because it thrust him as a colonial subject into the role of advancing the semicolonial project of the foreign powers in China. The expedition, moreover, represented a new stage in cooperation among the imperial powers (and Japan) at the dawn of a new century which brought to a close two decades of intense competition among them for Africa, Southeast Asia, and the Pacific islands.[11]

Throughout his text of 319 pages Singh shows himself to be keenly aware of defining himself in relation to the coalition that had assembled in China to confront the Boxers and the Qing state and ever conscious of his multiple notions of self and others—really an ensemble of others because he differentiates among the different Europeans yet lumps them together in relation to the Japanese, notwithstanding the Euro-American-Japanese collective role in the international expedition. (Americans are also highlighted in a number of different sections.)

Singh's subaltern outlook was no doubt also reinforced by his Hindu reformist beliefs. Whether he was formally affiliated in 1900 with the Arya Samaj, the Hindu reform organization that sought a return to a "purified" Hinduism is unclear, but his language and concerns in portraying China— and in comparing China to India—reveal a distinct Arya Samaj flavor. He consistently harks back to the Vedas as the sole repository of knowledge and he often refers to his country as "Aryavarta," an appellation favored by Swami Dayananda Saraswati (1824–1883), the founder of that movement, in order to claim it as the land where Aryans had been in residence from the very beginning of time. Singh also expresses considerable interest in such Arya Samaj issues as idolatry, child marriage, and the status of women. Nor would it have been unusual for a sepoy to be an Arya Samajist. Although some elements of that movement were known to oppose Indian involvement in the colonial military, others were known to proselytize sepoys.[12] A decade later he was openly identified as the author of various Arya Samaj tracts.[13]

Singh's account is also notable because it exhibits familiarity with some of the contemporary writings in English that were rushed into print in the aftermath of the Boxer Uprising and of the sensation that had been created around the world by the siege of the foreign legations in Beijing in the summer of 1900. Two works that the author specifically alludes to are Robert Hart's essays (especially the piece on "The Peking Legations: A National Uprising and International Episode," which first appeared in the *Fortnightly Review* in November 1900), which were subseqently issued as a collection of articles titled *These From the Land of Sinim* and which were much criticized for their seemingly sympathetic portrait of the Boxers and apparent attempt to convey "a Chinese point of view," and Neville P. Edwards's *The Story of China*.[14]

For Gadhadhar Singh, an Indian subaltern who marched under the flag of the British Empire, the Boxer movement was a *"bidroha,"* an uprising or revolt of peasants. Note his use of the term *bidroha* rather than *rajdroha*, which implies rebellion against authority, against government. In identifying it as an uprising, he anticipates its preferred designation in the current historiography.[15]

Singh's specific remarks on the Boxers opens with a caveat: the term "Boxers" he emphasizes is a word of foreign fiction. The Chinese term for them, he tells us, is "I ho chuan" or "Fists of Righteous Harmony," and he attributes their beginnings to the organization with the same name and to another body known as the Dadaohui (Big Sword Society). He does not divulge whether he arrived at this understanding based on his own personal knowledge or experiences while he was stationed in China. Certainly, he bases some of his information on the above-mentioned works by Hart and Edwards. In fact, he cites the latter's *Story of China*, specifically its observation about the "two societies . . . whom we call 'The Boxers.'" He also relies on its depiction of an initiation rite to convey a sense of their beliefs and practices.[16]

While echoing these two contemporaneous accounts, Singh's history of the Boxers also sounds different notes. His emphasis is apparent in the discussion that follows his reference to Hart's book, from which he quotes the following passage, first in English and then in translation: "One of the best shots in a Legation guard relates how he fired seven shots at one of the chiefs . . . less than 200 yards off: the chief stood there contemptuously, pompously waving his swords as if thereby causing the bullets to pass him to right or left at will: he then calmly and proudly stalked away unhit, much to the astonishment of the sharpshooter!"[17] Left out in Singh's quote is the next line in Sir Robert Hart's statement, which states, "Though professing to know nothing beyond the domain of sense, the Chinaman is really an extravagant believer in the supernatural, and so he readily credits the Boxer with all the powers he claims."

Singh, by contrast, follows up the legation guard story by aligning himself with the believers in such supernatural *shakti* (power or force). This kind of power is nothing new, he writes; it has many historical precedents. "Who has not heard of the supernatural deeds performed by the Prophet Muhammad, the Great Master Jesus and Guru Nanak [the sixteenth-century founder of the Sikh religion]? Was the Durgadutt sword of the Punjab ruler Govind Singh any less miraculous? Therefore, it is natural to think of great results emanating from a belief in supernatural strength. But such power is only a 'cause.' The 'material cause' of real strength is effort."[18] Elsewhere in his text, he amplifies this explanation by underlining the importance of having the knowledge and technology of war making. And he emphatically states that to depend solely on such *shakti*—meaning power derived from religious faith—was to lapse into *bhul* or error or forgetfulness. His country, Hindustan, he opined, had committed this fatal error and paid a heavy price for it because it was destroyed—by which he presumably means that it was conquered and controlled by Britain. The Boxers as well had mistakenly placed their faith in their "supernatural" power and, as a result of the error of their ways, had devastated their country, or, to employ his evocative phrase, "blanketed their entire country and polity in dust."[19]

The Boxer Uprising, in Singh's estimation, was instigated by the activities of Christian missionaries, or, to use his terminology, the *"padri log"* (clergymen) or *"padri dal"* (clergy faction). Although he echoes Hart and Edwards in viewing the uprising as an outgrowth of popular and government sentiment against Western demands imposed on China as well as Western missionary activities, he is much more pointed in his condemnation of Western excesses. Contrast, for instance, the more critical position taken by Hart (in comparison to Edwards) on the role of missionaries in China and the even more negative stance adopted by Singh. According to Hart, Chinese Christians "offended public feeling by deserting Chinese for foreign cults, next they irritated their fellow-villagers by refusing . . . to take part in or share the expenses of village festivals, and lastly, . . . they shocked the official mind, and popular opinion also, by getting their religious teachers, more especially the Roman Catholics, to interfere on their behalf in litigation." Hart also expresses disapproval of—as does Singh, clearly relying on his reading of Hart—the "arrangement by which missionaries were to ride in green chairs and be recognized as the equals of Governors and Viceroys."[20]

While obviously critical of the clergy—Singh's entire discussion, in fact, is subtitled "The Boxer Provocation"—he opens his consideration of their role by posing the following questions: "Who does not know that only one religion is predominant in the world? Only religion is entirely dedicated to spiritual achievement and is our other worldly companion in this world. Therefore, who can find fault with the Christian clergy if their lives validate this devotion?"[21]

Fault he does the Christian missionaries, nonetheless. In his eyes, they were the "advance guard" for the spread of European rule. As for their converts, they were an ulcer on the village body, inflicting pain on their fellow villagers through harassments that were always supported by the missionaries.[22] One Chinese response to the high-handedness of the missionaries and their converts— as Singh implies in a discussion that once again references Edwards and Hart but takes a different tack—was the killing of an English missionary named Brooks in Shandong. In the aftermath of this incident, as also before it, foreign powers extracted many concessions from China. These demands aroused the ire of the Chinese government and Chinese society, which grew troubled by seeing the destruction wreaked on the country by the foreign powers.

Singh then poses the rhetorical question about whether the Boxers should be characterized as "wicked" or not, or whether their actions should be viewed as generated by mental anguish, by the pain that the Chinese felt over the tragic events that had transpired, involving the foreign powers, the missionaries, and their converts, on the one hand, and the Chinese government and people, on the other hand. And in case his views on this issue are not spelled out forcefully enough, he adds that the natural law is to consider the weaker party the guilty party. Might makes right, in other words, and thus the Boxers were adjudged the offenders. Not surprisingly, he closes out this discussion by declaring that weakness is a great sin.[23]

Singh's account of the "Boxer Provocation" forms the backdrop to his narrative of the events immediately preceding the siege of the legations. He first describes what he terms the "First Relief," by which he means the small allied detachment that arrived in Beijing at the end of May to protect the legations, and the subsequent unsuccessful relief expedition launched by Admiral Edward Seymour from Tianjin on June 10. Next he turns to the events relating to the actual siege itself, concluding this part of his China "news" with the moment that the international expedition arrived in Beijing on August 14. The English force that was moving in the direction of the eastern gate, he writes, was seen by guards posted on the legation wall. News of their coming quickly spread across the legation. Parenthetically— this sentence is set off in brackets—he explains that the "English force" were "Hindustani," that is, Indian soldiers, like himself, who made up the bulk of the British force. One group sought to gain entry through the so-called "sluice gate" of the Forbidden City. At three o'clock in the afternoon the commanding officer of the British troops, Lieutenant-General Sir A. Gaselee, along with other officers, including Major Vaughan of the 7th Rajputs, arrived at the legations. "That time," in his words, "was an occasion of indescribable happiness."[24]

Gadhadhar Singh's discursive route to this moment of "indescribable happiness" is paved with talk of war. Understandably so, because to reach this August moment in Beijing, he has to march the reader through the thicket of events that he either experienced firsthand, read about in contemporary English-language works, or heard about from others in the field.

War is very much the leitmotif of the "news" that Singh presents in the first 122 pages of the book, which records, roughly in chronological order, the experiences of Singh's 7th Rajputs Battalion, beginning with its embarkation from Calcutta on board the *Palamcottah* on June 19, 1900, to almost three months later, when he and his men were among the first members of the allied force to enter the legations. Sprinkled throughout these pages as well are ruminations of one sort or another: some personal, some historical, and some philosophical, many of them proclaiming this subaltern's heightened notion of himself as a Rajput warrior and a Hindustani.

Meditations on war abound because of the high premium Singh places on its centrality to his professional and personal preoccupations. At one point he writes in English (and glosses in Hindi at the bottom of the page)—unquestionably influenced by the poet Rudyard Kipling's well-known couplet about "Four things greater than all things are, Women and Horses and Power and War"—that "Two things better than all things are, The first is power the second is war!"[25] He accords war such a place of honor that he pronounces "all knowledge . . . incomplete without knowledge of war." No wonder he expresses strong disagreement with those religious leaders who he says consider killing inhumane and equate war with the way of the jungle and not of civilization. Not so, he insists, offering as proof his contention that it was precisely a lack of fighting skills and knowledge of war that has historically led to bloodshed. In his reckoning, more blood was spilled in an earlier era when people only knew how to fight with swords. However, as warfare developed, such as with the advent of guns, the number of casualties declined.[26]

About power the Hindustani subaltern is relatively quiet, at least explicitly. Implicitly, however, much of what he says about war touches on power, especially when he correlates experience in and knowledge of warfare with power. In fact, he views the power of states and peoples as resting on a military foundation and military know-how as being a correlate of civilization. Noticeable is his obvious envy of "civilized" countries where he says there were twelve-year-olds who were knowledgeable about war.

Singh found his own countrymen and country wanting on this score. "Our" educated people—those who had BA and MA degrees and those who held professional offices—he laments, knew little about warfare and, lamentably, were not embarrassed about their ignorance. They were not familiar with the different kinds of military strategies involved in fighting in different terrains. Nor were they aware of the histories of foreign countries and of European naval warfare. He singles out European armies for praise, mentioning in particular that they were well-equipped and recruited from a variety of groups, including volunteers, peasants, lords, young people, and various castes and races. In his estimation, those people who were not knowledgeable or experienced in warfare, did not respect such knowledge, or did not consider it their duty to familiarize themselves with it had brains that were filled with the clods of earth from Beijing's Coal Hill.

To a large extent, Singh's reflections on war, especially about the lack of knowledge of it, were dictated by and centered on his concerns about the fate of nations. For "whatever country . . . was deficient in knowledge about war or did not care about war was poor and inferior in every which way."[27] Wealth and poverty, in other words, were outgrowths of martial strengths and weaknesses, respectively. India's colonial condition, he implies, resulted from its lack of knowledge about and experience in warfare. China stood perilously close to meeting this same fate, positioned as it was on the eve of destruction by the Euro-American-Japanese alliance for which he was a foot soldier.

By virtue of his military credentials, Singh belonged to the category of knowledgeable people. He credited his martial expertise in part to his experiences as a subaltern in the British colonial army, a role that he believed had enabled him to partake of the European world, which had all the requisite assets of power: military knowledge, technology, and experience.

There was, however, another source for his expertise, an almost innate basis for his military orientation: his caste and religion. No doubt he was especially conscious of these personal attributes because he was thrown into a hyperactive "contact zone," a setting which seemingly made him acutely aware of his sense of sameness and otherness in relation to the international cast of people around him. A combatant in war, he consistently underlines his martial and Rajput background in his story, two aspects of his identity that he always conjoins in his self-definition.[28] Thus, there are many rhetorical bows in the direction of his Rajput warrior identity, which he thought made him inherently martial. In his view, the Rajput *jati* or caste is predisposed to war, even born to wage war; Rajput livelihood, in fact, he emphasizes, centers on war, and it is the be-all and end-all of their lives. Talk about war frightened most people but not Rajputs; on the contrary, it warmed their blood.[29]

Singh's pronouncements on his Rajputness conform to what scholars term "the norms of the Kshatriya social order whose traditional calling was to rule as warriors," a culture prized if not emulated by Rajputs, especially elite Rajputs.

> They [Rajputs] were preeminently warriors and rulers, guardians of society's security and welfare. Feudal play, of which the highest expression was combat but which also included blood sports (pig-sticking, goat-cutting, hunting big and small game) and latterly polo, was a central occupation and preoccupation; its disciplines and austerities hardened the Rajput and prepared him for battle. Rajputs ate meat, took alcohol and opium (not as an underground or challenging counter-cultural practice, but to prepare for or to celebrate wars and weddings and as a support for ordinary social intercourse), kept concubines and enjoyed dancing girls. Their core value was not purity and the avoidance or eradication of pollution, but honour and the avoidance or eradication of dishonour. Courage, valour, and prowess animated the Rajput sensibility. Political, not religious, ritual expressed and regulated the allocation of honour.[30]

Furthermore, Singh's emphasis on his military and Rajput identity—a form of hypermasculinity—was reinforced by colonial ideology. General Leach, who addressed the regiment at Fort William on 29 June 1900, on the eve of its departure for China, underscored precisely this aspect of its identity. Hailing them as "Rajputs" on that occasion, he reminded them that their Hindustani Rajput predecessors had previously fought in China. And now, he continued, they were being entrusted with a special mission "because the *Hind sarkar* [Indian government] has faith in you . . . In China the representatives of 'world powers' [Singh's term is *"sansar shaktiyon"*] are suffering because of the actions of the followers of a new order or community (*sampradaya*) called Boxers. You should carry out the orders of the government, and quickly. Your force has previously gone on an expedition to China in 1858–59. So this is not a new trip (*yatra*) for you. We hope that you will be successful."[31]

Most of the Rajputs serving in the Bengal Army, as *The Sepoy Officer's Manual*[32] observes, were not from Rajasthan, one of the major areas populated by Rajputs. Indeed, few of the Rajputs serving in the Bengal infantry were actually from Rajasthan. Most soldiers of this "warrior caste," as was Gadhadhar Singh, who was from the Lucknow-Kanpur area, were recruited in north India, from the long-standing "military labour market in Hindustan": Awadh "and the banks of the Ganges and Jumna." Other upper but also lower castes from this area of present-day Uttar Pradesh were prized as well by the military. In the aftermath of the Mutiny/Rebellion of 1857 the Bengal Army became more upper caste[33] and more segregated by caste into separate companies. After 1892 the sixteen Hindustani or non-Punjabi infantry regiments remaining in the Bengal Army were all reorganized "as single-class regiments," that is, as single-caste regiments. Singh's 7th Rajput Regiment, as well as the 2nd, 4th, 8th, 11th, 13th, and 16th regiments were all Rajputs.[34]

Although a loyal soldier—he consistently refers to "our" English government or "*Angrezi sarkar*"—he was cognizant of the differential treatment meted out to "Hindustani" sepoys and white (*gore*) sepoys. Note that he employs the racial term *gore* rather than *angrez* (English or British) to refer to his fellow soldiers who were European, a usage that echoes the contemporary Indian distinction between those Europeans who were considered gentlemen or *sahib* or *sahib log* and ordinary soldiers in particular who were designated *gora-log* or whiteys or white people.[35] One conspicuous difference was in the equipment of Indian and British rank-and-file. Although Singh claims that his memory did not stretch back to a much earlier time—presumably a veiled reference to the Mutiny/Rebellion of 1857 and the conflict triggered by the use of Enfield rifles—he harks back to 1883, when Hindustani sepoys had "breechloaders" whereas "white soldiers" were equipped with Martini Henry rifles.[36] And when they acquired "magazine" guns during the campaign of 1887, Hindustanis were finally granted Martinis. Such disparities in weaponry, he states, was the eternal rule of the military. However, a change was made, just prior to leaving for China, ushered in by what he terms a desire not to have "black" (*kale*) sepoys (a term he employs to refer to his fellow Rajputs and himself) become the laughing-stock of the world by joining their allies on the international expedition armed only with the old Martini rifles. As he perceptively comments, lack of up-to-date rifles would have lowered the reputation of "our Britain." This "reform"—and he curiously uses the Hindi transliteration of "reform" to evoke parallels with concurrent social and cultural changes—resulted in Hindustanis receiving the very same Lee-Metfords that whites possessed. For Lieutenant-Colonel Vaughan, this change barely earns a mention: "We were to be re-armed with the Lee-Metford rifle before sailing."[37] Hardly more forthcoming is the regimental history which observes: "The 7th Rajputs were still armed with the Martini-Henry rifle, and as this would be quite inadequate against an enemy equipped with modern weapons, Lee-Metford rifles . . . [were] issued two or three days before sailing."[38]

Singh's observations in a section entitled "Loot and Atrocity or Outrage (*atyachar*)" similarly highlight his sense of self and difference, of his multi-layered identity as Rajput/Sepoy/Hindustani/Subaltern—and as a Hindustani who felt a sense of Asian kinship with the enemy Chinese.

Loot—the term itself embodies the Indian/Chinese/colonial/semicolonial connection—because it stems from the word for "Plunder; Hind. lut, and that from Skt. lotra, for loptra root lup, 'rob, plunder.'" *Hobson-Jobson* dates the word back to the late eighteenth century, when it came to be associated with plunder and pillage. Thereafter, it became part of the English vocabulary, gaining wider acceptance between the so-called "Chinese War of 1841, the Crimean War (1854–5), and the Indian Mutiny (1857–8)"; in short, it was a term that grew out of the colonial experience in India and was then extended beyond the frontiers of the subcontinent through the culture of colonialism, so much so that one *Nautical Glossary* of 1867 refers to "Loot, plunder, or pillage, [as] a term adopted from China."[39] James Hevia argues that "Chinese loot can be located within a pedagogy of imperialism, recruiting as it were volunteers for empire," that is, looting "suggests a relationship between the act of defeating China and the constitution of colonialist subjects. . . . What more commanding image could there be for the constitution of colonizing subjectivities than the appropriation of the signs of another 'sovereign' and the assimilation of those signs to oneself?"[40]

Irony frames Singh's discussion of loot, which he launches into by recounting an earlier episode in China, the Sino-Japanese War of 1894–1895. During this war English newspapers, he observes, condemned the victorious Japanese for committing atrocities. He reports that "we" (presumably referring to Hindustanis) joined in this criticism of the Japanese, who were depicted by the English press to have acted in a manner that no "civilized races" (*sabyajati*) of Europe would have ever done.

From this rhetorical flourish—a reference to events that he said had occurred not too long ago—he turns to interrogate his own times in the following manner: "Who of the eight nations present in China looted and snatched, how much, in what manner, and who was stationed where is difficult to know? But I can say this much, that nothing was left untouched by whoever had whatever form of control over whichever place." The Russians and Japanese he locates at the head of the list of looters of goods particularly, and the Russians and French first in snatching things and in committing atrocities. Hindustanis did not loot, he says, but "grabbed and ran." In his reckoning the entire international force was involved in looting and engaging in atrocities. Implicitly, at least, his scorecard reads that there were no civilized races present among the members of the international expedition.[41]

Other contemporary accounts have tended to narrate the story of loot in China in 1900–1901 in national terms, a praise-and-blame story in which the country or countries condemned are typically the "other" nations. British versions of this story often single out Russians for their "legendary" "brutality," notwithstanding the fact that virtually every one of the foreign powers participated in the sport of looting China, even the Australians, who supplied a small naval contingent as part of the international expedition. In many narratives the United States receives the least criticism. Perhaps this stems from the fact that the American "occupation" of Beijing (different powers were responsible for different quarters of the city) was notable (according to one historian) for maintaining law and order and for enforcing strict and severe penalties for looting. In this historian's view, the American occupation "ran with remarkable smoothness,"[42] an interpretation that accords well with Singh's account.[43]

Advocacy history has also meant that few accounts admit to atrocities. Thus, Indian troops, in Lieutenant-Colonel Vaughan's estimation, "did not get out of hand after the capture of Pekin, nor did they commit atrocities." He categorically denies newspaper reports of barbarous treatment of the Chinese by the troops, at least not "our soldiers, both British and native" who, he insists, were not involved in such acts. He knew of no "instance, nor heard of one, in which our men killed either women or children." But, of course, there were the "others": He was aware of "cases in which Japanese coolies, following in rear of the army, decapitated aged men and women whom the troops in their passage had spared." He also knew that "Russian methods are summary" and, therefore, he was not "surprised at a good deal of unnecessary slaughter being attributed to them."[44]

In Vaughan's story of looting in China, historical initiative and agency were the monopoly of the "other," namely, those other "foreign troops." Occasional lapses occurred among his own men, but only because his soldiers had found "foreign troops hard at work looting" and, consequently,

> parties . . . [were] sent out under command of officers with orders to bring in what they could find to the Prize Committee, which was now started. One of these found a mandarin's house, and the store of wine and tinned provisions in it formed a welcome addition to the commissariat rations we had been living on for so long. Large quantities of furs and silks were also found, which went to the Prize Committee. *Looting on the part of the British troops were carried on in the most orderly manner, and the houses of all those known to be friendly were protected.*[45]

The British looted discriminately, in other words; they differentiated between Chinese friend and foe, and what they appropriated were mostly intended to provide much needed dietary supplements; and what other kinds of things they "found" (notice the passiveness of this construction) were handed over to a committee in order to be redistributed in an "orderly manner." And, in case these extenuating circumstances are not sufficient justification, he reminds us

> that it is one of the unwritten laws of war that a city which does not surrender at the last and is taken by storm is looted. Numberless instances could be quoted, and considering the cowardly and unprovoked attack on the Legations, and the murder of Europeans, including helpless women and children, under circumstances of the most revolting cruelty, the Chinese were treated by

us far better than they deserved. Many reports were current that the troops of other Powers, one in particular, shot every person they saw, armed or unarmed, whether, man, woman, or child; but no instance of this ever came under my observation, beyond the fact that corpses of unarmed peasantry were seen lying about.[46]

Looting, according to Singh, was much more actively pursued and by virtually everyone. It began as soon as the foreign troops reached Tianjin, where the Japanese, Russians, and French pilfered much, the latter two especially appropriating several tons of silver. Although he does not directly implicate himself, he admits that sepoys were involved and that they snatched whatever they needed by threatening and even killing local inhabitants. The Chinese were treated miserably, like Doms, he says, a reference that he fleshes out by mentioning that this "Untouchable" scavenger caste were paid meager wages (two to four annas) by municipalities at home to kill dogs. His implication is that the Chinese were treated like dogs and the people recruited to mistreat them were not low caste but good people and good Hindus![47]

Again and again, he recalls graphic, eyewitness descriptions of atrocities perpetrated by soldiers (at one point he says of all races). His catalog of horrific incidents includes the story of a poor Chinese man who was kicked and thrown around like a football and of a "helpless" Chinese who was patched up by a Hindustani medical doctor only to be tortured to death by Japanese soldiers.[48]

At times, he only identifies the perpetrators as "foreign" troops. But, always, he documents acts of atrocities with great compassion and humanity. Innocent villagers—men, women, and children—he observes, were often hunted down as "*shikar*,"[49] as game. Some women, he writes, committed suicide rather than be captured by foreign troops. While his "foreign comrades" invariably blamed the Boxers for such deaths, he hewed a different line on the matter because he had personally witnessed a woman attempting to drown herself rather than fall into the hands of approaching international troops.[50]

The worst offenders, in Singh's experience, were Russian and French troops. Their modus operandi was to converge on a few houses in a village, kill a handful of its inhabitants, strip the houses of all their valuables, bayonet the crying children, and then rape and kill the women; or, as Singh put it euphemistically, they "destroy the religion of their victims before taking their lives." The troops would then emerge from the houses and set fire to them. Nor were the hands of his fellow countrymen any cleaner: Hindustani sepoys, too, were involved in the burning of villages.[51]

The subaltern account diverges substantively and substantially from that compiled by his commanding officer, Lieutenant-Colonel Vaughan. Consider their record of the events of 7 August 1900, when the 7th Rajputs were en route to Beijing. For Vaughan this was not an eventful day, as had been the previous days dating back to 4 August, for which period he has heroic tales to recount for virtually every day. The subaltern story follows a different plot; it refers to events that are entirely elided in the officer's version, including an incident that apparently involved the cruel torture and execution of a Chinese interpreter and the killing of a Chinese person who was spotted along the river. In Singh's earthy prose, the unfortunate Chinese victims are described as being crushed like bedbugs. He lumps Hindustani sepoys among the guilty in many such incidents, although he exculpates them somewhat by suggesting that they often fired instinctively and impulsively at innocent bystanders because their guns were within easy reach.[52]

Looting became a major preoccupation when the international expedition reached Beijing. There, in the third and fourth weeks of August, looted silver was available everywhere for bargain prices. Singh reports that the sellers were typically Russians and Japanese (and presumably therefore the agents provocateurs), the buyers the British and the Hindustanis. A number of other items were also available for cheap prices, and all these things were looted from the Chinese after they had been killed. What happened in China happened, and was bound to happen, he declares, almost as if to imply that the destruction he was an eyewitness and party to was the inevitable result of war and the obvious disparities in power between China and the member nations of the international expedition. Although seemingly intent on staking out a position that did not apportion blame and guilt among the various foreign powers, not surprisingly he concludes his remarks on "Loot and Atrocities" by doing precisely that. Once again, he resorts to the technique of having someone else speak on his behalf, in this case a Chinese doctor (*hakim*) with whom he recalls having a conversation and whose persona and voice enables him to veil his own personal judgments about looting. According to Singh, his purpose in talking to the Chinese doctor was in order to persuade him to appreciate the good deeds of the British, but the latter retorted that it was not enough just to criticize the Russians or any one party when all the powers competed with one another to loot and to wreak havoc upon China. Singh writes that he had no rejoinder to this observation, presumably because it accorded well with his own experiences. He then goes on to note that the British were no less implicated in looting and killing. Perhaps they had even rescued all the boys and children they had in order to recruit them for work in their camps. Moreover, these children were orphans because the British (along with other members of the international expedition) had killed their parents. And what of Hindustanis who are brothers and kinsmen of the Chinese? They, too, he acknowledges, had participated in the assault on China.[53]

A member of the international expedition that had advanced on China in retaliation for the Boxer Uprising, Gadhadhar Singh could not entirely dissociate himself from the assault on China. Nor did he seek to do so, in fact celebrating many of its achievements. However, his experiences in the "contact zone" of China led him also to develop a sympathetic attitude that is apparent throughout the book, and especially at the end as it closes with a comparative look at China and India, a perspective that enables this subaltern author to register his understanding of the similarities existing between what he characterized as the two principal countries of Asia. This comparative perspective also enables him to underline their differences from Europe.

Singh's sympathies toward China are articulated from the outset of the book. They surface for the first time in the text—by design, I believe—when he writes of the initial approach of his ship to Chinese soil, at Dagu, the entry point into Tianjin and Beijing. He remembers this moment as an occasion when he scanned the nearby landscape and detected many deserted and destroyed villages. On some broken buildings he saw French, Russian, and Japanese flags aflutter, and in some villages he espied a few people alive, skeleton-like old people standing upright with the help of their walking sticks.

"Even hearts of stone," Singh remarks, "would have melted and felt compassion." "It was not necessary for my heart to be moved by pity," he adds, "because I had come to fight against the Chinese. But . . . I felt an emotion that was born not out of duty but in the mind." In attempting to understand why he felt this way, he mentions that he realized that the "Chinese are Buddhists. (At that time I did not know about Confucianism.) They share this religion with the people of Hindustan. As neighbors and fellow residents of Asia, they are also of the same 'country.' There are not many differences in [presumably he means skin] color and customs. Why did God inflict times of trouble on them! Did God not want to help them?"[54]

Singh then highlights the similarities in the pasts of China and India, a consideration that leads him to envision a common future for them:

I developed a feeling of sympathy in seeing the distress of the Chinese people—gentle were also our ancestors who for Delhi would fight against Lahore and for Jaipur against Chitore [both Rajput states]. For [the Mughal Emperor] Akbar they would fight against Rathore [another Rajput state] and for the British against Ranjit [Singh, the Sikh ruler]. Did worms really infect their hearts and brains? And then it came to my mind that God had created these difficult times for the welfare of China. For China, too, would fall into the hands of our all powerful [British colonial] government and attain the sleep of happiness and carefreeness that our country of Aryavarta was looting. Then it became a matter of great happiness. May God look to your welfare—so it should be! Place China, too, in the hands of that great power in which Aryavarta has been placed. By creating a "Hindu Chinese" [country] establish a huge kingdom in Asia. So be it.[55]

These ruminations flow into an account of a conversation that Singh reports he had had with a "Bluejacket" (a member of the naval force) who greeted him in the tugboat that came to unload the troops from the ship in order to transport them to the shore. That he alludes to this incident right after he articulates sympathy for the Chinese is perhaps no coincidence. On the contrary, this passage, which closes out his account of the ocean voyage, seems intended to remind himself—and his reading public—that he harbored no seditious sentiments, even as he displayed positive feelings toward those he had come to fight against. Striking as well is the fact that the "ship soldier" who he had had this verbal exchange with was an Irish soldier, who apparently took an interest in him because he spoke English. But he then quickly adds that there were other Indian soldiers who spoke English and there were other Bluejackets present who did not seek him out.

The Irishman, according to the Indian subaltern, informed him about the battles that had taken place a few days earlier in Dagu and Tianjin and dispensed helpful advice based on the former's war experiences. Their discussion then veered off in a different direction. Singh remembers the Irish soldier telling him that he, too, was not English—he was Irish, that he also had come to wage war on behalf of the British government, and that he was acting in an appropriate manner because it was good to have "mutual sympathy." Furthermore, the Chinese were *"jangli"*—to use Singh's term for what the Irishman told him, presumably, that the Chinese were not civilized, that is, of the jungle or wild.[56]

Appreciative though Singh was of the Irishman's efforts to befriend him, he clearly did not agree with the latter's portrayal of China as uncivilized. On the contrary, his "mutual sympathy" clearly extended to China and its people. To him, China and India were comparable and compatible because they were the two most ancient civilizations of the world; the latter, moreover, he credits (erroneously) with having produced the oldest book in the world, the Vedas. These ancient civilizations had declined considerably in modern times, however. In fact, both countries were mired in poverty and lagged far behind Europe economically. He drives home this point by recounting a conversation he had had with an English missionary, who compared European standards of living with those of China and India. Wages were abysmal in China, especially in Shandong, where the Boxer movement had been active. In the estimation of his missionary informant, incomes in China or India were so low that they only amounted to what people in England made four hundred years ago.

Singh partly blames trade imbalances for these huge disparities in standards of living. China and India had once been rich and powerful, but no longer so because of Europe's commercial ascendancy. This dominance was evidenced by British control of the production and trade of commodities that had once made Asia prosperous; for instance, tea from China and cloth from India. He argues that the British gained control of the trade of the former and both the production and trade of the latter as their textile industry undermined India's indigenous cloth production. His line of reasoning verges on the "drain of wealth" argument that was increasingly gaining favor with contemporary Indian nationalists. Indeed, Singh's "news" about China and India followed on the heels of much publicized writings by such nationalist authors as Romesh C. Dutt, who had published articles in the 1890s blaming British rule for India's poverty and followed up with an extended polemic in 1901 entitled *The Economic History of India under Early British Rule.*[57]

In Singh's understanding, social problems were the other major source of the contemporary plight of China and India. His list of their many social shortcomings includes excessive spending, opium smoking (more in the case of China than India), female illiteracy, and belief in false gods. Understandably, he singles out issues that preoccupied Arya Samaj reformers.

Toward China Singh felt "mutual sympathy," about Japan he professed admiration. For him, the latter represented a model of what an Asian country could become and of what an Asian country had done to withstand Europe in a world where power and war were paramount. He recognized that its historical trajectory had followed a different course, certainly in contrast to the path that India had taken and that China seemed to be on the verge of hurtling down.

To employ Singh's metaphor, Japan, above all, had succeeded in the world because it had emerged from behind a veil of darkness. He appears to have based this assessment partly on his reading knowledge of that country—some of his observations about Japan are taken from the Edwards book—and partly on his many personal and overwhelmingly favorable encounters with Japanese soldiers, who constituted the single largest contingent in the international expedition. He repeatedly marvels at how effectively its leaders and people had willingly sacrificed their narrow partisan interests for the national cause, subordinating local loyalties for the nation. He knowingly traces its political, economic, and social achievements first under the Tokugawa Shogunate and then during the Meiji period. He is particularly laudatory about the Japanese willingness to embrace new ideas and new technologies, an openness that he clearly admires and contrasts with the close-mindedness of China and India. In fact, he characterizes India as closed off behind a *pardah*, a screen or a curtain that so enclosed people, places, and ideas that there was no room for commonsense and wisdom to surface.[58]

The project of "recovery of the subject" so central to the subaltern enterprise has to date tended to yield mostly insurgent subalterns. Notwithstanding Guha's broad definition of subaltern as anyone who is subordinated "in terms of class, caste, age, gender and office or in any other way,"[59] subaltern consciousness has been located only in the more dramatic actions of *bidroha*, actions that are most likely to stand out in the colonial noise that is sometimes all that we can hear from the colonial period because of the politics of archival production. But "no subaltern identity," as one historian has noted recently, "can be pure and transparent, most subalterns are both dominated and dominating subjects; depending on the circumstances or location in which we encounter them."[60]

To read Gadhadhar Singh's remarkable account of his adventures in the hyperactive "contact zone" of China during the Boxer Rebellion is to see a "consciousness" that is manifested in far more complex ways than can be encompassed by the current project of subaltern struggles. Given the limitations of the colonial archives, what is one to make of the "enunciatory position" of sepoys who as "dominated subjects" played a range of roles over the course of the eighteenth and nineteenth centuries? Consider the history of Gadhadhar Singh's regiment. In the eighteenth and early nineteenth centuries the unit had fought for the emerging empire both within the subcontinent (in Nepal, and against the Pindaris and the Sikhs) and abroad (Macao, Ceylon, Mauritius, Java), but they also deserted frequently. In 1824 they participated in the Barrackpore Mutiny, but in 1857 they were not involved in that mutiny, in part because they were shipped off to China.

But to see subaltern actions only through the lens of the binary oppositions of loyal/disloyal or subordinate/insurgent is to miss out on all the layers of identity and consciousness that constituted any individual or group in the colonial period or in any semicolonial society. Certainly, Gadhadhar Singh, engulfed in the "contact zone" of China in 1900–1901 defined himself in far more nuanced and multilayered ways. A loyal sepoy and the very model of a Rajput warrior, he was also a Hindustani who distinguished himself from his English superiors and from all the other foreigners who manned the international expedition to suppress the Boxer Uprising. Commanded to serve his British government against the new order of Boxers, he was a soldier's soldier but not blind to the outrages perpetrated in the name of Western civilization. Indeed, his China tour of duty prompted him to interrogate Western civilization, whose forces looted and ransacked and killed like scavengers and hunted down people for sport. From such experiences developed subaltern sentiments about the empire and civilization he collaborated with and a budding awareness of racial and cultural kinship between China and India—and even the rest of Asia—that anticipated the rising discourse about civilization and pan-Asianism in the decades to come.[61]

NOTES

1. The reference here is to the fundamental epistemological and hermeneutical issues that postcolonial scholars have raised about voice and agency in any colonial

society. Gayatri Spivak, for example, argues that "the testimony of . . . voice-consciousness" does not exist for subalterns. Such silencing, she contends, issues from the politics of archival production—silence exists because subalterns have no "enunciatory position"; they did not and do not have a subject-position from which to speak. See Gayatri Chakravarty Spivak, "Can the Subaltern Speak? Speculations in Widow Sacrifice," *Wedge* 7/8 (1985): 120–30 and, for debates on this issue the essays in Vinayak Chaturvedi, ed., *Mapping Subaltern Studies and the Postcolonial* (London: Verso, 2000).

2. Thakur Gadhadhar Singh, *Chin meh Terah Mas: (Chin Sangram)* (Lucknow: Thakur Gadhadhar Singh, 1902).

3. Shahid Amin, *Event, Metaphor, Memory: Chauri Chaura, 1922–1992* (Berkeley: University of California Press, 1995), 1. To continue in his words, "Peasants do not write, they are written about. The speech of humble folk is not normally recorded for posterity, it is wrenched from them in courtrooms and inquisitorial trials. Historians have therefore learned to comb 'confessions' and 'testimonies' . . . for this is where peasants cry out, dissimulate or indeed narrate." For similar observations about the problematics of recovering the "experienced past" of Boxers, see Paul A. Cohen, *History in Three Keys: The Boxers as Event, Experience, and Myth* (New York: Columbia University Press, 1997), 59–68.

4. Mary Louise Pratt, *Imperial Eyes: Travel Writing and Transculturation* (London: Routledge, 1992), 4, 6.

5. The allied force that set out for Beijing from Tianjin on 4 August numbered a little over twenty thousand men. The Japanese had the largest contingent (about ten thousand), the Russians five thousand, the British three thousand, and the Americans about two thousand, five hundred. France was represented by its Indochinese force of about eight hundred Vietnamese. William J. Duiker, *Cultures in Collision: The Boxer Rebellion* (San Rafael, Ca.: Presidio Press, 1978), 154–55.

6. Frank Dikötter, *The Discourse of Race in Modern China* (Stanford: Stanford University Press, 1992), 14, refers to the Chinese characterization of Indians as black devils during the Opium War. See also Arthur Waley, *The Opium War through Chinese Eyes* (Stanford: Stanford University Press, 1958), 111, 194, 218. The popular Chinese press in treaty ports often expressed contempt for "barbarian" continents such as India and Africa (Dikötter, 50). See also Hevia chapter in this volume.

7. Lt. Col. H[enry] B[athurst] Vaughan, *St. George and the Chinese Dragon* (Dartford, Kent: Alexius Press, reprint, 2000).

8. Susanne Hoeber Rudolph and Lloyd I. Rudolph, with Mohan Singh Kanota, eds., *Reversing the Gaze: Amar Singh's Diary, A Colonial Subject's Narrative of Imperial India* (New Delhi: Oxford University Press, 2000).

9. H[enry] G[eorge] Rawlinson, *The History of the 3rd Battalion 7th Rajput Regiment (Duke of Connaught's Own)* (London: Oxford University Press, 1941); L/Mil/5 and L/Mil/7 series, British Library, London.

10. Paul A. Cohen, *Discovering History in China: American Historical Writing on the Recent Chinese Past* (New York: Columbia University Press, 1984), 144.

11. Carleton Frederick Waite, *Some Elements of International Co-operation in the Suppression of the 1900 Antiforeign Rising in China with Special Reference to the Forces of the United States* (Los Angeles: University of Southern California Press, 1935), 45.

12. Lajpat Rai, *The Arya Samaj: An Account of Its Aims, Doctrines and Activities* (Lahore: Uttar Chand Kapur, 1932), 71–99; K[ripal] C[handra] Yadav and K[rishan] S[ingh] Arya, *Arya Samaj and the Freedom Movement, Volume One: 1875–1918* (New Delhi: Manohar, 1988), 156–71.

13. For example, see Gadhadhar Singh, *Karuna Kahani* (Ajmer: Prakash Book Depot, 1916), which is identified as "The Tale of Compassion. An Arya Samajist Narrative."

14. Neville P. Edwards, *The Story of China with a Description of the Events Relating to the Present Struggle* (London: Hutchinson, 1900); Sir Robert Hart, *"These From the Land of Sinim": Essays on the Chinese Question* (London: Chapman & Hall, 1901). On Hart's motives in writing these essays, see his personal correspondence. John King Fairbank, Katherine Frost Bruner, and Elizabeth MacLeod Matheson, eds., *The I.G. in Peking: Letters of Robert Hart, Chinese Maritime Customs, 1868–1907*, vol. 2 (Cambridge: Harvard University Press, 1975), 1232–49.

15. Joseph W. Esherick, *The Origins of the Boxer Uprising* (Berkeley: University of California Press, 1987), argues in favor of viewing the Boxer movement as an uprising and not a rebellion. Ranajit Guha, *Elementary Aspects of Peasant Insurgency in Colonial India* (Delhi: Oxford University Press, 1983), 4–13, translates *bidroha* as "insurgency" in order to emphasize peasant and rebel consciousness and to counter prior characterizations of peasant jacqueries, revolts, and uprisings as prepolitical or lacking in political consciousness.

16. Edwards, *Story of China*, 6, 98. Edwards provides an account of an initiation rite that he claimed was probably similar to what Boxers did and is drawn from Demetrius C. Boulger, *A Short History of China* (London: Allen, 1893).

17. Singh, *Chin*, 96–97. I have reproduced this passage from Hart, *"These From the Land of Sinim,"* 8, rather than from Singh because the latter has some typographical errors in his quote.

18. Singh, *Chin*, 97. Renowned as a warrior, Govind Singh was the tenth guru of the Sikhs. He is generally credited with transforming the Sikhs into a militant order.

19. Hart, *"These From the Land of Sinim,"* 8; Singh, *Chin*, 98.

20. Hart, *"These From the Land of Sinim,"* 4–5.

21. Singh, *Chin*, 99.

22. Singh, *Chin*, 98.

23. Singh, *Chin*, 99–100.

24. Singh, *Chin*, 121, also 102–121 for an account of the siege. See also Vaughan, *Chinese Dragon*, 81–91.

25. Singh, *Chin*, 21.

26. Singh, *Chin*, 13.

27. Singh, *Chin*, 13, 12–14.

28. Singh, *Chin*, 5, 13, passim.

29. Singh, *Chin*, 5, 12.

30. Susanne Hoeber Rudolph and Lloyd I. Rudolph, *Essays on Rajputana: Reflections on History, Culture and Administration* (New Delhi: Concept Publishing Company, 1984), 179.

31. Singh, *Chin*, 1.

32. Lt. Edmund George Barrow, *The Sepoy Officer's Manual: A Book of Reference for Officers of the Bengal Native Infantry*, revised and brought up to date by Lt. H. B.

Vaughan (Calcutta: Thacker, Spink, 1887). Singh's commanding officer, Vaughan, revised this manual when he was a lieutenant.

33. Dirk H. A. Kolff, *Naukar, Rajput and Sepoy: The Ethnohistory of the Military Labour Market in Hindustan, 1450–1850* (Cambridge: Cambridge University Press, 1990), 185–86. Of the 67,000 Hindus in the Bengal Army in 1842, 28,000 were identified as Rajputs and 25,000 as Brahmins, a category that included Bhumihar Brahmins. The Brahmin presence in the Bengal Army was reduced in the late nineteenth century because of their perceived primary role as mutineers in the Mutiny of 1857. Barrow, *Manual*, 94.

34. T[homas] A[nthony] Heathcote, *The Indian Army: The Garrison of British Imperial India, 1822–1922* (London: David & Charles, 1974); Rawlinson, *7th Rajput Regiment*, 62.

35. Col. Henry Yule and A. C. Burnell, *Hobson Jobson* (Delhi: Munshiram Manoharlal, 2nd. ed., 1968), 388, notes the following: "*gora* [plural: gore], 'fair-complexioned.' A white man; a European soldier; any European who is not a sahib."

36. After the Mutiny, Indian troops were issued improved weapons only after the British had discarded them. British units had the Snider breech-loading rifle in 1866 while Indian troops were equipped with Enfield rifles. When Martini-Henry rifles were issued to British troops in the early 1870s, Indian soldiers finally received the Sniders, which they retained until 1892. By then British soldiers were equipped with the bolt-action Lee-Metford rifles; their Martinis were then passed on to the Indian troops. This pattern of supplying inferior weapons to Indian troops continued into the twentieth century, until at least World War I. Heathcote, *Indian Army*, 56.

37. Vaughan, *St. George*, 15; Singh, *Chin*, 7.

38. Rawlinson, *7th Rajput*, 87.

39. *Hobson-Jobson*, 519–20, 525–26.

40. James L. Hevia, "Loot's Fate: The Economy of Plunder and the Moral Life of Objects from the Summer Palace of the Emperor of China," *History and Anthropology* 6, no. 4 (1994): 333. Hevia refers to the "plundering of colonized societies by colonizers" as a "common enough characteristic of empire building and warfare in general" which "took on special features during the period of capitalism's global consolidation in the second half of the nineteenth century. For one thing, such activities were increasingly referred to as looting, a word rich in connotation. It not only described theft, but referenced its own theft—it had been lifted from Hindi or Sanskrit."

41. Singh, *Chin*, 301.

42. Michael H. Hunt, "The Forgotten Occupation, Peking, 1900–1901," *Pacific Historical Review* 48 (1979): 503.

43. Bob Nicholls, *Bluejackets and Boxers: Australia's Naval Expedition to the Boxer Uprising* (Sydney: Allen & Unwin, 1986).

44. Vaughan, *St. George*, 163, 176–77.

45. Vaughan, *St. George*, 120–21.

46. Vaughan, *St. George*, 121–22.

47. Singh, *Chin*, 302–3.

48. Singh, *Chin*, 304.

49. His use of this term is loaded with irony. *Shikar*, a Hindi term derived from the Persian word for hunting, refers to sport in the sense of shooting or hunting.

Shikar, especially big-game hunting, was an "invented" colonial tradition that was redolent with imagery and symbolism expressive of the power and manliness of colonial civilization vis-a-vis the "uncivilized" natural order. For example, see William Kelleher Storey, "Big Cats and Imperialism: Lion and Tiger Hunting in Kenya and Northern India, 1898–1930," *Journal of World History* 2, no. 2 (1991): 135–73.

50. Singh, *Chin*, 306.

51. Singh, *Chin*, 306–7.

52. Singh, *Chin*, 305.

53. Singh, *Chin*, 308.

54. Singh, *Chin*, 17.

55. Singh, *Chin*, 17.

56. Singh, *Chin*, 17–18.

57. Romesh C. Dutt, *The Economic History of India under Early British Rule* (New Delhi: Government of India, reprint, 1970).

58. Singh, *Chin*, 2–3, 27–33.

59. Ranajit Guha, *Subaltern Studies I: Writings on South Asian History and Society* (Delhi: Oxford University Press, 1982), vii.

60. Florencia E. Mallon, "The Promise and Dilemmas of Subaltern Studies: Perspectives from Latin American History," *American Historical Review* 99, no. 5 (December 1994): 1491–1515.

61. Somewhat different were the China experiences of another Rajput soldier, the aristocratic Amar Singh. See Rudolph and Rudolph, *Amar Singh's Diary*. See also Prasenjit Duara, "The Discourse of Civilization and Pan-Asianism," *Journal of World History* 12, no. 1 (2001): 99–130; Rebecca E. Karl, "Creating Asia: China in the World at the beginning of the Twentieth Century," *American Historical Review* 103, no. 4 (October 1998): 1096–1118; Stephen Northup Hay, *Asian Ideas of East and West: Tagore and His Critics in Japan, China, and India* (Cambridge: Harvard University Press, 1970).

4

Reporting the Taiyuan Massacre

Culture and Politics in the China War of 1900

Roger R. Thompson

This study of the Taiyuan massacre looks at one of the most notorious and yet least studied events in the history of the Boxer Uprising.[1] A graphic account of Shanxi governor Yuxian's cold-blooded murder of forty-five foreigners, including women and children, in the outer courtyard of his government compound in the provincial capital of Taiyuan on 9 July 1900 has served as perhaps the defining representation of the madness of the Chinese state in the midst of the Boxer Uprising. From Arthur Smith's *China in Convulsion* (1901) and H. B. Morse's *International Relations of the Chinese Empire* (1918) to Peter Fleming's *The Siege at Peking* (1959), Sterling Seagrave's *The Soong Dynasty* (1985) and *Dragon Lady* (1992), Nat Brandt's *Massacre in Shansi* (1994), and Diana Preston's *Besieged in Peking* (1999) there appears, usually in an extended quotation, the same account of the Taiyuan massacre. Many readers in the years immediately following the Boxer Uprising must have found solace in this tragic tale of the brave martyrdom of forty-five foreigners. Although thousands of Chinese lost their lives, sometimes in large groups, only in Taiyuan was the foreign death toll so large. Close to two hundred foreigners perished in China in 1900, but in most other cases those who were killed died alone or with just a few of their compatriots. The enormity of the Taiyuan massacre in the eyes of Westerners was unique.

Elements of this story had consequences even in the midst of the Boxer Uprising. In the fall of 1900 Western and Japanese diplomats began discussing whom the Qing government must punish before hostilities could cease and negotiations begin. Two men and two events dominated the agenda: Yuxian and the Taiyuan massacre and Dong Fuxiang and the so-called siege of the legations in Beijing, which was lifted on 14 August when allied troops finally entered the imperial capital. Yuxian, as Shanxi governor, was held responsible for the massacre of missionaries in Taiyuan, and Dong Fuxiang, a commander of imperial troops in Beijing, was to answer for his role in the siege. While the foreign community in China was outraged at the treatment of all foreigners, Yuxian's fate was tied most closely to the clamoring within missionary circles and Dong Fuxiang's to the affronted diplomatic and business communities. Since the danger, excitement, and boredom of the siege of the legations was experienced firsthand by some of the Beijing negotiators, there was little need to investigate its circumstances, but Western authorities had neither eyewitnesses to rely upon nor the ability (nor apparent interest) to conduct an inquiry into the Taiyuan massacre. Unlike the siege, no Westerner fated to be in Taiyuan in July 1900 survived; it was not until early 1901 that a purported eyewitness account was even published. The Yong Zheng account, appearing first in the *North China Daily News* and then quickly reprinted in the missionary journal the *Chinese Recorder*, is the one that is still republished in popular accounts of the Boxer Uprising. Not until July 1901, when a missionary-led delegation reached Taiyuan, were there even informal inquiries; no diplomatic investigation would ever be conducted. Unlike the siege of the legations, which attracted the attention of diplomatic authorities around the globe and was soon documented by numerous first-person accounts, little was known in the fall of 1900 about the Taiyuan massacre. Nonetheless, the attention and vitriol heaped upon Yuxian in the fall of 1900 was even greater than the fury directed at Dong Fuxiang.

The oft-repeated narrative of the Taiyuan massacre was not the first one, only the most detailed, well-written, and compelling. Vivid as it is, however, scholars of the Boxer Uprising have wisely left it out of their monographs, preferring instead to simply say that Yuxian had supervised the executions of the foreigners gathered in Taiyuan.[2] Its descriptions, sometimes one by one, of the deaths of forty-five persons, complete with telling details of utterances, comportment, and appearance immediately raise suspicions. Dr. J. A. Creasey Smith, a missionary associated with the English Baptist Missionary Society (BMS), provided this account, which he attributed to a Chinese convert named Yong Zheng. Creasey Smith, who said he witnessed Yong Zheng's baptism in Shanxi in 1899, vouched for his trustworthiness. The more one reads this account, however, the less likely it seems that a terrified eyewitness could have recalled so much so well almost nine months later. Among the details reported were the names of some of the doomed foreigners and a direct quotation of the last words a Mrs. Lovitt spoke just before the two blows that killed her were delivered.[3]

Insufficient evidence makes it difficult to confirm or deny the presence of Yong Zheng at the scene he described, but most of the key elements of the story he related had already been circulating in treaty-port newspapers since September 1900. Moreover, the ways in which the death scenes were represented bear striking similarities to passages in a book that almost certainly would have been well-known to Creasey Smith: John Foxe's *Book of Martyrs.* This book, first published in Elizabethan England under the title *The Acts and Monuments of John Foxe,* had, in subsequent and somewhat vulgarized nineteenth-century versions with titles like *Fox's Book of Martyrs,* become important within the evangelical circles from which many British missionaries came.[4] The hagiographic literature published after the Boxer Uprising reflected the continuing influence of the *Book of Martyrs* in evangelical missionary circles. There were, for example, Robert Forsyth's *The China Martyrs of 1900: A Complete Roll of the Christian Heroes Martyred in China in 1900 with Narratives of Survivors* (1904) and Luella Miner's *China's Book of Martyrs* (1903), which begins,

> A new "Book of Martyrs" at the beginning of the twentieth century—how inappropriate it seems! . . . We have read with a sickening horror, yet with a glowing inspiration, the tales of faith and heroism; and have rejoiced in the thought that these things are records of a bygone age, that we live in a time when men have ceased to persecute the prophets, and stone those who preach against their corruptions.[5]

Later in her introduction Miner quotes from what appears to be a nineteenth-century version of the *Book of Martyrs* as she tries to convince readers that the butchery and cruelty rampant in China in 1900 had been seen before in sixteenth-century England.[6] A final example, based on events in Shanxi, comes from E. H. Edwards's *Fire and Sword in Shansi: The Story of the Martyrdom of Foreigners and Chinese Christians* (1903). In his introduction Alexander Maclaren writes:

> The page which these martyrdoms has added to the Book of Martyrs is of a piece with all the preceding pages—the same Christ-sustained heroism displayed by tender women, mothers, maidens, and children; the same meek forgiveness, the same unalterable constancy. Stephen need not be ashamed of his last successors. Nor were the Chinese converts a whit behind in their devotion.[7]

Edwards, too, follows the narrative structure established by John Foxe's *Book of Martyrs* when he casts Yuxian in the role of a "Chinese Nero."[8]

What is pertinent to this study, however, is not the general correspondence of these hagiographies with Foxe's work but rather the specific correlation of the Taiyuan massacre story with this familiar narrative structure.

Creasey Smith's sympathetic credulity and the lack of any semblance of cross-examination, the preternatural specificity of detail, and the stylistic similarities to *Fox's Book of Martyrs* prompt the conclusion that Yong Zheng's account requires, at the very least, further corroboration. More is at stake than the memories of martyred missionaries—our understanding of the Boxer Uprising, its documentation, and its significance in modern Chinese history is at the center of this inquiry. This will become clear when the "Taiyuan massacre" is placed in a different narrative—the China War of 1900—rather than that of the Boxer Uprising.

PROBLEMS OF DOCUMENTATION:
THE DEARTH OF EYEWITNESS ACCOUNTS

Why are the basic facts of the Taiyuan massacre so difficult to ascertain? One, there were no survivors among the Westerners in Taiyuan in June and July 1900. Two, there was no direct contact between Westerners in Taiyuan in those months and other Westerners in Shanxi who did survive. The burning of the Schofield Memorial Hospital in Taiyuan on 27 June was reported in a letter of 6 July from the pen of Dr. Millar Wilson; news based on this letter, containing the last information to come from the Taiyuan martyrs, did not reach Shanghai until early September.[9] Three, Westerners in Shanxi were barred from sending or receiving telegrams beginning on 6 July. What knowledge we do have of events in Taiyuan in July is based on Chinese accounts, some of which were written down in Shanxi by still-surviving Westerners in July. These Western voices, and the Chinese voices they relied upon, were silenced in August, either by death or by fleeing the province. Many of these voices would be heard, however, in 1901, when their journals and letters reached the hands of Westerners and were published in books like Marshall Broomhall's *Martyred Missionaries of the China Inland Mission with a Record of the Perils & Sufferings of Some Who Escaped* or in 1903 in E. H. Edwards' *Fire and Sword in Shansi*.

Layer upon layer of details were added before there could be a story of the Taiyuan massacre, so it is instructive to limit our first gaze to the sketchy details available in the weeks prior to the 14 August relief of the siege of the legations. Although Westerners were denied access to telegraphic services in Shanxi in early July, two China Inland Mission (CIM) missionaries in southwestern and central Shanxi, F. C. H. Dreyer in Pingyang and Alexander Saunders in Pingyao, who fled the province in August and July respectively, heard reports from yamen personnel that were based in part on telegraphic traffic. Both men also reported what they heard on the street. Similar sources inform the journals and letters of doomed missionaries gathered by Westerners like E. H. Edwards when they were finally able to return to Shanxi in July 1901. In addition to these Western sources, valuable information can also be found in the reports filed by one Zhang Zhiheng. Zhang was a Shanxi native whose conversion followed contact with the China Inland Mission in Pingyang. Zhang's testimony about his Christian beliefs was heard by CIM founder J. Hudson Taylor during his 1886 trip to Shanxi and in 1900 Zhang was an elder in the Yuncheng church in southwestern Shanxi connected with the Swedish Mission, which was affiliated with the China Inland Mission. With funds provided by the China Inland Mission Zhang Zhiheng gathered intelligence and disbursed emergency aid in the province.[10] He filed his first report from Xi'an, Shaanxi Province, on 26 July, soon after he fled the province. He went back to Shanxi on 31 July and, upon his return to Xi'an, sent letters dated 14 and 22 August and 19 September. Finally, we have the journal of Rev. C. W. Price, a missionary associated with the American Board of Commissioners for Foreign Missions (ABCFM). A member of the so-called Oberlin Band in Shanxi, Price and his wife Eva were stationed in central Shanxi at Fenzhou City. His journal contains a wealth of information, some of which can be corroborated, about the oral reports and rumors swirling in Shanxi in July. Price's sources of information included "yamen underlings," who were always on the premises of the mission compound, Chinese Christians, officials, and rumors he heard on the street.[11]

With these sources in hand, which were based on evidence gathered up to mid-August 1900, let us see what was known about the deaths in Taiyuan. C. W. Price's journal is a good starting point, for it establishes the range of information in oral reports and rumors. Significantly, his journal, which begins with a retrospective account to early June, contains no mention of massacres until an entry he made the night of 17 July, when he received a letter from missionary colleagues in nearby Taigu. Price learned that the missionaries in Taiyuan, as well as those who had just arrived in Taiyuan from Shouyang County, "were all killed while on their way to the Fut'ai's [i.e., governor's] yâmen [sic]. Later reports say but one man and one woman killed. Hard to say which report is correct."[12] Price's uncertainty continued at least until 25 July when he writes, "We are beginning to have more hope that the T'ai Yüan Fu friends have not been made away with. Everything goes by rumours. No word that can be depended on."[13] With an entry for 31 July, shortly before his own death, Price's journal falls silent; he is no more certain about the fate of the Westerners in Taiyuan than he was when he first heard the news.

Another Westerner then in Shanxi, F. C. H. Dreyer of Pingyang, a county located on the main trade route between Taiyuan and Xi'an, wrote up an account of his experiences after his arrival in Hankou on 28 August. He recalled that on 14 July yamen personnel in Pingyang said all foreigners in Taiyuan were massacred on the thirteenth day of the sixth lunar month (i.e.,

9 July). Similar information was relayed to Dreyer by yamen "underlings" in Yishi on 20 July and two days later in Puzhou, near the Shanxi-Shaanxi border. It is at the latter city that Dreyer hears for the first time specific numbers: thirty-seven foreigners and thirty natives had died in Taiyuan.[14] The only other contemporary report filed by a Westerner is that of Alexander Saunders, whose party escaped into Henan around 16 July. Unfortunately, Saunders mentions nothing of events in Taiyuan taking place after 28 June.[15]

The imprecision and uncertainty in these reports can be found as well in those filed by the CIM agent Zhang Zhiheng, whose letters from Xi'an dealt in part with his attempts to gather information on the massacre in Taiyuan. Not surprisingly, given that Zhang Zhiheng and Dreyer were traveling in the same part of southwestern Shanxi at about the same time—late July—their information is similar. The figure of thirty-seven foreigners and thirty natives appears in Zhang Zhiheng's letter of 26 July, but he states that the massacre took place in Taiyuan on 8 July (twelfth day of the sixth lunar month). Even though Zhang Zhiheng heard this in five other yamen he still did not consider this to be verified information and he reports in later letters that accounts still vary: some have it that forty-two foreigners died, some thirty-seven; some have a hundred Chinese deaths, some have forty.[16] Zhang Zhiheng's cautious approach to information derived from yamen sources was shared by F. C. H. Dreyer, who wrote, "We were dependent for our information on the conflicting and highly-colored reports from native official sources, which were specially calculated to develop the anti-foreign feeling among the people."[17]

First among the noteworthy elements in the stories circulating in Shanxi in July and early August of 1900 is the wide range of figures related, from no deaths to as many as forty-two foreigners and one hundred Chinese. Second, there is no mention of the role of Yuxian in the Taiyuan deaths, although he does appear in some of these accounts. This is especially true in C. W. Price's journal, where he expresses skepticism about the story that Yuxian was personally attending to the killing of Chinese Christians.[18] F. C. H. Dreyer mentions Yuxian, but only in the context of his popularity among the business community in Taiyuan, whose members successfully prevailed upon him to not leave for the "front" (i.e., Zhili Province) as he was supposed to have done on 5 July.[19]

In addition to these comments about the character of Yuxian we have evidence of Yuxian's actions in mid-July that are worth puzzling over. C. W. Price's journal entry for 18 July, for example, states, "Word also came to day that the Governor of the province had been shot in the trouble there on the 14th or 15th."[20] A 14 July telegram from C. H. S. Green, a missionary who was in Huolu County, just over the border in Zhili Province, stated that Taiyuan had been rioted, but there were no details.[21] If Green had access, as did his colleagues in Shanxi, to telegraphic traffic routed through county ya-men, this could correspond to the "trouble" mentioned by Price. These may be elements, then, of a counternarrative to the Taiyuan massacre story. However much the details vary in the telling, by mid-August this much was clear: foreigners and Chinese had died in Taiyuan and there were serious problems of local order, but these contemporary sources tell us little more.[22] This was a very thin layer of knowledge indeed and it was all that had reached the London headquarters of the China Inland Mission by 8 September.[23] It does not appear that any of this particular information was relayed to British consular officials in Shanghai or to the Foreign Office in London. The *Times* did, however, publish an in-depth report on 5 September 1900 based on information supplied by the China Inland Mission. In this article appears the following, which tallies with the reports being filed in Xi'an by their agent Zhang Zhiheng: "Reports have come from time to time of murders of missionaries there [i.e., Shanxi], but so far they have not been confirmed."[24]

The information, sketchy and conflicting, collected in Shanxi by Price, Dreyer, Saunders, and Zhang in the summer of 1900 bears little compari-son to three versions of the "Taiyuan massacre" that began circulating in China and abroad in the late summer and fall of 1900. These versions, which are associated with the high government official Wang Wenshao and two Chinese Christians, Fei Qihao and an Evangelist Zhao, appear to have been based on oral reports and rumors.[25] Yuxian is implicated in all three, with the variations turning on his personal involvement in the killings and whether or not Boxers were involved. All information in subsequent West-ern publications, mostly hagiographic martyrologies but scholarly studies as well, follows one of these three versions or their variants.[26] I have yet to uncover any evidence of a government investigation by Chinese or Western authorities, nor have I found any study or collection of reliable documents that goes beyond the testimony, based on oral reports, rumors, and hearsay, that is at the center of each of these versions. Even E. H. Edwards, who was certain he knew what had happened by the fall of 1900 after his interview with Evangelist Zhao, and whose trip to Shanxi in the summer of 1901 pro-vided him with much of the material that he published in *Fire and Sword in Shansi*, could only say, in the end, "As to what really occurred, the whole truth will probably never be known, but, from inquiries made on the spot, it seems certain that the Governor did not assault any with his own hand."[27] Edwards also backed away from attributing the violence to Boxers, saying that soldiers alone had carried out the massacre. Edwards's definitive ac-count, made after a trip to Taiyuan in 1901, conveyed fewer facts than he had gathered in the fall of 1900 from Evangelist Zhao. We have already seen how Shanxi was rife with rumor in 1900, and this phenomenon was char-acteristic of all China in this year of turmoil. Rumors, forgeries, and fraught communication channels not only enabled rumor to stand for fact, but also contributed to a documentary archive, including government documents, that combines the genuine with the spurious.[28]

One subsequent development in the reporting on the Taiyuan massacre is the publication in early 1901 of the graphic and oft-repeated Yong Zheng "eye-witness" account, mentioned above, by J. A. Creasey Smith. Creasey Smith, who was associated with the Baptist Missionary Society, had commissioned Evangelist Zhao's fall 1900 trip to Shanxi. Although Yong Zheng was not mentioned in the context of Evangelist Zhao's inquiries, the basic elements of his story were also collected by Zhao. Since Creasey Smith believed Yong Zheng's claims, he let his informant speak directly to the reader in the first-person account he published in the *North China Daily News*, but his colleague, J. Percy Bruce, faced a different task and was very meticulous in describing the efforts of Evangelist Zhao to gather information. Bruce also gives us some insight into what "eye-witness" could mean in BMS circles. Zhao's version of the Taiyuan massacre came from the Shanxi resident Liu Xidei, who learned the details from the Xinzhou evangelist Cui Lun, who "was practically an eye-witness, for though more or less in hiding he kept himself fully informed by friends . . . of all that was going on."[29] In Evangelist Zhao's version of the Taiyuan massacre, Yuxian decapitated the first three victims himself[30] while Yong Zheng's "eye-witness" account fixes the blame on an "executioner" and Yuxian's bodyguards.[31] The Yong Zheng account, which we have seen resembles *Fox's Book of Martyrs* in its manner of presentation, includes details that had already been published in the Evangelist Zhao and Fei Qihao versions of the Taiyuan massacre.

Neither the sketchy and conflicting details circulating in Shanxi before 15 August, nor the more elaborate, but still conflicting details available elsewhere after the relief of the Beijing legations contain the elements of a persuasive and authoritative narrative of the troubles in Shanxi in the summer of 1900. We still need new sources and a method that will make it possible to escape from this web of conflicting stories. The rewriting of this history in the archives presents almost insurmountable obstacles. Western sources are equally problematic. Take, for example, F. C. H. Dreyer's account of his escape from Shanxi, written shortly after his arrival in Hankou on 28 August, which was published in Marshall Broomhall's *Martyred Missionaries*. Dreyer subsequently published an expanded version entitled *The Boxer Rising*. In the first version Dreyer, whose Pingyang station was near the center of the storm, does not appear to have actually seen a "Boxer." Nor did he encounter any Boxers on the road. He did, however meet up with robbers who encouraged one another to kill the foreigners. When Dreyer talked about problems in Pingyang and in most other towns he always referred to "crowds" or "youths." But when he revised his account "crowds" became "Boxers" and "riots" became "Boxer riots."[32] Events he could not explain in

1900 were now understood to possibly be a result of Yuxian's machinations.[33]

It is this rewriting of the record that makes the conventional wisdom on the Taiyuan massacre very difficult to question, and many might wonder, why bother? The skeptic might ask, is there any other plausible narrative? Questions of historical significance will be addressed, but first it is necessary to rewrite yet again the history of the Taiyuan massacre. Sources ignored by most Qing officials, and historians both Chinese and Western, can be used to write a very different history. To engage in this task is not to justify what happened in Shanxi in 1900, nor is it to minimize the sufferings and sacrifices of the Christian community.

Because of the serious problems associated with the sources and extant narratives about events in Shanxi in 1900 it is necessary to apply very strict standards to the documentary base. For Western accounts I will use, as much as possible, only those produced in the summer of 1900. One exception to this rule concerns Dreyer's later version of Shanxi events, which can be compared to his 1900 version and corrected where necessary. In addition to Dreyer's account, C. W. Price's journal and the CIM agent Zhang Zhiheng's letters, all written in the period from June to September 1900, fit this profile of acceptable sources. But the most important sources, and ones that have seldom been used, are the memorials, court letters, decrees, and edicts that were exchanged between Taiyuan and Beijing in July and August. Yuxian himself wrote at least twenty memorials and attachments between 3 July and 6 August and his reporting is corroborated and elaborated upon by his subordinate Li Tingxiao, whose actions were praised by missionaries.[34] Let us put aside all of the problematic sources discussed so far and privilege, as much as possible, information contained in accounts by Westerners in Shanxi and in Chinese government documents written in 1900.[35]

WHAT HAPPENED IN SHANXI IN JULY 1900?

Here's how the situation looked to Yuxian. In late June conditions in Taiyuan deteriorated precipitously and threatened to match those in Beijing, which had already been overrun by rural insurgents in mid-June. Although there were fewer of them in the Taiyuan area and local security still seemed to be firmly in the hands of Yuxian and orthodox elites, the opening stage of the crisis, like in Beijing, was marked with rumor and fire. Yuxian said that Boxers (*quanmin*) had been talking about burning an English church in the city. While Yuxian did not implicate these Boxers, a terrible fire did break out on the evening of 27 June. In the midst of the chaos, presumably as the besieged foreigners were finally forced to flee the premises, shots from within the compound struck and killed four Chinese and wounded one. As for the foreigners, Yuxian relates, a few were burned to death. Five young Chinese girls were among the foreigners who had escaped the flames and Yuxian reports that he apprehended the girls and sent them back to their families.[36] Western accounts confirm that the besieged missionaries used firearms and put the death toll of Chinese at forty to fifty, including those who perished in the fire.[37]

At this point Yuxian had a serious problem of local order on his hands. There were rumors that great numbers of Christians from Taiyuan City and its suburbs had all fled to the mountains that ringed the city on three sides and were planning to retaliate. Yuxian wasn't entirely persuaded by these rumors but, on the other hand, he said the city's defenses had to be strengthened. The people, he added, were still fairly calm although he had received an unsubstantiated report that a church had been burned in Pingyao.[38]

Nevertheless, Yuxian made a fateful decision at this point. The riot in Taiyuan on 27 June was a major one, with deaths on both sides and extensive property damage. How should foreigners and Chinese converts in Shanxi now be treated? Could anything be done to quiet the populace? Yuxian issued a proclamation that called on Chinese Christians to end their association with foreigners (*chujiao*). Once this step was taken, local magistrates, who issued "certificates of protection," were obligated to protect them. Yuxian had at least two goals in mind: to restore local order and to minimize the opportunities for Chinese Christians to ally with foreigners in opposition to the state; this was not a manifesto for a religious war.[39] What was of particular concern to Yuxian was news of entrenched villages of Christians as well as reports of Catholics congregating in the massive cathedrals that had been built in recent years.[40] In Pingyang Prefecture F. C. H. Dreyer reported that Christians from two counties had fled to Yueyang County, where they were seeking shelter with Catholics "who seem to be well-armed."[41] Implicit in this account is the suggestion, which would make the situation even more difficult for Yuxian, that Chinese Catholics and Protestants were now cooperating. It is not apparent whether or not this directive went to the whole province, but Li Tingxiao said the proclamation had its desired effect in Yangqu County, with its county yamen in Taiyuan City, but was less effective in nearby Taiyuan County. Yuxian wanted peasants to return home and tend to their fields and, most important of all, give no indication, on the pain of death, that they were rebelling against state authority. His policy was implemented in advance of Beijing's, which issued an edict on 2 August that called for Chinese Christians to "turn over a new leaf" (*zixin*) and return to their villages. This edict was distributed throughout Shanxi as a provincial proclamation. It was this policy that was interpreted in Western circles as an order to renounce one's faith.[42]

Subsequently, news from central and south Shanxi, Inner Mongolia, and Zhili underscored the seriousness of the crisis. We do not know if Yuxian knew about the situation in Henan's Nanyang Prefecture, where Protestant missionaries passing through the province would claim that "Catholics under an Italian bishop or priest . . . were carrying on a little war of their own,"[43] but Yuxian did know about the situation in Xian County, Zhili. A court letter dated 1 July directed Yuxian to hurry without delay to Xian County, about two hundred miles east of Taiyuan, where a group of Chinese Christians was reportedly plotting trouble.[44] He was to lead two battalions, to use Boxers (*Yihetuan*), and to entrust the defense of Taiyuan to Li Tingxiao.[45] There was indeed a brewing confrontation in Xian County between non-Christians and a well-fortified and armed group of Catholics that included more than thirty foreigners and about five thousand Chinese Christians who had gathered from throughout southeastern Zhili in June.[46] Yuxian also was probably aware of battles between Christian and non-Christian villages in Baoding, situated between Xian County and the Shanxi-Zhili border.[47]

By the time Yuxian received these latest instructions, three days after they were issued in Beijing, the deteriorating situation in Shanxi was consuming his attention. In the past few days he had received detailed reports from magistrates in north Shanxi as well as the subprefectures (*ting*) in Inner Mongolia, for which Shanxi was administratively responsible, about serious conflicts between missionaries, their converts, and other Chinese. A similar report would be filed in November by a Western military officer who interviewed Catholics from the region.[48] The precipitating event, according to the report Yuxian based his memorial upon, was a Christian attack, led by a missionary, that had left nine people dead. Magistrates and prefects across northern Shanxi reported to Yuxian numerous instances of church burning. So too was the situation deteriorating in the Taiyuan area. Christians continued to remain in well-defended mountain strongholds and were planning, according to the spies Yuxian had sent out, evil deeds. In addition to collecting information, Yuxian said he was taking measures for defense such as rehabilitating militias (*tuanfang*).[49]

On 4 July Yuxian had received the court letter ordering him to leave for Zhili.[50] There then occurred a remarkable series of events, corroborated in F. C. H. Dreyer's account,[51] as news of this transfer became common knowledge in the Taiyuan area and Yuxian's preparations became evident. It had been his intention, Yuxian claimed, to follow the instructions of the just-received court letter and leave the next day for Zhili. It was then, according to both Yuxian and Li Tingxiao, that a broad-based mobilization of both elite and popular opinion forced Yuxian to remain in Taiyuan. According to their accounts, provincial officials and eminent local gentry visited his yamen to plead their case, which was also argued in numerous petitions. The case was also made with feet and physical presence, for a large group of persons, including gentry from both rural and urban settings in Taiyuan City and throughout Taiyuan Prefecture, as well as village elites, merchants, and other commoners, streamed into Taiyuan City and clogged its streets in a display associated with demonstrations against the imperial will when popular officials were transferred. Li Tingxiao, who estimated the number of persons coming into Taiyuan at about ten thousand, said that the people made good their demand by the refusal of carters to allow their carts to be used to carry the materiel to be taken by Yuxian's forces, which included a newly raised infantry battalion and a cavalry squadron, as well as by people guarding the gates of the yamen and the city to ensure that Yuxian stayed in Taiyuan.[52] Yuxian added force to his account by quoting from one of the petitions beseeching him to stay:

> After the burning of the church [i.e., the Schofield Memorial Hospital compound] the foreigners have been instigating the poisoning of wells and the Christians (*jiaomin*) have been fleeing to the mountains to plot revenge. The people are fearful and trembling and have been without food and rest. Fortunately the order has been received to rehabilitate the militia (*tuanlian*) and there has been a transfer of troops here so every place has been seriously preparing for defense. If you suddenly leave the province we're afraid that Taiyuan City cannot be protected and that the people (*baixing*) will have no one to rely on.[53]

We know that Yuxian was not exaggerating when he spoke of people's fears. On the evening of 5 July, the second day of these demonstrations in Taiyuan, a rumor had spread in nearby villages that an attack of Christians was imminent. Liu Dapeng, a member of the gentry, recalled the events of that night:

> The people were panic-stricken and everyone fled. Before long the inhabitants of [five villages] were in a state of utter turmoil. People screamed and cried out for help. Men, carrying their wives on their backs, sons their mothers, fled by the light of the stars in all directions. Some hid in nightsoil pits, others in pigpens, still others in reed fields, rice paddies, and lotus ponds. The bedlam lasted the entire night. Only when dawn broke did people discover that it was a false alarm.[54]

In the end Yuxian decided to remain in Taiyuan and delegated to an expectant official in Shanxi the task of leading a battalion to Xian County.[55] This solved the impasse; carters agreed to cooperate and preparations commenced for a departure scheduled for 9 July.[56]

Yuxian made this decision on 6 July and protests abated, but his receipt that day of another court letter, dated 3 July, gave him no respite. Yuxian and other governors and governors-general were reminded that hostilities had commenced between China and foreign countries and called for preparations to be made.[57] It was on the strength of this order that Yuxian barred foreigners from access to telegraph offices in Shanxi for incoming or outgoing telegrams. The next day a telegram from Shanghai sent by Sheng Xuanhuai, director of the Imperial Telegraph Administration and an official with close ties to the influential official Li Hongzhang, said that Westerners should be given access to telegraph offices throughout China; Yuxian was convinced this was a villainous fabrication and maintained his order, which was intended to limit Western access to news from Shanxi.[58] Although imperial communication lines, including telegraph lines (as the instruction from Sheng suggests), remained open, this order given in the context of what Yuxian perceived to be war seriously affected, as Yuxian had intended, Western knowledge about events in Shanxi.

Yuxian might have preferred to leave the province earlier, for the situation only worsened. The dispatch of troops based or mobilized in Taiyuan to points outside the province meant Shanxi remained seriously under-garrisoned. Yuxian said repeated requests by county magistrates for troops to help quell turmoil just could not be met. For example, in nearby Taiyuan County rural insurgents, falsely calling themselves Boxers (*Yihequan*), forced their way into the county yamen on 9 July, demanded food, and humiliated the magistrate.[59] In Yangqu County, the head county of Taiyuan Prefecture, a similar case occurred in Taiyuan City on the same day.[60] This was the day that would come to be given as the date of the Taiyuan massacre. It was also the day that Yuxian received a court letter sent from Beijing three days earlier that reminded officials to foster Christian–non-Christian amity. This letter also said, however, that Chinese Christians who defied state authority could be exterminated in accordance with circumstances.[61] The court was responding specifically to Yuxian's memorial about unrest in Inner Mongolia, but the situation in central Shanxi was analogous. Yuxian, who had heard reports that Christians and missionaries were plotting in Taiyuan, did not wait long to act. According to a memorial written by Li Tingxiao on 12 July: "[Yuxian] looked into the matter himself and took responsibility for rounding up each of the [Chinese] Christians who had been plotting trouble together and had them all executed."[62]

Yuxian described the tense atmosphere of 11 July in Taiyuan City when two people called out in the street that a force of several thousand Christians was only five miles away and was soon to attack the city. People converged on Yuxian's yamen, demanding action, and he sent out troops to investigate in order to calm fears.[63] Another one of Yuxian's worries at the time, also focused on the head county of Yangqu, concerned a Catholic named Li Fu, a second captain in a Qing unit stationed at Yu County. Li, according to Yuxian, was now fomenting trouble along with Westerners in

Taiyuan. According to Catholic sources the sixty-four-year-old Li Fu was an advisor to Franciscan missionaries in Taiyuan and had been arguing in the days after 27 June for a robust military defense of Catholic positions in Taiyuan.[64] Yuxian recommended that he be stripped of his rank and executed; permission was received.[65]

Taiyuan continued to be very unsettled. What had happened to the foreigners still in Taiyuan? The Chinese record reviewed here gives no clue and there are few in Western accounts. Alexander Saunders, the CIM missionary stationed in Pingyao, reported that on 28 June he met a native Christian about seven miles south of Taiyuan who had reported that "all foreigners were in the Baptist mission compound surrounded by a great mob who were threatening to burn it with all who were inside."[66] We know that the Schofield Memorial Hospital was burned in similar circumstances on 27 June. That the crisis reported on 28 June seems to have passed is indicated by the 6 July letter written by Dr. Millar Wilson that suggests that group at the Farthing residence compound (Baptist) was still alive.[67] A messenger, who had left Taiyuan on 7 July, delivered this letter to F. C. H. Dreyer and also reported that the local magistrate had asked all missionaries in Taiyuan to relocate to a single residence that could be more easily defended. But the messenger wasn't sure if that request had been complied with.[68] A *North China Herald* correspondent's report sent from Shandong (Weihaiwei) on 30 August noted that a story had been circulating in recent weeks that the foreigners had been burned to death in Mr. Farthing's house.[69] A more optimistic variation of this story, related by the Dreyer party to the Hankou correspondent of the *North China Herald* on 28 August, stated that the Baptist mission compound was set on fire and the foreigners escaped to the provincial yamen.[70]

Although these two late-August stories contradict one another we do know that missionaries might indeed try, in a crisis, to flee to government yamen. F. C. H. Dreyer described the strategy, decided upon in Pingyang in June, that if missionaries and their families were forced from a compound by a mob, "Our object in this was to throw ourselves upon the mercy of the magistrate, and, if his help was refused, die in the Yamen, under his eyes rather than on our own premises."[71] We need to keep this in mind when assessing Western reports about events in Taiyuan around 14 July. On that day C. H. S. Green reported that telegraphic news had arrived about a riot in Taiyuan.[72] C. W. Price, whose first journal entry (17 July) about the Taiyuan violence repeated the news received from nearby Taigu that all the missionaries in Taiyuan had been killed on their way to the provincial yamen, wrote in his journal the next day that there were troubles in Taiyuan on 14 or 15 July and that Yuxian had been shot.[73] One other significant event occurred on 14 July according to Catholic sources: Li Fu was executed.[74]

These sketchy Western reports of a Taiyuan riot and the various stories about continuing episodes of mob violence in Taiyuan conform to the broad outlines of the Chinese narrative just presented, which ends on 11 July. In that narrative we have already seen evidence of numerous instances in which crowds were near or in government yamen: the county yamen in Taiyuan City had been invaded by rural insurgents on 9 July and the provincial yamen was a focal point of demonstrations during 4–6 July as well as on 11 July.

The weight of evidence leads to a conclusion that mob violence, not Yuxian, was directly responsible for a massacre or massacres in Taiyuan that took place in July, probably on the fourteenth. This conclusion is also supported by Shanxi governor Cen Chunxuan's 1901 statement recorded on the officially sponsored memorial erected at a massacre site: foreigners were killed outside the provincial yamen.[75] Twenty years later a Western traveler in Shanxi, who passed this spot on his way to an interview with Governor Yan Xishan, reflected, "It seemed almost strange to walk so peacefully into his yamen through the same now rather tumble-down entrance at which more than twoscore foreigners were massacred by Boxer-influenced mobs in 1900."[76]

In 1900, however, nothing was known for certain and foreigners outside Taiyuan, based on little more than oral reports and rumors, had to make life-and-death decisions. Some, like F. C. H. Dreyer, negotiated with local officials and received the documents and protection that guaranteed their safe passage out of the province.[77] Dreyer and his party left Pingyang on 14 July. Catholic missionaries in Pingyang opted for the privately hired security details favored by Shanxi merchants when they traveled.[78] And others, such as C. W. Price in Fenzhou and his colleagues in Taigu, decided to stay. Their names would be added to the list of martyrs that would be compiled in the fall of 1900.

For these Westerners, and for the people of Shanxi, it became clear that the end of the turmoil was not near. The pattern of violence increased during July, with problems continuing in the north and worsening in central Shanxi, and magistrates' requests for help still coming into Taiyuan. In many cases Yuxian blamed the violence on bandits (*tufei*) who were falsely assuming the name of Boxers. Yuxian continued to be summoned by Beijing to go to Xian County and he still worried about provincial responsibilities for defense elsewhere on the Shanxi-Zhili border at Zhangjiakou and Huolu.[79]

From Yuxian's perspective China was at war, with regular troops and local militias in Shanxi preparing to meet the expected advance of allied troops. Unlike his peers in central and southern China, who were able to strike a neutrality pact with foreigners, one which should have reminded careful observers of similar examples of noninvolvement by provincial officials at a remove from hostilities during the Sino-French and Sino-Japanese wars in the two previous decades, Yuxian had no choice but to act in support of the strategic and tactical goals of the court as best he could. To that end Yuxian raised new troops, sanctioned the mobilization of local militia, insisted that Chinese Christians renounce their association with Westerners, executed Chinese Christians on charges of treason, suppressed bandits, and executed "false Boxers." For three weeks Taiyuan and its hinterland were in a state of turmoil that appeared at times to verge on anarchy. For that Yuxian and his subordinates were ultimately responsible. Other cities and towns in Shanxi and elsewhere were rioted, but nowhere was the loss of foreign lives as great as it was in Taiyuan. Taiyuan was witness to tragedy.

THE "TAIYUAN MASSACRE" OR MASSACRES IN TAIYUAN: QUESTIONS OF HISTORICAL SIGNIFICANCE

Why does this matter? This study of the Taiyuan massacre and its context rewrites the accepted historical record about events in Shanxi during the summer of 1900, as well as the general narrative of the Boxer Uprising. The richness of the oral reports and rumors that led to several versions of the Taiyuan massacre was no less evident elsewhere in China. When one looks at the range of events and the way they were perceived in June and July of 1900 it becomes more and more difficult to restrict one's inquiry to an embattled imperial court fighting a regional battle in the north. The bitterness of China's defeat at the hands of Japan in 1895, the euphoria experienced by the reformers associated with Kang Youwei and Liang Qichao in the spring and summer of 1898, the tragedy of the September coup in that year, and the struggle to determine the next emperor of China that broke out early in 1900 had all defined political fault lines that remained significant as spring turned to summer. Revolutionaries and reformers alike took advantage of the chaos and tried to advance their causes. Can we continue to rely on the documentation, produced by these antagonists in the struggle of the moment or in the months and years to follow, to understand what was happening in Beijing and north China in 1900? The goal, however, is not to just write a more detailed and accurate history of one region's vicissitudes in 1900, but rather one that views the events of 1900 from a truly national perspective. There was a Boxer Uprising in 1900, but it was one part of an extraordinarily complicated history that includes, as well as the China War, a series of anti-Christian and antiforeign outbursts in other parts of China and revolutionary battles fomented by followers of both Sun Yat-sen and Kang Youwei.

Political forces, both domestic and international, were being realigned in China during and immediately after the Boxer Uprising. That Yuxian's reputation has seemed to be irretrievably in tatters since September 1900 is evidence enough for the momentous nature of this sea change. In 1899 Yuxian, along with Li Bingheng and others, had many in China who were sympathetic to his position. It was the "militant conservative" position, defined by John Schrecker in his study of German imperialism in Shandong Province, that Yuxian exemplified. It was a position with a long and honorable lineage going back to the *qingliu* movement of the 1870s when a young official named Zhang Zhidong was one of its adherents. Yuxian, along with Li Bingheng, adopted this position in their dealings with foreigners in Shandong during the heightened imperialist challenges of the late 1890s. The Anglo-American voices that only recalled with hatred the seeming antiforeign sentiments of Yuxian in western Shandong neglected to mention that this was part of a nuanced approach to foreigners that also included, in eastern Shandong, a working relationship with German interests active in the concession area around Jiaozhou Bay in 1899.[80] Yuxian was not happy with this state of affairs and he would have agreed with Li Bingheng's argument in 1897 for armed resistance to the German invasion.[81] Li Bingheng was stymied in Shandong, but Yuxian and some of his Shandong officers would have another chance to pursue this policy in Shanxi in 1900.

Yuxian and his colleagues thought they were dealing with the repercussions of a Western invasion of China that was threatening both Tianjin and Beijing. By the time of the Schofield Memorial Hospital burning of 27 June China was on a war footing. The ill-fated Seymour Expedition had failed in its attempt to reach the besieged legations and a worldwide effort to mobilize the forces necessary to march on Beijing was underway. A countermobilization was taking place in China; Yuxian and Shanxi Province were central elements in the developing strategy.

This strategy had its critics within Chinese officialdom and when it collapsed few cared to remember it. Certainly Li Hongzhang, who was one of those critics, had little interest in explaining to Western negotiators in Beijing what had been going on in Shanxi during the summer of 1900. Li's efforts led in part to the imperial decree of 13 February 1901 that ordered Yuxian's death by beheading. In that edict Yuxian was pilloried in exactly the terms to be found in the Western press:

> When governor of Shansi he ordered killed many missionaries and native Christians. More than the others is he marked out by his crass stupidity and fierce cruelty—a criminal of the deepest dye and one of the chief ringleaders.[82]

Nowhere is there even a hint of the tremendous challenges that had faced Yuxian the previous summer. But even as Li and his allies eagerly offered up

Yuxian as one of the prime scapegoats of the Boxer fiasco, the strategy Yuxian had so desperately tried to support in Shanxi was still in place. It would take another two months before Yuxian's military subordinates would be ordered by another imperial decree, which also reflected Li Hongzhang's will, to yield to the Allies in April 1901.[83] Those with access to Chinese government documents could have pieced together the Shanxi story and at least suggested a more complex reality in Shanxi, but officials like Li Hongzhang had no desire to advance the cause of their factional enemies.

Even Chinese officials who might have supported Yuxian were not willing to risk the ire of Western negotiators in Beijing in the fall and winter of 1900 to1901 since they were desperately trying to persuade the allies to not make good on the threat to invade Shanxi. Zhang Zhidong, for example, made clear to Western authorities that with the announcement of Yuxian's punishment in September 1900, there was no longer any justification to move allied troops into Shanxi.[84] Zhang sent the first of these telegrams well aware, in all likelihood, that Yuxian was still in Shanxi aiding the new governor, Xiliang, whom Zhang Zhidong had dispatched to Shanxi during the summer of 1900 to aid Yuxian in his defense of the passes into the province. Yuxian remained in the province in a military capacity until November 1900.[85]

It is striking how quickly the honorable "militant conservative" position exemplified by Yuxian came to be identified during and after the Boxer Uprising as nothing more than the rabid, superstitious, and irrational antiforeignism associated with Boxers. This third way in foreign relations, which Schrecker lists with the accommodationist mainstream approach associated with Li Hongzhang and Yuan Shikai and the Western-style internationalist position championed by reformers like Kang Youwei, was no longer a viable option.[86] In 1900 many foreigners would have been surprised to learn that the hated Li Bingheng had been identified by Kang Youwei in 1895 as one of two civilian officials, the other being Zhang Zhidong, who could be depended upon to ably defend China.[87] The militant conservative position, not xenophobic irrational anti-foreignism, was at the center of debates in 1900. But the two were lumped together in the minds of many, and certainly the accommodationists and the internationalists could agree in the fall of 1900 that they now had an enemy in common. Deprived of an articulate spokesman like Zhang Zhidong, the position held by Yuxian, Li Bingheng, and Dong Fuxiang was beyond repair and would remain so for a generation. It would not be until the rise of the Chinese Communist Party that another political force in China possessed the will, determination, and resources to champion a militant position, one that, ironically, had an ideological foundation largely foreign in origin.

In 1900, however, the accommodationists and internationalists decided they could work together and both sides found allies among the foreigners, who now had new access to many areas in Chinese government, society, and economy. No one, in this new power equation, had anything to gain by calling attention to, supporting, or investigating Yuxian's role in the events of 1900. And with the facts that were known, or not known, Yuxian was perfectly suited to assume the role of benighted and brutal villain—the "Butcher of Shansi"—in the narrative of the New China being written as the fires of 1900 were extinguished and the ashes swept away. We may never know as much as we would like about what happened in Taiyuan in July 1900, but that should not distract us from the significance of this story. It is a story told in part by Yuxian himself, a provincial governor who played many roles and cast the people of Shanxi in a drama that addressed questions of identity, loyalty, and national survival in new and momentous ways. Further research may reveal significant continuities between this forgotten and easily ignored moment in Shanxi's history and the struggle to build a new China that would unfold in Shanxi in the years and decades to come.

NOTES

1. There are numerous Western accounts of events in Shanxi in general and Taiyuan in particular based on interviews and research conducted from 1901 on, but much of this material is hagiographical in intent and lacks corroborating evidence. A convenient guide to the Protestant literature, and a narrative based upon it, can be found in Nat Brandt, *Massacre in Shansi* (Syracuse: Syracuse University Press, 1994). The Catholic record was produced to provide a documentary basis for the canonization process. See Giovanni Ricci, *Barbarie e trionfi: Ossia le vittime illustri del Sansi in Cina nella persecuzione del 1900*, 2nd. ed. (Firenze: Associazioni Nazionale per Soccorrere i missionari Cattolici Italiani, 1910) and his *Avec les Boxeurs chinois* (Brive,Corrèze: Éditions Écho des grottes, 1949). In a multiauthor five-hundred-page work on the Boxer Uprising, published in China in 1981, fewer than three pages are devoted to events in Shanxi. See Liao Yizhong, Li Dezheng, and Zhang Zuru, *Yihetuan yundong shi* (A history of the Boxer movement) (Beijing: Renmin chubanshe, 1981). For a detailed account, based largely on post-1900 material, see Qiao Zhiqiang, "Shanxi diqu de yihetuan yundong" (The Boxer movement in the Shanxi area), in *Yihetuan yundong liushi zhounian jinian lunwenji* (Articles commemorating the sixtieth anniversary of the Boxer movement) (Beijing: Zhonghua shuju, 1961), 167–83. For an extensive account published in Chinese in 1909 under Catholic auspices, based in part on Western sources, see Li Di, *Quanhuo ji* (A record of the Boxer calamity) (Shanghai, 1909), 332–415. Recent Western accounts of the Boxer Uprising give limited coverage to events in Shanxi. See Joseph Esherick, *The Origins of the Boxer Uprising* (Berkeley and Los Angeles: University of California Press, 1987); and Paul A. Cohen, *History in Three Keys: The Boxers as Event, Experience, and Myth* (New York: Columbia University Press, 1997). (I thank Mark Allee, David Buck, Henrietta Harrison, Mark Lewis, Haun Saussy, Matthew Sommer,

Jonathan Spence, and Gary Tiedemann for their criticisms, suggestions, and assistance in the writing of this essay.)

2. Cohen, *History in Three Keys*, 51.

3. Yong Zheng [Yung Cheng], "The Martyrdom at T'aiyuanfu on the 9th of July, 1900. By an Eye-witness," *North China Herald*, 3 April 1901, 637. This account is available in Arthur H. Smith, *China in Convulsion* (New York, Chicago, and Toronto: Fleming H. Revell Company, 1901), vol. 2, 614–15. I have not seen the version that first appeared in the *North China Daily News*, but its sister publication, the weekly *North China Herald and Supreme Court & Consular Gazette* (hereafter *North China Herald*), published the Yong Zheng account, dated 29 March, in its issue of 3 April 1901. The *Chinese Recorder* reprinted this version, in a special expanded edition, in April 1901. Arthur Smith's version closely follows the one published in the *North China Herald*. Most differences are minor stylistic and punctuation changes, but the Smith version does include three additional substantive changes: "big beheading knives" becomes "heavy swords with long handles"; the sentence "I did not see them [i.e., native Christians] all, but I was told there were thirteen"; and the two sentences preceding the final sentence—"On the 11th July the remains were temporarily buried outside the great South Gate, to the West side. On the 10th July there were also killed many Catholic Christians, I heard sixty, and during the next few days a few more Protestants were also killed"—were dropped from the Smith version.

4. William Haller, *The Elect Nation: The Meaning and Relevance of Foxe's Book of Martyrs* (New York and Evanston: Harper & Row, 1963), 251–53. For passages in the *Book of Martyrs* corresponding to the Yong Zheng narrative see *Fox's* [sic] *Book of Martyrs; or, The Acts and Monuments of The Christian Church; being A Complete History of the Lives, Sufferings, and Deaths of The Christian Martyrs; from the Commencement of Christianity to the Present Period*, revised by the Reverend John Malham and re-edited by the Reverend T. Pratt (Philadelphia: J. J. Woodward, 1830), 116, 498, 500, 502–3, and 584.

5. Luella Miner, *China's Book of Martyrs: A Record of Heroic Martyrdom and Marvelous Deliverances of Chinese Christians during the Summer of 1900* (New York, Boston, and Chicago: The Pilgrim Press, 1903), 13.

6. Miner, *China's Book of Martyrs*, 23–24.

7. E. H. Edwards, *Fire and Sword in Shansi: The Story of the Martyrdom of Foreigners and Chinese Christians* (New York: Revell, 1903), 8–9.

8. Edwards, *Fire and Sword*, 21.

9. Marshall Broomhall, ed., *Martyred Missionaries of the China Inland Mission with a Record of the Perils & Sufferings of Some Who Escaped* (London: Morgan & Scott, 1901), 295.

10. Broomhall writes: "This man, whose name we do not publish, has organised a secret service with native Christians as his helpers, who have, at the risk of their lives, travelled throughout Shan-si to obtain all the information possible, and to succour any if not too late." See Broomhall, *Martyred Missionaries*, 21. Clues to the identity of "C.c.-h." can be found throughout Broomhall's work. Eva French refers to an "Elder Chang chih-heng of the Yun-ch'eng [Yuncheng] Church." See Broomhall, *Martyred Missionaries*, 271. Mr. Blom, of the Swedish Mission, entrusted "C.c.-h, elder of the Y———church" with funds to be given to "any missionary in case of need." See Broomhall, *Martyred Missionaries*, 263. That C.c.-h. was Chang

Chih-heng (Zhang Zhiheng in pinyin) is further substantiated by Broomhall's quotation of C.c-h.'s testimony in his *Martyred Missionaries*, 264, based on a passage in the China Inland Mission's *Days of Blessing in Inland China, Being an Account of Meetings Held in the Province of Shan-si* (London: Morgan & Scott, 1887), 127–28. Here the full name is given: Chang Chih-heng. Broomhall had only praise for Zhang: "He is one of the oldest Christians in the province, a man of considerable ability and strength of character." See Broomhall, *Martyred Missionaries*, 262.

11. For a discussion of the distinction between oral reports and rumors in Shanxi see Henrietta Harrison, "Newspapers and Nationalism in Rural China, 1890–1929," *Past and Present*, no. 166 (2000): 183. Harrison notes that "oral reports contained a record of their chain of transmission from a source that could be presumed to be reliable."

12. Edwards, *Fire and Sword*, 283.

13. Edwards, *Fire and Sword*, 287.

14. Broomhall, *Martyred Missionaries*, 115. See F. C. H. Dreyer, *The Boxer Rising and Missionary Massacres in Central and South Shan-si, North China, with an Account of a Missionary Band's Escape to the Coast* (Toronto: China Inland Mission, [1901?]), 37, for the date Dreyer was in Puzhou.

15. *North China Herald*, 22 August 1900, 410–11.

16. All four letters were published in Broomhall, *Martyred Missionaries*, 264–70.

17. Dreyer, *Boxer Rising*, 10.

18. Edwards, *Fire and Sword*, 286.

19. Broomhall, *Martyred Missionaries*, 115.

20. Edwards, *Fire and Sword*, 284.

21. Broomhall, *Martyred Missionaries*, 293.

22. Two documents that were published after 1900 could add more detail, but I am not certain of their authenticity. One is a diary extract from the Taigu missionary Rowena Bird, whose entry for 12 July stated that thirty-two foreigners and thirty Chinese had been massacred on 10 July at Yuxian's order. See Edwards, *Fire and Sword*, 293. While similar figures appear in the reports filed by F. C. H. Dreyer and Zhang Zhiheng, neither mentioned Yuxian's purported role. Further evidence that this text could have been corrupted comes from C. W. Price's journal. We know that he learned of the events in Taiyuan through Taigu missionaries like Rowena Bird and yet he never mentioned Yuxian in this context. The second document, a 1 August 1900 letter attributed to Price's wife Eva, states that thirty-three foreigners were beheaded on 8 July on orders of Yuxian. See Eva Jane Price, *China Journal, 1889–1900: An American Missionary Family during the Boxer Rebellion* (New York: Scribner's, 1989), 235. This document, too, is problematic. Again, the information bears no correlation to what appears in C. W. Price's journal, nor was it found by E. H. Edwards in his information-gathering effort in the summer of 1901. Eva Price had not written a letter since 6 June, preferring to write instead in a diary; C. W. Price's last journal entry was dated 31 July, the day an escape was planned. It seems highly unlikely that C. W. Price, who had been keeping a journal faithfully since the end of June, would not have added another entry that dealt definitively with the problem he had been wrestling with since 17 July. If something had happened to Rev. Price on 31 July, it should have been worthy of mention in a letter written by his wife on 1 August. Our confidence in this letter is not strengthened by the words of Robert

Felsing, the editor of Eva Price's letters: "How Eva Price's letter of August 1, 1900, made its way from Fen Cho fu [Fenzhou fu] will always be a bit of a mystery." See Price, 237. This collection of letters was in the possession of family members prior to their publication in 1989. According to Roland M. Baumann, archivist of the Oberlin College Archives, the original letters were to have been deposited at the Oberlin College Archives. It appears that some letters were lost in the process of publication and Eva Price's 1 August 1900 letter may be among the missing. Roland M. Baumann, e-mail message to author, 18 July 2002. The two main elements in the Bird diary entry and the Price letter—the number of deaths (thirty-two or thirty-three) and Yuxian's role—are characteristic of accounts dating to late August and September rather than July and early August.

23. Broomhall, *Martyred Missionaries*, 293–96.

24. *Times*, 5 September 1900, 8. Others reporting from Xi'an, with much less information in hand, were more certain. On 1 August the Foreign Office received a telegram from Consul Warren in Shanghai, based on information gathered by a Baptist Missionary Society representative in Xi'an: "Fifty missionaries murdered, fear welfare of Christians." See Great Britain, Parliament, *China No. 1 (1901): Correspondence respecting the Disturbances in China*, Cd. 436 (February 1901), 44. Similar information, although presented without attribution, accompanied the *New York Times* article published on 21 July 1900, 2. Under the headline "Sixty Missionaries Killed in Shan-si," the article stated that word from Shanghai reached London on 20 July. Boxers also massacred one hundred Chinese Christians according to this dispatch. I have not found any evidence that the Baptist Missionary Society had funded an intelligence and relief operation on the scale mounted by the China Inland Mission's Zhang Zhiheng.

Catholic reports coming from Shaanxi in August 1900 contain similar information. The apostolic vicar of north Shaanxi, Amatus Pagnucci, reported on 18 August 1900 that Yuxian himself had killed the Catholic bishop in Taiyuan and ordered his soldiers to kill the rest. See *Acta Ordinis Fratrum Minorum* 19 (1900): 192. This report included information written by Barnabas Nanetti, a Franciscan missionary from the Taiyuan area who reached a safe haven in Mongolia in August. His 7 August letter states that Yuxian ordered everyone to his yamen and had them killed, beginning with the bishop. See *Acta Ordinis Fratrum Minorum* 19 (1900): 191. I thank Henrietta Harrison for providing me with photocopies of this Franciscan publication. I thank my colleague, Professor Haun Saussy, and Don Lavigne, a graduate student at Stanford University, for helping me with translations of these Latin texts.

25. This context also informs the jottings of a member of the Shanxi gentry named Liu Dapeng who lived near Taiyuan. Liu was an inveterate diarist for over three decades and much could be learned from his diary for 1900, but this year is missing from the manuscript in the Shanxi Provincial Library. See Henrietta Harrison, *The Man Awakened from Dreams: One Man's Life in a North China Village, 1857–1942* (Stanford: Stanford University Press, 2005), 7. Liu's retrospective account of the Taiyuan massacre has elements that can be found in Western accounts. See Liu Dapeng, "Qian yuan suoji" (Sundry information from the Qian Garden), in *Yihetuan zai Shanxi diqu shiliao* (Historical materials on the Boxers in the Shanxi area), ed. Qiao Zhiqiang (Taiyuan: Renmin chubanshe, 1980), 31–32.

26. Wang Wenshao version: a story filed from Tianjin on 5 September 1900 attributes the following to a "prominent member" of the Zongli yamen who accused Yuxian of "inviting all the foreigners in Tai-Yuan into his yamen under pretense of escorting them in safety to the coast, and having them all put to death." See *New York Times*, "Atrocities by Chinese," 4 October 1900, 2. A story in the 26 September 1900 issue of the *North China Herald*, 657, identified a grandson of Wang Wenshao to be the source of this story.

Fei Qihao version: on 1 September 1900 Fei Qihao, a Christian associated with the Tongzhou and Fenzhou missions of the American Board of Commissioners for Foreign Missions, reached Tianjin after his escape from Shanxi. He was interviewed by missionaries, consuls, and military officers. The British officer Col. H. Boxer's account of his questioning of Fei can be found in Great Britain, Parliament, *China No. 5 (1901): Further Correspondence respecting the Disturbances in China*, Cd. 589 (May 1901), 36–38. The Fei Qihao version can also be found in the *Peking and Tientsin Times* issue of 8 September 1900, 70, in a story written by Mrs. Arthur Smith and reprinted in the *North China Herald* on 26 September 1900, 676–77. Mrs. Arthur Smith also published an account, dated 26 November 1900, entitled *Mr. Fei's True Story* (Chicago: Woman's Board of Missions of the Interior, [1901?]). Luella Miner included her version of Fei's first-person account in *Two Heroes of Cathay* (New York: Fleming H. Revell, 1903). Robert Forsyth published Mrs. Smith's version in *The China Martyrs*.

Evangelist Zhao version: Evangelist Zhao, like Fei, had also escaped from Shanxi but returned at the request of Robert Forsyth, who was associated with the Baptist Missionary Society (BMS), to gather more information in the fall of 1900. Zhao was interviewed by Robert Forsyth, J. Percy Bruce, and E. H. Edwards. Forsyth's "Narrative of Massacre in Shansi, July 1900" was published in the *North China Herald* on 28 November 1900, 1155–57. See also E. H. Edwards, "More Particulars about the Shansi Murders, Account of Some of the Shansi Massacres as Narrated by Evangelist Chao Who Escaped from the Station of Hsin-cheo, but Subsequently Returned to Ascertain the Fate of the Missionaries," *Peking and Tientsin Times*, 24 November 1900, 114–15. The most complete account of the Zhao version was written by J. Percy Bruce on 10 November 1900 for the benefit of BMS headquarters in London. See J. Percy Bruce, "Massacre of English Baptist Missionaries and others in Shansi," *Chinese Recorder*, March 1901, 132–37.

These three versions characterized Anglo-American coverage of Protestant victims in Taiyuan. Less attention was paid to the Roman Catholics in Taiyuan, but on 19 August the British Foreign Office did receive a 17 August telegraphic report from Consul Carles in Tianjin that many foreigners had been executed in the provincial yamen of Taiyuan. See Great Britain, *China No. 1 (1901)*, 96. On 12 October the Foreign Office received Carles's full report, which included a translation of Father Becker's account of the Taiyuan massacre, based on the testimony of a Roman Catholic soldier who claimed to have deserted from Taiyuan on 29 July and returned to his home in Xian County, Zhili. Father Becker had relayed this news from Xian County to the French consul-general in Tianjin. The key points in this narrative include a 2 July edict ordering missionaries to leave without escort for the coast; Yuxian's 9 July invitation for all Europeans, Catholic and Protestant, to come to the

yamen; the presence of five hundred soldiers; Yuxian's interrogation of the missionaries; and his order for them to be executed. The soldier also claimed that on 14
July two hundred Chinese Christians were killed because they refused to apostatize.
Women and children, however, were spared. See Great Britain, *China No. 5 (1901)*,
25–27. These detailed Protestant and Catholic accounts were not consistent with respect to the question of escort, where the massacre took place, who killed the missionaries, and how many were killed.

27. Edwards, *Fire and Sword*, 72; and Edwards, "More Particulars about the Shansi
Murders," 114–15.

28. In the aftermath of the Boxer Uprising the doctoring of archival records and
the creation of fictitious "true accounts" such as Jingshan's infamous diary were
common. For the latter see Hugh Trevor-Roper, *Hermit of Peking: The Hidden Life of
Sir Edmund Backhouse* (Harmondsworth: Penguin, 1978), 212. Wu Xiangxiang's dis-
coveries in Beijing in 1947–1948 marked the beginning of increased access to
archival documentation that makes possible the rewriting of this history. Of particular concern to historians is Wu's realization that the *Veritable Records (Shilu)* for the
Guangxu period (1875–1908), completed in manuscript form in 1921 and published in Changchun in 1937, was not completely reliable. See Wu Xiangxiang, "Gugong cang juanluan shiliao zhushi" (Notes on the archives concerning the Boxer
Uprising kept in the Palace Museum), *Guoli Zhongyang yanjiuyuan Lishi yuyan yanjiusuo jikan* 23 (1951): 161–98; Wu Xiangxiang, "Qing Dezong Shilu benji de zhengben" (On the original version of the *Veritable Records* of the Guangxu Period), *Dalu
zazhi* (Taibei) 2, no. 12 (30 June 1951): 7–10; and Knight Biggerstaff, "Some Notes
on the *Tung-hua lu* and the *Shih-lu,*" *Harvard Journal of Asiatic Studies* 4, no. 2 (1939):
101–15. For scholars of the Boxer Uprising this finding is particularly troubling
since Chester C. Tan's *The Boxer Catastrophe* (1955; repr., New York: Octagon Books,
1975), still regarded as the best single account of the events of 1900 from the perspective of the court, relied heavily upon the 1937 Changchun publication, based
on the Shenyang manuscript, of the *Shilu*. Fortunately, the editors of *Yihetuan dang'-
an shiliao* used a different and more accurate version of the *Shilu* available in Beijing,
the Huangshicheng manuscript. For information on this manuscript see Endymion
Wilkinson, *Chinese History: A Manual*, 2nd ed. (Cambridge: Harvard University Asia
Center, 2000), 941. The editors of *Yihetuan dang'an shiliao* carefully noted differences in the two versions. For example, an edict dated 31 July 1900 (GX26/7/6) in
the Shenyang manuscript of the *Shilu* reads: "If the Christian converts (*jiaomin*)
come out they won't be harmed," but the Beijing manuscript reads "If Christian
rebels (*jiaofei*) come out to plunder then it is ordered that they will be dealt with
forcefully." See *Yihetuan dang'an shiliao* (Archival materials on the Boxers), ed. Gugong bowuyuan Ming-Qing dang'an bu (Beijing: Zhonghua shuju, 1959), vol. 1, 2
(hereafter *YHTDASL*). There are numerous instances in which a term like *jiaofei* was
changed to *jiaomin* in the documentary record. Sue Fawn Chung also called into
question the authenticity of a number of edicts issued in 1900 and writes, "There is
no doubt that many edicts and memoirs were either tampered with or forged." See
Sue Fawn Chung, "The Much Maligned Empress Dowager: A Revisionist Study of
the Empress Dowager Tz'u-hsi in the period 1898 to 1900" (PhD diss., University of
California at Berkeley, 1975), 258, note 83. For Chung's careful assessment of the issue see "Much Maligned Empress Dowager," 240–49. For discussion of an elite-

sponsored forgery of an imperial edict in Hunan see Cohen, *History in Three Keys*,155.

29. J. Percy Bruce, "Massacre of English Baptist Missionaries," 133.

30. Bruce, "Massacre of English Baptist Missionaries," 134.

31. Yong Zheng, "The Martyrdom at T'aiyuanfu."

32. Compare Broomhall, *Martyred Missionaries*, 108 and 117, with the corresponding passages in Dreyer, *Boxer Rising*, 19 and 52.

33. Compare Broomhall, *Martyred Missionaries*, 103, with the corresponding passage in Dreyer, *Boxer Rising*, 6. Another example of this rewriting can be seen in Dreyer's account of the Taiyuan massacre. In 1900 he put the number of deaths at thirty-seven, which he repeats in his 1901 text, but he also interpolates, later in this 1901 text, that the "definite news" received at this time was forty-five. This latter figure corresponds to the number in the Yong Zheng account published by J. A. Creasy Smith in early 1901; it does not appear in Dreyer's 1900 text. See Broomhall, *Martyred Missionaries*, 115, and Dreyer, *Boxer Rising*, 69 and 123.

34. Approximately twenty Yuxian memorials and attachments, dating from 3 July to 6 August, can be found in *YHTDASL*, 225–440. One memorial, dated GX26/6/14 (10 July), is too problematic to be used. See *YHTDASL*, 281. In this memorial Yuxian concentrates entirely upon the troubles with foreigners and Chinese Christians in June and July 1900. The memorial gives a narrative of events beginning with the burning of the Schofield Memorial Hospital, claims that foreigners were plotting against the state and engaging in actions like poisoning wells, and tells of the execution first of forty-four foreigners—men, women, and children— and seventeen Chinese Christians, and then of seven foreigners from Shouyang, and mentions as well the firing of a church at the North Gate of Taiyuan. A close reading of Yuxian's memorials for this period reveal the 10 July 1900 memorial to be very different in terms of style, structure, and content. Yuxian almost always starts his memorials with reference to a document, whether it be a memorial, an edict, or a lower official's report, and often packs his memorials were specific details like names and dates. Also, when Yuxian refers to capital punishment it is usually foregrounded by receipt of permission from Beijing or at least specific reference to established procedure. See *YHTDASL*, 225, 320–21, 396–98, and 437–39. It is rare as well for Yuxian himself to write narratives of events, although he will often quote from others who do. None of these characteristics can be found in the 10 July memorial. Fortunately, Yuxian's subordinate Li Tingxiao submitted a memorial on 12 July (GX26/6/16) in which he described recent events, including executions, that can be used in place of Yuxian's 10 July memorial. See *YHTDASL*, 293–95. In a separate essay I explore in much greater detail the reasons why I suspect the authenticity of Yuxian's memorial, which appears closely related to the Wang Wenshao version of the Taiyuan massacre.

35. For an indictment of contemporary Western sources and the studies of the Boxer Uprising based on them, as well as a complaint about the lack of Chinese material see Lo Hui-min, "Some Notes on Archives on Modern China," in *Essays on the Sources for Chinese History*, ed. Donald D. Leslie, Colin Mackerras, and Wang Gungwu (Columbia: University of South Carolina Press, 1973), 215–16.

36. Yuxian memorial GX26/6/3 (rescript date GX26/6/5). See *YHTDASL*, 205–6. This section is based on Roger R. Thompson, "Military Dimensions of the 'Boxer

Uprising' in Shanxi, 1898–1901," in *Warfare in Chinese History*, ed. Hans van de Ven (Leiden: Brill Academic Publishers, 2000), 306–11.

37. Broomhall, *Martyred Missionaries*, 115.

38. Yuxian memorial GX26/6/3 (rescript date GX26/6/5). See *YHTDASL*, 205–6.

39. For Yuxian's discussion of this policy see Yuxian memorials GX26/6/10 (rescript date) and GX26/6/20 (rescript date), attachment A, *YHTDASL*, 225 and 319–20. For a facsimile of a "certificate of protection" given to a Christian in Yangqu County see Edwards, *Fire and Sword*, 110.

40. For photographs of these imposing edifices see Ricci, *Barbarie e trionfi*.

41. Dreyer, *Boxer Rising*, 61.

42. Edict GX26/7/8. See Jian Bozan et al., eds., *Yihetuan* (The Boxers) (Shanghai: Shenzhou guoguang she, 1951), vol. 4, 34. For an English translation see Great Britain, *China No.1 (1901)*, 152–53. In Li Tingxiao's discussion of this policy he includes a quote from the edict. Li's memorial of GX26/8/1 also gives a retrospective account of the policy's implementation. See *YHTDASL*, 508–9.

43. Dreyer, *Boxer Rising*, 78.

44. In the court letters of GX26/6/5 and GX26/6/12 the Christians in Xian County are called *jiaomin* and *jiaofei* respectively. See *YHTDASL*, 215 and 264.

45. Court letter GX26/6/5. See *YHTDASL*, 215.

46. Liao Yizhong, et al., eds., *Yihetuan da cidian* (A Boxer dictionary) (Beijing: Zhongguo shehui kexue chubanshe, 1995), 432. For an account of this incident see Jean-Paul Wiest, "Catholic Images of the Boxers," *The American Asian Review* 9, no. 3 (1991): 41–65.

47. Court letter GX26/6/9 to Ting Yong. See *YHTDASL*, 239–40.

48. Great Britain, Parliament, *China No. 6 (1901): Further Correspondence respecting the Disturbances in China*, Cd. 675 (August 1901), 64–68.

49. Yuxian memorial GX26/6/7. See *YHTDASL*, 225.

50. Court letter GX26/6/5 received by Yuxian on GX26/6/8. See *YHTDASL*, 215. Yuxian mentions the receipt date in his memorial GX26/6/12 (rescript date). See *YHTDASL*, 263–64.

51. Broomhall, *Martyred Missionaries*, 115.

52. Li Tingxiao memorial GX26/6/16 (rescript date GX26/6/19). See *YHTDASL*, 293–95.

53. Yuxian GX26/6/12 (rescript date). See *YHTDASL*, 263–64.

54. Cohen, *History in Three Keys*, 158.

55. Yuxian GX26/6/12 (rescript date). See *YHTDASL*, 263–64.

56. Li Tingxiao memorial GX26/6/16 (rescript date GX26/6/19). See *YHTDASL*, 293–95.

57. Court letter GX26/6/7. See *YHTDASL*, 221.

58. Yuxian memorial GX26/6/11 (rescript date). See *YHTDASL*, 257.

59. Yuxian GX26/6/19 (rescript date). See *YHTDASL*, 313.

60. Yuxian GX26/6/19 (rescript date). See *YHTDASL*, 313.

61. Court letter GX26/6/10. See *YHTDASL*, 249.

62. Li Tingxiao, GX26/6/16 (rescript date GX26/6/19). See *YHTDASL*, 293–95. The published version of this memorial contains a mistaken transcription of the Grand Council draft copy (*lufu zouzhe*) of this memorial. The passage should read: "[Yuxian] looked into the matter himself and took responsibility for rounding up

(*lian na*) each of the [Chinese] Christians who had been plotting trouble together (*tong mo luan ge jiaomin*) and had them all executed (*yibing zhengfa*)." The published version switches *na* and *tong*. I thank my colleague, Professor Matthew Sommer, for obtaining a photocopy of Li Tingxiao's memorial from the No. 1 Historical Archives in Beijing.

63. Yuxian memorial GX26/6/20 (rescript date), attachment C. See *YHTDASL,* 320.

64. *Acta Ordinis Fratrum Minorum* 30 (1911): 182–83.

65. Yuxian memorial GX26/6/20 (rescript date), attachment B. See *YHTDASL,* 320.

66. *North China Herald,* 22 August 1900, 410–11. See also "An Escape from Shansi to Han-kau," *Times,* 29 September 1900, 12, Letter to the Editor from Alexander R. Saunders.

67. Wilson's letter is mentioned by F. C. H. Dreyer, who received it from a Chinese servant on 13 July. See Broomhall, *Martyred Missionaries,* 115. Dreyer carried the letter out of the province and elsewhere it is stated that it was dated 6 July. See Broomhall, *Martyred Missionaries,* 295.

68. Broomhall, *Martyred Missionaries,* 115.

69. *North China Herald,* 12 September 1900, 549.

70. *North China Herald,* 5 September 1900, 492. The story goes on to say that when the foreigners arrived at the yamen Yuxian asked Boxers to come in and kill them.

71. Dreyer, *Boxer Rising,* 20.

72. Broomhall, *Martyred Missionaries,* 293.

73. Edwards, *Fire and Sword,* 283–84.

74. Ricci, *Barbarie e trionfi,* 642–43.

75. *Shanxi sheng gengzi nian jiaonan qianhou jishi* (A complete account of the church difficulties in Shanxi province in 1900), in *Yihetuan* (The Boxers), 1:510. For a description of the 11 June 1902 dedication ceremony of this memorial see Edwards, *Fire and Sword,* 132–34.

76. See Harry A. Franck, *Wandering in Northern China* (New York and London: The Century Co., 1923), 260.

77. Broomhall, *Martyred Missionaries,* 117–19.

78. Broomhall, *Martyred Missionaries,* 109. See also Dreyer, *Boxer Rising,* 23; and Thompson, "Military Dimensions," 297–98.

79. Yuxian memorial GX26/7/3 (rescript date). See *YHTDASL,* 396–98.

80. John E. Schrecker, *Imperialism and Chinese Nationalism: Germany in Shantung* (Cambridge: Harvard University Press, 1971), 104–11. See also Esherick, *Origins of the Boxer Uprising,* 190–204.

81. Schrecker, *Imperialism and Chinese Nationalism,* 36.

82. William W. Rockhill, "Report of Commissioner to China," in *Papers Relating to the Foreign Relations of the United States, 1901* (Appendix) (Washington, D.C.: Government Printing Office, 1902), 89.

83. Thompson, "Military Dimensions," 311–18.

84. For Zhang Zhidong and Liu Kunyi's telegram to the Chinese legation in London see Great Britain, *China No. 5 (1901),* 108. Zhang Zhidong had already sent a similar telegram to the legation on 25 October. See Great Britain, *China No. 5 (1901),* 52.

85. See also Paul H. Clements, *The Boxer Rebellion: A Political and Diplomatic Review* (1915; repr., New York: AMS Press, 1967), 160.

86. Schrecker, *Imperialism and Chinese Nationalism*, 43–48.

87. Schrecker, *Imperialism and Chinese Nationalism*, 57.

5

Looting and Its Discontents

Moral Discourse and the Plunder of Beijing, 1900–1901

James L. Hevia

The suppression of the Boxer Uprising by European, American, and Japanese forces draws attention to the sharp distinction made by the end of the nineteenth century between civilization and barbarism in East Asia. In most cases, contemporary Western observers and interpreters outside of China located barbaric behavior squarely with the Boxers and on those members of the Qing administration who supported them—had not innocent women and children been murdered by the "savage" Chinese? The activities of military and civilian actors from "civilized" North Atlantic nation-states, with only a few exceptions, were generally exempt from critical scrutiny. In contrast, Chinese historians have long drawn on contemporary Chinese-language accounts to detail the violence directed against Chinese bodies by the allied expeditionary forces.[1]

Yet regardless of which population's behavior is called into question, often ignored is another kind of violence common in north China at the time, one that was directed not at persons, but at their possessions. In contrast to atrocities committed against Chinese people, the assault on Chinese objects, either through their destruction or plunder, did draw the attention of Western and Japanese observers in and outside of China. Critical voices were raised in protest not only to the scope of looting—it included Qing imperial palaces, residences of the Qing nobility, and private homes, as well as Tianjin and the towns and villages around Beijing—but also to the pervasiveness of the practice among all of the armies in north China, which some saw as a scandal.

Just why this was the case, why looting appears to have shocked the moral sensibilities of some contemporary observers, is the issue explored here. I begin with a discussion of the sack of Beijing in 1900, with comparative references to the looting of the Summer Palace in 1860 by a joint Anglo-French force. The comparison will highlight specific differences between these two looting episodes and help to clarify unique features of events in 1900–1901. I then address the moral confusion that looting seems to have involved for some of the participants. Lastly, I provide an overview of the debate in Europe and North America concerning looting, which will help to focus attention on what appears to have been the fundamental issue that it posed for Euro-American perceptions of just warfare at the time.

"A CARNIVAL OF LOOT"

Almost immediately after the lifting of the siege of the legations on 14 August, members of the eight armies turned to looting in Beijing. Within a day, they were joined by the diplomats and missionaries they had rescued.[2] Speaking at a distance, the *Sidney Morning Herald* characterized the mad scramble for plunder as a "carnival of loot"; on the scene, W. A. P. Martin, a siege survivor, spoke of a riot "in the midst of booty."[3] These characterizations suggest that the sack of Beijing was similar to what had occurred at the Summer Palace forty years earlier; that a loot fever gripped the armies and Euro-American civilian population in Beijing, and a wild orgy of plunder ensued, one in which few if any could resist temptation.[4]

Yet, as much as the initial stages of this second looting episode at Beijing resembled the frenzy of its 1860 predecessor, there were certain differences. For one thing, no one stepped forward as Garnet Wolseley had done in 1860 to safely contain looting by declaring it to be a tendency among ordinary soldiers, as opposed to officers.[5] Secondly, the loot itself did not have attached to it the aura of a proper name such as "from the Summer Palace of the Emperor of China." Given the self-righteous conduct of Euro-American diplomatic and military personnel in China, particularly as it was articulated through rhetoric that demanded "retributive justice" for "savage" and "barbaric" Boxer assaults on Christian missionaries and defenseless legations, this is something of a surprise. One would expect to find references in museum collections of objects from the Forbidden City or Beijing 1900 taken during the Boxer episode. But only a few items so labeled seem to have surfaced in London then or later.[6] Nor were there sales of Boxer Rebellion loot in London and Paris auction houses like those that took place in the 1860s[7]; also not seen were public displays of objects looted from Qing palaces as had occurred in both cities in 1861 and 1862.[8]

The reasons for these absences are, perhaps, not too difficult to discern. First, as noted above, looting in 1900 was a major point of contention and public debate in China, the United States, and Western Europe. Second, with respect to the proper names of Chinese art objects, the great auction houses and museums in London, Paris, other European capitals, and the United States had already begun to adopt a new standardized nomenclature for Chinese art, a descriptive language produced between 1870 and 1900 by a group of art experts, such as the Englishman Stephan Bushell, who were based in the legations and Imperial Maritime Customs at Beijing.[9] New knowledge and its adoption allowed looted objects to be slipped almost imperceptibly into markets and museums in Europe and North America.

Other differences are also evident. Consider, for example, the physical geography of looting. In 1860, it was more or less confined to the area in and around the Yuanming Gardens or Summer Palace. In 1900, it included all of Beijing, the new Summer Palace, and virtually every city and town of Zhili province. Moreover, unlike in 1860 when plundering lasted two to three days, looting in 1900 began with the occupation of Tianjin in late July and stretched well into October in Beijing. Outside of the Qing capital, it continued even longer as armies searched the countryside for Boxer remnants.

At the same time, there were also certain features shared by the two episodes. While many accounts attempted to minimize the extent of looting by their compatriots and shift the blame to the soldiers of other armies, it is clear when the accounts are pieced together that all of the armies plundered to a greater or lesser extent, including the Japanese army.[10] Common in both cases was the carnival-like atmosphere of unregulated plunder noted by the Australian reporter quoted above. Drunken Frenchmen were robbed of their loot by Sikhs, and soldiers ransacked pawn shops, the premises of curio dealers, and private homes, leaving chaos in their wake. Street bazaars where soldiers sold off some of their plunder spontaneously appeared. Even members of the otherwise dignified *corps diplomatique* joined in the mayhem. Lady Claude MacDonald, wife of the British minister, who was reported to have been at the head of one looting expedition, is said to have exclaimed, after having already filled eighty-seven cases with "valuable treasure," that she "had not begun to pack."[11]

As had occurred in 1860, much was broken and destroyed as soldiers searched for precious metals, jewels, and furs.[12] And while several British accounts claimed that their archrivals in Asia, the Russians, were the worst of the looters,[13] Bertram Lenox Simpson, a siege survivor, argued that everyone had been made "savage" by the loot fever.[14] Such "savagery" was confirmed by another eyewitness, Gadhadar Singh, a soldier in the 7th Rajputs of the British India Army, whose book on the campaign found little to distinguish one group from another in their lust for plunder (see Yang, this volume).

FROM LOOT TO PRIZE AND TROPHY

The period of unregulated plunder lasted for several days. By the end of August, however, serious attempts were being made by some of the allied commanders to control or manage looting. The British army took the lead in systematizing loot by establishing a prize commission. Echoing General Hope Grant in 1860,[15] the British commander, General Gaselee, explained in a report to the War Office that he had been compelled to set up the commission in order to maintain the "contentment and discipline" of his forces "under the demoralizing conditions of this particular campaign."[16] At the same time, he claimed that he was "unacquainted with the rules under which prize funds were established after Delhi, Lucknow and Pekin 1860."[17] While this may indeed have been the case, Gaselee seems to have had at least a passing acquaintance with the practices of the British army in India and China a half century earlier and with the often ambiguous rules on plunder to be found in military law and army regulations,[18] for he had little difficulty in putting together a prize committee that apportioned shares on the basis of rank and race. Indian soldiers were given one share less than British soldiers of equivalent rank, while native officers, regardless of rank, were held to be the equivalent of British warrant officers.[19]

The fund itself was raised through the public auction of booty brought in by authorized "search parties" and held on the grounds of the British legation. Pictures of auctions were published in London illustrated newspapers such as *Black & White* and *The Graphic* (see figure 5.1).[20] By 22 August sale of plunder appears to have become a daily occurrence, and word had spread to other units. George Lynch, a reporter on the scene, provided one of the few descriptions of the auctions themselves. As in 1860, the sales were lively affairs and, at least in the first days, included the British generals as well as Sir Claude MacDonald, the British ambassador. In addition, members of each of the regiments of the British contingent, including native soldiers of the India army, Japanese, American, and German soldiers, legation members, and even Chinese traders were present. Although this constituted a much larger pool of buyers than in 1860, the bidding was moderate, with many valuable items, particularly furs, going for just a few dollars.[21] Even so, General Stewart suspected that the foreign residents and legation members—the "knowing ones" as he called them—probably got even greater bargains.[22] A reporter for the *London Daily Express* added that legation members "had a decided advantage over the relievers, inasmuch as they were familiar with localities and the whereabouts of precious things. They got in 'on the ground floor.'"[23]

Soon, residents of other treaty ports and eventually curio shop owners from Shanghai and Hong Kong, some of whom were reported to have commissions from European auction houses and art dealers, arrived to partici-

Figure 5.1.   Scene of an auction at the British legation, *The Graphic*, 15 December 1900.

pate.[24] Later, as replacement troops filtered in, they too had the opportunity of acquiring valuable Chinese curios. People seemed to come from the "ends of the earth" to join in the plunder.[25] By mid-October, the auctions, which had been held daily except Sundays for almost two months, had generated a prize fund of more than $50,000.[26] Eventually the fund rose to $330,000. When divided up, it yielded $27 per share.[27]

The allotment was, as Sir Claude MacDonald later argued, orderly, fair, and moderate.[28] It also had the added virtue, as had been demonstrated in 1860, of drawing a distinction between the disciplined British forces and those of the other countries involved in the expedition. Morever, as before, auctions served to reproduce the army by order of rank and seal it off from the moral chaos of plunder, while maintaining a clear distinction between white Englishmen and Indian native soldiers.

Regardless of whether they understood the full import of the British "system," most observers who commented on it were impressed. The correspondent for the Paris weekly *L'Ilustration* called it "*procèdent systématique-ment,*" while Arthur Smith, an American missionary, thought it "scientific" in comparison to the behavior of other armies, who seemed (with the possible exception of the Japanese units, see below) on the whole to have no

method at all.[29] Discussing the behavior of the American forces, Army chaplain Leslie Grove told his wife, "Our rule against [looting] is utterly ineffec-
tual & those who disobey do so with impunity & get many interesting articles thereby."[30] It was not until 21 September 1900, in fact, that General
Adna Chaffee, the American commander, acted. Faced with open violation
of U.S. Army general orders in time of war,[31] Chaffee followed the British
lead by ordering that all loot be called in and auctioned off. But instead of
becoming a prize fund, the proceeds from the sale of "captured property"
went into a "Public Civil Fund" that was used to pay a portion of the cost
of the American occupation of Beijing in the coming year.[32]

These formal measures for dealing with plunder were accompanied by
the emergence of "extemporized" and "extremely picturesque" street
bazaars.[33] With Chinese merchants and Western missionaries also partici-
pating in the sales, business was apparently brisk. Some buyers even wrote
home to let their wives know of their good fortune.[34] While soldiers and
civilians bought and sold plunder in various quarters of Beijing, army commands set their sights on collecting trophies for their national and regimental collections.

In the British case, this included gathering captured European-manufac-
tured field guns and shipping them to London, Edinburgh, Sidney, and
Dublin.[35] Meanwhile, the 4th Prince of Wales' Own Gurkha Rifles made off
with a temple bell and a block of stone from the Great Wall of China, which
was placed in the walls of the regimental headquarters in India and inscribed "China, 1900."[36] For their part, the American forces shipped examples of Chinese weapons, Boxer flags, and a statue of the Chinese god of
war, Guandi, to the recently established trophy room at West Point.[37] In addition, two of the units involved, the 9th and 14th infantry regiments, incorporated yellow dragons into their insignias and took new nicknames,
the "Manchus" and "Golden Dragons," respectively.[38]

In these and other ways, the meanings attached to Summer Palace objects
were easily transposed onto 1900 loot. Objects could stand for the orderly
reconstitution of armies (in this case, the British and American contingents), while highlighting the differences between disciplined and undisci-
plined forces. They could also act as signs of humiliation, of taste and dis-
cernment, of the triumph of civilization over barbarism, and of military
trophy collecting and regimental "heritage."

By 1900, however, there appears to have been a more sophisticated approach to plunder among some of the looters. Officers in the Japanese
army, for example, were especially interested in Chinese art and antiquities,
and even issued guidelines to soldiers distinguishing various grades of
plunder, ranging from those for the imperial household, for display in museums and schools, and for military trophy.[39] Such signs of taste and dis-
cernment were not unique to the Japanese army, however. While he makes

light of it, George Lynch, a reporter on the scene, observed that "when offered a china cup or saucer, the correct thing to do is to look at the mark at the bottom as if one understood what it meant, and shake the head."[40] What these "knowing ones" were looking for were imperial reign date ideograms, meticulously recorded in the publications of Stephan Bushell and others, that provided authenticity and indicated the value of objects.

VARIATIONS ON A THEME

The shift of understanding in the value of Chinese objects was matched by other novel forms of plunder. Perhaps the most controversial of these involved Christian missionaries, who also engaged in the looting of Beijing and its environs. In some cases, missionaries were reported to have seized the homes of imperial princes and wealthy urbanites and sold off their contents.[41] In addition, American missionaries pioneered another kind of plunder—tribute expeditions into rural areas where missions had been attacked and destroyed. Initially, these operations were conducted with the cooperation of U.S. forces. The first seems to have occurred on 20 September 1900 when a patrol of the 6th Cavalry, accompanied by the Reverends William Ament and Robert Coltman, entered a village outside the capital. Ament identified signs of Boxer activities, and after commiserating with a group of Chinese he identified as Christians, apparently sanctioned their looting of several of the homes in the village. Captain Forsyth, the commander of the unit, objected, insisting that the property be returned, or he would immediately go back to Beijing.[42] Incidents like this led higher officers in the American command to surmise that they were being used by the missionaries. As Colonel Dickman noted in the official campaign diary, "the missionaries wanted to show the troops simply for future effect by impressing the natives with the power of the foreign devils apparently at their disposal."[43]

Paralleling the missionary activities in rural areas were punitive expeditions designed to collectively punish communities. As armies swept through villages, they created an enormous amount of disorder, which contributed to the ranks of roving bands of robbers. Some of these groups may have been Boxer remnants, but most were probably persons displaced by six months of warfare in the region. In a case noted in December, local bands were reported carrying the flags of one or another of the allied forces and "levying tribute upon and plundering villages."[44] In other instances, deserters from the allied armies engaged in similar operations.[45] In what was perhaps the most spectacular such case, two American privates forced several Chinese at gunpoint to help them hold up a village outside Tianjin. As the wagons were being loaded, a French patrol caught them in the act. With the testimony of the commandeered Chinese as evidence, the two were tried, convicted, dishonorably discharged, and sentenced to twenty-one years at Alcatraz.[46]

Although the American soldiers failed in this illicit activity, others appear to have been more successful. At least one case later surfaced to suggest even the "well-disciplined" British soldiers found ways of circumventing prize procedures. In 1926, a story circulated about the theft of two golden bells from the Temple of Heaven by officers of the 16th Bengal Lancers. Claiming them as "trophy," the officers had spirited them off with other items ostensibly destined for the officers' mess. Sometime around 1905, they decided to melt down one of the bells and divide the spoils, but one of their number objected, claiming the share allotted to him was insufficient.[47] This tale of "enterprise" and "initiative" is perhaps indicative of the enormous scale of the plunder of Beijing and Zhili province, a scale that to this day defies easy reckoning because with the exception of trophy, so little is known about where all the loot finally came to rest.

CIVILIZATION AND BARBARISM

In addition to enriching the plunderers, the scale of looting had other effects, one of which was to raise questions about the nature of the military expedition itself. For many in Europe and North America the allied intervention into north China was morally and politically just. From this perspective, the Boxers and the Qing government had violated international law, murdered Christian missionaries and converts, and destroyed the public and private property of foreigners in China. The expedition to relieve the legations was a high-minded mission founded on rational international law. Thus, activities such as looting could, in various ways, blemish the moral and legal principles upon which the relief expeditions were launched.

One result of these attitudes was to attach a stigma to all Chinese objects, regardless of how they had been acquired. Major-General Norman Stewart, commander of one of the British units, noted the phenomenon in his campaign diary. Expressing discomfort with the behavior of other officers and the men and women of the diplomatic corps, Stewart exclaimed that he had come to hate the sound of the word "loot." "If you happen to pick up an article which seems good, and for which you have paid the price," he observed, "you are at once asked 'Where did you loot that?' Even those who ought to know better seem to doubt your honesty. *Life under such conditions is a bit degrading.*"[48]

Stewart's sense that the honesty and integrity of Europeans and Americans, even officers, was under scrutiny is borne out in other sources, some of which acknowledge participation in the opportunities available to obtain Chinese objects, while privately expressing moral doubts about the conditions of acquisition. For example, Leslie Grove, a U.S. Army chaplain, initially wrote his wife of the unique opportunity he had to acquire valuable Chinese curios. However, as he became more fully aware of the extent of the looting, the American missionary involvement in it, and the degree to which plunder was made acceptable through prize sales, Grove found great cause for concern. Among other things, he told his wife that he would no longer buy at the British auctions and that he was certain the missionary complicity in looting would deal a severe blow to their cause.[49]

Grove's instincts were right, but perhaps more significantly, his observations about possible consequences at home points directly to one of the major differences between 1900 and 1860—the huge explosion in media coverage of events in China. Wholly new mechanisms of information processing were in place to exploit the story on a scale unimaginable in 1860. Vastly expanded transportation and communication systems linked the east coast of China into a global steamship and railroad network capable of rushing reporters to the scene in two to three weeks. Submarine cables across the Pacific and through the Indian Ocean made it possible for newsmen to communicate by telegraph with Europe and North America at high speed. New printing technologies, particularly able to accommodate large numbers of photographs, packaged and delivered the sensational developments in China at a velocity and in a form that made information itself a spectacle, allowing for a vast expansion of vicarious audience participation in events. And audiences were not entirely predictable in their responses.

Added to this were the dramatic elements that the event itself offered for exploitation. The reports of missionaries having been killed were not only sensational news, but recalled other instances of atrocities committed against whites in the colonial world. Thus, when contact with the legations in Beijing ceased after the telegraph line to Tianjin was cut in July and the fate of the hundreds of other missionaries in China and members of the legations was unknown, the relief expedition took on epic proportions, fed by speculation and fantasies of oriental cruelty.

It was into this new media climate that "news" from north China entered. Newspaper reporters were present from the moment the allied armies landed at Dagu. Their accounts of the campaign, including vivid descriptions of looting and in some cases of atrocities committed by allied soldiers not only appeared in their own newspapers, but were picked up by others in the treaty ports and in review magazines in Europe and North America. In addition, some accounts from 1860 were republished and comparisons between the two campaigns were immediately made.[50] Even if such reports contained no negative judgments, they gave a sense of the scale of violence and the sheer breadth and scope of plunder, both of which seemed to require evaluation.

In most cases, editors and commentators justified the use of force against Chinese "barbarism" either on the grounds of retributive justice or as a timeless feature of warfare. Looting, on the other hand, appears to have been less easily reconciled with Euro-American values. That bastion of foreign privilege and treaty rights in China, the *North-China Herald*, expressed concern over reports coming from Tianjin early on. Recalling 1860, when looting had been "authorized" as a means of "punishment of the Peking Government," the editors seemed perplexed by the plunder of private, as opposed to government, property in Tianjin. The editors concluded that

> it will be a shock to the modern sentiment of the civilised world if such orgies . . . are to be the regular thing. Wherein will the much-boasted civilisation of the West appear if such deeds are the outcome of it? Our troops have come to do a necessary duty. They have to get the upper hand of a savage and sanguinary enemy, to whom murder and pillage are but the incidents of an ordinary day's work. It is to exterminate this demon, *not imitate him*, that the United Powers of Europe have sent troops, and we shall be much mistaken if the plunder of civilians in the shameless manner depicted does not raise a howl of execration from one end of the civilised world to the other.[51]

Of import here are three elements that would become central to many other critiques of looting. First, and perhaps most importantly, was the problem plunder posed to civilization. Could one be civilized, or claim the superiority of European nations, if one looted? The second, and related issue, was that question of mimicry—how could the "victims" of Chinese "barbarism" retain the moral high ground if they slavishly copied the behavior of savages? Third, looting appeared to have occurred without a sense of shame. This was not only akin to the practices of the uncivilized, but invited criticism from throughout the civilized world. When reports arrived in Shanghai of a repetition of the loot "orgy" in the Qing capital, the paper added one more element to the mix—it referred to the sack of Beijing as a "scandal." The only solace it found was in the fact that "the loot taken by the British troops was brought back to the Legation and sold by auction for the general benefit."[52]

As the *Herald* predicted, when word reached Europe of the carnival of loot, it caused a sensation. The *London Daily Express* observed that once the mission to China was accomplished, "civilization" ought to "have the grace to blush."[53] In an editorial, the *Review of Reviews* argued that the news from China was "calculated to make Europeans hang their heads for shame." Pointing to looting, loot sales in the British legation, and Russian massacres in Manchuria, the editorial concluded "we have flung aside the garb of civilization, and are acting like our piratical ancestors in the days of the Vikings. Civilization is but skin deep, and the restraints that conscience endeavours to place upon the human brute have snapped under the strain of events in China."[54] In France a similar pattern emerged. As early as 25 August 1900, *Le Monde Illustré* fantasized about China's future *revanche* against the harsh treatment of the allies. Another French weekly, *La Vie Illustrée*, critically discussed *"La Guerre et Le Pillage en Chine"* (see figure 5.2) in great detail in its 1 February 1901 issue. In the face of such criticism, the government returned a bronze lion sent as trophy to Paris by the French com-

Figure 5.2.   The War and the Pillage of China, cover, *La Vie Illustrée*, 1 February 1901.

mander General Frey. Similar outrage at plunder was expressed in the pages of the Japanese newspaper *Yorozu Chōhō*, which published a series of exposes between November 1901 and March 1902 (see Middleton, this volume).

Other sources echoed the sense of outrage and concern evident in the newspaper accounts. Robert Hart, the head of the Imperial Maritime Customs and a longtime resident of Beijing, noted that a bit of temptation placed before a European easily led to a "retrogression to barbarism." More importantly, he worried that "for a century to come Chinese converts will consider looting and vengeance Christian virtues!"[55] According to James Ricalton, a photographer on the scene, Li Hongzhang, the eminent official and Qing representative to the "peace" conference that would produce the Boxer Protocol, was also puzzled by the behavior of members of Western civilization. As the story went, after consulting the "Mosaic decalogue," Li suggested that "the eighth commandment should be amended to read, Thou shalt not steal, but thou mayst loot."[56] Li's criticism was all the more telling because it indirectly pointed to Christian missionary involvement in the looting.

In the United States, once word of missionary actions had circulated in American newspapers, there was an uproar. Some of the earliest reports of questionable behavior on the part of missionaries appeared in the *New York Sun*, under the byline of Wilbur Chamberlain. But what elevated the missionary question into a cause célèbre was an interview that Chamberlain conducted with the Reverend William Ament. The *Sun* published it on Christmas Eve, 1900. In it, Ament not only justified looting, but in a most un-Christian spirit, echoed other missionaries in arguing that "the soft hand of the Americans is not as good as the mailed fist of the Germans. If you deal with the Chinese with a soft hand they will take advantage of it."[57] The logic of Ament's argument prompted a response from no less a figure than the essayist, novelist, and humorist Mark Twain, one of the leading critics of American expansion into the Pacific. In an article entitled "To the Person Sitting in Darkness" (*North American Review*, February 1901), Twain lampooned missionary morality and likened it to questionable American activities in the Philippines. Twain's caustic indictment generated, in turn, a defensive apologetics on the part of the American Board of Commissioners for Foreign Missions. Both Judson Smith and Gilbert Reid (independent missionary, formerly a member of the American Presbyterian mission) claimed that missionary looting was "high ethics," and added that American missionaries had only looted to provide money for the relief of Chinese Christians, a proposition that Twain gleefully shredded in his reply, "To my Missionary Critics."[58] Somewhat at a disadvantage in this exchange, missionary leaders nevertheless attempted to influence opinion in treaty port China; Arthur Smith joined Reid and Judson Smith in writing letters to the *North-China Herald* justifying missionary actions and criticizing Twain.[59]

While missionaries and their critics appear to have been bounded by the discursive regularities of a Christian moral universe, others attempted to mobilize history and international law to make their arguments. This was the case with John MacDonnell, who, in a piece that appeared in the *Contemporary Review*, drew attention to British prize laws. Drawing upon an 1864 Parliamentary commission on army prize procedures, which investigated instances dating back to 1807, MacDonnell argued that rather than acting as a deterrent, prize procedures, because they gave a disproportionate amount of a prize fund to officers, encouraged common soldiers to loot more.[60] But British prize procedures were only part of the issue. MacDonnell also pointed to the contradictory relationship between prize law and international agreements involving warfare that had emerged since France's defeat by Prussia in 1871.

Following that war, many European countries had acted to professionalize their armies by integrating new organizational and weapons technologies into them and improving their officer corps.[61] Over the same period of time, the rapid change in military technology led to discussions concerning the establishment of international standards for the conduct of warfare. The results of these discussions were embodied in the Hague Convention of 1899. In the sections dealing with rules of land warfare, as MacDonnell pointed out, plunder and the seizure of private property were outlawed without qualification.[62] All of the nations that invaded China in 1900 were parties to the convention, as was the Qing government.[63] While these developments did nothing to prevent a spectacular instance of looting in Beijing, they could not help but call into question the behavior of the allied armies.

For MacDonnell, therefore, the "letter and the spirit of the Hague Convention" had been violated in China. As he put it, the theory of the convention was "all that could be desired," but when dealing with "Oriental nations," if opportunity presented itself, "the old outrages were repeated." Those outrages, he added, were rooted in the practices of the British army in India, which had not only shaped prize law in the nineteenth century, but produced the most extreme examples of plunder to date.[64]

MacDonnell was not alone in pointing out that the Hague Conventions had been violated by the allied powers. Plunder was, however, only part of the issue. The *North-China Herald*, for example, while finding little fault in British prize procedures, did point to what it thought were a number of specific violations concerning "Rules and Usages of War." These included the atrocities committed by Russian forces, the punitive expeditions launched by the allied powers, the looting of the Beijing observatory, and the "charity from loot practiced by some American and British missionaries."[65] Like the *Herald*, George Lynch was also disturbed by the violation of the Hague Conventions, but perhaps more importantly, Lynch used the issue of lawlessness to raise questions about the level of and kinds of violence directed at China by Western powers over the course of the nineteenth century.[66] Lynch's ruminations on this issue led him to conclude that the West had mistaken speed for progress, which was "propelling us like a herd of Gadarene swine over an abyss of God knows what."[67]

In "The Chinese Wolf and the European Lamb," published in the *Contemporary Review* in early 1900, E. J. Dillon also drew attention to the scale of violence leveled against the population of north China by the armies of "civilization." Like contemporary articles published by Chinese observers,[68] Dillon provided a detailed account of executions, slaughter, and all other manner of atrocities committed by the allied forces. The catalog ran from July into September and drew occasionally for emphasis on the graphic interviews about German atrocities published in the *Bremer Bürger-Zeitung* and the *Frankfurter Zeitung* in October and November. Dillon concluded his piece with the following question: "Why should cultured and more or less truth-loving people persist in speaking of the glorious work of civilising China, when it is evident that they are ruining her people and demoralizing their own troops besides?"[69]

Dillon's concerns were repeated by Thomas F. Millard, an old China hand, in the pages of *Scribner's Magazine*. The allies' insistence upon revenge, Millard charged, was criminal. "Seized with a vertigo of indiscriminating vengeance," he wrote, "the powers are trifling with the peace of the world. Events such as the months of September, October and November brought to China have carried war back to the Dark Ages, and will leave a taint in the moral atmosphere of the world for a generation to come."[70]

These critical interventions into discussion of civilization and barbarism are quite significant; they indicate that neither the events that transpired in China nor the way Euro-Americans, to say nothing of Chinese, thought about them existed in a vacuum. A central element in explaining and justifying the sorts of activities that disturbed many of the writers cited here was the issue of racial difference, and especially the link between race and the progress of civilization. Directly or indirectly, race was not far from the thinking of either critics of or apologists for the actions of the allied powers in China. Moreover, race was a continual undertone throughout the campaign and the occupation of Beijing. Few accounts could not, for example, avoid mention of how surprisingly impressive the Japanese army was or ignore the presence of large numbers of Indian soldiers that made up the British contingent. One British officer even thought that contempt was being shown the British due to their having "practically no white troops" among the occupation forces.[71] Yet, whether or not this was actually the case, one cannot help but be reminded of one of the central "racial" issues of empire—were whites altered by contact with "lesser" races? Did racial degeneration occur through contact with "brown" men, "black" men, and "yellow" men?

These questions existed, in turn, in a far broader context than the China coast, and it is probably best contextualized in widely diffused apprehensions about atavistic primitivism in the last quarter of the nineteenth century. As a kind of repressed element within bourgeois sensibilities about the stark division between the civilized and the savage, such concerns focused not only on "racial" mixing,[72] but on the possibility that contact with "inferior" civilizations or peoples would awaken latent desires or primitive remnants in the European psyche.[73] Thus, when real events such as the spectacular plunder of Beijing and north China or the violence directed against Chinese people exceeded rational expectations and seemed to converge with fiction, tropes from the latter were readily available for representing the meaning of European and American behavior in other than triumphalist terms. And, although there was not a thorough inversion of meaning, insofar as atrocities and plunder could serve as signs of degeneration, it was more difficult to construct the events of 1900 in the clear terms of European moral superiority that had dominated the constructs and rationales of the 1860 invasion of China.

There is a disturbing sense, evident in contemporary critiques, that the line between civilization and savagism, perhaps more than anything else, distinguishes 1860 from 1900. It also distinguishes the latter episode from earlier imperialist incursions into China and helps to explain why no great public display of 1900 occurred in Europe, North America, or Japan and why it remains difficult to identify actual 1900 loot—the bulk of it was apparently "laundered" through the art market. At the same time, some of the plunder is not completely invisible. Various objects still sit on display as "legitimate" trophy from the Boxer "Rebellion" in national and regimental museums of the countries that invaded China in 1900. However, as far as I have been able to discern, since the government of France refused to accept the "trophies" of General Frey, there has been only one instance of repatriation. In 1955, Otto Grotewohl, an official of the now defunct German Democratic Republic, returned a Boxer banner and other artifacts taken by the German army in 1900 to Zhou Enlai at a ceremony held in Beijing.[74]

Outside of this gesture of socialist solidarity, looting in China by civilian and military representatives of Euro-American imperial powers and Japan has been forgotten or ignored. As is the case with objects taken from colonial Africa and Asia, public institutions that hold verified or suspected China loot cloak themselves in the garb of curators of human heritage and seldom acknowledge the dubious provenance of their collections. This remains a curious stance, especially at a time when the issue of looting during World War II in Europe has not only been raised, but repatriation and monetary compensation has occurred. The failure to address the issue of plunder will continue to haunt relations between the West and the former colonial world until contemporary nation-states find an equitable way to deal with the legitimate grievances stemming from past wars. This is no less an issue for postcolonial African and Asian nationalists today than it is for their counterparts in China.

NOTES

Portions of this essay appeared in James L. Hevia, *English Lessons: The Pedagogy of Imperialism in Nineteenth Century China* (Durham and Hong Kong: Duke University Press, 2003).

1. Among recent Chinese scholarship, the most comprehensive account is Li Decheng, Su Weizhi, and Liu Tianlu, *Baguo lianjun qinhua shi* [A history of the Eight Power invasion] (Ji'nan: Shandong University Press, 1990). Also see articles and materials collected in Su Weizhi and Liu Tianlu, eds., *Yihetuan yanjiu yibai nian* [One hundred years of Boxer studies] (Ji'nan: Qi-Lu shushe, 2000).
2. Reverend Roland Allen, *The Siege of the Peking Legations* (London: Smith, Elder & Co. Allen, 1901), 231.
3. The *Herald* cited in Bob Nicholls, *Bluejackets and Boxers: Australia Naval Expedition to the Boxer Uprising* (Sidney: Allen & Unwin, 1986), 111, and W. A. P. Martin, *The Siege of Peking* (New York: Fleming H. Revell Co., 1900), 134.
4. See Polly Condit Smith's account of succumbing to the lure of plunder in Mary Hooker, *Behind the Scenes in Peking* (1910; reprint edition, Hong Kong: Oxford University Press, 1987), 189–90.
5. Garnet Wolseley, *Narrative of the War With China in 1860* (1862: reprint edition, Willmington, DE.: Scholarly Resources Inc., 1972), 225–27.
6. *The Celestial Empire*, March 6, 1901, notes that a British private had sold some items through the Stevens house. In 1913, Stevens sold a Chinese drum said to have been captured by the 39th Regiment at Beijing during the Boxer Rebellion. See National Art Library, London, auction house catalogues, 23.ZZ.
7. On London and Paris auctions see James L. Hevia, "Loot's Fate," *History and Anthropology* 6, no. 4 (1994): 326, 341–42, and *English Lessons* (Durham: Duke University Press, 2003), 91–95.
8. See Hevia, "Loot's Fate," 326–31.
9. See James L. Hevia, "Looting Beijing: 1860, 1900," in *Tokens of Exchange*, ed. Lydia Liu (Durham: Duke University Press, 1999), 201–3.
10. Most of the contemporary sources acknowledge as much. The American periodical *Harper's Weekly* even ran two pieces on the sack of Tianjin that discussed different patterns of looting among the various armies. See Oscar King Davis, "The Looting of Tientsin," *Harper's Weekly* 44 (September 15, 1900): 863–64, and Charles Denby, "Loot and the Man," *Harper's Weekly* 44 (27 October 1900): 1008–9.
11. Lady MacDonald's involvement in looting was reported by Peter Fleming, *The Siege of Peking* (New York: Harper & Brothers, 1959), 243. G. E. Morrison, *Times* cor-

respondent in Beijing, noted in his diary that General Norman Stewart complained in the officers' mess about the MacDonalds' having at least 185 crates of plunder by November; see Cyril Pearl, *Morrison of Peking* (Sydney: Angus & Robertson Ltd., 1967), 151. The number of crates comes from Whiting's unpublished journal cited in Frederic Sharf and Peter Harrington, *China, 1900* (London: Greenhill Books, 2000), 222–23. Also see Susanna Hoe, *Women at the Siege, Peking 1900* (Oxford: Holo Books, 2000), 196.

12. Alfred Waldersee, *A Field Marshal's Memoirs*, trans. Frederic White (London: Hutcheson & Co., 1924), 221, and W. Meyrick Hewlett cited in Sterling Seagrave, *Dragon Lady* (New York: Vintage Books, 1992), 367.

13. Stanley Smith, *China From Within: Or the Story of the Chinese Crisis* (London: Marshall Brothers, 1901), 128; Richard Steel, *Through Peking's Sewer Gate*, ed. George W. Carrington (New York: Vantage Press, 1985), 59; and the diary of Lieutenant Colonel Gartside-Tipping, National Army Museum (London), 6902/3, no. 2, p. 20.

14. B. L. Putnam Weale [pseud. Bertram Lenox Simpson], *Indiscreet Letters from Peking: Being the Notes of an Eye-witness, Which Set Forth in some Detail, from Day to Day, the Real Story of the Siege and Sack of a Distressed Capital in 1900, the Year of Great Tribulation* (London: Hurst and Blackett, 1907; reprinted, New York: Arno Press & the *New York Times*, 1970), 334, 349, 354.

15. Hevia, "Loot's Fate," 321–24.

16. Norman Stewart, *My Service Days* (London: John Ouseley, 1908), 241–42.

17. Rules for prize commissions had been well established by parliamentary law and military regulations for some time; see Hevia, "Looting Beijing," 194–96. According to a War Office report of 1903, investigators found only a few instances of prize funds actually being allocated in any military actions from the Crimean War forward. This led them to conclude that prize was "a thing of the past." It had gradually been phased out and replaced by a cash gratuity for hardship and campaigning; see WO33/6338. This could also explain why Gaselee expressed doubts and confusion over invoking prize procedures.

18. The War Office's *Manual of Military Law* (first edition 1884), in a section entitled "The Customs of War," noted that the seizure of scientific or art objects was "incompatible with the admitted restrictions" of depriving the enemy of war-making resources, and "could only be justified as a measure of retaliation." Within a page, however, the editors acknowledged that officers should attempt to prevent pillage *and* noted procedures, identical to those found in prize law, for dealing with its results. At the same time, they indicated that the regulations therein were compiled only for the use of officers and had no official authority. See War Office, *Manual of Military Law* (London: Her Majesty's Stationary Office, 1887), 311–13. This is the second edition. The sections cited here are the same in the third and fourth editions of 1893 and 1899.

This seeming uncertainty and confusion over the status of plunder in time of war was also evident in army regulations. *The Queen's Regulations* of 1868, for example, forbade plunder and indicated that officers had a duty to prevent it—no mention was made of prize money; see *Queen's Regulations and Orders for the Army* (London: Her Majesty's Stationary Office, 1868), vol. 2, 186. In contrast, the *King's Regulations* of 1901 contained a section on prize, noting that it was the property of the crown and therefore subject to acts of parliament; see *King's Regulations and Orders for the Army* (London: His Majesty's Stationary Office, 1901), 50.

19. Public Record Office, London, War Office 28 [Records of Military Headquarters, 1746–1926], 302: 28–29. Cited hereafter as WO.

20. Remarkably, *Black & White* printed a photograph of the sales at the British legation as early as 20 October 1900. The caption claimed that the items were "found in deserted homes." The same issue contained a drawing of axe-wielding soldiers "looting a mandarin's house in Pekin," 644. The drawing from *The Graphic* appeared in the 15 December 1900 issue on p. 885.

21. George Lynch, *War of Civilizations* (London: Longmans, Green, and Co., 1901), 177–80, William Oudendyk, *Ways and By-ways of Diplomacy* (London: Peter Davies, 1939), 107–8; and Hoe, *Women at the Siege*, 374. In contrast, Gartside-Tipping complained that the prices were too high; see National Army Museum Archives, London, 6902/3, no. 2, 22. Others such as Edmond Backhouse hoped there would be another opportunity to procure such good furs; see Hui-min Lo, ed., *The Correspondence of G. E. Morrison* (London: Cambridge University Press, 1976), vol. 1, 201.

22. Stewart, *My Service Days*, 256.

23. Cited in *The Celestial Empire*, 14 January 1900, 55–56.

24. *The Celestial Empire*, 19 November 1900, 617.

25. Eliza Skidmore, *China, the Long-lived Empire* (New York: The Century Co., 1900), 196.

26. See *Peking and Tientsin Times*, 18 October 1900.

27. Presumably, the figure was in Mexican dollars, the standard currency of the treaty ports, which was equivalent to about 2 U.S. dollars at the time. *The North-China Herald*, 24 April 1901, 784 printed the following on the allocation of shares: "Lt. General commanding, 10 shares; General Officers, 8 shares; Field Officers, 7 shares; Captains , 6 shares; Subalterns, 5 shares; Warrant Officers and Native Officers, 4 shares; British NCOs, 3 shares; Native NCOs, 2 shares; British Soldiers, 2 shares; and Native Soldiers (Indian and others), 1 share."

28. *The Celestial Empire*, 22 April 1901, 4.

29. *L'Illustration*, 12 January 1901, 19, and Arthur Smith, "The Punishment of Peking," *The Outlook* 66 (1900), 497.

30. United States Military History Institute, Carlisle, Pa., Grove Correspondence, 22 August 1900. Hereafter cited USMHI.

31. According to Wilson, it is General Order No. 100, written by Professor Francis Lieber in 1863; see James H. Wilson, *China* (New York: D. Appleton and Co. 3rd edition, 1901), 389.

32. For sources related to Chaffee's decision see United States, National Archives and Record Administration (hereafter, NARA), RG203, entry 4, 54–56; Chaffee's letter of 8 March 1901 is in RG395.4, 898, "Letters Sent, 1900–1901"; and the Office of Finance, *Ledgers of Emergency Fund Account, 1898–1909*, the China Relief Expedition section indicated that loot was transformed in Washington into "Money received from auctions sales of captured property in China, Special order no. 36, Gen'l. Chaffee."

33. *The Celestial Empire*, 19 November 1900, 617.

34. Stewart mentions the Chinese shopkeepers; see *My Service Days*, 257. Also see Wilbur Chamberlain, *Ordered to China* (New York: Frederick A. Stokes Co., 1903), 101–2 and USMHI, Grove Correspondence, 11 October 1900.

35. India Office Records (IOR), London, L/MIL/7/16765, 11. This IOR L/MIL series of documents is a miscellaneous collection of published and unpublished materials on the Boer War and the China Expedition.

36. Ranald MacDonnell and Marcus Macauley, comps., *A History of the 4th Prince of Wales's Own Gurkha Rifles, 1857-1837* (Edinburgh and London: William Blackwood and Sons, 1940), vol. 1, 228.

37. NARA, RG395.4, 944, Circular 4, 24 September 1900. Chamberlain mentions the war god; see *Ordered to China*, 119. Something labeled as such is in Earl McFarland, *Catalogue of the Ordnance Museum, United States Military Academy* (West Point, N.Y.: United States Military Academy Printing Office, 1929), 41, which also contains other Boxer trophies. Also see Lloyd Leonard, *Catalogue of the United States Military Academy Museum* (West Point, N.Y.: United States Military Academy Printing Office, 1944), where the Boxer items are grouped together.

38. See the web sites <www.perso.hol.fr/~nguiffen/manchu.html> (31 May 2001) and <www.25thida.com/14thinf.html> (31 May 2001).

39. See Jordan Sand, "Was Meiji Taste in Interiors 'Orientalist'?" *Positions* 8, no. 3 (Winter 2000), 654.

40. Lynch, *War of Civilizations*, 170.

41. See Simpson, *Indiscrete Letters*, 374; Steel, *Sewer Gate*; and Martin, *Siege*, 135.

42. NARA, RG395.4, 913, no. 19.

43. War Department, *Reports on Military Operations in South Africa and China* (Washington: U.S. Government Printing Office, 1901), 512. Another such case was detailed by a Lieutenant Guiney, whose cavalry column accompanied the Reverend E. G. Tewksbury on what the latter termed a "fact-finding" tour. Upon entering a village, Tewksbury immediately began to collect bullion. Guiney reported that Tewksbury refused to give an accounting of what was being collected and soon after the military escorts ended; see NARA, RG395.4, 906, box 2, 14 October 1900.

44. NARA, RG395.4, 898, 472, order to Captain Forsyth to be on the lookout for these bands, dated 17 December 1900. See also RG395.4, 968, reports dated 17 December 1900 and 19 January 1901.

45. WO32 [War Office and successors: Registered Files (General Series)], 6417, Colonel Grieson's staff diary reports that a band of sixty Sikh deserters were marauding in the countryside; see entry for 10 January 1901. See also NARA, RG395.4, 968, 18 April 1901.

46. NARA, RG395.4, 944, 5 and 906, box 4.

47. IOR, L/MIL/7/16819.

48. Stewart, *My Service Days*, 252.

49. USMHI, Grove correspondence, letters of 22 August, 9 and 13 September, and 11 and 16 October, 1900.

50. S. P. Read, "Russia in North China," *Independent* 53 (1901): 486-89.

51. *North-China Herald*, 8 August 1900, 277-78, emphasis added.

52. *North-China Herald*, 12 September 1900, 542.

53. Cited in *The Celestial Empire*, 14 January 1901, 56.

54. *Review of Reviews* 22 (1900): 52.

55. Robert Hart, "China and Non-China," *Fortnightly Review* 75 (1901): 278-93 and *These from the Land of Sinim* (London: Chapman & Hall, Ld. Hart, 1901), 87-89.

56. James Ricalton, *China through the Stereoscope* (New York: Underwood & Underwood, 1901), 233.

57. Chamberlain's reports are cited in Marilyn Young, *The Rhetoric of Empire: American China Policy, 1895–1901* (Cambridge, Mass.: Harvard University Press, 1968). Also useful on missionary justifications for the use of violence is Stuart Creighton Miller, "Ends and Means: Missionary Justification of Force in Nineteenth Century China," *The Missionary Enterprise in China and America*, ed. J. K. Fairbank (Cambridge, Mass.: Harvard University Press, 1974), 249–82.

58. For the Twain-missionary exchange see Mark Twain, "To the Person Sitting in Darkness," *North American Review* 172 (1901): 161–76, and "To My Missionary Critics," *North American Review* 172 (1901): 520–34; and Judson Smith, "The Missionaries and Their Critics," *North American Review* 172 (1901): 724–33, and Gilbert Reid, "The Ethics of Loot," *Forum* 31 (1901): 581–86, and "The Ethics of the Last War," *Forum* 32 (1902): 446–55. See also *The Literary Digest* 23, no. 2 (1901): 36–37; and William Ament, "The Charges against Missionaries," *Independent* 53 (1901): 1051–52, and "A Bishop's Loot," *Independent* 53 (1901): 2217–18.

59. *North-China Herald*, 27 March 1901, 602–3; 3 April 1901, 660–61; and 19 June 1901, 1193–94.

60. See WO33 [Reports, Memoranda, and Papers], 6337 and Parliamentary Papers for 1864. Also see the index to the latter under the entry "Prize Money, Prizes, Salvage, &c." for a list of acts of Parliament concerning prize.

61. In Great Britain, several parliamentary commissions recommended reform and reorganization of the army, and these changes had begun to be implemented by the 1880s. Officers faced increasingly stringent written tests for promotions; new training manuals were written and regulations reformulated. Advanced training exercises and maneuvers, particularly with new artillery, automatic weapons, and small arms, became a normal part of unit evaluations. By the end of the century, European armies were exchanging observers and intermilitary standards were being established.

62. Charles I. Bevans, *Treaties and Other International Agreements of the United States of America, 1776–1949* (Washington, D.C.: U.S. Government Printing Office, 1918–1930), vol. 1, 260.

63. Formal ratifications were delivered at the same moment the looting of Beijing was underway. See Carnegie Endowment for International Peace, *Signatures, Ratifications, Adhesions, and Reservations to the Conventions and Declarations of the First and Second Hague Peace Conferences* (Washington, D.C.: Carnegie Endowment, 1914), 2–4.

64. John MacDonnell, "Looting in China," *Contemporary Review* 79 (1901): 444–52, especially 446–50. One of the few other references to the Hague can be found in the *Review of Reviews* 22 (1900): 52.

65. *North China Herald*, 24 April 1901, 784.

66. Lynch, *War of Civilizations*, 303, 311–16.

67. Lynch, *War of Civilizations*, 317.

68. See the discussion in Paul Cohen, *History in Three Keys* (New York: Columbia University Press, 1997), 181–94 and the contemporary Chinese sources he draws on.

69. E. J. Dillon, "The Chinese Wolf and the European Lamb," *Contemporary Review* 79 (1901): 1–31.

70. Thomas F. Millard, "Punishment and Revenge in China," *Scribner's Magazine* 29 (1901): 187–94.

71. See the reports of Colonel Grierson in WO32, 6413, 6422, 6423, 6425, 6426, and 6427, where he discusses various incidents involving the India army troops. Grierson was disturbed especially by the behavior of the German forces, who he seems to have expected something better of; see his comments in WO32, 6423, letter dated 2 April 1901 and WO32, 6415, diary entries of 20–29 December 1900.

72. See Robert Young, *Colonial Desire* (London: Routledge, 1995).

73. Patrick Brantlinger has pointed out that popular fiction and dissident literature during this period were rife with such concerns: see *Rule of Darkness* (Cornell: Cornell University Press, 1988), 227–54.

74. I am grateful to Klaus Mühlhahn for bringing the incident to my attention. See Roland Felber and Horst Rostek, *Der "Hunnenkrieg" Kaiser Wilhelms II.: Imperialistische Intervention in China 1900/0* (Berlin: VEB Deutscher Verlag der Wissenschaften, 1987), 43.

6

Scandals of Empire

The Looting of North China and the Japanese Public Sphere

Ben Middleton

THE NORTH CHINA INCIDENT AND
THE JAPANESE PUBLIC SPHERE

In Japan, what is today known as the Boxer War (*giwadan sensō*) was a popular little war. As was the case with the Sino-Japanese War that had ended with resounding success five years earlier, no voices of dissent were raised in the mainstream Japanese media when troops were dispatched in mid-June 1900 to intervene in what contemporaries called the North China Incident (*Hokushin jihen*). Although there was an overarching unity in the foreign policy goals of the government, the people's parties, and the main extraparliamentary opposition groups, imperialist desire and imperialist fantasy were, if anything, stronger in the public sphere than in the government.

Hesitating to enter what it perceived to be a minefield of machinations by the Western great powers, the transcendental cabinet headed by Field Marshal Yamagata Aritomo initially balked at sending a large force. Finally, on 15 June 1900, it approved the dispatch to Tianjin of an advance force of two infantry battalions from the Hiroshima-based 5th Division under the command of Major General Fukushima Yasumasa.[1] Only after English diplomats in Tokyo urgently requested the dispatch of sizable reinforcements, arguing that the Western powers were dependent upon Japan to provide the backbone of the force to relieve the legations in Beijing, did the cabinet decide to dispatch the remainder of the 5th Division under Lieutenant General Yamaguchi Soshin (Motoomi).[2]

The Japanese government's strategy of holding back to attain maximum diplomatic advantage was ultimately successful, but appeared as mere vacillation to many in the public sphere. It was roundly condemned as such by large sections of the press, which viewed the situation as an opportunity to realize Japan's civilizing mission—for Japan to assist benevolently a languid, torpid neighbor that lacked the subjectivity to maintain order in its own house by spreading the virtues of right, humanity, and civilization.

However, after fighting broke out and the North China Incident rapidly transmogrified into the North China War from about mid-July 1900, opposition mounted in sections of the Japanese press, especially the *Yorozu Chōhō* (Complete Morning Report), the most popular Tokyo newspaper of the day. The *Chōhō*'s journalists, at first enthusiastic supporters of the war effort, were instrumental in developing a critique of it. This arose from several factors, including a new awareness of Chinese subjectivity, based on reports from war correspondents of the staunch resistance put up by Boxer and Qing forces at Tianjin and elsewhere; a contention that the allied forces were overstepping the bounds of legitimacy by waging war against China per se rather than merely subduing the Boxers; a perception that the imperialism of the Western powers was predicated on anti-Asian racism; a change in focus from state's rights in the international arena to the effects of state policy on the nation at home; and disaffection at tax increases to pay for the war.

This critique of the North China Incident soon collided with a discourse on imperialism, which had just begun making waves in the Japanese public sphere in response to the "new imperialism" of the Euro-American powers and the development of a "social imperialist" response by the Japanese state to the social problems spawned by economic restructuring and regional tensions following the Sino-Japanese War.[3] The result was the development of a powerful, general critique of militarism and imperialism in the months after the official end of the Boxer conflict. This tended to re-radicalize extraparliamentary opposition politics, giving rise to new social movements espousing various forms of liberalism, social democracy, and socialism. These included the first Japanese Social Democratic Party (Shakai minshutō, or SDP), the Risōdan (Band of Idealists), established by the *Chōhō* in the wake of the SDP's proscription, and the Heiminsha (Commoners' Society), which subsequently led opposition to the Russo-Japanese War.

These anti-imperialist currents, although always a minority movement, received a tremendous fillip from a scandal that rocked Japan from late 1901. The *Yorozu Chōhō*, in a fifty-part serialized article entitled, "The Scandal of the Looting of North China," which was published between December 1901 and January 1902, revealed that during the Boxer campaign, the Japanese Imperial Army had engaged in a vigorous yet clandestine campaign of looting in north China. There was thus approximately a one-year lag between this Japanese loot scandal and the reporting of looting in the European and American public spheres, as discussed in this volume by James Hevia and others.[4]

This chapter, relying mostly on contemporary Japanese newspaper sources, will analyze the form and contours of this scandal. The import of this is fourfold. First, it counters the entrenched prejudice that the conduct of Japanese forces during the Boxer campaign was "exemplary." When the scandal broke, the Yokohama-based *Japan Weekly Mail* expressed astonishment: "What this is all about the foreign public cannot tell. Nothing was heard of Japanese looting while the campaign was in progress. A great deal was said about other nationals, but the Japanese escaped unnoticed."[5] The "exemplary" tag has remained to this day, with no less a historian than the late Marius Jansen contending that "in contrast to the looting by other elements of the allied force, Japanese troops behaved in exemplary fashion." Military historian Robert Edgerton has likewise taken at face value a report by English war correspondent Henry Savage Landor, writing that "the few Japanese who looted did so in a 'silent, quiet and graceful way.'"[6] Second, it thereby discredits the view that war crimes committed by Japanese forces during the Asia-Pacific War were exceptional in the context of those forces' own histories. Third, it casts light on the construction of the Meiji public sphere and on negotiations between the press and governing elites. Finally, it highlights the limits of late Meiji politico-moral critique.

THE *YOROZU CHŌHŌ* AND THE BIRTH OF A SCANDAL

Before outlining the contours of the scandal, I should first describe in more detail the character of the newspaper that broke it. The *Yorozu Chōhō* was one of the most popular and successful Tokyo newspapers of the day. Founded in 1892 as an unabashedly commercial enterprise, the *Chōhō* inherited an aggressively antiauthoritarian and reformist yet nationalistic agenda from the Freedom and Popular Rights Movement (*Jiyū minken undō*). Although often derided as an *aka shimbun* or red newspaper—the Japanese equivalent of the English yellow journal—by 1900 the *Chōhō* was moving to attract students and the educated classes by improving the intellectual quality of its articles.[7] The editor, Kuroiwa Ruikō, headhunted leading talent from other papers and hired young, politically committed writers such as Kōtoku Shūsui, Uchimura Kanzō, Sakai Toshihiko, and Taoka Reiun.[8] Their magnetic writing, guided by Kuroiwa's astute leadership, forced circulation well over 80,000 by 1901.[9]

A focus on East Asian geopolitics, especially the "China problem," was integral to the paper's new perspective, and was a major concern of its most famous writer, Kōtoku Shūsui. Best known for his role in founding the Social Democratic Party, his leadership of the anti-imperialist Heiminsha, his later anarchism, and his execution in 1911 for allegedly plotting to assassinate the Emperor Meiji in the so-called high treason incident, Kōtoku remains an *enfant terrible* of dominant narratives of modern Japanese history. However, like most *Chōhō* journalists, Kōtoku was a steadfast imperialist until well into the Boxer campaign.[10] He took a paternalistic line toward China and strongly supported the subjugation of the Boxers. However, by late 1901 he had come to adopt a position that was anti-imperialist and antimilitarist but still staunchly nationalistic. This is strongly reflected in his writings on "The Scandal of the Looting of North China."

Kōtoku did not construct the scandal alone, but it may reasonably be assumed that he was the point man.[11] His interest in the problem of looting and other violations of international law by the Japanese army is certain, for he published at least ten articles on related topics.[12] Further, of all the *Chōhō* journalists, he was at this stage the most vocal critic of imperialism and militarism.[13] But while the serialized scandal articles did not carry bylines, it may also be assumed that Sakai Toshihiko, Kobayashi Tenryū, and Taoka Reiun, who had been war correspondents in north China, were involved. Initially all champions of the Boxer War, their fervor was tempered by their battlefield experiences, such that by 1901 they too were following trajectories of dissent. The Christian intellectual Uchimura Kanzō was another likely participant. Others may well have been involved, but Kobayashi Kazumi's thesis that these men formed the core group is quite plausible.[14]

The scandal itself had a life of its own in the public sphere before the *Yorozu Chōhō* addressed it. This can be surmised from the many readers' letters offering details of returned officers' carousing and also reports from Hiroshima offering colorful descriptions of the "souvenirs" that officers had brought back from the front. As they did not report them during the war, *Chōhō* journalists probably did not witness the crimes they sensationalized, instead obtaining details mostly from veterans.

Yet the *Chōhō* did not immediately break the scandal. Its first move was to attempt to persuade the government to investigate:

> When we went to rebuke Prime Minister Katsura Tarō, his response was that he was not unaware of the matter, but that because if it were exposed to the public it would greatly harm the prestige of the state. Therefore his wish was that we keep the affair under wraps. Although we are naturally not men who happily work to harm the prestige of the state . . . if crimes have been committed we will certainly castigate them, so we cannot readily accept the prime minister's argument. Thus, henceforth we shall publish the truth of the affair of the plunder of North China.[15]

It was thus Katsura's attempt to cover up the affair that led to the birth of the scandal. The *Chōhō* kept the scandal alive for nearly two months in over fifty installments. The most prominent kind of loot involved—silver ingots in the rough shape of a horseshoe—gave the scandal the name by which it is still known: the *bateigin jiken* or "Horseshoe Silver Affair."[16]

DIMENSIONS OF THE SCANDAL

For the most part, the *Yorozu Chōhō* fought its battle alone, but with seemingly much public support. Most other newspapers actively responded to the scandal only when the military refused to defend itself.[17] It is difficult to gauge precisely public reaction to the scandal, but given that the *Chōhō* published some twenty letters to the editor from across the country, all indicating heightened local concern, it is probably fair to conclude that public support for the paper's agenda was strong.

Certainly if Mitsukawa Kametarō can be taken as representative of the paper's student readership, the incident had a strong impact. Just thirteen at the time, Mitsukawa became famous in the 1920s with Ōkawa Shūmei and Kita Ikki as one pole of the so-called trinity of the ultranationalist state reconstruction movement. In his 1935 book, *Sankoku kanshō igo* (After the Triple Intervention), Mitsukawa recalled that after the Boxer War, a time of "great trust that military men were all patriots . . . an incident broke out that mercilessly obliterated my pure white, squeaky clean mental state of youth and made me sink down into a bottomless abyss of lament." This was the Horseshoe Silver Affair. Mitsukawa thought he "must have been dreaming" when he read that officers, whom he had held to be "as noble as the gods," had looted. "Thieves emerged from the ranks of the military! What a shameful disclosure! For the first time I felt that I understood society."[18] Given the level of support for the Risōdan at this time, many would have shared Mitsukawa's moral outrage.

The scandal also spread to the Diet, where the small 34 Club—recently formed when thirty-four members of the *Kensei hontō* (Real Constitutional Party) party split in opposition to its support of the government's decision to raise taxes to pay Boxer War expenses—urged the government to prevent a "national disgrace" and "salvage the prestige of the Imperial Army."[19] Progressive Party politicians further demanded that Katsura Tarō either "take action against" the *Chōhō* to clear the name of the accused, or else discipline the army. The government responded by trying to ignore the problem, arguing the need for proper investigation.[20] The *Chōhō* in turn castigated not only the government but also all the major parties for being more concerned with factional advantage than the "fate and security of the nation." Casting suspicion on the integrity of "the current crop of politicians," it asserted that if they were soldiers, "they would be a mob who would commit even worse looting than the soldiers of today."[21] Despite all of this, the government felt only mildly pressured.

THE HORSESHOE SILVER AFFAIR AND BOXER WAR LOOT

For the most part, the scandal articles were written in episodic form, with each article making specific charges against certain officers or units. The highest-ranking officer accused was Lieutenant General Yamaguchi Motoomi, commander of the 5th Division. Others accused included brigade commanders Major Generals Manabe Bin (Akira)(9th Infantry) and Tsukamoto Shōga (21st Infantry), regimental commanders Colonels Awaya Kan (11th Infantry), Kobara Yoshijirō (41st Infantry), and Nagata Hisashi (5th Artillery), and surgeons Shibaoka Madatarō and Hosono Ken'yū (commanders of the 1st and 2nd field hospitals). Despite the length of the series, the *Yorozu Chōhō* did not accuse any officer ranked lower than major, although it regretfully noted that a high proportion of all Japanese troops looted.[22]

The *Chōhō* spent much time trying to quantify the amount of loot senior officers ran back to Japan past a cordon of *kempeitai* (military police) inspections. By late January 1902, as the ballooning scandal provoked investigations by both military and civil police in the Hiroshima region, the *Chōhō* reported that "the ringleaders in the looting affair"—Yamaguchi, Manabe, Awaya, and Kobara—had secretly repatriated some 8,000,000 taels or ¥12,000,000, mainly as horseshoe silver. At least some of this seems to have been converted into currency. Yamaguchi, after finding local companies unwilling or unable to manage the job of selling "his" silver overseas, eventually turned to Jardine Matheson in Yokohama. Manabe and Awaya also contracted with Jardine through the good offices of Kōno Tazaburō, described by the *Chōhō* as "a businessman of ill repute." The *Chōhō* learned from Kōno himself that Jardine had undertaken to pay ¥45 per 50 taels, and intended to sell the silver in Hong Kong for ¥75 per 50 taels.[23] Further, according to Kōno at least one shipment of 1,800,000 taels from Hiroshima-Ujina to Hong Kong had taken place by early December 1901.[24]

Where the remainder of this loot ended up remains unclear. Junior officers seem to have had their smaller quantities of loot worked into decorative objects and jewelry. For example, the *Chōhō* reported that "the very heavy pure-gold chain that [army surgeon] Hosono Ken'yū drapes around his neck is in fact the reincarnation of golden bracelets that had adorned corpses in the caskets he dug up at Dongyuemiao."[25] Yet such instances were of minor consequence compared to the vast amount of silver looted by senior officers that was "probably still hidden in various warehouses in the Hiroshima and Yamaguchi regions, hidden in empty ammunition boxes and soy-sauce barrels, or hidden under the floorboards of their concubines' houses."[26]

As the scandal spiraled in February 1902, the *Chōhō* suddenly ran the headline "Plundered Silver Appears as a Phantom in the Exchequer." In addition to the ¥1,900,000 of looted silver that the government had already confirmed was in the exchequer, a new supplementary income from loot of ¥1,860,000 suddenly appeared. The *Chōhō* suspected that this silver was "spat up by the thieving officers who had custody of it" to mollify their critics in the army and indemnify themselves against harsh punishment.[27] To the *Chōhō* this implied that the scandal was not just an issue of military corruption, but corruption at the highest levels of state.

Horseshoe silver was not the only loot, but it seems to have been the most common. A complete accounting of all the looted objects the *Chōhō* mentions is impossible here, but no portable items of value seem to have been overlooked, including gold bullion, "marble and rare foreign woods,"[28] "countless jewels, splendidly ornamented clocks that are works of art, . . . rolls of silk . . . , gemstones, writing brushes, ink and paper in unknown quantities,"[29] huge temple bells wrought of "four parts gold, six parts bronze,"[30] "calligraphic works, paintings and antiques,"[31] "golden necklaces, jewels rare to the world and other items of tremendous value" robbed from "the graves of dignitaries,"[32] and to cap it all, a commodity as mundane and quotidian as rice.[33] Other items mentioned include scrolls and statues, such as "a statue of the Buddha in white jade worth well over ¥10,000."[34] Generals were also rumored to have decked out their messes with chairs of pure gold decorated with jewels that had belonged to the Dowager Empress.[35] This catalog is but a sample!

Soldiers were not the only ones accused. The *Chōhō* also charged that "although most of those in our long-besieged legation in Beijing were incorruptible, both Sugi Ikutarō and Oka Shōichi gained extremely bad reviews." Sugi, who had been a journalist, was a character who "thought nothing of pillaging before breakfast," and received considerable bounty for leading the looting of the Qing Treasury. So did Oka, a legation official, who "on his own initiative repeatedly broke into the mansions of wealthy families, purloining objects that took his fancy, piling them onto horse-drawn wagons and carting them back to his temporary official residence behind the Japanese legation, which he bedecked ostentatiously with several boxes containing 1,000 taels of horseshoe silver."[36]

The economy of loot also centered on Japanese, Chinese, and English businessmen as willing buyers and conveyors. None of the Chinese are mentioned by name, although they are portrayed as being willing participants in this black economy. Japanese firms involved in varying degrees included the following *zaibatsu*: Ōkura-gumi, Arima-gumi, Fujita-gumi, Mitsui, and Yasuda.

Most of the looting of Beijing seems to have occurred in the two days after advance units of the Japanese army entered the city on 15 August 1900. After the surrender of the Chinese forces within the city, Yamaguchi, like his British counterparts, banned looting by individuals and ordered that loot be turned over to unit headquarters.[37] The *Chōhō* recognized that an attempt was made to enforce this ban, citing one occasion where Yamaguchi "in a blaze of anger court-martialed one major and two field officers" who had looted in the Forbidden City after the parade celebrating the entry of the allied army into Beijing. Yet it regarded such actions as the height of farce. Accusing Yamaguchi of being a more than competent looter himself, it was "forced to laugh. Thieves being punished by one who rakes a percentage off thieves is a unique occurrence in all of history."[38] For the most part the ban was anyway ineffective as checks were easily evaded, so that "the menacing and plundering of Chinese people's homes carried on as before, but now both covertly and overtly in the name of requisitioning."

Further, in similar fashion to the British army's loot auctions discussed in this volume by James Hevia, Japanese company headquarters started openly selling loot. "This gradually became so ridiculous that at night [soldiers] began paying calls on newspaper reporters and translators, offering to unload objects for extremely low prices, and if they could not pay, proposed scheming with Chinese who they had contact with to exchange the objects for cash." Objects that did not sell were simply abandoned by the roadside; this was evidently blatantly visible within the Japanese garrison area on the morning of 20 August. Such practices ended when Japanese merchants entered Beijing from late September.[39]

Attempting to dispel any notion that the looting was the result of sporadic breakdowns in discipline, as has often been claimed of excesses by Japanese imperial forces, the *Chōhō* argued that senior officers simulated innocence while looting actively:

> Plundering upon plundering! What was the conduct of the bigwig generals at this time? . . . [They] adorned themselves with a façade that if broken would have revealed that they were pillaging left and right. An adroit system . . . whenever they witnessed looting by enlisted men or junior officers, they exclaimed angrily that it was a disgrace to the military. . . . they hauled this loot to divisional headquarters, where especially valuable items were distributed among the bigwigs while the remainder was disposed of in a manner convenient to maintaining a show of appearances.[40]

Finally, it must be stated that the scope of the scandal was focused rather narrowly on looting and other property crimes. The *Chōhō* generally and inexplicably overlooked physical violence the Imperial Army perpetrated on Chinese civilians.

SCANDAL AS "GOSSIP MADE TEDIOUS BY MORALITY"?

Given the secondhand nature of the reportage, can it be dismissed as "gossip made tedious by morality," as Oscar Wilde once memorably defined scandal? The answer is not entirely, for the articles do claim a certain verac-ity. This comes not only from the copious detail—names of perpetrators, dates, times, places, and circumstances, and so on—but also from the *Chōhō's* declaration that if articles did contain errors, it would correct them and issue an apology. And indeed it did on several occasions. For example, the twenty-fourth article accused Lieutenant Colonel Shiba Gorō—who had achieved fame during the siege as the dashing military attaché responsible for the defense of the Japanese legation—of misappropriating 130,000 taels of looted silver that the *kempeitai* had earlier confiscated. It charged Shiba with repatriating the proceeds through the Beijing branch of the Hong Kong & Shanghai Bank, and using it to build a house in an expensive Tokyo sub-urb. Two days later, the *Chōhō* completely retracted its "false charges against Shiba Gorō" after he protested his innocence. However, it maintained that the basic details of the story were correct—funds had been sent in Shiba's name from Beijing in a legitimate if irregular transaction, although "not a single *rin* found its way into Shiba's account."[41] The legation official, Oka Shōichi, also appealed his innocence and the *Chōhō* subsequently issued a retraction.

The *Chōhō* challenged prime targets of the scandal, such as Yamaguchi Motoomi, to clear their names in similar fashion.[42] They deigned not to. Their inaction did nothing to challenge the *Chōhō's* credibility. Pointedly, the *Chōhō* was never censored or sued for libel. The veracity of the accusa-tions is further supported by the overwhelming consistencies between them and stories of looting published in contemporary French newspapers, dis-cussed in this volume by Anand Yang in his account of assertions by an In-dian soldier that Japanese were among the leading sellers of looted silver.[43]

More telling of the veracity of the allegations is the account of booty given in the official military history of the Boxer War, published by the Japanese army in 1904. This account is interesting in that it openly alludes to the plun-dering of silver bullion, yet legitimizes it as state policy. That this was not even more scandalous is indicative of both the military's dismissive attitude and the desire of the editor, Major General Fukushima Yasumasa, commander of the initial expeditionary force, to minimize disgrace to his division:

> When [Japanese forces] occupied Beijing, they discovered silver bullion . . . The total amounted to 2,914,856 ryō . . . On 14 September, War Minister Katsura commanded Divisional Commander Yamaguchi to dispose of the plundered silver (*rokaku ginkai*), ordering the use of one part (214,286 ryō) for expenses in North China and the remittance of the remainder to Japan (the greatest part was remitted through the Tianjin Specie Bank . . .) The plundered silver from Beijing was packed into boxes under the guard of the divisional adjutant . . . From 22 September, logistics, ammunition and victuals were transported to Tongzhou under military escort to be repatriated . . . 1,928,571 taels were transferred to the Central Treasury, the remainder to the War Ministry.[44]

Such effacement of individual looting was the general tactic the military adopted to try to regain honor. Major General Manabe Bin, one of the few 5th Division officers to speak to the press, took a similar stance when interviewed by Hiroshima's *Chūgoku shimbun* newspaper. What is especially interesting about Manabe's statement is his semantic acrobatics. Angered by charges that his regiment had looted, he contended that it had instead simply "carried off" items of value. An example he gives is that

> while chastising the bandits, a certain company commander in the 42nd Regiment stabbed to death the ringleader, who wore a sharp Japanese sword at his hilt. The company commander brought the sword home as a souvenir. Also these chairs [three chairs in the regimental commander's residence with elaborate jewel-embossed ebony frames and delicate artwork], we brought home from headquarters in Beijing because they were such wonderful curios. They're in all the official residences, which is by no means inappropriate.[45]

Such matter-of-fact justifications ultimately did Manabe little benefit.

Yet back in Japan, the taking of "war trophies" seems to have been common knowledge. At the local level, there was not only recognition but even some pride at such exploits. This is brought out in a fascinating exchange of letters between a young soldier named Mori Gihei, sent with his unit to northern China, and his family. Although in the surviving letters Gihei does not mention whether he was directly involved in looting, a reply sent to him by his father expresses the happiness felt in their town not only at the Imperial Army's great victories but also at the loot: "The great victory at the Tianjin forts has seen joy enter into the houses of all the neighborhoods. . . . The large amount of plunder from northern China is above all else a great exploit. All the people of this country are rejoicing."[46] Exhibitions of lesser "war trophies" such as Boxer flags and the uniforms of Chinese commanders at local town halls and schools throughout Japan doubtless helped whip up this enthusiasm.[47] This not only lends further credence to the *Chōhō* articles but also helps explain why they focus on attacking corrupt policy and corrupted senior officers.

THE DISCOURSE OF THE SCANDAL

Morality figured prominently in the discourse of the scandal. The *Chōhō* was as concerned as many of its European counterparts with what James Hevia calls the question of "mimicry"—how Japan could appear virtuous if it had "copied the behavior of savages."[48] However, none of the *Chōhō* articles denigrated the army per se or questioned its role in the Boxer War. Indeed, the *Chōhō* presented the scandal as a means of restoring "the honor of Japanese soldiers" by provoking a full inquiry and purge of corrupt elements.[49] Behind this lay an upsurge of nationalistic sentiment. This attitude is epitomized in Kōtoku's editorial, "Touchstone":

> I venture that the situation is not serious enough to indict our whole army sim-
> ply because in it there are soldiers who looted. . . . However, we cannot but re-
> alize that buckets of mud have been smeared over the face of our army . . . and
> that attempting resolutely to dispel this shame, to wash it out is in fact first of
> all the primary responsibility of our army, and that second, it is the primary re-
> sponsibility of our entire nation. Therefore, if our army cannot face its ex-
> tremely important and extremely pressing responsibility to separate swiftly the
> sweet from the foul and the gems from the gravel so as to wipe this mire from
> its own face, they are only a violent, hollow-eyed family of little rats.

Kōtoku argues that the way this problem is dealt with would become a "touchstone for our army and our nation." Yet his conclusion was as grim as it was nationalist. Distrusting the "military authorities," the only place he could put his trust was in "our nation of forty million, in the true *bushidō* of the majority" as "final judgment resides with the nation."[50]

Yet morality and nationalism were not the only grounds on which the *Chōhō* attacked. Many articles intertwined such sentiments with legalistic arguments, such as the following:

> International law expressly prohibits the looting of property other than mili-
> tary equipment and provisions. Yet, our army purports to be an army that pro-
> tects humanity and justice through a discourse of civilization (*bunmeishugi*).
> Our countrymen have been especially proud of this honor since the war of
> 1894–95. . . . This looting! . . . It has resulted in the most outrageous disgrace
> to the military, the most appalling national disgrace to Japan![51]

Elsewhere, the *Chōhō* argued that from the viewpoint of international relations, the looting would destroy Japan's relations with China.[52] It contended moreover that

> the dispatch of troops to north China was not undertaken to wage war against
> China, but to assist China and to pacify the insurgent bandits. Thus, we may
> tolerate the confiscation of materiel and provisions belonging to the bandits,
> calling this bounty and calling it helping China pacify the bandits. However,
> . . . breaking open the treasuries of China, which we ought to be assisting, . . .
> is clearly an act of spoliation.[53]

Therefore Kōtoku avowed that "the so-called bounty, the stolen loot in the national treasury must be returned to China."[54] Further in this legalistic vein, Kōtoku presciently lamented that the tremendous pressure being brought to bear on the judicial system would destroy any hope for "the independence of judicial authority" in Japan, leaving it heavily influenced by the political sphere.[55]

The *Chōhō* also argued that not disciplining the offenders not only set an appalling precedent, but contradicted the precedent that Yamagata Aritomo himself had set in 1894 when, as commander of the 1st Army, he had "bawled out" General Yamaji Motoharu for the massacre at Port Arthur. Kōtoku demanded to know why Yamagata refused to "bawl out" the offenders in the Boxer War.[56] Concerned that a disturbing trend was emerging, the *Chōhō* suggested that the government's overlooking the small amount of looting during the Sino-Japanese War had produced the current round of looting. An editorial thundered, "Should it go unpunished this time around, we cannot know how much more heinous an incident will be given rise to next time. If someone were to prophesy that the senior officer corps of the Japanese army were openly to become bandits, we could not with any certainty regard it as a lie."[57]

CONSEQUENCES OF THE SCANDAL

Despite these prophetic words, the army establishment found no ready consensus on the "loot question." It was aware of the matter at least as early as the spring 1901 divisional commanders' conference, yet it launched no systematic investigation. Many senior officers seemed to support the resolution of the "clean and incorruptible" General Nogi Maresuke that two officers, then under his command, who had been implicated in looting, should be "stripped of their decorations and expelled from the army." According to the *Chōhō*, Nogi had even retired from the active list to take responsibility for this disgrace, using ill health as a pretext. Contemporary historians have supported this suggestion.[58]

After the scandal broke, the *Japan Weekly Mail* reported that "Viscounts Torio and Miura advocate the settlement of the loot question by removing to the retired list the senior officers who took part in the affair. Viscount Terauchi and Baron Ozawa, on the contrary, are in favor of allowing matters to rest, whereas other officers of the Head Quarter Staff take a very strong view."[59] However, the *Mail* did not state what that view was. On the other hand, according to the *Chōhō*, Yamagata held that "because the offenders were all officers who had distinguished themselves in the field, it would be a slight to the army to punish them for looting."[60]

Yamagata's position prevailed and a cover-up ensued. Unsurprisingly, this immediately became the subject of new scandals. The first was "The Slander Affair in the Aftermath of the Looting." Three witnesses to the *kempeitai* investigation of the Horseshoe Silver Affair were charged with slander for supposedly making unsubstantiated claims. The *Chōhō* was scandalized and cried that the charges were beaten up. Lasting from 31 January to 3 February 1902, this affair fizzled under *kempeitai* censorship, only to transmogrify immediately into "The Generals' Custodial Theft Affair," published in twelve parts from 3 to 18 February 1902.[61] These articles detail the relationship of the three "slanderers" and their attempts to sell loot on behalf of senior 5th Division officers. By this stage, the scandal had spread from the *Chōhō* to other papers, increasing pressure on the government and military establishment to resolve the affair.

In the end, the loot scandal led neither to a full-scale purge of corrupt elements from the military nor to a rectification of the relationship between the army and the state. While the political impasse over raising taxes to pay for the Boxer War had brought down the fourth Itō Hirobumi cabinet in mid-1901, the loot scandal had nowhere near the same effect. Nonetheless, it still claimed several scalps. Lieutenant General Yamaguchi was pushed to resign as commander of the 5th Division on 17 March 1902 to take responsibility for the scandal.[62] The army maintained face by promoting him to general and transferring him upstairs to the General Staff. Later, he was made a viscount just before his death in 1904.[63] Manabe, who had meanwhile been promoted to divisional commander, was court-martialed and suspended from duties. However, after being reinstated, he fought with distinction in the Russo-Japanese War, was promoted to lieutenant general, and eventually was made a baron.[64]

In mid-April, Majors Sugiura Kōji and Yonekura Kyōichirō "were stripped of their decorations and commissions."[65] Two other officers, notably Colonel Awaya Kan, and several enlisted men were also hauled before a court-martial that May. But with the government frantically attempting to cover up the scandal to prevent a loss of international prestige, they were predictably cleared. The *Jiji shinpō* newspaper reported that this decision was justified legalistically: "The court-martial conducted various investigations into the conduct of Colonel Awaya Kan and those under him, concluding that the so-called plunder was public plunder (*kōkyō no bundori*) and thus in other words, a type of war bounty, and that there was not a trace of what could be recognized as pillage (*ryakudatsu*)."[66] In other words, looting on behalf of the state was permitted, but looting for private gain was not.

However, although the soldiers were cleared of the sin of private looting, the force of public opinion against the military forced the army's hand into suspending them. The *Jiji shinpō* approvingly noted that "while the court-martial exonerated them, because administratively this was something that could not be overlooked, it was ordered that they be suspended from duties." The *Jiji shinpō* also reported that General Yamaguchi was to resign as commander of the 5th Division to take responsibility.[67]

Several civilian contractors were charged with a variety of offences, and in a move the *Chōhō* regarded as "the height of farce," the 5th Division banned purveyors implicated in the scandal from its bases.[68] Perhaps the most serious consequence of the scandal, not noted at the time, was that it cast a

dark cloud over the Chōshū faction in the army, indirectly ending its monopoly over the army high command. The suspension of Manabe opened
the door for officers from other regions, such as Uehara Yūsaku from Sat-
suma. This was quite a blow to the Chōshū faction because Manabe was regarded as the great hope of the faction, a potential successor after Tanaka
Giichi to power brokers Katsura Tarō and Terauchi Masatake.[69]

CONCLUSION

"The Scandal of the Looting of North China" was the major scandal stemming from the Boxer War. Launched by the *Yorozu Chōhō*, a major Tokyo
daily, in the face of the government's obdurate unwillingness to investigate
allegations brought to Prime Minister Katsura Tarō in late 1901, the scandal
focused not only on looting and the disposal of loot, but on the hypocrisy
of the army and its political mentors, and the consequences this implied for
Japan's diplomatic and world-historical position. The *Chōhō* thus aggressively targeted not "the highest organs of Meiji state power," as Kobayashi
Kazumi has argued,[70] but only what it regarded as corrupt or malignant elements within these organs because, politically, the scandal combined a
radical nationalist imaginary with an antiestablishment zeal that in itself
was not yet explicitly antistate or antimilitary.

The Horseshoe Silver Affair was not simply a moralistic critique of the
systematic, clandestine pillaging carried out during the war, but an attack in
the mode of scandal on the military's growing domination of the state. At
issue for the *Yorozu Chōhō* was nothing less than the fate of the Japanese nation. Emboldened by this recalcitrant nationalism, the *Chōhō* was remarkably successful in generating a widespread public outrage that sustained the
scandal for over three months. This outrage became a catalyst in the deep-
ening of anti-imperialist sentiment in Japan. It gave focus to the considerable energies of writers such as Kōtoku Shūsui, stimulated the impetus of
the *Chōhō*'s new political organization, the Risōdan, and laid the foundations of the vanguard opposition movement during the Russo-Japanese
War, the Heiminsha. The Horseshoe Silver Affair thus greatly influenced the
subsequent course of extraparliamentary opposition politics in Japan.

Ultimately the scandal dissipated in the face of a half-hearted *kempeitai*
and civilian police investigation that resulted in several courts-martial and
resignations. There was no broad purge, as desired by the *Yorozu Chōhō*. The
army itself was not held legally accountable, nor were its political mentors.
Only a fraction of those who had looted were disciplined and the loot was
never returned to China. Although the *Chōhō* cast clouds over the reputation of the army, the limits on the effectiveness of critique in the public
sphere had become obvious. The sea of fire and blood and hysteria of the

Russo-Japanese War finally restored the military's image, but it took much longer for the tainted image of the North China War to be forgotten.

NOTES

1. On the machinations behind Japanese official policy, see Stewart Lone, *Army, Empire and Politics in Meiji Japan* (New York: St. Martin's Press, 2000), 74–88, and Ian Nish, "Japan and the North China Incident of 1900" (paper presented at the 1900: The Boxers, China and the World conference, June 2001).

2. Lone, *Army, Empire,* 79–80; *Kokushi daijiten* (Tokyo: Yoshikawa kōbunkan, 1979–1997) vol. 12, 694. The *Yorozu Chōhō* frequently used on-yomi of names in its *rubi*—hence Soshin. However, the general's given name is usually pronounced, "Motoomi." Except for major historical figures, I follow the *Chōhō*'s pronunciations.

3. This is not to deny that imperialist ideas were in circulation well before this time. Cf. Yamaizumi Susumu, "Ikioi to shinkaron," in *Seijigaku,* ed. Kataoka Hiromitsu (Tokyo: Seibundō, 1980). For a recuperation of the concept of new imperialism, see C. A. Bayly's chapter in this volume, "The Boxer Uprising and India: Globalizing Myths."

4. The chapters by James Hevia, Lewis Bernstein, and Anand Yang in this volume all discuss the Western context of the loot question.

5. "The Loot Question," *Japan Weekly Mail,* 14 December 1901, 624.

6. Marius Jansen, *The Making of Modern Japan* (Harvard University Press, 2000), 487. Robert Edgerton, *Warriors of the Rising Sun* (New York: W.W. Norton, 1997), 80–81.

7. Kubota Tatsuhiko, *Nijūichi daisenkaku kisha den* (Osaka: Osaka mainichi shimbunsha, 1930), 310, 321. Yamamoto Taketoshi, *Shimbun to minshū* (Tokyo: Kinokuniya shoten, 1978), 137–40. For a general treatment of the *Chōhō*'s politics of scandal, see Oku Takenori, "*Yorozu Chōhō* ni miru shakai genshō no sokumen," *Shakai kagaku tōkyū* 40, no. 3 (1995): 25–52.

8. Itō Masatoku, "Sōsei kara Meiji-ki," in *Nihon shimbun hyakunen shi,* ed. Nihon shimbun hyakunenshi kankōkai (Tokyo: Nihon shimbun hyakunenshi kankōkai, 1960), 279–80.

9. Yamamoto, *Shimbun to minshū,* 95–96; Itō, "Sōsei kara Meiji-ki," 279–80. Between 1895 and 1897, *Chōhō* circulation increased from 48,000 to 82,000. Thereafter, circulation figures diverge. Itō reports that it reached 120,000 in 1903; Nishida, however, puts it at 85,000, though this may ignore regional circulation. Nishida Nagahisa, "Tōkyō-to shimbun shi sono II," in *Nihon shimbunshi,* ed. Nihon shimbun kyōkai (Tokyo: Nihon shimbun kyōkai, 1956), 136.

10. For a discussion of Kōtoku's imperialist period, see Ben Middleton, "Kōtoku Shūsui to teikokushugi e no kongenteki hihan," *Shokishakaishugi kenkyū* 12 (1999): 134–93.

11. Kobayashi argues that "there is no mistaking that [Kōtoku] was the person most responsible." Kobayashi Kazumi, *Giwadan sensō to Meiji kokka* (Tokyo: Kyūko shoin, 1986), 372.

12. Most of these articles are reproduced in Kōtoku Shūsui zenshū henshū iinkai, ed., *Kōtoku Shūsui Zenshū,* vol. IV (Tokyo: Meiji bunken, 1972). Hereafter KSZ IV.

13. Kōtoku's most important book of this period, published in April 1901, is *Imperialism: The Spectre of the Twentieth Century*. My annotated translation should be published in the near future.

14. Kobayashi Kazumi, "Bateigin jiken to Meiji no genronjin," in *Chūgoku genkindaishi ronshū*, ed. Shingai kakumei kenkyūkai (Tokyo: Kyūko shoin, 1985), 157.

15. "Hokushin bundori no kaibun (1)," *Yorozu Chōhō*, 1 December 1901. Hereafter, articles in "The Scandal of the Plunder of North China" series are cited as HBK. Unless specified, all references to newspaper articles are from the *Yorozu Chōhō*.

16. Miyashita Tadao, following Wagel's 1915 essay, *Currency in China*, offers "Sycee taels" as another translation of *bateigin*. While there had been a long commerce between China and Japan involving these ingots, *bateigin* was only used from the time of the 1894–1895 Sino-Japanese War as a direct translation of "horseshoe silver"—a term used by Westerners in China and not the Chinese, who simply called the ingots *yuan bao*. Miyashita Tadao, *Chūgoku kasei no tokushu kenkyū* (Tokyo: Nihon gakujutsu shinkōkai, 1952), 2, 83.

17. Kobayashi, *Giwadan sensō*, 408.

18. Mitsukawa Kametarō, *Sankoku kanshō igo* (Tokyo: Gendai jānarizumu shuppankai, 1977), 44–45.

19. "34-ha no bundori shitsumon," *Yorozu Chōhō*, 25 January 1902; "Bundori mondai semaru," 26 January 1902.

20. "Bundori mondai shūgiin ni izu," 24 January 1902.

21. "Bundori mondai to gikai," 3 February 1902.

22. For details, see HBK (6), 6 December 1901.

23. "Bundori jiken no yōryō," 27 January 1902.

24. "Bundori jiken no yōryō," 28 January 1902. The *Chōhō* printed many articles about police uncovering evidence of loot sales, for example, "Hiroshima daisōsaku zokuhō," 15 February 1902.

25. HBK (17), 17 December 1901.

26. "Bundori jiken no yōryō," 27 January 1902.

27. "Bundorigin kokko ni genshutsusu," 5 February 1902. Cf. also "Bundori jiken no yōryō," 27 January 1902.

28. HBK (8), 8 December 1901.

29. HBK (9), 9 December 1901.

30. HBK (12), 12 December 1901.

31. HBK (13), 13 December 1901.

32. HBK (14), 14 December, (15), 15 December, and (17), 17 December 1901.

33. HBK (27), 27 December 1901, and (34), 3 January 1902.

34. "Ōkura no kainyūhin," 12 February 1902.

35. "Seitaikō no isu," 22 February 1902.

36. HBK (5), 5 December 1901.

37. Cf. James Hevia, "Looting and Its Discontents," in this volume.

38. HBK (5). Yet the Imperial Army was not totally corrupted. For an account by a Japanese soldier of attempts at preventing Russian looting, see Fujimura Shuntarō, *Aru rōhei no shuki: hiroku hokushin jihen*. (Tokyo: Jinbutsu ōraisha, 1967), 241–43.

39. HBK (4), 4 December 1901, and HBK (6).

40. HBK (5). HBK (20) (20 December 1901) makes similar allegations.
41. The *Chōhō* also published a letter from a veteran in the thirty-seventh article vouching for Shiba's integrity. HBK (37), 6 January 1902.
42. HBK (38), 7 January 1902.
43. Anand Yang, "(A) Subaltern('s) Boxers," in this volume. See also Régine Thiriez, "Imaging the 1900 China Events" (paper presented at the 1900: The Boxers, China and the World conference, June 2001): 7–9.
44. Sanbō honbu (ed.), *Meiji 33-nen Shinkoku-jihen senshi*, vol. 4 (Tokyo: Senryūdō, 1904), 162.
45. *Chūgoku shimbun*, 16 February 1902, cited in Kobayashi, *Giwadan sensō*, 409.
46. Mori Yukimasa, ed., *Hyakunenme no kenshō: wakakushitesatta Gihei no shōgai.* (Takashima: Kaiyōsha, 2005), 91.
47. Mori Takehiro cites contemporaries recounting these exhibitions in "Shinkoku hahei wo meguru Gihei no ashiato," in *Hyakunenme no kenshō,* ed. Mori Yukimasa, 89–94.
48. Hevia, "Looting and Its Discontents," in this volume.
49. HBK (7), 7 December 1901.
50. "Shikinseki," 31 January 1902, in KSZ IV, 28–30.
51. "Rikugun no daiojoku," editorial December 1901. For legalistic arguments, see also HBK (3) and Kōtoku, "Seija no mondai," 29 January 1902 in KSZ IV, 23–24; Kōtoku, "Bundori ni taisuru shokan," *Keisei*, 25 February 1902, in KSZ IV, 361–65.
52. "Rikugun no daiojoku," editorial December 1901.
53. Kōtoku, "Bundori ni taisuru shokan."
54. Kōtoku, "Bundori ni taisuru shokan."
55. "Shihōken no dokuritsu," 29 January 1902, KSZ IV, 25.
56. "Rikugun no daiojoku." While exact details of the events at Port Arthur are shrouded in uncertainty, Yuki Tanaka notes that "[i]t is said that a large but unspecified number of Chinese soldiers and civilians" were massacred at Lushun between 22 and 24 November 1894. Yuki Tanaka, *Hidden Horrors* (Oxford: Westview Press, 1998), 229, note 84.
57. "Kodama rikushō ni atau," 21 January 1902.
58. HBK (2), 2 December 1901. On Nogi stepping down, see Ōhama Tetsuya, *Nogi Maresuke* (Kawade shobō shinsha, 1988) and Sasaki Hideaki, *Nogi Maresuke: yo wa shokun no shitei wo koroshitari* (Kyoto: Minerva shobō, 2005), 96.
59. "The Loot Question," *Japan Weekly Mail*, 624.
60. "Shushō rikushō no sekinin wa ikan," 9 February 1902.
61. The first affair was called the *Bundori yoha no bukoku jiken,* the second the *Rikugun shōkan no kanshutō jiken.*
62. "Kodama rikushō no danwa," 20 February 1902; "Yamaguchi Soshin no jihyō," 21 February 1902.
63. "Yamaguchi Motoomi," *Nihon jinmei daijiten*, vol. 6 (Tokyo: Heibonsha, 1979), 332.
64. "Manabe Akira," *Nihon jinmei daijiten*, vol. 6 (Tokyo: Heibonsha, 1979), 4.
65. HBK (2).
66. "Bundori shōkō no muzai to teishoku no riyū" and "Dai-5 shidanchō no shintai," *Jiji Shinpō*, 15 May 1902.

67. See for example "Hiroshima no gunpō kaigi," 14 February 1902; "Awaya, Hayashi ryūchi," 15 February 1902; "Gunpō kaigi hirakaren," 17 February 1902; "Awaya ra shūkansu," 1 March 1902.

68. "Dai-5 shidan mizukara kaichokusu," 19 March 1902. *Jiji shinpō* 15 May .

69. On factional struggles in the Imperial Army, see Tanida Isamu, *Jitsuroku: Nihon rikugun no habatsu kōsō* (Tokyo: Tenbōsha, 2002). Cf. Kobayashi, *Giwadan sensō*, 428.

70. Kobayashi, *Giwadan sensō*, 373.

7

After the Fall

Tianjin under Foreign Occupation, 1900–1902

Lewis Bernstein

After Tianjin was occupied by allied troops during the Boxer Uprising, it was governed by an allied military government, the Tianjin Provisional Government (TPG), for twenty-five months. Although the TPG changed the city's physical appearance, its activities constitute an almost overlooked chapter in Tianjin's administrative history. It attracted some contemporary Western attention but has been almost completely ignored by scholars since then, including those writing about Yuan Shikai and/or Tianjin.[1] This blind spot is understandable given the specialized state of contemporary Western scholarship, but general histories of Tianjin and local government published during the Republican period and in the last twenty years also ignore the TPG. Gazetteers and general histories contain detailed chronologies that record the founding of the city, its various administrative functions, the attempt of the Taipings to seize it, Seng-ko-lin-ch'in's repulse of the Anglo-French expeditionary force in 1858, and the "skirmish" in June to July 1900. The subsequent occupation and the TPG's activities and accomplishments are ignored, or rather the physical changes are reported but they are attributed to no human agency. The same can be said for works on the evolution of urban governance.[2]

Nothing has been published in a Western language since 1927 about this brief episode in Chinese history. The reasons appear obvious; the TPG's activities represent a cultural victory of Western imperialism and civilization in China. Because imperialism as a way of life and thought is out of intellectual fashion, Westerners may wish to forget this episode. Because they were militarily and culturally humiliated and forced to learn from their conquerors, the Chinese do not wish to remember it. Nevertheless, it is important because it drastically changed the city's physical shape, showed the imperial government how cities could be turned into money-making machines using modern administrative methods, and was one of the few times foreign powers temporarily occupied, administered, and returned territory to China. In fact, three Chinese cities were occupied and administered by foreign troops between 1857 and 1902: Canton in 1857, Tianjin in 1859–1860 and 1900–1902, and Beijing in 1860 and 1900–1901.

Material for these earlier occupations should exist in British and French archives although the published sources do not take note of them. The only extended treatment of a foreign occupation of Beijing (1900–1901) may be found in an article by Michael H. Hunt.[3] This article is instructive and points up the differences between the occupations of Beijing and Tianjin. To begin with, the allies occupied Tianjin for twenty-five months but were in Beijing only for thirteen months, until the Boxer Protocols had been signed. The American contingent left north China in May 1901, several months before that event, thus serving as an occupation force for only ten months. Tianjin was treated as a single entity and part of its hinterland was included in the zone of occupation, while Beijing was divided into sectors and the occupying powers did not extend their formal administrative reach into the countryside surrounding the capital. In addition, according to Hunt's account, the Americans found Chinese officials in Beijing with whom they could cooperate. That occupation was indirect, with the forces in the American sector working with an informal Chinese administration. The TPG found no Chinese officials with whom it could cooperate. Finally, the occupying forces in Beijing were under the intense scrutiny of the diplomatic community while the Tianjin occupation was strictly a military affair of little interest to those in the capital and isolated from the glare of publicity.

A history of the TPG's activities has been relatively difficult to piece together. The most accessible account of its activities may be found in H. B. Morse's magisterial work on Sino-foreign relations.[4] His account is based on the "Proces Verbaux des Séances du Conseil du Gouvernement Provisoire de la Cite de Tientsin," which was "given to the author by the Secretary General," Charles Denby Jr.[5] The most extensive published report of the TPG's activities was an article in a French military journal by an officer who may have been a member of the provisional government.[6]

After seizing the walled city on 14 July 1900, the allies were confronted with the ordinary problems of governing a city of approximately 750,000 people, "complicated by the chaos of capture, looting, and military occupation . . . trade in even the necessities of life had undergone a seemingly irreparable upheaval; and everywhere the poisoning presence of grim reminders of a fallen city and endangered the health of Native and Foreigner alike."[7] In addition, the unity the powers displayed while in danger from the Boxers was rapidly disappearing, to be replaced by enmity over extension of territorial concessions.

At an impasse and faced with the necessity of governing Tianjin and the surrounding territory, the allied commanders agreed "that only the military could restore order, peace and security."[8] To accomplish this "a centralized government was created" and "endowed with absolute power."[9] To avoid the "disagreeable wrangles that would interrupt the smooth running of affairs," civilians would be excluded from the executive body of the government, which would be composed of "officers from each of the powers."[10]

This body was eventually made of representatives of "each of the allied powers that participated in the 1900 campaign."[11] The powers added or withdrew members and the governing council usually consisted of six members. The council, and through it, the TPG itself, was not an autonomous body. It was a creature of the allied commanders-in-chief and they suppressed any attempt to claim independent status.[12] Council members were regarded as equals, and as representatives of their respective military commanders given freedom from diplomatic interference.

The council was given broad executive power. It could make and promulgate rules and regulations on those matters "of interest to the provisional Government." Its authority over the Chinese was absolute; it could tax, confiscate, and sell property as well as police and administer justice. It had no authority over foreigners, civilian or military. In fact, all foreigners arrested on any charges by TPG authorities had to be turned over to the "appropriate military or consular authority" with the complete "record of interrogation . . . within twenty-four hours."[13]

At first, the TPG's administrative boundaries were narrow, consisting of "the city of Tientsin and the surrounding territory within the limits of the mud wall" except for the foreign concessions and those places occupied by foreign troops. Thus, its jurisdiction was limited to those business and residential areas occupied by the Chinese. After several months, the TPG's operational zone was expanded to give it jurisdiction over enough territory to assure the safety of communications with the outside world and the city's food supply. This meant the TPG's jurisdiction extended "16 kilometers on either side of the river" from the Gulf of Beizhili to a line "about 25 kilometers to the west and northwest" of the city.[14] These jurisdictional boundaries mirrored those of the Chinese xian administration.[15]

This jurisdictional expansion gave the TPG increased responsibilities for policing rural areas as well as for the extirpation of river piracy and banditry. Its overall tasks had not changed. It was still responsible for reestablishing and maintaining public law and order by securing supplies for famine relief and "finding, pursuing, arresting or otherwise dispersing bands of robbers, looters, rebels or other miscreants."[16] To this end, it could "build and maintain necessary public works, maintain river and canal communications" to ensure free passage of goods between the city and the sea and "survey the environs of Tianjin and see to their improvement."[17] It was also responsible for providing the occupation troops with a labor force, draft animals, and transportation as well as inventorying and safeguarding abandoned Chinese property and enforcing public health measures to guard against the spread of epidemic disease.[18] It was also empowered to "take whatever measures" were "necessary to mobilize the population to undertake"[19] these goals.

The TPG council was the executive body of the organization that supervised the work of the various departments. According to Morse,[20] it met three times a week, but everyday operations were carried out by its department heads. There were seven departments: 1) the General Chancellery; 2) Police and Fire Department; 3) Board of Health, which was also responsible for public works and social welfare; 4) Treasury; 5) Custodian of Abandoned Property; 6) Judicial; and 7) Military. Each of the six council members was responsible for overseeing the operations of one of the departments—the Military Department was a liaison office between the occupying forces and the TPG. Departmental functions were "defined by name only; as to details, they shall be bound by the special instructions of the council."[21] Each department was staffed according to need; both civilians and soldiers were used in the administration. The Russians claimed the right to oversee the General Chancellery office of the secretary general. The Chinese Secretariat, the office through which the TPG communicated with the Chinese under its jurisdiction, was supervised by the Japanese. The Police and Fire Department was supervised by the German member, Treasury by the British, Justice by the American (and after their withdrawal by the Italian), and the Board of Health by the French.[22]

The TPG's accomplishments may be listed under five headings: 1) finance; 2) public health; 3) public order; 4) public works; and 5) social welfare. The government's most pressing need was for money to fund its operations. It was initially funded by grants from the principal powers that were to be repaid from the revenues it would collect later. This debt was easily retired as the "growing appreciation of the advantages of systematic rule oiled the wheels of trade and progress."[23] In a less poetic vein, the TPG began to collect all of the taxes normally collected by the Chinese government and supplemented them with license fees for boats, vehicles, brothels, opium dens, and other places of entertainment. After its jurisdictional boundaries were increased, its tax base grew. It also received authority to collect customs duties and *lijin*. Before it began collecting these fees, the amount remitted to Beijing by the local authorities never exceeded 100,000 taels. By 1904, using TPG collection methods, revenue increased almost 1500 percent to 1,420,024 taels.[24]

The second most pressing problem the TPG faced was public health. The most immediate need was to clean up the city after a month-long siege and series of pitched battles. When the immediate disposal of corpses and debris was accomplished, the Public Health Department concentrated its energies on thoroughly cleaning the city and providing its inhabitants with adequate sewage and water supply arrangements as well as a campaign to control infectious and venereal disease.

The TPG found it almost impossible to organize and immediate clean up because "the hands needed to do the task were lost since all coolies were immediately requisitioned by the troops." Foreign troops were detailed to help with this job, but the problem was solved by making "the leaders of each ward" responsible for this project. Working under the supervision of the police and public health authorities, the local residents cleaned their neighborhoods "at their own expense." In the fall of 1900, the Public Health Department undertook a thorough cleaning of the city, draining cesspits and eliminating trash pits. Two thousand metric tons of garbage were collected and burned during this period.[25] While garbage was collected and burned, plans were made and carried out to construct adequate water supply and sewage disposal systems for the city. The former system brought clean, filtered water into the city at a nominal user cost. The latter proved more difficult to construct because of drainage problems, but was completed after the TPG's tenure following the plans it drew up. Both systems served the city and the foreign concessions.[26]

The Public Health Department also worked to contain the spread of smallpox, cholera, plague, and venereal disease. Smallpox was relatively easy to contain through a program of free public vaccination. Plague and cholera were controlled by quarantine camps and public hospitals. The TPG's major problem was that it could not fully prevent infected people from entering Tianjin. To combat these diseases, the Health Department revitalized a Chinese benevolent society to support these hospitals; eleven were founded. Although their sanitary and medical regulations were established with foreign advice and assistance, this project was supported, organized, and managed by the Chinese.[27] Venereal disease was also a major public health problem, albeit one that primarily concerned the foreign occupation troops. The generals "demanded that appropriate measures be taken to protect the troops." The TPG eventually established licensed brothels, operated by its own licensees and inspected by its own public health doctors.[28]

Thus far, the sources I have uncovered offer neither information nor guidance regarding the mechanics of the TPG's police and judicial powers. Nevertheless, it is possible to discuss briefly the dimensions of police power. It is apparent that the first TPG police were foreign troops aided by Chinese auxiliaries, who became the backbone of this force. A foreign correspondent reported, "They did excellent work and became a smart, serviceable set of men."[29]

In common with other police forces, its first priority was the maintenance of public security and order by suppressing banditry, secret societies, Boxer remnants, and river piracy. The police operated through a network of informants and through Chinese officials using Article 10 of the Boxer Protocol as a means of forcing foreign cooperation.[30] Chinese officials were less than enthusiastic in their cooperation. However, consultation gave the TPG the excuse to "confiscate whatever real property" suspected criminals left behind and "this proved to be a sufficient deterrent." Law and order was rapidly restored to the city and the surrounding district. This was attributed to the "constant activity and presence of the police" as well as the end of organized resistance after Beijing was captured. As it became apparent that the TPG police was effective, "villages were rapidly repopulated, business conditions improved and fields were cultivated." In fact, the police were "efficient enough that the German and Japanese consuls, on separate occasions, asked the TPG to assign its police to patrol their concessions." Restoration and maintenance of public order were not the only functions of the police force. It was also responsible for enforcing the TPG's sanitary regulations, naming all streets and numbering all buildings, controlling vehicular pedestrian traffic, surveying locations for electric streetlights, and undertaking "the preparatory work for a census" of the city and the surrounding district. Its work was evidently a success because the Chinese attempted to hire the foreign officers after the retrocession and accepted the Chinese rank and file into the new Tianjin police department.[31]

Physical construction, that is, public works, was the TPG's most enduring legacy. Although I have not been able to uncover statistical evidence that would show the speed and extent of the reconstruction, it undertook several projects that benefited Tianjin.[32] Its first major public works project demolished the city's wall and the fortifications and arsenals that lay in its jurisdictional area. This demolition and the fires that destroyed approximately two-thirds of the city made it possible for the TPG to impose some kind of order on the broad, open spaces that became available for rebuilding. Chinese property owners were forced to abide by a rudimentary building and zoning code: "Property owners were required to construct houses, stores and workshops in block-like checkerboard patterns, leaving space for wide avenues and sidewalks, so the buildings would stand apart from each other."[33]

Tianjin's major streets were also widened. Major arterial roads were laid out with an engineer's logic—in straight lines "and the particular interests of merchants and property owners were not taken into account." Streets and sidewalks were widened and storefronts pushed back.[34] The owners of all property "intruding on the trace, were summarily ejected, but were fully compensated either in money or by land elsewhere."[35] The new roads "turned the town into a city; stylish and airy yet proper, with easy communications" between its various parts.[36]

The new construction served several purposes. The rebuilt houses and the destroyed walls allowed the city "to breathe easier." The wide boulevards eased traffic problems, embellished Tianjin, and made future insurrections on the 1900 model easier for foreign troops to suppress. The TPG also supervised the beginnings to the construction of an electric street lighting system and an electric streetcar system. The latter would circle the city's perimeter and connect to a line running through the foreign concessions. It would also run on Tianjin's major thoroughfares. Work was not started on the system until the city had been returned to Chinese jurisdiction and was completed within eighteen months, between March 1904 and September 1905. Bridges were also built linking the Chinese city and the foreign concessions on the western side of the river with the concessions and the railroad station on the river's east bank. There were two boat bridges, one east and one north of Tianjin, linking the two banks of the river.[37] The TPG also decided to build a third bridge, an iron swing bridge that would not interfere with river traffic.[38] There was more physical construction in both the city and the foreign concessions. Unfortunately, we have no records of what was built and when it was built. However, given the amount of physical damage sustained in both the city and the concessions, as well as the latter's expansion, the amount of building must have been considerable.

A serious, immediate problem the TPG faced was feeding the city's population in the aftermath of the siege and battles. Tianjin was a smoldering ruin, the surrounding countryside was either devastated or deserted; all normal trade had come to a halt. One of the TPG's first acts was to commandeer all private food stocks and requisition tribute rice stored by the China Merchants Steam Navigation Company.[39] The city's inhabitants were saved from immediate starvation and fed through the winter.

Tied to this problem were the issues of food relief distribution and work relief. Traditionally, food for the poor had been distributed by charitable societies underwritten by rich Chinese. These organizations were closely supervised by and acted as surrogates for the local administration. The TPG wished to avoid relying on the local administrative apparatus. At the same time, Protestant missionary societies were trying to control local food distribution and use it to gain new converts. The TPG acted to bring all food relief under its jurisdiction. It made all private relief groups its agents and used the police to supervise food relief distribution. This was a temporary solution; a more permanent one was linked to planned almshouses and work relief. The solution focused on eliminating street begging and providing the poor with jobs. Tianjin had always made provision for poor relief. However, the Boxer Uprising destroyed the endowments and the buildings and the charitable foundations. The Public Health Department was placed in charge and established a poor relief program that concentrated on turning almshouses into "homes, pure and simple," and providing the inhabitants with work. They either joined a corps of public health coolies or workshops in the asylums. Former beggars and bandits were given work and were able to support themselves while reimbursing the asylum. "We were able to harness desperation and put it to good use." The Chinese government continued this program after it returned to the city.[40] These projects cast an interesting light on the goals of the men who ran the TPG. Although one is tantalized by these hints of a social welfare program, there is a sense that its origins may be found in the general air of progressive reform in the Atlantic world as well as in the colonial civilizing enterprise.[41]

The TPG was born in trying political circumstances and existed for twenty-five months in an uncertain and difficult environment. It had to balance a set of contradictory issues against each other; the particularistic and often contradictory and acrimonious interests of the foreign powers, while balancing the often conflicting goals of foreigners and Chinese against each other and against the powers. It also faced the systematic, covert opposition of the Chinese government, which actively advocated its abolition. Despite this chaotic environment, the TPG survived and changed the physical geography of the city.

It had frequent differences of opinion with the missionaries in Tianjin. The most acrimonious clash was over control of famine relief. The missionaries, like the Red Cross, were accused "of using famine relief to extend their own influence," of making it "a closed purse," not wishing to ameliorate the sufferings of the poor. Protestant missionaries were said to "assume that Protestant employees of the TPG must do their bidding." The missionaries were called "intolerant" because of their frequent demands that the TPG destroy "mosques and Chinese temples" in the area under its jurisdiction. They were also seen as being "out of control" in demanding excessive reparations.[42] This opinion was echoed by the diplomats who complained of excessive missionary damage claims and of the indiscriminate support they received back home and who urged that consular officials on the scene be given more discretion.[43]

Nevertheless, it was the Chinese government and its officials that provided the most determined opposition to the TPG. It was "their self-esteem, personal interests as well as their purses [that] were damaged when Tianjin was under foreign occupation." First, they attempted to discredit it with the local population, then registered false complaints against it with the consular body and the allied commanders, tried to use missionary opposition to further their own ends and finally attempted to act as liaison between it and the Chinese people. They were unsuccessful in every attempt.[44]

The most telling criticism of the provisional government was that "it failed entirely in the first principle of good administration that the work should be done through the Chinese themselves."[45] Chinese officials were not permitted "to open an office in the city, even if they could set foot in it with safety."[46] We know very little of how the ordinary Chinese reacted to the TPG. I have not yet discovered any Chinese account of its operations. The leading English language newspaper in Tianjin reported that a Chinese newspaper wrote, "Anti-foreign spirit is very strong in Tientsin."[47] It also reported "rather vicious placards have been the order of the day . . . prophesying that when the Chinese officials return to Power, all who have been connected with the Provisional Government, foreign or Chinese, will be 'flayed alive' and similar amiable suggestions."[48]

Given these incidents and problems, could the rule of the TPG be called a success? Arthur Smith stated that "within a certain radius" its successes "were many."[49] It did change Tianjin's physical appearance. The sewage system was transformed and a public health department was created to combat infectious and epidemic diseases. A modern water supply system, bringing filtered, potable water to the city was also created. The city and its surrounding district were well policed and a modern street lighting and urban transportation system was begun. There was also a "fixed system of taxation and the freedom of the Civil Court of the Judicial Department, where citizens could have their disputes adjudicated without submitting to delays." A public library was established, "containing the best Chinese works, together with magazines and periodicals of all kinds and books in other tongues for those who could enjoy them."[50]

Charles Denby called "its acts beyond all praise." However, despite its enlightenment, he admitted its rule was "an iron military rule."[51] It achieved success because it rested on undeniable military power. In a little more than two years it transformed the city, realizing reforms and changes that in normal times would have been met with determined opposition. It changed Tianjin; its rule had many good results. The wonder of it all was that all of its good works were accomplished under anomalous conditions. It had no independent power but was fortunate that neither the generals nor the consuls nor the ministers in Beijing took much interest in the way Tianjin was governed or in its internal improvements. Another explanation for its successes was that its staff was, in large part, men who shared a common profession, with similar values, customs, practices, and outlooks, even though they were of different nationalities. A contemporary wrote, "Tianjin's population was grateful to it for all the good it had done; its good name will live in history."[52]

Nevertheless, this was Captain Condamy's opinion. The picture of the TPG's activities has been based on material written by men who were unabashed imperialists. The TPG must have looked quite different from the Chinese side. It could be arbitrary, capricious, and dictatorial, taking no heed of the wishes or desires of the Chinese inhabitants of Tianjin and the surrounding countryside. It did what it did, not because it had any love or affection for them, but because these measures were good for their general health and well-being and were going to be accomplished regardless of local wishes. The reforms, especially the physical construction, must have caused much inconvenience and no little hardship to some of Tianjin's citizens. Even those measures that were indisputably beneficial, like a modern water supply system, the TPG bestowed on Tianjin and its people with an altruism that seemed to be liberally laced with contempt. However, the TPG posed no threat to the established social and political order. It resolutely opposed the excessive reparations and indemnity claims of Christian missionaries and their converts. From the point of view of the local elites and the common people, those who collaborated with it, the TPG may have appeared similar to the local magistrate. Like him, its first concern was maintaining law and public order and administering justice. It also collected taxes and attended to the social welfare needs of the community, working with local collaborators.

The Boxer Rebellion and the allied occupation of Tianjin dramatically changed the city. After the TPG's tenure, things could never be the same. The maps in the 1842 *Jinmen baojia tushuo* present a particular view of the city and its suburbs, giving the reader a visual orientation for the xian while the text provides a bureaucratic picture of the population. The events of the rest of the nineteenth century did little to upset Tianjin's socioeconomic equilibrium. Tianjin suffered more physical damage than any other large city in north China in the Boxer Rebellion. The siege and battles devastated the surrounding countryside and leveled large portions of the walled city and the foreign concessions. At its finish, many doubted Tianjin would be rebuilt.

The TPG controlled the city for twenty-five months and physically transformed it, building a sewage system and a water supply system that provided potable drinking water for the inhabitants. It also created a unified municipal police and fire departments, a public health department, a plethora of straightened, widened, paved, and named streets with numbered houses facing them, a new system of poor relief, and provided relatively honest tax collection and a rudimentary zoning code. It demolished the city's wall and other fortifications in the area and began to straighten and deepen the Haiho between Tianjin and the sea.[53] At the same time, foreign powers added to the existing concessions and created new ones by annexing large tracts of land outside the former city wall.

The traditional orientation of the walled city and its suburbs was destroyed and the *Jinmen baojia tushuo* maps made obsolete and irrelevant. There was no way to locate oneself in the walled city and its suburbs because they had disappeared, the wall replaced by a wide perimeter boulevard, the suburbs by new foreign concessions. Tianjin was physically transformed. After 1902, there was no clear demarcation line between the

Chinese and the foreign cities. The only way to mark one's passing from the Chinese city to the foreign concessions or from one concession to another was a change in architectural style. Urban services were similar in both cities and the transportation network bound them together.

NOTES

This paper is based on the fifth chapter of the author's PhD dissertation, "A History of Tientsin in Early Modern Times, 1800–1911" (PhD diss., University of Kansas, 1988).

1. The last time it was mentioned in an English language book was by Otto D. Rasmussen, *Tientsin: An Illustrated Outline History* (Tianjin: Tientsin Press, 1927). Aside from the author's dissertation chapter, the only extended discussion is Mori Etsuko, "Tenshin toto gamon ni tsuite" (On the Tianjin Provisional Government), *Toyoshi Kenkyu* 47, no. 2 (September 1988): 86–115. Recent work about Yuan includes Jerome Ch'en, *Yuan Shih-k'ai* (2nd ed., Stanford: Stanford University Press, 1972); Ernest P. Young, *The Presidency of Yuan Shih-k'ai: Liberalism and Dictatorship in Early Republican China* (Ann Arbor: University of Michigan Press, 1977); and Stephen R. MacKinnon, *Power and Politics in Late Imperial China: Yuan Shikai in Beijing and Tianjin, 1901–1908* (Ann Arbor: University of Michigan Press, 1980). Recent work about Tianjin includes Kenneth G. Lieberthal, *Revolution and Tradition in Tientsin, 1949–1952* (Stanford: Stanford University Press, 1980); Gail Hershatter, *The Workers of Tianjin, 1900–1950* (Stanford: Stanford University Press, 1986); and Kwan Man Bun, *The Salt Merchants of Tianjin: State-Making and Civil Society in Late Imperial China* (Honolulu: University of Hawaii Press, 2001). Other recent works include Wang Jiajian, *Qingmo minchu woguo jingcha zhidu xiandaihua de licheng (1901–1928)* (The progress and modernization of Chinese police organization in the late Qing and early Republican eras, 1901–1928) (Taibei: Commercial Press, 1984); Roger A. Thompson, *China's Local Councils in the Age of Constitutional Reform, 1898–1911* (Cambridge: Harvard University Press, 1995); Zhang Xiaobo, "Merchant Associational Activism in Early Twentieth Century China: The Tianjin General Chamber of Commerce, 1904–1928" (PhD diss., Columbia University, 1995); Ruth Rogaski, *Hygienic Modernity: Meanings of Health and Disease in Treaty-Port China* (Berkeley: University of California Press, 2004); Brett Sheehan, *Trust in Troubled Times: Money, Banking and State-Society Relations in Republican Tianjin, 1916–1937* (Cambridge: Harvard University Press, 2003).

2. Representative examples include Song Yunpu, ed., *Tianjin zhilue* (A brief account of Tianjin) (Tianjin, 1931, reprint ed., Taibei: Chengwen chubanshe, 1969); and Tianjin congkan bianji weiyuanhui, ed., *Tianjin shi zhengfu* (The government of the City of Tianjin) (Tianjin: Tianjin shi zhengfu mishichu bianyi shi, 1948). General works include Liu Nai-chen (Liu Naizhen), "Reform of Chinese City Government based on European Experience" (PhD diss., 2 vols., University of London, 1930); Pan Rushu, "Zuijin ershinian zhi Zhongguo shizheng," (Municipal administration in China during the last twenty years), *Qinghua zhoukan* 35, nos. 8/9 (2 May

1931): 128–69 and 35, no. 10 (12 May 1931): 98–125; Chang Yu-sing (Zhang Youxin), *L'autonomie local en China* (Nancy: impr. de Grandville, 1934); Loo Kou-tung (Li Gantong), *La vie municipal et l'urbanisme en Chine* (Lyon, 1934); Chen Kyi-ts'ung (Chen Jizhen), *Le systeme municipal en Chine* (Gembloux, Belgium: Duculot, 1937); Henry Leonidas Wen, (Wen Lingxiong), "Comparative Study of Municipal Structure and Activities in the United States and China" (PhD diss., Indiana University, 1942); Frank Y. C. Yee, "Police in Modern China" (PhD diss., University of California, Berkeley, 1942); and Li Zonghuang, *Zhongguo difang zizhi conglun* (A complete account of local self-government in China) (Taibei: Zhongguo difang zizhi xuehui, 1954).

3. Michael H. Hunt, "The Forgotten Occupation: Peking, 1900–1901," *Pacific Historical Review* 45 (1979): 501–29. One of his main sources, the papers of the American China Relief Expedition held by the National Archives and Records Administration of the United States in Record Group 395 (Records of the United States Army, Overseas Operations and Commands, 1898–1942) in files 896–973, offers tantalizing partial glimpses of the TPG. However, the American commander, General Chaffee, took little interest in the activities in Tianjin.

4. Hosea Ballou Morse, *The International Relations of the Chinese Empire, Vol. 3: The Period of Subjection, 1894–1911* (London: Longmans, 1918), 291–300, 357, 364–65.

5. The quotation is from Morse, *International Relations of the Chinese Empire*, 493. Professor S. A. M. Adshead, in a personal communication received in 1995, informed me that a copy of this document exists in the Harvard University Library system, while Professor Ruth Rogaski wrote that a Chinese translation of the document is located at the Tianjin Academy of Social Sciences.

6. Capitaine Condamy, "Histoire du Gouvernement provisoire de Tien-tsin (1900–1902) par le Capitaine Condamy," *Revue des Troupes colonial* 1 (1905): 168–80, 248–64, 414–41, 507–29; 2 (1905): 17–45, 164–85.

7. Rasmussen, *Tientsin*, 225.

8. Condamy, "Histoire du Gouvernement provisoire," 1 (1905): 171.

9. Charles Denby Jr., "The Capture and Government of Tientsin," in Charles Denby Jr., *China and Her People* (2 vols., Boston: L.C. Page & Co., 1906), 2: 204.

10. Condamy, "Histoire du Gouvernement provisoire," 1 (1905): 172.

11. "La ville actuelle de Tien-tsin et l'Oeuvre de Gouvernement militaire provisoire," *A travers du monde* 10 (1904): 366.

12. Morse, *International Relations of the Chinese Empire*, 294.

13. Condamy, "Histoire du Gouvernement provisoire," 1 (1905): 174–75.

14. Condamy, "Histoire du Gouvernement provisoire," 1 (1905): 173–75; Rasmussen, *Tientsin*, 223.

15. See *Jinmen baojia tushuo* (Explanation of the Tianjin household register map) (Tianjin, 1842), passim. A picture of the city itself is presented in *juan* 12 while the first eleven deal with the administrative geography of the entire prefecture. Another useful source is Wu Huayuan, et al., comps., *Xu Tianjin xianzhi* (Renewed gazetteer of Tianjin county) (Tianjin, 1870), 1: 1–3b; as well as Wu Tinghua and Cheng Feng-wen, comps., *Tianjin fuzhi* (Tianjin prefecture gazetteer) (Tianjin, 1739, reprint ed., Taibei, 1971), 1: 1–8a. See also Zhang Tao, *Jinmen zaji* (Notes on Tianjin) (Tianjin, 1884; reprint ed., Taibei: Wenhai chubanshe, 1969); and Zhao Zhencheng, *Qingdai*

dili yenko biao (Successive geographic changes of the Qing period) (Beijing: Zhonghua shuju, 1955), 5 and the chart in chapter 1.

16. Condamy, "Histoire du Gouvernement provisoire," 1 (1905): 178.

17. Condamy, "Histoire du Gouvernement provisoire," 1 (1905): 254.

18. Rasmussen, *Tientsin*, 221; Condamy, "Histoire du Gouvernement provisoire," 1 (1905): 174.

19. Condamy, "Histoire du Gouvernement provisoire," 2 (1905): 255.

20. Morse, *International Relations of the Chinese Empire*, 293.

21. Rasmussen, *Tientsin*, 222–23; Condamy, "Histoire du Gouvernement provisoire," 1 (1905): 176–77.

22. Morse, *International Relations of the Chinese Empire*, 292–293; Condamy, "Histoire du Gouvernement provisoire," 1 (1905): 176.

23. Rasmussen, *Tientsin*, 225.

24. Morse, *International Relations of the Chinese Empire*, 294–95.

25. Condamy, "Histoire du Gouvernement provisoire," 2 (1905): 25, 27.

26. Rasmussen, *Tientsin*, 227; Condamy, "Histoire du Gouvernement provisoire," 2 (1905): 28–29, 167–68.

27. Condamy, "Histoire du Gouvernement provisoire," 2 (1905): 32–38, especially 37–38.

28. Condamy, "Histoire du Gouvernement provisoire," 2 (1905): 30–31.

29. Harry Crauford Thomson, *China and the Powers: A Narrative of the Outbreak of 1900* (London: Longmans, Green, and Co., 1902), 82.

30. U.S. Congress, House of Representatives, 57th Congress, 1st Session, *Papers Relating to the Foreign Relations of the United States, with the Annual Message of the President, Transmitted to Congress, December 3, 1901*, "Appendix: Affairs in China: Report of William Rockhill, Late Commissioner to China, with Accompanying Documents" (Washington, D.C., 1902) [hereafter "Report of William Rockhill"], 316–17, 331–33.

31. Condamy, "Histoire du Gouvernement provisoire," 2 (1905): 21, 22.

32. In particular, Sabatier wrote of the construction of the French Army Engineers in Tianjin and lists a phenomenal amount of building, see Aubin Sabatier, *La Génie en Chine: Period d'Occupation, 1901–1906* (Nancy: Berger-Levrault & cie., 1910), 23–28, 40–44, and 105–8.

33. Condamy, "Histoire du Gouvernement provisoire," 2 (1905): 24.

34. Condamy, "Histoire du Gouvernement provisoire," 2 (1905): 167.

35. Morse, *International Relations of the Chinese Empire*, 296.

36. Condamy, "Histoire du Gouvernement provisoire," 2 (1905): 187.

37. In the eighteenth and nineteenth centuries there were four boat bridges, two on the north side of the city and two on its eastern side. There were also numerous ferries crossing the river to supplement the bridges. For further information on these bridges, see Wu Huayuan, et al., *Xu Tianjin xianzhi*, 25: 9–10b and Wu Tinghua and Cheng Fengwen, *Tianjin fuzhi*, 3: 2–8b.

38. Condamy, "Histoire du Gouvernement provisoire," 2 (1905): 171–73, Morse, *International Relations of the Chinese Empire*, 296.

39. Morse, *International Relations of the Chinese Empire*, 295; *Peking and Tientsin Times*, 29 September 1900, 83.

40. Condamy, "Histoire du Gouvernement provisoire," 2 (1905): 40–45.

41. For the Atlantic world see Daniel T. Rodgers, *Atlantic Crossings: Politics in a Progressive Age* (Cambridge: Belknap Press, 1998), especially chapters titled "The Self-Owned City," "Civic Ambitions," and "City Planning in Justice to the Working Population," 112–208. A foreign-drawn picture of Tianjin just before the Boxers may be found in Pierre Bure, "Tientsin," *Bulletin de la Société Royale belge de geographie* 23 (1899): 232–68, 24 (1900): 312–39. For a similar glimpse of Seoul and Japanese colonialism in Korea, see Todd A. Henry, "Sanitizing Empire: Japanese Articulations of Korean Otherness and the Construction of Early Colonial Seoul, 1905–1919," *The Journal of Asian Studies* 64, no. 3 (August 2005): 639–75.

42. Condamy, "Histoire du Gouvernement provisoire," 1 (1905): 259–60.

43. Ernest Satow believed that missionary and merchant reparation claims would have to be reduced by 25 percent before they could be considered reasonable. Satow Papers, Papers of Sir Ernest Mason Satow (Kew: The National Archives, PRO 30/33), Satow to Lansdowne, 1/30/01, PRO 30/33/14/1. Several months later, Lansdowne agreed with Satow's observation that the missionaries received too much "indiscriminate" support and that the consuls should be give greater freedom of action. Lansdowne to Satow, 4/09/01, PRO 30/33/14/1. The issue of missionary claims and looting is also examined in Marilyn B. Young, *The Rhetoric of Empire: American China Policy, 1895–1901* (Cambridge: Harvard University Press, 1968), 191–95 and Stuart Creighton Miller, "Ends and Means: Missionary Justification of Force in Nineteenth Century China," in John K. Fairbank (ed.), *The Missionary Enterprise in China and America* (Cambridge: Harvard University Press, 1974), 274–80. More specific discussions of looting may be found in the chapters in this volume by James L. Hevia and Ben Middleton.

44. Condamy, "Histoire du Gouvernement provisoire," 1 (1905): 260–62.

45. Arthur H. Smith, *China in Convulsion* (New York: Fleming H. Revell Company, 1901), 585.

46. *Peking and Tientsin Times*, 23 March 1901, 182.

47. *Peking and Tientsin Times*, 19 January 1901, 146.

48. *Peking and Tientsin Times*, 2 February 1901, 155.

49. Smith, *China in Convulsion*, 585.

50. Rasmussen, *Tientsin*, 225–26.

51. Denby, "The Capture and Government of Tientsin," 2, 205.

52. Condamy, "Histoire du Gouvernement provisoire," 2 (1905): 184.

53. The river straightening project was undertaken by a joint Sino-foreign board, the Haiho Conservancy. A representative of the TPG sat on the board in place of the Chinese governmental representative from the Tianjin administration. Begun in 1898, this was a project to deepen and straighten the river channel between Tianjin and the sea. The war destroyed all the work that had been accomplished. Part of the project was to cut a passage through the Dagu Bar. Material on the Haiho Conservancy may be found in "Report of William Rockhill", 257–78, Morse, *International Relations of the Chinese Empire*, 297–98, 380, Rasmussen, *Tientsin*, 238–40, Herbert Chatley, "The Port of Tientsin: The Shipping Center of North China," Dock and *Harbour Authority* 20, no. 234 (April 1940): 129–34, and Margaret A. Hitch, "The Port of Tientsin" (master's thesis, University of Chicago, 1924), and Margaret A. Hitch, "The Port of Tientsin and Its Problems," *Geographical Review* 25 (1935): 367–81.

8

The Boxer Uprising and India

Globalizing Myths

C. A. Bayly

This paper examines some international reactions to the Boxer Uprising. It focuses on the ideologies of imperialism and nationalism, especially within India and the wider British empire, as they were expressed during the years around 1900. Paul Cohen remarks of the Boxer Uprising that it stirred immediate international interest and engagement in a way that the Taiping Rebellion before it had not done. I hope to demonstrate that the process of mythmaking about the Boxers in the international arena occurred almost simultaneously with the events themselves, both in official discourse and the public sphere. The interpretation of the Chinese crisis, however, remained quite ambiguous for both British and Indian opinion within India.

I turn first to India toward the end of the year 1900. The subcontinent was then in the determined grip of the conservative viceroy and former Foreign Office China expert, George Nathaniel Curzon. Lord Curzon was an imperial revivalist. Like his contemporaries Lord Cromer in Egypt and Lord Milner in South Africa, he was attempting morally to rearm the British empire against the industrial and diplomatic threats of the German empire, a restive France, and a newly assertive United States. He hoped to assist the Indian National Congress to its grave and participated energetically in the suppression of the Transvaal and Orange Free State. Among Indians, Curzon remained temporarily popular because his first attempts at imperial self-strengthening were directed against the British Indian Army and the racism of British expatriates. Yet already India itself was suffering a degree of low-level social turbulence that was in some ways comparable with contemporary events in China.

In 1899 there had been sporadic revolts among forest tribes in central and western India.[1] During 1900 the failure of rainfall over much of the western sector of the country resulted in a severe famine in Gujarat and Maharashtra. This climatic conjuncture seems to have been connected with the contemporary drought in China and it raised the level of popular dissidence in both regions. Vernacular circular letters, predicting the coming of the millennium and the imminent end of British rule, were implicated with peasant revolt in Gujarat during 1899 and 1900.[2] Bubonic plague had also been rife in northern and western India since 1896. Attempts to control it had precipitated conflict between frightened European residents and Indians in major commercial cities.[3] There was a full-scale riot in the northern industrial city of Kanpur where "wild rumours" circulated that patients were being killed in plague camps.[4] Rigorous quarantine measures had alienated conservative Indians who found their homes invaded by medical officers and their servants confined to large detention camps.

Hostility to the government had already fanned a campaign of terrorism among young people that the government blamed on radical nationalists such as Bal Gangadhar Tilak. A powerful strand of violent Hindu revivalism, centered on devotion to the popular elephant-headed god, Ganpati, permeated Tilak's movement. Within four years, Curzon was himself facing a sustained campaign of terrorism and noncooperation in Bengal. This *swadeshi*, or nativistic, movement wove together popular religiosity and national self-assertion in a manner distantly comparable with the events of the Boxer Uprising.

By 1900 this alienation of the Indian middle class from British government and once-admired Western modes of thought was already palpable. During the course of the year 1900, Rabindranath Tagore, the great Bengali poet and first Asian Nobel laureate, was becoming darker in mood. Tiring of the life of a rich *zamindar* or landholder and approaching his fortieth year, he voiced increasing disenchantment with the West and its soulless exploitation of Asia. He wrote to the scientist Jagadishchandra Bose, sarcastically comparing the weakness and lack of determination of Bengalis with the cruel efficiency of Lord Roberts, commander in chief of the British Indian Army.[5] Roberts was currently mounting a punitive expedition against the Boers at the height of the South African War. On 31 December 1900 Tagore completed a Bengali poem, the "Sunset of the Century." He wrote, "The century's sun has set in blooded clouds./There rings in the carnival of violence/from weapon to weapon, the mad music of death."[6]

Tagore had in mind the suppression of the Boxer Uprising as well as the conflict in South Africa. In both of these short and bloody colonial wars, Indian troops of the so-called martial races were taking part. Tagore's poem ended, "Abandoning shame and honour/in the name of nationalism, with heinous injustice./They wish to sweep away *dharma* [ethics, or right conduct] in the wash of violence./Gangs of poets shriek rousing terror./The fighting song of tussling dogs on the burning ghat." This image of the imperial poet laureate, Rudyard Kipling, as a mangy pariah dog, chewing at the half-burned limbs of corpses on the burning ground, is arresting, to say the least.

Tagore's own interest had been fixed on China for several years since the opium trade, lucrative to Indians as well as the British, had become a point of controversy among the intelligentsia of Calcutta. Even most nationalists still saw the trade as a boon to India, but the spread of the opium habit among coolies in the tea estates of Assam to the north was forcing a re-assessment. A few months after he wrote his poem, Tagore favorably reviewed *Letters from John Chinaman*. This small book, published in London but immediately noticed in India, was purportedly written by a Chinese official and denounced British policy toward the Qing. "John Chinaman" contrasted the "cockpit of egotistical forces" of Western modernity with the golden mean of embattled Confucianism. He demanded to know how the British would react "if the Chinese had permanently occupied Liverpool, Bristol [and] Plymouth."[7] In fact, the letters had been written by Tagore's future acquaintance, the British radical poet Goldsworthy Lowes Dickinson. But it spoke to the resentful and reactive cultural nationalism which Tagore believed was boiling up within all Eastern peoples as the first sign of a new pan-Asian identity.

The Indian intelligentsia almost universally agreed with Tagore that the Europeans were themselves responsible for the Boxer Uprising. The *Maratha*, a Pune newspaper, connected with the radical Tilak, argued that the Boxers were a "patriotic movement incensed by the audacious inroads of foreigners" into China.[8] A Madras editor asserted, "It is not a government now but a people aroused to patriotism by the aggressions of foreigners."[9] Almost universally too, English-language and vernacular papers blamed European missionaries "who ridicule the religion of the Chinese and offend them in many ways."[10] This was a period when missionary societies had redoubled their activities in India and the resentment stirred up by their appearance in the bazaars and villages was a potent cause of the rise of Hindu revivalist organizations. The *Maratha* editor cleverly turned this mood against the British by quoting Curzon's own earlier book, *Problems of the Far East*, which was distinctly hostile to missionaries. The viceroy had denounced the employment of unmarried Chinese girls in proselytization.[11] The celebrated Oxford Sanskritist Friedrich Max Müller also blamed the missionaries for the uprising[12] and was quoted with approval by the Indian press. Another publication made the Indian analogy explicit, saying that China was now in a similar situation to India in the eighteenth century, "when . . . owing to anarchy . . . it became prey to foreigners."[13]

Yet the Indian press also set these events in an international framework and this was testament to the recent expansion of the telegraph and to the cheap access which Indian editors now had to news through popular British publications such as W. H. Stead's *Review of Reviews*. India had recently been transfixed by the South African War and generally took some pleasure in the humiliation of British forces by "40,000 Boer farmers." One newspaper drew the obvious conclusion that the Boxer Uprising was "probably due to Boer instigation."[14] The successes of the Boers were certainly known in China. Another quoted an interview by a Boer general in a Cairo newspaper in which the Boer welcomed the Boxer Uprising as an aid to the independence of his own country.[15] This last example is interesting because it shows the Indian intelligentsia were making direct connections with nationalist leaders and other spokesmen of non-European societies. The *Maratha*, for instance, printed an interview on the crisis with Li Hongzhang, which had originally appeared in the *North-China Herald*.[16] Citing the *Review of Reviews*, the newspaper seemed to take comfort from the fact that the British empire was "overstretched" across the world, with forces recently victorious in the Sudan, embattled in southern Africa, and now engaged in China.[17]

It should also be said, however, that conduct of the Boxers themselves summoned up varying degrees of ambivalence among Indian editors, their correspondents, and their readership. Suppressed Indian patriotism broke forth, of course, with one newspaper declaring that "as soon as the Indian Army was landed in China, the Tatar and Chinese forces retreated."[18] More significantly, some Muslim journals with close links to the Arabic newspapers of Cairo republished the order of the Ottoman Khalifa to the Chinese Muslims, urging them to refrain from supporting the Boxers.[19] Istanbul at this time was currying support in Germany and could not really afford a breach with any of the European powers. Much as Egyptian and Indian Muslims reacted with glee to the embarrassment of the British, many of them wanted to uphold the authority of the Khilafat. At the same time, they were inclined to regard the Boxers as idolatrous fanatics. This view also surfaced in the Hindu press. The *Kerala Samachar* declared that the Boxers were "a danger to civilisation,"[20] not least because they would give an excuse to the powers to partition China. This theme of civilization and barbarity became more prominent as the siege of the legations wore on. Li Hongzhang's view that the Boxers were "ignorant fanatics" caused a sobering reassessment, as did the murder of Japanese diplomatic personnel by the rebels. To many Indians, "only Japan has the zeal and power necessary to preserve the ancient civilisations of the east and may Japan succeed."[21] Indian nationalists toyed with themes of sacrifice and invoked antique martial heroes and the blood-drinking goddess Kali in their own anticolonial mythology. But true manifestations of martial popular religiosity frightened them considerably because they threatened both subaltern insurrection and pollution. For instance, the Kerala newspaper's fear of fanatical religiosity has to be seen in the context of continuing outbreaks of "little-tradition" Muslim violence in the region. These so-called Moplah (*Mappila*) uprisings centered around martial arts institutions and targeted wealthy Hindus as well as Christians. The parallel with the Boxers must have been fairly clear to the Kerala intelligentsia.

One point to bear in mind is that the most politically advanced Indian regions of 1900 were precisely those which had not participated in the Great Mutiny and Rebellion against the British from 1857 to 1859. Their citizens had been and remained frightened by the popular violence that it summoned up. Though the parallel was too dangerous to make openly, memories of the Mutiny still colored Indian views of the Boxer Uprising, especially in regard to the culpability of missionaries for both outbreaks. For the British, to whose reaction I now move, the parallel was immediately subject to open discussion. B. L. Putnam Weale's *Indiscreet Letters from Pekin*, published shortly after the relief of the legations, stated that the rebellion was already "as famous as the Indian Mutiny."[22] The events fitted into the mythical narrative pattern of the mutiny like a hand in a glove. In both cases, an ancient and effete dynasty of central Asian origin had fomented and then set itself at the head of an outbreak of popular "fanaticism." The murder of Europeans and Indian Christians by Nana Sahib in Kanpur in 1857 was paralleled by the murder of European priests and Chinese Christians at Beijing's Catholic cathedral in 1900. Once again, the martial races of India, loyal to the empire, had come to the rescue of heroic, besieged Europeans. Putnam Weale writes tellingly of the moment in Beijing in the late summer when a tumult below the ramparts seemed to signal a final Boxer attack: "With tremendous-heart beating. I looked over and it was the smell of India. Into the quadrangle and beyond hundreds of native troops were filing and piling arms."[23] They demanded *"pani, pani!,"* "water water!" of the exhausted defenders. Shortly afterward in 1904, G. H. Henty, the boys' adventure novelist, turned such eyewitness accounts into a story worthy of the still best-selling genre of mutiny novels. He published *With the Allies to Pekin*, a romance of the siege of the legations replete with oriental devilry and European heroism. The difference was that, forty years on, Britain could no longer do it alone. This may well have been the first time that the term "Allies" was used to refer to the principled white guardians of the "international order." It was a theme which was to recur throughout the twentieth century. It was first directed at the Hun, who ironically had made his first bow in the Kaiser's 1900 speech against the Boxers. Later the Turk, the Jap, and the Arab were brought to heel by "the Allies."

Yet as with the Indian observers the historical myths that bedded down the narrative of the Boxer Uprising were complemented with visions of a strenuous future. Many British commentators, haunted by millenarian fears at the end of one century and the beginning of the new, were making similar connections. The outbreak within a few years of Mahdist purism in the

Sudan (1895–1898), the Boxer Uprising (1900), Pan-Islamic organization in Egypt, Indian terrorism (1896–1899 and 1905), and more ambivalently, the martial resurgence of Japan (1904–1905) represented the return of the "dreadful irrationalism" of the East, only half submerged by a century of the Christian civilizing mission. It was ferocious indigenous resistance to American imperialism in the Philippines, of course, which caused Kipling himself to refer to Asians and Africans as "sullen captive races, half devil and half child." In a more scholarly vein, the British Indian scholar-official, Sir Alfred Lyall warned of "that unquiet spirit . . . which has been spreading over the Eastern continent particularly manifest in countries under European governments."[24] Lyall wrote these words in the introduction to *Indian Unrest*, a book by Valentine Chirol, deputy editor of the *Times*, who specialized in analyzing "fanatical" religious revolt among Asians and Middle Eastern Muslims.

What seems to be clear then is the interconnectedness—and indeed the intertextuality—of the pervasive sense among both the imperial elite and Asian subjects and semi-subjects that a new phase in the history of empire and indigenous resistance had been reached about 1900. This sense of change of pace provided the context for the historical arguments which activists and scholars produced over the next few years. The liberal J. A. Hobson argued that huge commercial conglomerates were corrupting the liberal constitution and dragging Britain into war in southern Africa and the Far East. The Chinese concessions were, he believed, "the crowning instance of irrational government."[25] Rosa Luxembourg believed that under-consumption by impoverished working people at home drove European powers and the United States to find markets for goods and services abroad. Lenin asserted that a new phase of capitalism had been reached as great financial combines redivided the resources of the world. The activities of French capital in Siberia, Manchuria, and Turkestan provided him with a spectacular example.

In the last half century, however, the idea of the "new imperialism" of the 1880s and 1890s has been marginalized by historians. Jürgen Osterhammel's expert treatment of British "informal empire" in China in the new *Oxford History of the British Empire* does not note any particular change in this era. The *Oxford History* as a whole has no chapter or discussion anywhere of what contemporaries and the first generation of theorists of imperialism regarded as its high point. The two most influential recent analyses of nineteenth-century imperialism explicitly reject the idea of the new imperialism. Ronald Robinson and John Gallagher saw an essential continuity in the official mind from 1800 to 1914. Peter Cain and Anthony Hopkins saw little change in what they called British "gentlemanly capitalism" between 1848 and 1948.

I think it may well be time to revive the idea of "the new imperialism." What characterized it was not perhaps the emergence of any novel diplomatic, ideological, or economic trend in itself. But what was striking was the interlinking of economic and diplomatic rivalries in China and elsewhere with an enormous explosion of information and what Thomas Richards calls "the redeployment of the stock of romanticism to secure the ends and aims of empire."[26] It was the sheer reach of the global desire of the denizens of the foreign offices, legations, editorial offices, and oriental societies of the years around 1900 that is so amazing. Telegraphic information and the regular printing and circulation of intelligence reports gave an immediacy to supposed foreign threats to security. In the case of Britain's Indian empire, a new intelligence bureau associated with the Quarter Master General's office in Simla collated information on Russian aims from the Balkans to north China. In 1894 to 1895 its data was brought together into a large geopolitical compendium: "Reports on Russian Advances in Asia." These reports and later consular dispatches from China, Afghanistan, Persia, and Central Asia establish a close linkage between national trade concessions, the diplomacy of loans to the Chinese government, the forward movement of national railway companies, and overall strategic security.[27] Lenin may have been incorrect in seeing the conscious machinations of a newly energized international capitalism behind this. Yet the complicity of government with big firms in all this is very clear.[28] War was good for business, too. One consequence of the British government's embarrassment during the revolt was the construction of a new seaborne extension to the telegraph line into China through Weihaiwei.[29]

Still more striking were the animal instincts and what one might call the geopolitical longings of Western commentators in all this. Of course, during the Boxer crisis itself, the British government displayed all its most endearing—and enduring—qualities of ineptitude. Salisbury only bothered to come to London two days a week, continuing to reiterate his mantra that in China, "We have no partition of territory in view. We only aim at a partition of preponderance."[30] Policy toward China vacillated from day to day. Curzon for his part was well aware that India could bear no additional taxation and that the further dispatch of its white garrison army to South Africa or to China would endanger the balance between Indian and white troops which had been maintained since 1858. Ironically, the ultimate dispatch of Indian troops to China was something of a relief to the Indian authorities because it restored that balance in the Indian garrison.[31] So, at the level of events, British commitment to war in China was apparently halting, reactive, and grudging. On the face of it, it does not seem to bear the imprint of a dynamic new imperialism. Yet that new imperial drive lay more in guiding assumptions and predispositions than in any one set of policies. The myth of European supremacy which played so well to the Boxer panic was immanent in all the papers and discussions of the era. The Director of Military Intelligence wrote at the end of 1898 that the British should build a British China Army similar to the British Indian Army. The Chinese, though "not deficient in military qualities" would be officered by British soldiers "following our Indian precedents."[32] Curzon himself would have preferred to keep China united as a huge buffer state for India against the Russians. But, in a passage of breathtaking visionary longing, he stated that "should our Yang-tse sphere ever crystallize into anything like a protectorate, or even an actual possession, it might be desirable to have a railway [from Burma into Yunnan] to bring up Sikhs and Goorkhas from India" into China.[33] The new imperialism of the 1890s, like the new nationalism, is perhaps to be found not in policies or programs, so much as in the generation of new, world-scale mythologies of past crises and future dominance. It was into this global mythoscape that the legend of the Boxer Uprising erupted and to its reach that it contributed.

NOTES

1. Birsa Munda had proclaimed to the tribal Munda people of central India in 1899 that British rule was at an end.
2. Vinayak Chaturvedi, "Colonial Power and Agrarian Politics in Kheda District (Gujarat), c. 1890–1930" (PhD diss., Cambridge University, 2001).
3. Rajnarayan Chandavarkar, "Plague Panic and the Epidemic Politics of India, 1896–1914," in *Imperial Power and Popular Politics: Class, Resistance and the State in India, c. 1850–1950* (Cambridge: Cambridge University Press, 1998), 234–66.
4. E. B. Alexander, Commissioner Lucknow to Chief Secretary, Govt. North Western Provinces, 1 May 1900, cited in Patrick Macartan McGinn, "Governance and Resistance in North Indian Towns, c. 1860–1900" (PhD diss., Cambridge University, 1993), 295 passim.
5. Andrew Robinson and Krishna Datta, *Rabindranath Tagore: The Myriad Minded Man* (London: Bloomsbury, 1995), 128.
6. Rabindranath Thakur, *Naibedya* (Allahabad, 1902), poem 64. The translation is by Deep Kanta Lahiri-Choudhury, to whom I am very grateful.
7. G. Lowes Dickinson, *Letters from John Chinaman* (London: R. Brimley Johnson, 1901), 61. Some of the letters were first published in article form in *Saturday Review*, 1899.
8. *Maratha*, 17 Jan. 1900.
9. *Jayadhwaja*, 11 August 1900, Madras Vernacular Press Reports 1900, India Office Records, British Library.
10. *Vrittanta Chintamani*, 11 July 1900, ibid.
11. *Maratha*, 17 June 1900.
12. Stanley P. Smith, *China from Within: or the Story of the Chinese Crisis* (London: Marshall Brothers, 1901), 235.

13. *Jayadhwaja,* 2 Deccember 1899, MVPR, British Library.

14. *Vrittanta Patrika,* 21 June 1900, British Library.

15. *Naier i -Asifi,* 18 October 1900, British Library.

16. *Maratha,* 15 July 1900.

17. *Maratha,* 8 July 1900.

18. *Mulk-o Millat,* 25 August 1900, MVPR, British Library.

19. *Shams-ul Akhbar,* August 1900, MVPR British Library; coastal Muslim communities still used a form of language called Tamil-Arabic. Not only was Arabic literature commonly available in these southern ports, but social and political contacts existed quite independently of the networks of north India Persian-leaning communities.

20. *Kerala Samachar,* June 1900, MVPR British Library.

21. *Vrittanta Chinatamani,* 11 July 1900, MVPR British Library.

22. B. L. Putnam Weale [pseud. Bertram Lenox Simpson], *Indiscreet Letters from Peking: Being the Notes of an Eye-witness, Which Set Forth in some Detail, from Day to Day, the Real Story of the Siege and Sack of a Distressed Capital in 1900, the Year of Great Tribulation.* London: Hurst and Blackett, 1907, introduction, i.

23. Putnam Weale, *Indiscreet Letters,* 203.

24. Alfred C. Lyall, "Introduction," in Valentine Chirol, *Indian Unrest* (London: Macmillan, 1910), x.

25. Ronald Hyam, "The British Empire in the Edwardian Era," in *Oxford History of the British Empire, Vol. 4, The Twentieth Century,* ed. Judith M. Brown and William Roger Louis (Oxford, 2000), 51. Hobson, *Imperialism: A Study,* was published in 1902.

26. Thomas Richards, *The Imperial Archive: Knowledge and the Fantasy of Empire* (London: Verso, 1993), 5.

27. "Reports on Russian Advances in Asia," compiled by Intelligence Bureau, Quarter Master General's Dept., Indian Army, Curzon Papers, F111, 700, British Library.

28. See, for example, Foreign Office Correspondence, "Affairs of China" 1898, C. MacDonald to Salisbury 28 September 1897, Curzon Papers, 78A. While Jardine's and other companies intended to set up cloth mills in Hong Kong to penetrate what is assumed to be a huge China market, government and its consular representatives seem to be active in facilitating and even soliciting this outcome, lending some support to Hobson if not to Lenin.

29. Daniel R. Headrick, *The Tentacles of Progress* (New York: Oxford University Press, 1998), 107.

30. Salisbury to N. O'Connor, 28 January 1898, Curzon Papers 78A, India Office Records.

31. David Dilks, *Curzon in India,* vol. 1 (London: Rupert Hart-Davis, 1969), 208.

32. Major General Sir John Ardagh, Director Military Intelligence, note 16 June 1898 on the future of the China Internal Division, Curzon Papers, F111, 78B.

33. Memorandum by Curzon on "the exit of our railway system into western China and Yunnan," 12 June 1898, Curzon Papers, F111, 78B.

9

The Boxer Uprising and British Foreign Policy

The End of Isolation

T. G. Otte

It is generally accepted by modern historians of China that the Boxer events of the summer of 1900, China's military humiliation by the foreign powers, the imperial court's flight to Xi'an in August, and the Boxer Protocol of September 1901 as a postscript to these events constituted a watershed in the history of the late Qing dynasty.[1] Still, the significance of the Boxer Uprising for turn-of-the-century international relations has scarcely been given the attention it deserves. Indeed, the events of 1900 not only provide a prism through which to study the changing dynamics in great power relations, but they also throw into sharper relief two simultaneously occurring crises: the "China Question" as potentially the most volatile contemporary international flashpoint, and the Boxer crisis as a crisis of British foreign policy that called into question the virtues of "isolation." The eschewing of binding peacetime alliances was, perhaps, more a policy reflex than a consciously pursued policy. Indeed, the historian ought to beware not to let talk of "isolation," splendid or otherwise, obscure the complexity and flexibility of British foreign policy. Nevertheless, at the close of the nineteenth century, to the minds of many contemporaries, Britain's international aloofness appeared to entail grave risks to the country's imperial interests and security.[2] The late 1890s were a period of fast changes in international politics. Britain's traditional imperial rivals, France and Russia, had formed a new diplomatic and military combination in 1894. Germany was beginning to flex her industrial and naval muscles and the United States and Japan established themselves as new great powers. At the same time, the older empires of the Near and Far East, Turkey, Persia, and China, seemed on the verge of implosion. Combined these developments had the effect of increasing international pressure on Britain, and of reducing her freedom of maneuver. In the face of these new uncertainties, the existing foreign policy consensus, centered on the isolationist reflex, disintegrated, and in this the Boxer crisis had catalytic function.

The "China Question" arose as a direct consequence of China's defeat in the 1894 to 1895 Sino-Japanese War. Japan's victory had revealed China's armed forces, the Qing state even, as a "paper tiger." In the Social Darwinian parlance of the day, China had become a link in that chain of seemingly "dying nations" whose fate now preoccupied the great powers. Indeed, it seemed that "China had taken the place of Turkey as the preeminent Sick Man."[3] For the next decade the "Chinese Question" overshadowed all other international issues. China's weakness coincided with and stimulated a new expansionist dynamic in international relations. The Qing state became an object of great power politics. World politics, born in Europe, was projected onto the Asian arena; and China and Europe, in Philip Joseph's classic phrase, "were fused into one political system."[4] However, even though great power relations in China became increasingly competitive, and even though the imminent break-up of China was frequently predicted by the pundits, there was a tacit understanding among the statesmen of Europe that, unlike Africa, China was not to be partitioned. Such considerations were influenced by a mixture of endogenous and exogenous factors. Unlike Africa, China was not an identifiable power vacuum that needed to be filled. China might have appeared to be, in the words of one British diplomat, merely "a group of loosely federated satrapies."[5] Nevertheless, given her relatively high degree of cultural and ethnic homogeneity, direct foreign rule was always likely to meet with fierce resistance by the Chinese population. Moreover, the ensuing great power scramble for railway, mining, and other concessions after 1895 profoundly changed the nature of China's relations with the foreign powers. Such concessions entailed capital export, and this, in turn, required political stability and a compliant, though internally relatively strong, Chinese central government. The preservation of China was, therefore, in the logic of financial imperialism.[6] This, of course, did not preclude the establishment, by means of coercive diplomacy, of foreign bridgeheads on Chinese soil, usually in the shape of naval bases surrounded by a "sphere of influence."[7]

These two conflicting tendencies also shaped British policy toward the "Chinese Question" in general, and during the Boxer crisis in particular. In light of Britain's dominant position in the China trade, official British policy adhered to the idea of maintaining China's territorial integrity, and of preserving an open China market. Yet, faced with vigorous and concentrated competition from the other powers, the British government saw no option but to acquiesce in the establishment of spheres of influence. Britain's position in China deteriorated especially vis-à-vis Russia; as indeed the Great Game in Asia seemed to tilt in Russia's favor.[8] Given the latter's closer geographical proximity to China, Russia's *"pénétration pacifique"* of Manchuria could not be resisted. Instead, the British prime minister and foreign secretary, Lord Salisbury, concentrated on preserving the prosperous and commercially more profitable Yangzi provinces as Britain's own informal sphere of special interest. This was also the aim of the Anglo-Russian delimitation of (railway) spheres of influence in the Scott-Muraviev agreement of April 1899. Salisbury envisaged it as a tool for the preservation of the status quo in China, though in the final analysis it was no more than a holding operation.[9]

All of this was called into question by the outbreak of the Boxer rising. The event found British policy makers unprepared. The first stirrings of Boxer activities were certainly registered, most notably the murder of the Anglican missionary S. M. Brooks in the Feicheng district of Shandong on 31 December 1899. It was in this context that the British minister at Beijing, Sir Claude MacDonald, mentioned for the first time "an organization known as the 'Boxers' [which had] attained special notoriety" on account of its anti-Christian and antimissionary activities.[10] Nevertheless, there had been only few forebodings of an impending crisis. British policy toward the Boxer phenomenon was essentially reactive. It was shaped by two mutually reinforcing factors: MacDonald's often conflicting reports, and Salisbury's and the Foreign Office's deeply ingrained caution. MacDonald, frequently ill during the spring of 1900 and due to be transferred to Tokyo, was slow to notice the straws in the wind until the crisis was upon him.[11] Throughout the first half of 1900, he failed to realize both the nature and extent of the growing unrest. It was not as though the minister had altogether failed to report on the Boxers; nor did he remain wholly inactive. Indeed, MacDonald and the other foreign diplomatic representatives were clearly aware of the various secret societies. In early March 1900, for instance, they admonished the Zongli Yamen for not mentioning the *Dadaohui* as well as the *Yihequan* in a requested imperial decree.[12] A general awareness of the multifarious nature of the antiforeign "movement" ought not to be construed, however, into an assumption of an in-depth understanding of the phenomenon. Throughout the Boxer episode, and indeed in its aftermath, Foreign Office analyses of the Boxers tended to be based on rather vague assumptions about their antimissionary and antiforeign zeal.[13] The joint efforts by the foreign diplomatic representatives at Beijing in February and March to pressure the Zongli Yamen into publicly denouncing the secret societies and taking active measures for their suppression, met with the kind of delaying tactics that had come to characterize Sino-Western diplomatic relations at the end of the 1890s. On 10 March, alarmed by the open recruiting and drilling activities of the Boxers in the vicinity of Tianjin and Beijing, the foreign diplomats sent yet another note (the fourth since 27 January) to the Zongli Yamen. The ministers all agreed "that the strongest pressure was necessary to awaken the Imperial Government to a sense of the danger of international complications ensuing if these Societies were not promptly and vigorously dealt with." They warned the Yamen that, in the event of Beijing's noncompliance with their demands, their respective governments would "adopt other measures for the protection of the lives and property of their nationals in China."[14] To gain further leverage over the central government, the foreign representatives also agreed on a combined naval demonstration off the Dagu Forts. Although two British men-of-war were eventually dispatched to northern Chinese waters on 24 March,[15] Salisbury and his officials were anxious to rein in the soldier-diplomat MacDonald's enthusiasm for gunboat diplomacy. Salisbury in particular was concerned that Britain's ongoing military campaign against the South African Boers might minimize British influence in China in the event of an escalating crisis: "Stupid of [MacDonald] to do this . . . . One of the demonstrating powers will take the opportunity of appropriating something nice & we with our engagements in South Africa will have to grin and look pleasant."[16]

This sense of the constraints placed on Britain's ability to deal with a crisis in China also informed Foreign Office thinking as regarded another potential dispute between the foreign diplomats and the imperial government in Beijing. On 15 March the official gazette announced the appointment of Yuxian, the conservative and well-known antiforeign former governor of Shandong, as governor of Shanxi. MacDonald and his colleagues were outraged by the promotion of a man whom they regarded as the real culprit behind Brooks's murder and earlier unrest in Shandong.[17] Again, the officials in London urged caution. F. A. Campbell, the experienced senior clerk of the Foreign Office's Far Eastern department, warned that "we must have some influence in high quarters, unless indeed as many people believe, the secret societies are really favoured by the Government. In either case nothing but threats of force will suffice to remove him."[18] Rumors and conjecture, however, do not furnish a firm basis for formulating policy. Moreover, desirous not to exacerbate the situation further, the Foreign Office deemed it best to let the matter of Yuxian's appointment rest. At any rate, the tone of MacDonald's reports now grew less alarming, despite violent disturbances along the boundary of the British leased territory of Wei-hai-Wei in early May.[19] When later that month the Boxers began to spread rapidly across Shandong and Zhili, the minister pointed to the long continued drought as the main cause of the unrest, and added reassuringly that "a few days' heavy rainfall . . . would do more to restore tranquillity than any other measure which either the Chinese or foreign Governments could take."[20] In consequence, officials in London were convinced that what seemed to be cases of sporadically erupting, local popular excitement were in no way different from antimissionary incidents in the mid-1890s; an attitude of firmness was all that was required.[21] Thus, when the tone of MacDonald's communications became more urgent at the end of May, Salisbury and his clerks were not as yet unduly alarmed. With good reason, historians of the Boxer events have identified the summoning of the legation guards from Tianjin by the foreign diplomatic representatives on 28 May as a crucial decision which precipitated the course of events.[22] Relying on MacDonald's reports, the Foreign Office failed to assess accurately the strength of competing factions at the imperial court, and so did not appreciate that the calling up of the guards strengthened the pro-Boxer faction. Thus, when MacDonald first telegraphed the intention of the foreign representatives to reinforce the legation guards, Salisbury saw only the possible international ramifications of this step: "I do not look forward to a 'Concert of Europe' in China."[23] The foreign secretary in particular underrated the gravity of the situation. Two days before the siege of the Beijing legations began, he still assured the British minister at Tokyo that the "[Boxer] business will not come to much."[24] MacDonald's former legation secretary, now safely ensconced in Whitehall, supported Salisbury's caution, arguing as late as 19 June that, in light of the Boxer's lack of organization, leadership, and equipment, there was "no real cause for anxiety respecting the lives of Europeans in the capital."[25]

The news of the siege at Beijing and the Chinese court's declaration of war on the foreign powers stirred public opinion in Europe and North America. The British press neglected the ongoing war in South Africa, and concentrated on events in China.[26] What Paul Cohen has called the "'false bad news' phenomenon" produced an abundance of rumors and wholly unfounded stories. In July, Reuters reported from Shanghai that the legation quarter in the capital had been stormed and the entire diplomatic community massacred. Even the usually reticent *Times* published the obituaries of MacDonald, Sir Robert Hart, the inspector-general of the Chinese Maritime Customs Service, and its own China correspondent, Dr. G. E. Morrison.[27] With the rail and telegraph links to Beijing severed, the Foreign Office was now without any reliable information on the situation in the Chinese capital. W. R. Carles, the consul at Tianjin, supplied London with some information. But even that was not always accurate, and certainly not up-to-date, and so the officials in Whitehall were "living on rumours and conjecture as to the fate of our Legation."[28] Increasingly, however, they were resigned to accept the apparently inevitable. A letter from the permanent undersecretary, Sir Thomas Sanderson, also serves to illustrate the emergence of a new image of the Chinese. Whereas previously the Chinese had been seen as, though excitable, nonetheless easily cowed by a display of firmness and resolution, they had now acquired decidedly evil attributes:

> It makes me quite sick to think of those poor people shut up in Peking, and the now almost certain termination of their mission. . . . MacDonald will probably have to shoot his wife, sister-in-law, and two children to save them from torture.[29]

Despite the public outcry and clamoring for action in Parliament, Lord Salisbury refused to let himself be rushed into reinforcing Admiral Sir Edward Seymour's small relief force operating from Tianjin. He reasoned that no vital British interests had been affected as the Yangzi provinces remained tranquil and trade there was not impaired. Any further foreign interference seemed to him like the opening of Pandora's box, bringing down the Qing dynasty and quite possibly hastening the partition of the Middle Kingdom.[30] Salisbury saw the crisis in China within the wider international context of Britain's global interests and commitments: With her military resources tied down in South Africa, Britain was in no position to prevent the partition of China or any further encroachment upon Chinese territory by the other powers.[31]

Salisbury's "wait-and-see" approach struck a growing number of his ministers as irresolute. The secretary of state for India, Lord George Hamilton, complained that Salisbury and the Foreign Office were "in a hopeless state of flabbiness. . . . To let things drift seems now to be the accepted policy of that Department or at any rate of its chief, and the misfortune is that time is not on our side, and the longer we wait, the worse position we find ourselves in."[32] Salisbury's own parliamentary undersecretary at the Foreign Office, St. John Brodrick, was equally dissatisfied. Like many among the younger generation of government ministers, he took a keen interest in the "Chinese Question," and was generally an advocate of a strong forward policy. Salisbury's inactivity in the face of the Boxer events he deemed no longer masterly.[33] In his memoirs he later claimed that there had been a disposition at the Foreign Office "to set me 'in the forefront of the battle,' when the permanent officials wished to vary [Salisbury's] decisions."[34] Regarding his own role in the events of 1900 this was something of an understatement. Off his own bat, but with the concurrence of three senior Cabinet ministers (Arthur Balfour, Colonial Secretary Joseph Chamberlain, and First Lord of the Admiralty George Joachim Goschen), he advocated a military understanding with Russia and Japan with a view to quelling the uprising and restoring order in Northern China.[35] Salisbury rejected Brodrick's idea of a "tripartite military alliance" as it would ultimately be dominated by Russia, and might lead to the firmer entrenchment of Russia's position in China.[36] When Brodrick raised the matter again, this time coupled with the idea of a mandate for Japan to relieve the besieged legations at Beijing, Salisbury remained adamant. The foreign secretary was not prepared to take any risks.[37]

Salisbury agreed only reluctantly to the dispatch of further Indian army troops to Zhili after Seymour's relief column was forced to return to Tianjin.[38] In early July he withdrew to his country mansion, convinced that the diplomacy of coercion had brought about the crisis. He was in no doubt "that the Legations have been slaughtered . . . [and that] the great object, the rescue of the Diplomatic Body, appears to be no longer possible."[39] Salisbury only returned to the capital at the beginning of August, after telegraphic communication with Beijing had been briefly restored, and it became clear that the foreign community there was still holding out.[40] Nevertheless, throughout July British foreign policy seemed to be adrift while the other powers prepared for joint military action. The victory of the international forces over Chinese troops at Tianjin on 14 July emboldened the allied commanders. In early August they began the advance on Beijing without awaiting further augmentation and took the Chinese capital on 14 August.[41] Already at the end of June, Admiral Seymour had warned the Admiralty that in the event of a march on Beijing "there would have to be *one* commander of the combined forces." To his political masters in London this suggestion was anathema.[42] When Count Lamsdorff, the interim head of the Russian foreign ministry, suggested an international agreement to "secure unity of action and direction" of the relief operation in northern China, the ministers were appalled: A Russian commander in chief of the international forces would have undermined Britain's prestige as the dominant foreign power in China.[43] Nonetheless, the cabinet was divided. The chancellor of the exchequer, Sir Michael Hicks Beach, opposed further expenditure on a China expedition, on the grounds that Britain's South African commitments were already draining Treasury funds. He also argued that Britain's interests lay in the central and southern provinces of China.[44] Other ministers were driven by a more urgent sense of crisis, and were prepared to accept the appointment of a foreign, though not Russian, commander in chief.[45]

Salisbury held the balance between the two groups, but he delayed a decision for some time. No doubt, age and ill health had begun to take their toll. The double burden of Foreign Office and premiership had worn him out. His wife's death in 1899 had been another blow. At the cabinet meetings in the summer of 1900 he "sat a crumpled heap, like Grandpa Smallweed."[46] His real motivation for temporizing, however, was to keep a free hand until the situation had become clearer. Moreover, suspecting the other powers of harboring designs on Chinese territory, he was anxious to avoid any steps that would facilitate these ambitions. Ultimately, Salisbury's cool response to the Russian initiative laid it to rest.[47] Still, Salisbury failed to elucidate his foreign policy rationale to his cabinet colleagues. His handling of the Boxer crisis exasperated a growing number of them: "We are all most unhappy about China. We cannot get the Prime Minister either to state a policy, or to adopt any definite line. He seems disposed to let things settle themselves, which may mean the massacre of every Christian in China. . . . Heaven knows where we shall finally drift."[48] This distinct sense of drift prevailed especially among the younger ministers. The premier was now regarded as a liability, "a strange, powerful, inscrutable, brilliant, obstructive dead-weight at the top."[49] The government, they argued, "wants badly new blood, and the Prime Minister is tired and absolutely . . . out of touch with public opinion"; it seemed clear to them that *"no* policy is possible here till L[ord] S[alisbury] goes and [the] Cabinet is reconstructed."[50]

Meanwhile, the issue of the chief command over the international forces resurfaced again, this time raised by German Foreign Secretary Count von Bülow. The latter hoped to induce Salisbury to propose to the other powers the appointment of Prussian Field Marshal Count von Waldersee as commander in chief. Waldersee's appointment, Salisbury was informed, was the best means of forestalling Russian intrigues in China and the possible recrudescence of the Far Eastern *triplice* of 1895. Salisbury was unimpressed: "I think I have heard some of this before."[51] He had always mistrusted the German emperor. Now he suspected him of having "big designs in China."[52] At the end of July, he informed the German ambassador that in light of the novel and experimental character of the idea of a supreme international commander he could not accept Bülow's proposal.[53] In contrast to the earlier Russian proposal, Salisbury did not at any stage consult the cabinet about the German initiative. The ministers became involved only after Bülow, having failed to win Salisbury's approval, obtained Russian support for Waldersee's appointment. Salisbury resented being pushed into accepting a fait accompli. It seemed clear that Russia had ulterior motives. At the same time, senior Foreign Office officials warned that it would be impolitic to refuse Waldersee.[54] The cabinet assembled on 9 August to discuss the Prussian's appointment. Most ministers had already used the parliamentary recess to leave the capital. Bereft of Hicks Beach's support, Salisbury now found himself in a minority. According to Brodrick, the ministers present at the meeting, Balfour, Chamberlain, Goschen, and Hamilton, as well as the lord president of the council, the Duke of Devonshire, and the secretary of state for war, Lord Lansdowne, "were all strongly in favour of this [Waldersee's appointment]."[55] The issue was one, as Salisbury informed the queen, "in which there are serious objections both to accepting and refusing." His ministers did not dare to overrule him, and the outcome of the meeting was a compromise. Ultimately, the British government accepted Waldersee's *"supreme direction,"* but not his "supreme command," subject to his acceptance by the other powers.[56]

However, not only did the Wilhelmstrasse have to wait until 14 August for the final acceptance of Waldersee's chief command by all the powers. In a further ironic twist, Beijing was taken by the international relief column on that same day. The stated objective of Waldersee's mission had thus been accomplished some six weeks before the field marshal would set foot on Chinese soil.[57] Germany was now no longer in a position, as Wilhelm II had hoped, to play the role of *kapellmeister,* conducting the concert of Europe in China.[58] Worse still for Germany, Lamsdorff now announced Russia's complete withdrawal from the Chinese capital, combined with an invitation to the other powers to follow the Russian example. First indications of the plan reached the German government through Austrian diplomats on 21 August, well before Lamsdorff's circular note to the powers on 28 August.[59] It would have been acutely embarrassing for the government in Berlin had the kaiser's *Weltmarschall* arrived in China only to find that his international expeditionary force had already dispersed. Whether intended as a deliberate insult or not, German diplomacy had to respond speedily to the altered situation. In consequence, Bülow now sought a China agreement with Britain. By recognizing British preponderance in the Yangzi valley he hoped to induce Britain to oppose Russia's advance in Manchuria. Such an agreement would allow Germany to avoid the dreaded humiliation implicit in the Russian withdrawal; and it would allow Berlin to play off the other two powers against each other, thereby increasing Germany's diplomatic freedom of maneuver.[60] Thus, in a long arranged private meeting between the kaiser and the prince of Wales on 22 August the emperor hinted at the desirability of an Anglo-German China agreement. He anticipated further Russian encroachments on Manchuria, and suggested as a countermove a firm pledge on the part of the British government to maintain the "Open Door" in the Yangzi basin. If such an undertaking were given, he assured the prince and the accompanying British ambassador, Sir Frank Lascelles, the British "would find the German Government on their side."[61] Wilhelm was clearly under the impression that "an understanding" had been come to "regarding . . . the policy to be followed in the Yangtze region."[62] Still, the wording of his overture was so general that Lascelles failed to grasp its precise nature. The Foreign Office was thus unaware that the kaiser had in fact proposed a formal Anglo-German understanding on the future of the Yangzi.[63] Moreover, the overture was not only vague in its wording, it was also ill-timed. Salisbury had left Britain after the cabinet meeting of 9 August, and was now taking the waters in the Vosges mountains. The prime minister's absence, the secretary of state for India complained, hampered the conduct of British diplomacy: "[Salisbury] does not confide his ideas to any subordinates or his colleagues, and so we have to be constantly telegraphing to him; and not only is there a delay, but there is also a want of unity of purpose and of idea which is dispiriting and most annoying."[64]

At Hamilton's suggestion, but with Salisbury's concurrence, an informal cabinet committee was established, which had the "power to act during the recess within certain limits."[65] Hamilton's proposal was the result of his growing irritation with Salisbury's lack of leadership. Nineteenth-century British imperial policy, of course, tended to be little more than a continual exercise in improvisation. However, the absence of a permanent mechanism to coordinate all branches of politics affecting imperial and external

relations seemed never more glaring than in August 1900. If the prime minister failed to give coherent shape to Britain's foreign policy, the cabinet as
a collective body seemed unable to fill the gap. Hamilton lamented that the
cabinet "was a most *effete* organization. This is mainly the Chief's fault. . . .
If it was not for the regard felt for him by his colleagues & their efficiency,
the whole concern must long ago have tumbled to pieces."[66] Quite clearly,
then, the newly established committee had to give a sense of direction to
foreign policy. Its ostensible function was to coordinate and supervise the
military operations in China. Inevitably, therefore, the nucleus of the committee was formed by Hamilton himself, whose Indian troops provided the
bulk of the British China expeditionary force, and the two service ministers,
Lansdowne and Goschen. At a later stage they were joined by Chamberlain
and Hicks Beach.[67] The committee's proceedings were dominated by the announcement of Russia's withdrawal from Beijing, and by the kaiser's proposal of an Anglo-German China agreement. There was no doubt in the
minds of the ministers that the two issues were interlinked. The committee's work, however, progressed only slowly. Its responsibilities had not
been defined clearly, and the ministers were reluctant to take decisions
without Salisbury's consultation or, indeed, without his consent.[68]

The Hamilton-Goschen combination was the driving force behind the
committee's work.[69] The India secretary opposed the withdrawal of the
British contingent from the Chinese capital. Logistical considerations apart,
he realized that the matter was a "question of policy": the evacuation of Beijing would harm Britain's prestige in the Far East by creating "an impression
of vacillation & weakness." Withdrawal, therefore, was tantamount to abdi-
cating Britain's claim to be the leading power in Asian affairs.[70] Maintaining Britain's dominance in Asia and thwarting Russian designs to replace
her was the twin leitmotif of Hamilton's policy throughout the turbulent
summer months of 1900. But Hamilton also appreciated the opportunities
Russian withdrawal proffered to British diplomacy: "We have an opportunity such as we never had before of separating Germany from Russia. The
Emperor ought to thank us if we save him from the humiliation of having
his expedition made the laughing stock of civilization."[71] Hamilton was
gravely concerned about Britain's international isolation. He was convinced
that an alliance with a European power had become necessary. In view of
Russia's constant threat to Britain's Indian possessions and her alliance with
France, and her intrigues against Britain during the early phase of the South
African War, Germany seemed to be the inevitable choice.[72]

The first lord of the Admiralty held similar views. He urged the prime
minister to respond favorably to the German overture. However, unlike
Hamilton, Goschen did not necessarily advocate a full alliance with Germany. His approach was altogether more cautious: "I don't say that Germany is sincere, but if we keep the Emperor at arm's length, we are certain

to have him against us. If we are candid with him, there is at all events a chance of his working with us."[73] The prime minister was not to be moved. Whatever Britain's future policy in China might be, he declared,

> it cannot . . . be founded on so slender a basis as the half-dozen words which Lascelles has reported from the German Emperor. . . . I do not know with any precision what the "policy of the open door" means; still less do I know what is meant by having "Germany on our side," which is the consideration we are to receive for announcing our adherence to the "policy of the open door." These vague utterances may indicate the basis of future undertakings but they certainly do not furnish it.[74]

Salisbury's eventual response to the increasingly impatient government in Berlin was dilatory at best. Even the usually reticent Lansdowne was exasperated by his conduct: "Salisbury is very provoking: he deals with the ministers & sovereigns of foreign powers as if they were Hatfield solicitors."[75] Goschen gloomily warned that Salisbury's refusal to enter into talks with Germany was "A *non possumus* in every direction. . . . I cannot express myself too strongly . . . absolute isolation is playing the devil."[76] Moreover, failure to cooperate with Germany also entailed risks for Britain's position in China. While British diplomacy was drifting, German gunboats were steaming up the Yangzi river.[77]

Ironically, Salisbury's policy rationale was almost exclusively conditioned by those very events in the Yangzi basin. Although the southern and central parts of China had remained largely unaffected by the Boxer movement, the international merchant community at Shanghai and Pelham Laird Warren, Britain's energetic acting consul-general there, demanded the occupation of a series of strategic points along the Yangzi as a precautionary measure.[78] Salisbury initially rejected such suggestions. However, after some hesitation, and not without some misgivings, he finally agreed to the landing of some three thousand troops at Shanghai.[79] He soon came to regret this decision, for other powers now dispatched forces to the mouth of the Yangzi. By the end of August, French, German, and Japanese contingents had been disembarked at Shanghai. "Warren's greediness to steal a diplomatic advantage," Salisbury complained to Goschen, "has landed him in an international occupation of the Yangtze."[80]

For Salisbury himself the international occupation was an embarrassing setback, revealing the extent to which Britain's position in the Yangzi basin had been weakened. The appearance of German troops and vessels at Shanghai was particularly worrying: Germany, like Russia, had not recognized British claims to exclusive rights in the Yangzi region. Salisbury's long-held suspicions of the German emperor were thus given new grounds. They were reinforced by a report from the military attaché at Berlin, who had been questioned about Chinese affairs by an admiral in the kaiser's entourage. The attaché warned that "perhaps an attempt may be made later to prejudicially [sic] affect our interests in the valley of the Yangtze-Kiang."[81] Thus, the events in and around Shanghai are crucial for the understanding of Salisbury's attitude toward the kaiser's overture of 22 August. Furthermore, Salisbury and his advisers were by no means certain that the Boxer events might not lead to a civil war situation, in which case it seemed best to wait until "a strong man comes out on top."[82]

Salisbury's cool response to the German proposal did not bring this episode to a close. The cabinet's China committee now renewed its efforts to force the prime minister to agree to a change of policy. Goschen and Hamilton were adamant that British diplomacy had to grasp the opportunity "to drive a wedge between Germany and Russia by taking sides with the Germans." In this they were supported by Balfour, Chamberlain, and Lansdowne.[83] At Hamilton's suggestion the committee, with Chamberlain joining the discussions for the first time, met at the Admiralty on 4 September to formulate a coherent policy alternative and to bring pressure to bear upon Salisbury.[84] In Hicks Beach's absence, Lansdowne was the only member in favor of "a drawing in of our horns all over the world."[85] After some discussion, however, he was persuaded by the other ministers to advise Salisbury to keep British troops at Beijing. The ministers also urged him to seize "the opportunity . . . to detach the German Emperor from Russia & bind him more closely to our interests."[86] The combination of Goschen, Chamberlain, Lansdowne, and Hamilton was formidable, but it failed to move Salisbury: "The idea of developing this resolution into general acceptance of German policy is more dangerous and requires careful reflection." There were two fundamental questions which had to be addressed, he argued: "What does Germany want from us? What can she give us in return?"[87] Salisbury felt strong enough to resist the committee's recommendation. He had the chancellor's support and, independently of each other and in moves unconnected with the China crisis, Lansdowne had offered to resign from the War Office, and Goschen had announced his wish to retire from politics altogether. Although Salisbury refused to accept the resignation of his war minister, both Lansdowne's and Goschen's influence within the government was weakened.[88]

Still, Salisbury's promise to discuss the German proposal of a China agreement after his return from the continent did not placate his other anti-isolationist critics. "We do what is needed and get nothing for it," a desperate Brodrick complained to Chamberlain. "[W]e shall ultimately have to make some overture to Germany."[89] A first-rate opportunity to lead Britain out of her potentially dangerous diplomatic isolation, it seemed to Salisbury's critics, slipped through their hands when action was urgently required. The committee reconvened on 7 September, this time under participation of Hicks Beach as well as Chamberlain, though once again the chancellor remained strongly opposed to an agreement with Germany.[90] The continued deadlock now was an incentive for Chamberlain to intervene more forcefully in the debate. Until the end of August he had viewed the events in China with relative equanimity.[91] Now, he saw the situation in China as a useful opportunity to relaunch his pet project of an Anglo-German understanding. In a lengthy memorandum of 10 September he expounded the anti-isolationists' case. It was a scarcely veiled attack on Salisbury's passive disposition "to allow matters to settle themselves." Britain's primary interest in China, Chamberlain argued, was the maintenance of the country's integrity and of the "Open Door" against Russia. Russia's withdrawal from Beijing enabled her to pose as China's friend and protector, whilst simultaneously continuing her *"pénétration pacifique"* of Manchuria. Russian policy was thus the main source of Britain's short- and long-term problems in the Far East. But it also offered new opportunities; the circumstances seemed propitious for an attempt to detach Germany from her Eastern neighbor. German foreign policy, Chamberlain argued, was "largely dependent on the idiosyncrasy of the Emperor," who had now been placed "in a most difficult position" by the Russian withdrawal from Beijing: "But, if he is to escape from his humiliation, he must largely rely upon us to save him. . . . We have it in our power to do him a great service, and we ought to be able in return for our assistance to obtain satisfactory assurances."

Undoubtedly, Chamberlain's September memorandum was intended as the anti-isolationists' answer to Salisbury's blunt question as to what Germany could deliver in return for an agreement on China. But, the colonial secretary foresaw further advantages in a rapprochement with Germany. He shared Salisbury's pessimism about the political future of the Chinese empire; Russia's absorption of Manchuria and other parts of northern China could probably not be prevented. Therefore, he argued that "both in China and elsewhere it is our interest that Germany should throw herself across the path of Russia. An alliance between Germany and Russia, entailing as it would the cooperation of France, is the only thing we have to dread, and the clash of German and Russian interests, whether in China or Asia Minor, would be a guarantee for our safety." Chamberlain's argument was the almost exact mirror image of Bülow's rationale. The clash of German and Russian interests in the geostrategic periphery of European politics would have rendered impossible any revival of the Franco-Russian-German combination in Asia that was feared so much by so many in 1899–1900. It would have enhanced significantly Britain's imperial security, and it would have increased Britain's diplomatic freedom of maneuver, thus, ironically, lessening the need for the wholesale abandonment of "isolation." Whether, however, Germany would be so obliging as to risk antagonizing Russia was a question Chamberlain carefully avoided posing. Nevertheless, he urged

Salisbury to foster good relations with Germany. An Anglo-German agreement on China, based on the mutual recognition of respective spheres of interest and influence in Shandong province and the Yangzi valley, was a first step leading toward a general understanding with Germany. In conclusion, he pointed out, "We are not likely to take possession of any territory in the interior ourselves; but we ought to try for some understanding which will keep off all others, and make it easy to maintain the 'Open Door' in at least this, the most important, portion of the Chinese Empire."[92]

Salisbury returned to England on 12 September, and immediately met with the Goschen-Hamilton committee at the Foreign Office. In Hicks Beach's absence, and with his only support coming from Foreign Office officials, he found himself in an untenable position. No longer able to resist the anti-isolationists, he was forced to begin negotiations with Count Hatzfeldt, the German ambassador.[93] The result of these talks was the China agreement of 16 October 1900, a vague statement of almost commonplace principles which did not bind either party.[94] Salisbury had opposed the agreement from the start. But, having lost control over his cabinet, he was forced to pursue a "policy of pleasing Germany to which so many of our friends are attached."[95] It was the first step toward departing from what Salisbury's critics regarded as his isolationist policy, and the catalytic event bringing about this departure was the Boxer Uprising.

In terms of its day-to-day conduct, British foreign policy throughout the Boxer crisis gave the appearance of vacillation and temporization. It reacted to the events in northern China rather than trying to anticipate or, even less so, shape them. Policy decisions were made on an ad hoc basis, though they tended to be rooted in broad assumptions about Britain's regional and global imperial interests, and to be informed by general axioms derived from past experience of dealing with China. There was nothing in that experience to prepare policy makers for the Boxer phenomenon. Lack of adequate and accurate information from Beijing, and the constraints placed on Britain's resources by that other imperial crisis in 1900, the Boer War, reinforced the tendency to react. Beneath the troubled surface of crisis diplomacy by telegraphy, however, there emerged a dynamic new conceptualization of Britain's imperial and external policies. In its wake the old laissez-faire foreign policy consensus disintegrated. At the level of events, the Boxer crisis marked the beginning of the slow search for a way out of the country's international isolation. At a more profound level, Britain's Boxer experience was about more than specific policies or diplomatic tactics. The China crisis of 1900 helped to crystallize new guiding assumptions among the younger ("Edwardian") generation of policy makers who now began to fill responsible positions in Whitehall and Westminster, assumptions which embraced a new imperial ideal, and which recognized the need for foreign policy to operate on a vaster geostrategic scale. In this respect, the internal foreign debate in 1900 was linked to the wider paradigmatic shift in British political thinking about empire and international politics.[96] In terms of the consequences for British policy in China, the Boxer events reinforced the determination of Salisbury and his successors at the Foreign Office to consolidate China. But from now on there was also a lingering fear lest future disputes with China provoked another Boxer-style rising: "1900 is a warning."[97] The events of the long, dry summer of 1900, then, were not only a watershed in the history of late Qing China, but also of late nineteenth-century British foreign policy.

NOTES

1. For a useful corrective of some older views cf. Paul A. Cohen, *History in Three Keys: The Boxers as Event, Experience, and Myth* (New York: Columbia University Press, 1997), 22 and 56.

2. C. H. D. Howard, *Splendid Isolation: A Study in Idea* (London: Macmillan, 1967), *passim*; T. G. Otte, "A Question of Leadership: Lord Salisbury, the Unionist Cabinet and Foreign Policy Making, 1895–1900," *Contemporary British History* 14, no. 4 (2000): 1–26.

3. A. J. P. Taylor, *The Struggle for Mastery in Europe, 1848–1918* (Oxford: Oxford University Press, 1954), 391. The phrase of the "dying nations" was coined by Lord Salisbury, cf. *Times* (18 May 1898).

4. Philip Joseph, *Foreign Diplomacy in China, 1894–1900: A Study in Political and Economic Relations with China* (London: George Allen & Unwin, 1928), 416; W. C. Costin, *Great Britain and China, 1833–1860* (Oxford: Clarendon, 1937), 228.

5. Satow Papers, Satow diary, 8 Oct. 1901, Public Record Office, Kew, PRO 30/33/16/3.

6. H. Feis, *Europe: The World's Banker, 1870–1914* (New York: W.W. Norton, repr., 1965), 435–41; E. W. Edwards, *British Diplomacy and Finance in China, 1895–1914* (Oxford: Clarendon, 1987), chapter 1; Francis E. Hyde, *Far Eastern Trade, 1860–1914* (London: Adam & Charles Black, 1973), 197–215.

7. For the "bridgehead" concept see John Darwin, "Imperialism and the Victorians: The Dynamics of Territorial Expansion," *English Historical Review* 112, no. 3 (1997), 629–30; also Arthur Lewis Rosenbaum, "The Manchuria Bridgehead: Anglo-Russian Rivalry and the Imperial Railways of North China, 1897–1902," *Modern Asian Studies* 10, no. 1 (1976): 41–64. China, therefore, does not neatly fit into Renouvin's notion of the late nineteenth century as *"l'époque du 'partage du monde',"* Pierre Renouvin and Jean-Baptiste Duroselle, *Introduction à l'histoire des relations internationales* (Paris: Librairie Armand Colin, 1964), 113.

8. David Gillard, *The Struggle for Asia, 1828–1914* (London: Methuen, 1977), 153–66. For a detailed study of Britain's commercial position in China see D. C. M. Platt, *Finance, Trade, and Politics in British Foreign Policy, 1815–1914* (Oxford: Clarendon, 1968), 278–90.

9. Bertie Papers, Min. Salisbury, 20 May 1899, British Library, Add MSS 63013. The text of the agreement can be found in J. V. A. MacMurray, ed., *Treaties and Agreements with and concerning China* (New York: Macmillan, 1921), vol. 1, 204–5.

10. Great Britain, Foreign Office Archives (Kew: The National Archives), Mac-Donald to Salisbury (no. 5), 5 January 1900, PRO, FO 17/1411. On the murder itself see Victor Purcell, *The Boxer Uprising: A Background Study* (Cambridge: Cambridge University Press, 1963), 290–91.

11. On MacDonald's ill health see Hart to Campbell (Z/854), 29 April 1900, in John K. Fairbank, et al., eds., *The I.G. in Peking: Letters of Robert Hart, Chinese Maritime Customs, 1868–1907* (Cambridge, Mass.: Belknap Press, 1975), vol. 2, no. 1167. A useful account of aspects of MacDonald's term in Beijing is Mary H. Wilgus, *Sir Claude MacDonald, the Open Door, and British Informal Empire in China, 1895–1900* (New York: Garland Publishing, 1987).

12. In this case, it was Baron von Ketteler, the German minister, who emphasized this omission, Great Britain, Foreign Office Archives, MacDonald to Salisbury (no. 47), 5 March 1900, FO 17/1411.

13. Great Britain, Foreign Office Archives, Memo, Bertie, 10 June 1900, FO 17/1440.

14. Great Britain, Foreign Office Archives, MacDonald to Salisbury (no. 54), 16 March 1900, FO 17/1412; cf. tel. d'Anthouard to Delcassé (no. 33), 11 March 1900, *Documents Diplomatiques Français (1871–1914)*, edited by Ministère des Affaires Étrangères, 1st ser., vol. xiv (Paris: Imprimerie Nationale, 1949), no. 99.

15. Great Britain, Foreign Office Archives, Min. Campbell, 24 March 1900, FO 17/1418; Great Britain, Admiralty Records, Bertie to Admiralty, 24 March 1900, ADM 116/116; and Great Britain, Foreign Office Archives (Kew: The National Archives), tel. Salisbury to MacDonald (no. 37), 25 Mar.1900, FO 17/1419.

16. Great Britain, Foreign Office Archives, Min. Salisbury, on tel. MacDonald (no. 33), 10 March 1900, FO 17/1418. The desired imperial decree was finally published in the *Peking Gazette* on 18 April 1900, cf. Great Britain, Foreign Office Archives, MacDonald to Salisbury (no. 71), 18 April 1900, FO 17/1412.

17. Great Britain, Foreign Office Archives, MacDonald to Salisbury (no. 54), 16 March 1900, FO 17/1412. For Yuxian's role see Joseph W. Esherick, *The Origins of the Boxer Uprising* (Berkeley: University of California Press, 1987), 190–91.

18. Great Britain, Foreign Office Archives, Min. Campbell, 29 March 1900, on tel. MacDonald to Salisbury (no. 40), 29 March 1900, FO 17/1418.

19. Great Britain, Foreign Office Archives, Dorward to MacDonald, 9 May 1900, enclosed in MacDonald to Salisbury (no. 92), 11 May 1900, FO 17/1413; Pamela Atwell, *British Mandarins and Chinese Reformers: The British Administration of Weihaiwei (1898–1930) and the Territory's Return to Chinese Rule* (Hong Kong: Oxford University Press, 1985), 33–38.

20. Great Britain, Foreign Office Archives, MacDonald to Salisbury (no. 96), 21 May 1900, PRO, FO 17/1413; but see tel. Ministère des Affaires Étrangères, ed. *Documents Diplomatiques Français (1871–1914)*, Pichon to Delcassé (no. 92), 5 June 1900, *DDF* (1) 16, no. 161.

21. Great Britain, Foreign Office Archives, undated min. Campbell on tel. Mac-Donald to Salisbury (no. 65), 17 May 1900, PRO, FO 17/1418.

22. Esherick, *Origins of the Boxer Uprising*, 287; also Purcell, *Boxer Uprising*, 246–48, who makes an even more emphatic case.

23. Great Britain, Foreign Office Archives, undated min. Salisbury on tel. Mac-Donald to Salisbury (no. 73), 21 May 1900, FO 17/1418.

24. Satow papers, Satow diary, 12 June 1900, PRO 30/33/16/3. For a useful summary of the events, see J. E. Hoare, *Embassies of the East* (London: Curzon Press, 1999), 40–50.

25. Memo, Bax-Ironside, "Local Situation in Peking," 19 June 1900, Hatfield House Papers, 3M/A/106/30.

26. Bill Nasson, *The South African War, 1899–1902* (London: Edward Arnold, 1999), 211, is accurate in his summary of the press, though the tone of surprise is misplaced.

27. *Times* (17 July 1900). A special memorial service for Hart at St. Paul's Cathedral was only postponed after a last-minute appeal to Lord Salisbury, *I.G. in Peking* 2, 1234, n. On the rumors in general see Cohen, *History in Three Keys*, 160–62.

28. Sanderson to O'Conor (private), 26 June 1900, O'Conor Papers, Churchill College Archive Centre, Cambridge, OCON 6/1/25. Carles's telegraphic reports on the events around Tianjin and Dagu can be found in Great Britain, Foreign Office Archives, PRO, FO 17/1429; also W. Meyrick Hewlett, *The Siege of the Peking Legations, June to August 1900* (Harrow-on-the-Hill, Mdx: The Harrovian, 1900), 2–3.

29. Sanderson to Scott (private), 4 July 1900, Scott Papers, British Library, Add.Mss.52298; and to O'Conor (private), 24 July 1900, OCON 6/1/25.

30. Great Britain, Foreign Office Archives, MacDonald to Salisbury (no. 96), 21 May 1900, FO 17/1413; Bertie Papers, Salisbury to Bertie, 18 June 1900, Add.Mss. 63014.

31. Great Britain, Foreign Office Archives, Undated min. Salisbury on tel. MacDonald to Salisbury (no. 33), 10 March 1900, FO 17/1418.

32. Hamilton to Curzon, private, 6 June 1900, Hamilton Papers, British Library Oriental Collection, Mss.Eur.C.126/2; Lansdowne to Chamberlain, 11 June 1900, Lansdowne Papers, Lans (5) 20.

33. Brodrick to Salisbury, 11 June 1900, Midleton Papers, Papers of William St. John Brodrick, later ninth Viscount and first Earl of Midleton, Kew: The National Archives, PRO 30/67/5; Brodrick to Selborne (private), 16 August1898, Selborne Papers, Bodleian Library, Oxford, Ms. Selborne 2. See also his anonymous article "The Problem of China," *Edinburgh Review* (July 1899), 244–66; for Brodrick's authorship, Platt, *Finance*, 289–90.

34. Earl of Midleton, *Record and Reactions, 1856–1939* (London: John Murray, 1939), 107.

35. Midleton Papers, Brodrick to Salisbury, 12 June 1900, PRO 30/67/5; Brodrick to Curzon (private), 15, 22 and 29 June 1900, Curzon Papers, British Library Oriental Collection, Mss.Eur.F111/10A; Ian H. Nish, *The Anglo-Japanese Alliance: The Diplomacy of Two Island Empires, 1894–1907* (Westport, Conn.: Greenwood, repr. 1976), 83–91.

36. Midleton Papers, Salisbury to Brodrick (private), 15 June 1900, PRO 30/67/5; Claude M. MacDonald, "The Japanese Detachment during the Defence of the Peking Legations, June–August 1900," *Transactions and Proceedings of the Japan Society* 12, no. 1 (1914): 2–19.

37. Midleton Papers, Memo, Brodrick, 25 June 1900, PRO 30/67/5.

38. Great Britain, War Office Records, Hamilton to Curzon, 29 June 1900 (copy), and min. Knox, 4 July 1900, PRO, WO 32/6144; Ministère des Affaires Étrangères, unnumbered tel. Chaylard to Delcassé, 29 June 1900, *DDF* (1) 16, no. 205.

39. Great Britain, Cabinet Office Records, Salisbury to Queen Victoria, 20 July 1900, PRO, CAB 41/25/45; memo. Salisbury, 2 August 1900, 3M/A/86/27.

40. Hamilton Papers, Hamilton to Curzon (private), 3 August 1900, Mss.Eur.C126/2; Great Britain, Foreign Office Archives, unnumbered tel. MacDonald to Salisbury, 3 August 1900, FO 17/1418.

41. Great Britain, Admiralty Records, Naval Intelligence Report no. 587, "Diary of Principal Events in China during the Boxer Insurrection, 1900," PRO, ADM 232/32; Frances Wood, *No Dogs and Not Many Chinese: Treaty Port Life, 1843–1943* (London: John Murray, 1998), 161–63; P. D. Coates, *The China Consuls: British Consular Officials, 1843–1943* (Hong Kong: Oxford University Press, 1988), 287.

42. Great Britain, War Office Records, tel. Seymour to Admiralty (no. 384), 27 June 1900, WO 32/6145. For the command question of the Dagu and Tianjin operations see L. K. Young, *British Policy in China, 1895–1902* (Oxford: Oxford University Press, 1970), 150.

43. Great Britain, Foreign Office Archives, Scott to Salisbury (no. 215), 11 July 1900, FO 65/1600; tel. vice versa (no.107), 15 July 1900, FO 65/1603; Ministère des Affaires Étrangères, ed., Montebello to Delcassé (no. 68), 12 July 1900, *DDF* (1) 16, no. 225; Keith Neilson, *Britain and the Last Tsar: British Policy and Russia* (Oxford: Clarendon, 1995), 210–11.

44. Hamilton Papers, Hamilton to Curzon (private), 28 June 1900, Mss.Eur.C126/2; Hicks Beach Papers, Salisbury to Hicks Beach (private), 12 August 1900, Gloucestershire Record Office, PCC/72/2; cf. Lady Victoria Hicks Beach, *Life of Sir Michael Hicks Beach, Earl of St. Aldwyn* (2 vols, London: Macmillan, 1932) 2, 124–26.

45. Hamilton Papers, Hamilton to Curzon (private), 20 July 1900 (1st letter), Mss.Eur.C.126/2; Midleton Papers, memo, Brodrick, 12 July 1900, PRO 30/67/5.

46. M. V. Brett, ed., Esher journal, 4 Dec.1900, *Journals and Letters of Reginald, Viscount Esher* (2 vols., London: Ivor Nicholson and Watson, 1934), 1, 270.

47. Great Britain, Foreign Office Archives, tel. Scott to Salisbury (no. 73), 22 July 1900, and min. Salisbury, [23 July 1900], FO 65/1604; Great Britain, Cabinet Office Archives, Salisbury to Queen Victoria, 20 July 1900, CAB 41/25/45.

48. Hamilton Papers, Hamilton to Curzon (private), 20 July 1900 (2nd letter), Mss.Eur.C.126/2.

49. Midleton Papers, Curzon to Brodrick (confidential), 19 July 1900, British Library, Add.Mss. 50074.

50. Hamilton Papers, Hamilton to Curzon (private), 8 August 1900, Mss.Eur.C.126/2; Curzon Papers, Brodrick to Curzon (private), 13 July 1900, Mss.Eur.F.111/10B.

51. Hatfield House Papers, memo, Barrington, 18 July 1900, and min. Salisbury, [19 July 1900], 3M/A/122/87; Norman Rich, *Friedrich von Holstein: Politics and Diplomacy in the Era of Bismarck and Wilhelm II* (2 vols., Cambridge: Cambridge University Press, 1965), 2, 619–20.

52. Satow Papers, Satow diary, 30 May and 20 August1900, PRO 30/33/16/3; cf. T. G. Otte, "'The Winston of Germany': The British Foreign Policy Elite and the Last German Emperor," *Canadian Journal of History* 36, no. 3 (2001), 488–9.

53. Friedrich Thimme et al., eds., *Die Grosse Politik der europäischen Kabinette,* (40 vols., Berlin: Deutsche Verlagsanstalt, 1924), 16, nos. 4595 and 4596, tel. Derenthall

to Hatzfeldt (no. 253), 31 July 1900, and tel. Hatzfeldt to *Auswärtiges Amt* (no. 469), 31 July 1900.

54. Scott Papers, Scott to Salisbury (private), 9 August 1900, Add.Mss. 52303; Great Britain, Foreign Office Archives, min. Bertie, 8 August 1900, on tel. Lascelles to Salisbury (no. 21), 8 August1900, FO 64/1496.

55. Hicks Beach Papers, Brodrick to Hicks Beach (private), 9 August1900, PCC/72/2; Lansdowne to Hamilton, 16 August 1900, Lansdowne Papers, Lans (5) 28.

56. Hatfield House Papers, tel. Salisbury to Queen Victoria, 9 August 1900, 3M/A/84/117; Great Britain, Foreign Office Archives, tel. Salisbury to Lascelles (no. 117), 9 August 1900, FO 64/1496; Great Britain, War Office Records, min. Lansdowne, 9 August 1900, WO 32/6410.

57. Ministère des Affaires Étrangères, ed., tel. Delcassé to Boutiron (no. 63), 14 August 1900, *DDF* (1) 16, no. 276; Great Britain, War Office Records, Great Britain, War Office Records, Grierson staff diary, 25 September 1900, WO 32/6411.

58. J. C. G. Röhl, ed., *Philipp Eulenburgs Politische Korrespondenz*, (3 vols., Boppard: Boldt Verlag, 1983) 3, no. 1423, Eulenburg to Wilhelm II (private), 11 August1900,; Hans-Otto Meissner, ed., *Denkwürdigkeiten des General-Feldmarschall Alfred Grafen von Waldersee*, 3 vols. (Stuttgart: Deutsche Verlagsanstalt, 1923), 3, 4–5.

59. Great Britain, Foreign Office Archives, tel. Scott to Salisbury (no. 93), 29 August 1900, FO 65/1604; Ministère des Affaires Étrangères, ed., tel. Lamsdorff to Urusov, 12/25 August 1900, *DDF* (1) 16, no. 285; cf. B.A. Romanov, *Russia in Manchuria, 1892–1906* (Ann Arbor, MI: University of Michigan Press, 1952), 185–87.

60. Norman Rich and M. H. Fisher, eds., *The Holstein Papers* (4 vols., Cambridge: CUP, 1955) 4, no. 741, Holstein to Hatzfeldt (private), 23 August1900.

61. G. P. Gooch and H. W. V. Temperley, eds., *British Documents on the Origins of the War, 1898–1914* (11 vols., London: HMSO, 1926–1932) 2, no. 8, Lascelles to Salisbury (no. 228), 23 [*recte* 22] August 1900 (for the correct date see the original of the dispatch in Great Britain, Foreign Office Archives, PRO, FO 64/1494).

62. Hans-Otto Meissner, tel. Wilhelm II to Waldersee, 25 August1900, Waldersee, *Denkwürdigkeiten* 3, 10–1; memo, Wilhelm, 23 August 1900, *GP* 16, no. 4618.

63. Lascelles Papers, Lascelles to Salisbury (private), 1 September 1900, PRO, FO 800/17; Bertie Papers, Bertie to Lascelles (private), 5 September 1900, PRO, FO 800/162.

64. Hamilton Papers, Hamilton to Curzon (private), 22 August 1900, Mss.Eur.C.126/2.

65. Hatfield House Papers, Hamilton to Salisbury (private), 2 August 1900, 3M/E/Hamilton (1898–1902).

66. Hamilton Papers, Hamilton to Curzon (private), 12 September 1900, Mss.Eur.C.126/2. See also Robert V. Kubicek, *The Administration of Imperialism: Joseph Chamberlain at the Colonial Office* (Durham, NC: Duke University Press, 1969), chapter 2; Thomas Richards, *The Imperial Archive: Knowledge and Fantasy of Empire* (London: Verso, 1993), 3–7.

67. Hatfield House Papers, Goschen to Salisbury (private), 4 September 1900, 3M/E/Goschen (1899–1900). For a detailed discussion of the committee see T. G.

Otte, "'Heaven knows where we shall finally drift': Lord Salisbury, the Cabinet, Isolation, and the Boxer Rebellion," in *Incidents and International Relations: People, Power
and Personalities*, edited by Gregory C. Kennedy and Keith Neilson (Westport, Conn.:
Greenwood, 2002), 32–37.

68. Hamilton Papers, Hamilton to Curzon (private), 29 August 1900,
Mss.Eur.C.126/2.

69. Hatfield House Papers, Hicks Beach to Salisbury (private), 2 September 1900,
3M/E/Hicks Beach (1899–1902).

70. Hicks Beach Papers, Hamilton to Hicks Beach (private), 20 August and 2 September 1900, PCC/72/1; Hatfield House Papers, Hamilton to Salisbury (private), 31
August1900, 3M/E/Hamilton (1898–1902).

71. Hamilton Papers, Hamilton to Curzon (private), 5 September 1900,
Mss.Eur.C126/2; Young, *British Policy in China*, 201.

72. Hamilton Papers Hamilton to Curzon (private), 27 April 1900,
Mss.Eur.C126/2; Hatfield House Papers, Hamilton to Salisbury (private), 16 July
1900, 3M/E/Hamilton (1898–1902).

73. Great Britain, Foreign Office Archives, Goschen to Bertie (private), 7 September 1900, FO 800/162; Hatfield House Papers, Goschen to Salisbury (private), 27
August 1900, 3M/E/Goschen (1899–1900).

74. Balfour Papers, Salisbury to Goschen (private), 29 August1900 (copy),
Add.Mss.49706.

75. Lansdowne to Hamilton, 31 August 1900, Lansdowne Papers, Lans (5) 28;
tels. Lascelles to Salisbury (no. 30), 30 August 1900, and vice versa (no. 151), 31 August 1900, *BD* 2, nos. 9 and 11.

76. Julian Amery, *The Life of Joseph Chamberlain* (4 vols., London: Macmillan,
1932–1951), Goschen to Chamberlain (private), 2 September 1900, 4, 139.

77. Balfour Papers, Goschen to Balfour (private), September 1900,
Add.Mss.49706.

78. Great Britain, Foreign Office Archives, unnumbered tel. Warren to Salisbury,
14 June 1900, FO 17/1427. For the situation in the Yangzi basin see Great Britain,
Foreign Office Archives, Fraser to Warren (no. 145, confidential), 18 June 1900, FO
671/257; Chester C. Tan, *The Boxer Catastrophe* (New York: Columbia University
Press, 1955), 83–91.

79. Great Britain, Foreign Office Archives, tels. Warren to Salisbury (nos. 12 and
31), 24 June 1900, and 7 July 1900, FO 17/1427; tel. vice versa (no.85), 16 August
1900, FO 17/1426; J. D. Hargreaves, "Lord Salisbury, British Isolation and the
Yangtze Valley, June–September 1900," *Bulletin of the Institute of Historical Research*,
30 (1957), 62–75. On Shanghai, see Robert Bickers's very instructive *Britain in
China: Community, Culture and Colonialism, 1900–1949* (Manchester: Manchester
University Press, 1999), 123–26.

80. Balfour Papers, Salisbury to Goschen (private), 29 August 1900 (copy),
Add.Mss. 49706; Hatfield House Papers, tel. Sanderson to Salisbury, 15 August
1900, 3M/E/Sanderson (1866–1903).

81. Great Britain, Foreign Office Archives, memo, Col. Waters, 3 September 1900,
FO 64/1494; Otte, "Winston of Germany," 489–90.

82. Bertie's assessment as summarized in Satow Papers, Satow diary, 20 and 24
August 1900, PRO 30/33/16/3.

83. Great Britain, Foreign Office Archives, Goschen to Bertie (private), 4 September 1900, FO 800/162; Chilston Papers, Balfour to Akers-Douglas (private), 30 August 1900, Kent Archive Office, Canterbury, C/22/18.

84. Hatfield House Papers, Hicks Beach to Salisbury (private), 2 September 1900, 3M/E/Hicks Beach (1899–1902); Hicks Beach Papers, Hamilton to Hicks Beach (private), 2 September 1900, PCC/72/1.

85. Hicks Beach Papers, Lansdowne to Hicks Beach (private), 7 September 1900, PCC/84; Hatfield House Papers, tel. Lansdowne to Salisbury (private), 31 August 1900, 3M/A/89/69.

86. Hatfield House Papers, tel. Goschen to Salisbury (private), 4 September 1900, 3M/A/89/70; also in George W. Monger, *The End of Isolation: British Foreign Policy, 1900–1907* (London: Thomas Nelson, 1963), 18.

87. Hatfield House Papers, tel. Salisbury to Goschen 5 September 1900, 3M/A/89/73.

88. Lansdowne to Salisbury, 26 August 1900, Lansdowne Papers, Lans (5) 49; Hatfield House Papers, Goschen to Salisbury (confidential), 7 August 1900, 3M/E/Goschen (1899–1900); Lord Newton, *Lord Lansdowne: A Biography* (London: Macmillan, 1929), 186.

89. Chamberlain Papers, Brodrick to Chamberlain (private), 7 September 1900, Birmingham University Library, JC/11/8/2; Balfour Papers, Brodrick to Balfour (private), 7 September 1900, Add.Mss.49720.

90. Hicks Beach Papers, Hicks Beach to Salisbury (private), 2 and 11 September 1900, PCC/34; Hicks Beach, *Life of Hicks Beach* 2, 124–25.

91. Chamberlain Papers, Chamberlain to Salisbury (private), 31 August 1900, JC/11/30/198.

92. Great Britain, Cabinet Office Records, memo, Chamberlain, "The Chinese Problem," 10 September 1900, CAB 37/53/56; Nish, *Anglo-Japanese Alliance*, 92–93.

93. Akers-Douglas diary, 12 September 1900, F/28; Hicks Beach Papers, Hicks Beach to Salisbury, private, 11 September 1900, PCC/34; Balfour Papers, Devonshire to Balfour (private), 16 September 1900, Add.Mss.49769; Bertie Papers, memo, Bertie, 13 September 1900, *BD* 2, no.12.

94. Salisbury to Lascelles (no. 224), 15 October 1900, *BD* 2, no. 17; Hamilton Papers, Hamilton to Curzon (private), 24 October 1900, Mss.Eur.C.126/2.

95. Midleton Papers, Salisbury to Brodrick (private), 8 October 1900, PRO 30/67/5; Curzon Papers, Salisbury to Curzon (private), 17 October 1900, Mss.Eur.F.111/222.

96. C. A. Bayly, "The Boxer Rebellion and India: Globalizing Myths" [in this volume]; Andrew S. Thompson, "The Language of Imperialism and the Meanings of Empire, 1895–1914," *Journal of British Studies* 36, no. 2 (1997), 147–77.

97. Great Britain, Foreign Office Archives, tel. Satow to Warren (no. 3), 5 January 1906, FO 228/2510. The centrality of the Boxer experience remained a key feature of the British presence in China until the 1930s: see Bickers, *Britain in China*, 195.

10

Humanizing the Boxers

Paul A. Cohen

Ever since the Boxer Uprising took place, just over a century ago, there has been a powerful tendency to caricature the Boxers and, at least at certain junctures, their sisters-in-arms, the Red Lanterns. This has been true both in China and the West. The caricaturing in the West has, with some exceptions, been stridently negative, the Boxers, for most of the past century, being equated with barbarism, cruelty, irrational hatred of foreigners, and superstition.[1] This process of demonization began while the uprising was still in progress. In the years immediately after its suppression, the Boxers became a prime focus of Yellow Peril demonology. During the heightened nationalism and antiforeignism of the 1920s, many Westerners sought to discredit Chinese nationalism by branding it a revival of "Boxerism" (see figure 10.1) and at the time of the Cultural Revolution in the late 1960s Westerners resurrected the stereotype of the Boxers as fanatical, uncivilized xenophobes and pinned it on the Red Guards. In short, the Boxers and "Boxerism" have been used by Westerners as a kind of free-floating arsenal of negative symbols whenever we've been of a mind to denigrate or belittle some aspect of Chinese behavior.

The caricaturing of the Boxers on the Chinese side has been less one-dimensional. During the late Qing educated Chinese generally displayed strongly negative views of the Boxers, repeatedly referring to them as "bandits" (*fei*) and scoffing at the Boxers' and Red Lanterns' religious and magical claims. At the same time there was widespread popular support for the movement, and we have a number of full-color patriotic woodcuts hailing the Boxers and Red Lanterns as heroes and excoriating their foreign adversaries.[2] These contradictory images of the Boxers continued in the years following the original event. Chinese intellectuals, at the time of the New

Figure 10.1. Sapajou, "MAKING THINGS MOVE. The Boxer with the match: 'Ah ha! Something's going to happen now!'" Foreign use of the Boxer image—as well as that of Bolshevism—to denigrate Chinese nationalism reached a high-water mark in the early months of 1927 at the time of the Northern Expedition and the accompanying upsurge of Sino-foreign tension. This cartoon combines both images in the form of a "Russo-Boxer," portrayed as an inciter of mob violence. From *North-China Daily News*, 27 January 1927.

Culture Movement in the second decade of the twentieth century, often saw the Boxers as symbolizing everything about the old China that they wanted to replace: the xenophobia, the irrationality, the barbarism, the superstition, and the backwardness. As a reflection of the growing political radicalism of the 1920s, on the other hand, Chinese revolutionaries began to rework the Boxers into a more positive set of myths, centering on the qualities of "patriotism" and "anti-imperialism." This more affirmative vision of the Boxers as heroic battlers against foreign aggression reached a high-water mark among Chinese on the mainland during the Cultural Revolution of the 1960s and 1970s. During these years praise was also lavished on the Red Lanterns, in particular for their alleged rebellion against the subordinate status of women in the old society (see figure 10.2). Most recently, in the

Figure 10.2. Cultural Revolution Depiction of Red Lantern. A Red Lantern is here portrayed as a fiercely rebellious warrior, who, sword in hand, takes her place side by side with male Boxers in the fight against the foreigner. From *Hongdengzhao* (Shanghai, 1967).

modernizing Deng Xiaoping and post-Deng decades, the Boxers, no friends of modernity, have come in for their share of mockery and ridicule, especially in the literary realm, although in locales where the Boxers first emerged shrines honoring the movement's founders have been erected and in nationalistic rhetoric, official and popular, the Boxers are still held up as patriotic heroes.[3]

The fact that the Boxers are a live—and sometimes quite emotionally charged—symbol in both the West and China means that when historians try to understand them more or less in their own terms, we encounter a lot of intellectual static that needs to be silenced. In this chapter I want to try to do that, with a view not to portraying the Boxers as either good or bad, heroes or savages, but to understanding them as human beings who, faced with the multifaceted crisis that enveloped the North China Plain in the last years of the nineteenth century, responded in ways that were not all that unique from the perspective of Chinese history, or, for that matter, the histories of other peoples in other places and times. (C. A. Bayly, for example, points in his chapter to a number of fascinating parallels between the Boxers and popular dissident movements in India in the closing years of the nineteenth century.)

My efforts to reconstruct what it was like to be alive and conscious in north China in the spring and summer of 1900, when the Boxer Uprising was at its height, draw heavily on contemporary sources, in particular the published notices of the Boxers themselves, the diaries and eyewitness chronicles of contemporary Chinese, and the letters and journals of foreign participants and observers. I also make extensive use of Boxer oral history transcripts to corroborate the claims made in elite Chinese and foreign sources. In reading through these materials it quickly becomes apparent that there were certain aspects of the experiential setting of north China in 1900 that were attracting just about everyone's attention. Among them were the social and psychological effects of the prolonged drought afflicting the region, the religious and magical beliefs of the Boxers and Red Lanterns, the unusual credulousness of the populace as reflected in its eagerness to accept as true the most far-fetched rumors, and the ubiquitous experience of violent and horrific death. Since these were the things that were on people's minds at the time (foreigners, it turns out, as well as Chinese), we can tell a great deal about the world the Boxers and their Christian adversaries inhabited by looking more closely at these areas of contemporary experience.

Take, for example, the experience of death, a theme that as far as I know no Boxer historian in China or the West has ever focused on. When the story of the Boxer Uprising is told, the high points, depending on one's point of view, are generally the characteristics of the Boxers as a movement (their superstition, backwardness, xenophobia, patriotism) or the place of the uprising in the history of Chinese resistance to imperialist aggression or the martyrdom endured by the Christian community or the righteousness and heroism of the foreign military response or the consequences of the Boxer crisis for China's subsequent history. We of course hear of the deaths that occurred. But, more often than not, this part of the story is told in the flat, impersonal language of statistics. Death, in such accounts, becomes a collective marker. It stands as a metaphor for the cruelty of the Boxers or the brutality of the foreign relief forces or the suffering of the Christians or the slaying of innocents. But its meaning as an expression of individual experience is largely lost.[4]

Apart from such actualized death, there was the much broader phenomenon of death *anxiety*, which was pervasive in north China in 1900. Impoverished farmers idled by the continued failure of the rains in the spring became progressively more hungry and also progressively more nervous, especially (one imagines) those of them over thirty who retained vivid memories of the catastrophic drought of the late 1870s when close to ten million people in north China starved to death (see figures 10.3 and 10.4). (The life-and-death importance of water for the farming population of central Shanxi, including access to it and control over its sources, is a key ingredient in the argument Henrietta Harrison develops in her chapter.)

Young Boxers spent many hours practicing invulnerability rituals designed to confer immunity to death—invulnerability rituals, incidentally, that had an ample history in China both before and after the Boxer Uprising. Much of the Boxers' magic, moreover, was specifically directed either at ensuring the death of their foes or protecting against the death of their supporters among the general population. The anxiety rumors that were rampant throughout the region in the spring and summer typically had as their central content images of death or grave bodily harm; even the wish rumors that also had wide circulation may plausibly be seen as providing emotional release from the fear of death. Finally, as if other sources of death anxiety were not already abundant enough, notices posted all over north China repeatedly concluded with dire warnings of the terrible fate certain to befall those who chose to ignore the Boxers' message (see figure 10.5).

Different individuals in 1900 experienced death in different ways. Some were victims, others perpetrators, still others witnesses. Some wrote of the sights and sounds of death—and of death's distinctive smells. Others described the terrors that they personally or people they knew or had observed had gone through in the face of death. And many recounted the fearful choices that had to be made. The experience of death, in short, like the experience of anything, was a highly individual matter.

Much of the general literature on death, I discovered when I first looked, is concerned with the formal and informal rituals people in different cultures have devised to ease the transition across this greatest, and most final, of life's divides. However, as the following eyewitness description from the

Figures 10.3 and 10.4. Images of Starvation from North China Famine of Late 1870s. These images originally appeared in a Chinese pamphlet. In figure 3 the starving stand in pools of blood; in figure 4 a corpse is being carved up to provide food for the living. From Committee of the China Famine Relief Fund, *The Famine in China* (London: C. Kegan Paul, 1878).

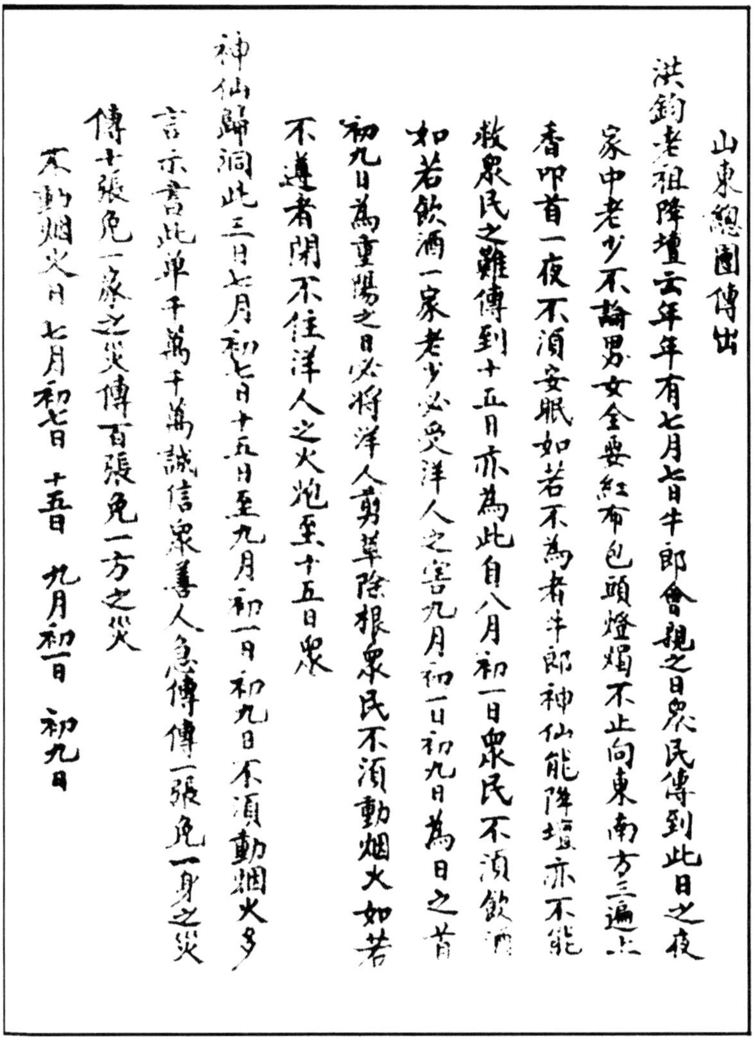

山東總團傳出

洪鈞老祖降壇云年年有七月七日半夜郎會觀之日眾民傳到此日之夜

家中老少不論男女金要紅布包頭燈焰不止向東南方三遍北

香叩首一夜不須安眠如若不為者牛郎神仙能降壇亦不能

救眾民之難傳到十五日亦為此自八月初一日眾民不須飲酒

如若飲酒一家老少必受洋人之害九月初一日初九日為日之首

初九日為重陽之日必將洋人剪草除根眾民不須動烟火如若

不遵者開不住洋人之火炮至十五日眾

神仙歸洞此三月七月初七日十五日至九月初一日初九日不須動烟火多

言示齊此單干萬千萬誠信眾善人急傳傳一張免一身之災

傳一張免一家之災傳百張免一方之災

天勅烟火月七月初七日 十五日 九月初九日

Figure 10.5. Boxer Notice. This fairly representative Boxer notice, issued from Shandong, contains a variety of instructions to the populace. Those who disobey the instructions, the notice asserts, will be defenseless against foreign gunfire. By circulating the notice people will safeguard themselves and their families against calamity. From *Yihetuan dang'an shiliao* (Beijing: Zhonghua, 1959), vol. 1.

Tianjin area makes clear, a great deal of the death that people in China experienced in the summer of 1900 was raw death, unmediated by ritual of any kind:

> There were many corpses floating in the river. Some were without heads, others were missing limbs. The bodies of women often had their nipples cut off and their genitalia mutilated. . . . There were also bodies in the shallow areas by the banks, with flocks of crows pecking away at them. The smell was so bad we had to cover our noses the whole day. Still, no one came out to collect the bodies for burial. People said that they were all Christians who had been killed by the Boxers and the populace dared not get involved.[5]

And, so, death, the ultimate object of the anxiety that was so pervasive at the time, also, because of the way in which it was encountered, became an added source of this very anxiety (see figure 10.6).

Another way to put a human face on the Boxers, to make them seem less exotic and mysterious, is to compare aspects of their experience with similar phenomena in other cultural settings. Let me offer a few examples. In Boxer notices that were widely circulated in the first half of 1900, the pervasive drought then gripping the North China Plain was consistently portrayed as resulting from the anger of the gods over the growing influence of the foreigner and in particular of the foreign religion Christianity. Rain would again fall and the drought lift, the notices explicitly stated, only after all foreigners had been killed and foreign influence in China eradicated. The predication of a supernatural connection between lack of precipitation and some form of inappropriate human action—the intrusion in this case of a foreign religious rival—reflected a pattern of thinking that had been deeply etched in Chinese cultural behavior for centuries. What I find fascinating is that it is a pattern that has also been widely displayed in other cultures (especially agrarian ones) in many different historical eras.

There is a classic statement of the logic informing it in the Hebrew Bible (Deuteronomy 11:13–21), where God announces to His chosen people that if they heed His commandments and love and serve Him faithfully, He will favor their land with "rain at the proper season," assuring ample harvests and an abundance of grain for their cattle. But, if they are "tempted to forsake God and turn to false gods in worship," His wrath will be directed against them, and "He will close the heavens and hold back the rain." Other examples abound. Muslims in Nigeria in 1973 interpreted the drought of that year as a sign of "the wrath of Allah against mankind." For Christians in late Elizabethan England, the famine of the 1590s "showed that God was angry with the people."[6] In Botswana in the nineteenth century it was widely believed that a prolonged drought was caused by the incursions of Christianity, especially after a renowned rainmaker, upon being baptized, abandoned his rainmaking practices.[7]

Figure 10.6.   Dead Defenders at South Gate of Tianjin's Chinese City. James Ricalton, who claimed that the bodies belonged to Boxers, took this photograph immediately after the foreign entry into the walled native city on 14 July 1900. Courtesy of Library of Congress.

A second example relates to the core religious practice of the Boxers as they fanned out across the North China Plain in the spring and summer of 1900. This was spirit possession—a transformative religious experience in which a god (or spirit) descended and entered the body of an individual who then became the possessing god's instrument. The anthropological literature on spirit possession, as it has been manifested in China and in many other parts of the world, is extensive, and perusing it helps to place Boxer possession in a wider context, thereby clarifying its meaning and functions within the movement. Erika Bourguignon, for example, looking at possession trance globally, distinguishes between societies, such as Palau (in the western Pacific), in which possession trance plays a predominantly *public* role, serving the needs of the community, and societies, like the Shakers of St. Vincent in the West Indies or the Maya Apostolics of Yucatán, in which the function of trance is a mainly *private* one, focusing on its importance for the individual, "who believes himself 'saved' as a result of the experience and . . . derives euphoria and personal strength from it."[8] Bourguignon sees these ideal-typical functions of trance, the public and the private, as endpoints of a continuum and she recognizes that, in some societies, possession appears to serve both roles simultaneously. Certainly this was the case with the Boxers, among whom entering into a trance state was closely tied to invulnerability beliefs affording protection in combat. In fact it would not be wide of the mark to argue that the broad range of individual (or private) needs spirit possession satisfied within the context of the Boxer movement constituted a major reason for the ease with which Boxer possession developed into a mass (or public) phenomenon in the last years of the nineteenth century. Self-preservation, in an immediate sense, and national preservation, on a more abstract level, were mutually reinforcing.

As another example, the population of north China was in a nervous and jittery state in the spring and summer of 1900, and in this setting rumors flourished. By far the most widely circulated rumor—there are frequent references to it in Harrison's chapter—was one that charged foreigners and Christians with contaminating the water supply by placing poison in village wells. The well-poisoning charge, according to a contemporary, was "practically universal" and "accounted for much of the insensate fury" directed by ordinary Chinese against Christians.[9] An interesting question has to do with the content of the hysteria in this instance. Why mass poisoning? And why, in particular, the poisoning of public water sources? If one accepts the view that rumors convey messages and that rumor epidemics, in particular, supply important symbolic information concerning the collective worries of societies in crisis, one approach to answering such questions is to try to identify the match or fit between a rumor panic and its immediate context. In the case of kidnapping panics, which have a long history not only in China but in many other societies as well, the focus of collective concern is the safety of children, who (as the term *kidnap* seems to imply) are almost always seen as the primary victims. Rumors of mass poisoning, on the other hand, are far more appropriate as a symbolic response to a crisis, such as war or natural disaster or epidemic, in which *all* of the members of society are potentially at risk.

A look at the experience of other societies amply confirms this supposition. Charges of well poisoning and similar crimes were brought against the first Christians in Rome and the Jews in the Middle Ages at the time of the Black Plague (1348). During the cholera epidemic in Paris in 1832 a rumor circulated that poison powder had been scattered in the bread, vegetables, milk, and water of that city. In the early stages of World War I rumors were spread in all belligerent countries that enemy agents were busy poisoning the water supplies.[10] Within hours of the great Tokyo earthquake of 1 September 1923, which was accompanied by raging fires, rumors began to circulate charging ethnic Koreans and socialists not only with having set the fires but also with plotting rebellion and poisoning the wells.[11] Newspaper accounts in 1937, at the onset of the Sino-Japanese War, accused Chinese traitors of poisoning the drinking water of Shanghai.[12] And rumors of mass poisoning proliferated in Biafra during the Nigerian civil conflict of the late 1960s.[13]

In many of these instances, the rumors targeted outsiders (or their internal agents), who were accused, symbolically if not literally, of seeking the annihilation of the society in which the rumors circulated. This, of course, closely approximates the situation prevailing in China at the time of the Boxer Uprising. Like the charge that the foreigners were the ones ultimately responsible for the lack of rain in the spring and summer of 1900, rumors accusing foreigners and their native surrogates of poisoning north China's water supplies portrayed outsiders symbolically as depriving Chinese of what was most essential for the sustaining of life.[14] The well-poisoning rumor epidemic thus spoke directly to the collective fear that was uppermost in the minds of ordinary people at the time: the fear of death.

Yet another strategy for humanizing the Boxers is what the anthropologist Paul Rabinow has called the "anthropologization of the West."[15] The ultimate objective of anthropologizing the West is the creation, as far as is humanly possible, of a level playing field between the Western inquirer and the non-Western object of his or her inquiry. Rabinow calls on Western anthropologists to accomplish this by showing how culturally specific and exotic the West's own understanding of reality has been. My inclination, basically, is to turn Rabinow on his head. I fully share his objective. However, I prefer to achieve it by emphasizing how *un*exotic, even universally human, was the Boxers' understanding of reality. With this in mind, in looking at the various aspects of the experiential world of the Boxers, I try, wherever possible, to counteract the Boxers' exceptionalism, to remove them from the realm of the strange and exotic.

For example, in contrast with almost all Chinese historians, I scrupulously avoid using pejorative terms like "superstitious" or "ignorant" or "backward" to describe the beliefs and practices of the Boxers. To define such beliefs and practices as "superstitious" is, in my view, to adopt an essentially adversarial stance toward them, making it more difficult to acquire a deeper appreciation of how they appeared to the Boxers themselves and the functions they served in the Boxers' intellectual and emotional worlds. Another way of rendering the Boxers in less exotic, more human, terms is

by paying close attention to the extraordinary emotional climate that characterized north China in 1900—the unusual levels of excitement, anger, jit-
teriness, and above all fear and anxiety that prevailed among all groups,
Chinese and foreign. Emotions are a great leveler. Finally, without denying
for a moment the importance of culture and its shaping influence on human behavior, I am convinced that in important respects the Boxers' responses to the problems they faced bore remarkable similarities to the responses of people in other cultures, including the cultures of Europe and
America, when faced with comparable difficulties.

Let me illustrate. We have already seen how common it is the world over
to view drought as supernatural in origin. Predictably, among people who
hold to such a view, both in China and elsewhere, a characteristic response
to drought is direct propitiation of the gods or some other supernatural entity through prayer or other rain-inducing ceremonial practices. Our intu-
ition, however, prompts us to reserve such a response to "backward" societies with low educational attainments; it is not something we would
anticipate encountering, say, in modern secular America, with its general
trust in scientific explanation of the physical world and its extraordinary
technological capability. How surprising, then, to discover that when a serious drought hit the Midwest in the summer of 1988, Jesse Jackson, then
campaigning for the Democratic nomination for president, prayed for rain
in the middle of an Iowa cornfield, and an Ohio florist flew in a Sioux med-
icine man from one of the Dakotas to perform a rainmaking ceremony,
which thousands came to watch.[16]

Another example has to do with magic and how people in different cultures respond when magic doesn't work. Chinese, as well as foreigners, who
have written on the Boxer movement, either as contemporary witnesses or
latter-day scholars, have consistently ridiculed the movement's vaunted
magical powers. This mocking stance has, for reasons that are plain enough,
been displayed with greatest frequency in connection with the Boxers' invulnerability claims. "If the bandits' magic can protect against gunfire," one
staunchly anti-Boxer official intoned, "how is it that on the seventeenth and
eighteenth days [of the fifth month of *gengzi*, i.e., 13–14 June 1900], when
the [Boxer] bandits launched repeated assaults against the legation quarters
on East Jiaomin Lane [Legation Street], the foreign soldiers' firing instantly
killed several bandits?"[17] An American missionary, after reporting that a
group of thirty to forty Boxers had scattered when fired on by marines in
Beijing on June 14, quipped, "These bullet-proof Boxers don't seem to like
the smell of foreign powder!"[18] Chinese scholars in more recent times,
while honoring the Boxers for their patriotic resistance to foreign aggression, have been equally dismissive of Boxer magical claims.[19]

There are a number of points to be made here. First, we have compelling
evidence that the Christian antagonists of the Boxers operated from a per-

spective, with respect to magicoreligious protection, that was broadly similar to that of the Boxers themselves: Chinese Catholic survivors in southeastern Zhili apparently believed that the appearance of the Virgin Mary above their church was instrumental in safeguarding them from a number of Boxer attacks between December 1899 and July 1900,[20] and foreign missionaries (Protestant as well as Catholic), threatened by fire during the siege of the legations, regularly attributed life-saving shifts in the direction or strength of the wind to the hand of God.[21]

Second, I would argue that the empirical-efficacy test applied by all critics of Boxer magical beliefs, generally leading to the conclusion that these beliefs were ineffective, largely misses the point. When the rites of medieval Catholics failed to result in miracles, people didn't stop performing them. When Protestant prayers for deliverance in the summer of 1900 went unanswered, the Christian faith of those who survived often became even stronger. Prayers and other ceremonies designed to induce rain sometimes "work" and sometimes don't, yet it seems an invariable rule the world over that when drought conditions prevail the stock of rainmakers goes up. Empirical efficacy, as a test of magicoreligious validity, is the ultimate cheap shot and as such has been universally used to discredit other people's beliefs. And yet people, even of "high cultural level," continue to believe. They continue to make, as hardheaded psychologists who study superstition are apt to put it, "false correlations between a particular act and a particular result."[22] Why?

This is a difficult question, and it is answered differently in different religious settings. One answer contests the very premise on which the challenge to magicoreligious ritual is often founded, to wit, that such ritual must be immediately and discernibly efficacious. Thus, the anthropologist Mary Douglas writes of the Dinka herdspeople of the southern Sudan: "Of course Dinka hope that their rites will suspend the natural course of events. Of course they hope that rain rituals will cause rain, healing rituals avert death, harvest rituals produce crops. But instrumental efficacy is not the only kind of efficacy to be derived from their symbolic action. The other kind is achieved in the action itself, in the assertions it makes and the experience which bears its imprinting." "So far from being meaningless," Douglas adds, "it is primitive magic which gives meaning to existence."[23]

In responding to the same question, Christian missionaries at the turn of the century would certainly have put the emphasis elsewhere. Prayer, for Christians, might indeed inform existence with subjective meaning. But the inner logic of events, in objective terms, was knowable only to God. God could be counted on to "bring forth the good to the *greatest number*," and one could be certain that, whatever transpired, in the end it would be for the furtherance of His kingdom. But, in the daily workings of human life, His plan was often beyond comprehension, and all Christians could do in the face of this was trust in it absolutely, even when their prayers were of no avail.[24]

The Boxers had yet other ways of accounting for the inefficacy of their rituals without imperiling the belief system on which they were based. Sometimes, when Boxer rituals failed to work properly, it was explained in terms of the insincerity or spiritual inadequacy or insufficient training of the person enacting them. But much more often the Boxers pointed to sources of pollution in the external environment (the most powerful of which were things relating to women, most especially uncleanness in women)—countervailing magical forces that had the power to destroy the efficacy of the Boxers' own magic.

For all that separated the Dinka, the Christians, and the Boxers, in the ways in which they dealt with the issue of ritual efficacy, there was one thing that drew them—and perhaps all other religious practitioners—tightly together. Their religious and magical practices had as a paramount goal the affording of protection and emotional security in the face of a future that was indeterminate and fraught with danger and risk. Through their rituals, each sought to exercise some degree of control over the uncertainty—or, as I like to call it, the outcome-blindness—that is one of the defining marks of human experience.[25]

One last means of constructing a more human picture of the Boxers is to take note of the counternarratives that appear with some frequency in the sources—narratives that offer alternative perspectives on some of the more stereotyped images by which the Boxers were known at the time or have come to be known. Since the Boxer Uprising as an event had to do, above all, with war and violence and death, it is not surprising that the more compelling of these counternarratives are often war stories. I will conclude by relating a few of them.

Although, as we have seen, the tendency among both elite Chinese and foreigners was to deride the performance of the Boxers in combat, there were those in both camps who took at least partial exception to this judgment. Yang Mushi, a Qing army officer who fought against the Boxers in late May and early June, reported that the Boxers' main strength lay in their numbers and the fact that they were "not afraid to die." Ai Sheng, a persistent Boxer critic, also conceded that, when in a possessed state, the Boxers "invariably faced death unflinchingly." Herbert Hoover, a young engineer in China at the time of the uprising, made much the same point, at least implicitly, in his account of the behavior of Boxer fighters on the first day of the Chinese assault on the railway station in Tianjin (June 18). And Roland Allen, a British chaplain in Beijing, after making a similar appraisal of Boxer fighting valor, as displayed in a battle on 20 August between Bengal Lancers and a small band of Boxers armed only with swords and spears, commented that this was "only another proof that the Chinese can fight and will fight, in his own cause, whilst he will not fight when led by officers in whom he reposes no trust, in a cause which he does not understand."[26]

Along with frequent demonstrations of personal courage, the Boxers, as their casualties mounted in fighting against adversaries who were almost invariably better armed, also became progressively more frightened. Offsetting formulaic Communist-era depictions of the Boxers as heroic resisters against foreign aggression are contemporary accounts portraying them in a far more vulnerable light. On 19 August a group of Boxers with antiquated rifles ran into a foreign force over a thousand strong west of Tianjin. The foreigners waited until the Boxers' ammunition was spent, then surrounded them and fired volley after volley into their midst. "Unfortunately," wrote Liu Xizi, a Chinese from the area, "the spirit soldiers of yore were suddenly turned into spirits [*gui*]." But "the most unbearable thing of all to see and hear," he added, reminding us that many Boxers were little more than boys, was the "children in their early teens lying by the roadside, with wounds to their arms and legs, crying out for their fathers and mothers."[27]

One final example, admittedly of a rarer sort, is especially compelling. Although "Boxerism" in the West has become, in the minds of many, a metaphor for extreme brutality and there is no lack of substantiation of Boxer cruelty in contemporary accounts, the Boxers were also capable of hollowing out a quiet space in the noise of war for the demonstration of personal compassion. Luella Miner recounts an incident involving the thirteen-year-old son of a Chinese pastor from Baoding, whose entire immediate family had been killed by Boxers. The boy was later caught by a group of Boxers sixteen miles south of Baoding and was about to be put to death when one of his captors, after discovering that he was all alone in the world, stepped forward and announced that he would adopt the boy as his own son. The boy's deliverer, whom Miner identifies as one of three bachelor brothers, "all notorious bullies," kept the boy in his home for three months, "tenderly providing for every want," and when it was found out that he had an uncle, also a pastor, who was still living, personally escorted him to Baoding to reunite them. The interesting thing about Miner's account is its demythologization of the Boxers. Even as Boxer behavior *in general* is represented by such characteristically lurid adjectives as "cut-throat" and "blood-thirsty," a lone Boxer, described in the story as "the terror of the region," is acknowledged to have feelings of tenderness and compassion. The fact that the author of this account happens to have been an American missionary who was among the besieged in the legations in Beijing in the summer of 1900 only makes it the more remarkable.[28]

Let me wind up by saying a word or two about what I've been doing in the foregoing pages and how it fits in with some of the broader themes of this volume. A number of the other chapters—James Hevia's scrutiny of looting and other forms of foreign "punitive" behavior in the aftermath of the siege, Ben Middleton's probing of the shifting views of Kōtoku Shūsui on Japan's imperialist project—discuss contemporary Western and Japanese criticism of the conduct of foreigners in China during the Boxer episode and the uncomfortable questions this conduct raised at the time concerning the allied forces' self-appointed "civilizing mission."[29] The general thrust of these contributions, however, is not to reconceptualize the Boxers (or, more broadly, the Chinese side); it is to turn the moral spotlight on the West and Japan.[30] Indeed, in press accounts quoted by Hevia, the Chinese are expressly described by such terms as "savage," "barbaric," and "sanguinary," and the main issue posed is whether China's adversaries, if they persist in behaving in the same way, are justified in claiming for themselves the mantle of "civilization."

What I do in my chapter is quite different from this, in that the focus of the demythologization is not on the West (or Japan), but on the Boxers themselves. In my efforts to counteract the caricaturing of the Boxers that has been pervasive in both China and the West and to present them in a more human guise, I've stayed as close as possible to the experiential side of the Boxer episode: the emotions actuating the participants, the ways in which both Boxers and Christians responded to the unusual circumstances in which they found themselves in north China in 1900, how they constructed their respective worlds. Also, in the course of doing this—and this is a second way in which my chapter, at least indirectly, picks up on a larger theme of the volume—I've made it a special point to highlight aspects of the Boxer story that resonate with the experiences of people elsewhere, emphasizing the universally human over the culturally particular. A number of the chapters in this book—I would draw attention, in particular, to those by Anand Yang and C. A. Bayly (presenting a range of Indian perspectives on the Boxers) and by T. G. Otte (exploring the implications of the Boxer War for British foreign policy)—put the events of 1900 in larger contexts of one sort or another. I try to do this also. But I do it in a different way, by challenging arbitrary and misleading distinctions between "China" and the "West," making it possible thereby to imagine the Boxers less as prototypically exotic—the West's all-purpose "other"—and more as plausibly human.

As noted earlier, I don't at all intend by this emphasis on the human dimension to disparage the importance of culture. Indeed, in my book on the Boxers I devote a fair amount of attention to culture. But culture, in addition to forming the prism through which human communities express themselves in thought and action, also has the potential to distance one community from another, thereby facilitating processes of stereotyping, caricaturing, and mythologization. In light of the unusual degree to which the Boxers have been subjected to just such processes over the years, it seemed especially important to me in my essay to focus on what they share with, rather than what separates them from, human beings in other historical and cultural settings. The point is not to deny the Boxers their particularity (nor, certainly, to portray them as angels); it is, rather, to rescue them from the aura of dehumanizing exceptionalism and distortion that has surrounded their history almost from the beginning.

NOTES

Although many of the details in this chapter are drawn from my book, *History in Three Keys: The Boxers as Event, Experience, and Myth* (New York: Columbia University Press, 1997), the analytic emphasis is on a theme—the humanity of the Boxers—that is only dealt with implicitly in the book.

1. The exceptions, emanating occasionally from contemporaries but more commonly, over time, from the political left, may also be seen as caricatures, insofar as they assume "love of country" to have been a primary attribute of the Boxer cause. The most prominent example of such positive mythologization among contemporaries was Sir Robert Hart, who viewed the Boxers (in my view uncritically) as "patriots" (*"These from the Land of Sinim": Essays on the Chinese Question* [London: Chapman and Hall, 1901], 4, 53–54). Arthur von Rosthorn, the Austrian chargé d'affaires at the time of the siege, also saw the Boxers as "patriots," whose anger toward the foreigners was entirely justified (Colin Mackerras, *Western Images of China* [Oxford: Oxford University Press, 1989], 69–70). Editorial sentiment favorable to the Boxers was widely expressed in the contemporary Russian press (David Schimmelpenninck van der Oye, "Russia's Ambivalent Response to the Boxers," *Cahiers du Monde russe* 41, no. 1 [January–March 2000]: 57–78). In the non-West, Indian intellectuals, as noted in C. A. Bayly's chapter, expressed a range of views at the time of the uprising.

2. Several of these patriotic woodcuts (in black and white) are in Cohen, *History in Three Keys*, 140, 153–54. James Flath dealt with them in his contribution to the "International Conference on '1900: the Boxers, China, and the World'" (London, 2001); he has since published his findings in *The Cult of Happiness: Nianhua, Art, and History in Rural North China* (Seattle: University of Washington Press, 2004). See also Jane E. Elliott, *Some Did It for Civilisation, Some Did It for Their Country: A Revised View of the Boxer War* (Hong Kong: Chinese University Press, 2002), plates 3.10(a), 3.10(b), 3.16, 3.18, 3.20, 3.21.

3. See, for example, the fiery speech delivered by the respected historian Dai Yi at the opening ceremonies of the conference marking the hundredth anniversary of the Boxer Uprising, held in Ji'nan, Shandong, 9–12 October 2000. The text is in *Yihetuan yanjiuhui tongxun* [The Boxer Study Association newsletter] 25 (March 2001): 8–11.

4. This is certainly true of the several chapters in this book—those authored by James Hevia, Henrietta Harrison, Roger Thompson, Anand Yang, and R. G. Tiedemann—that allude in one way or another to death. None of them deals with death in an *experiential* sense.

5. Guan He, *Quanfei wenjian lu* [A record of things seen and heard concerning the Boxer bandits], in *Yihetuan* (The Boxers), ed. Jian Bozan, et al., 4 vols. (Shanghai: Shenzhou guoguang she, 1951), 1: 482.

6. Both examples are cited in David Arnold, *Famine: Social Crisis and Historical Change* (Oxford: Basil Blackwell, 1988), 15.

7. R. K. Hitchcock, "The Traditional Response to Drought in Botswana," in *Symposium on Drought in Botswana*, ed. Madalon T. Hinchey (Gabarone, Botswana: Botswana Society in collaboration with Clark University Press, 1979), 92.

8. Erika Bourguignon, "An Assessment of Some Comparisons and Implications," in *Religion, Altered States of Consciousness, and Social Change*, ed. Erika Bourguignon (Columbus: Ohio State University Press, 1973), 326–27.

9. Arthur H. Smith, *China in Convulsion*, 2 vols. (New York: Fleming H. Revell, 1901), 2: 659–60.

10. These examples are all drawn from Richard D. Loewenberg, "Rumors of Mass Poisoning in Times of Crisis," *Journal of Criminal Psychopathology* 5 (July 1943): 131–42.

11. Andrew Gordon, *Labor and Imperial Democracy in Prewar Japan* (Berkeley: University of California Press, 1991), 177.

12. Loewenberg, "Rumors of Mass Poisoning," 133–34. Another report from Shanghai, published in a Japanese newspaper, stated that Chinese dropped bacteria into wells before retreating from the city (Loewenberg, 135).

13. Nwokocha K. U. Nkpa, "Rumors of Mass Poisoning in Biafra," *Public Opinion Quarterly* 41, no. 3 (Fall 1977): 332–46.

14. It should be noted that "outsiders" in this context need not refer exclusively to non-Chinese; it could also, as Harrison's discussion of central Shanxi makes clear, embrace Chinese (she calls them "vagrants") who were not native to the locality and therefore were targets of suspicion.

15. Paul Rabinow, "Representations Are Social Facts: Modernity and Post-Modernity in Anthropology," in *Writing Culture: The Poetics and Politics of Ethnography*, ed. James Clifford and George E. Marcus (Berkeley: University of California Press, 1986), 241.

16. Boston radio station WEEI, 19–20 June 1988. The general consensus of the onlookers in Ohio, according to the radio announcer (Charles Osgood), was to believe in rather than doubt the potential efficacy of the rainmaking ceremony.

17. Yuan Chang, memorial of *gengzi* 5/22 (18 June 1900), in *Yihetuan* 4:162.

18. Luella Miner, Journal, Beijing, 14 June 1900, in Luella Miner Papers (North China Mission), American Board of Commissioners for Foreign Missions, Papers (Houghton Library, Harvard University), box 1, file 1.

19. See, for example, Yang Tianhong, "Yihetuan 'shenshu' lunlüe" [A summary discussion of the "magical powers" of the Boxers], *Jindaishi yanjiu* (Studies in modern Chinese history) 5 (1993): 194.

20. Albert Vinchon, S.J., "La culte de la Sainte Vierge du Tche-li sud-est: Rapport présenté au Congrès marial de 1904," *Chine, Ceylan, Madagascar: Lettres missionnaires français de la Compagnie de Jésus (Province de Champagne)* 18 (March 1905): 132–33.

21. When a heavy wind was on the point of spreading a blaze from the Hanlin Academy to the British legation, according to Mary Porter Gamewell, the wind suddenly died down: "The same voice that spoke to the sea 1900 years ago spoke that violent wind into quiet." Gamewell, "History of the Peking Station of the North China Mission of the Woman's Foreign Missionary Society of the Methodist Episcopal Church," 61, in Miscellaneous Personal Papers, Manuscript Group No. 8, box

no. 73, China Records Project, Divinity School Library, Yale University. See also Sarah Boardman Goodrich, "Journal of 1900," 28 June 1900, 29, in ibid., box no. 88; Bishop Favier, diary, 15 June 1900, in J. Freri, ed., *The Heart of Pekin: Bishop A. Favier's Diary of the Siege, May–August 1900* (Boston: Marlier, 1901), 26.

22. Jane E. Brody, "Lucking Out: Weird Rituals and Strange Beliefs," *New York Times*, 27 January 1991, S11.

23. Mary Douglas, *Purity and Danger: An Analysis of the Concepts of Pollution and Taboo* (New York: Routledge, 1991), 68, 72.

24. The quotation is from Sarah Boardman Goodrich, letter, Tong Cho [Tongzhou], 25 May 1900, in Miscellaneous Personal Papers, Manuscript Group No. 8, box no. 88, China Records Project.

25. Gustav Jahoda writes of "superstition"—and I would make the same claims for religious and magical ritual generally—that it provides "at least the subjective feeling of predictability and control," thereby reducing the anxiety that is apt to be aroused in threatening situations marked by uncertainty as to probable outcome. Jahoda, *Psychology of Superstition* (Harmondsworth, Middlesex, Eng.: Penguin, 1969), 130, 134.

26. Yang Mushi, *Gengzi jiaoban quanfei dianwen lu* [Selected telegrams concerning the suppression of the Boxer bandits in 1900], in *Yihetuan* 4:347; Ai Sheng, *Quanfei jilüe* [A brief account of the Boxer bandits], in *Yihetuan* 1:447; Hoover, "History, June, 17th. to 23rd., 1900," 3, in Lou Hoover Papers, Boxer Rebellion: Drafts, Herbert Hoover Presidential Library, West Branch, Iowa; Allen, *The Siege of the Peking Legations* (London: Smith, Elder, 1901), 288.

27. Liu Xizi, *Jin xi biji* [A cautionary account of the area west of Tianjin], in *Yihetuan* 2:87–88.

28. Miner's account was published, under the title "Ti-to and the Boxers: A True Story of a Young Christian's Almost Miraculous Escape from Death at the Hands of Bold Cut-throats," in *The Ram's Horn*. The version used here is in Luella Miner Papers, box 4, file 1.

29. Two other papers presented at the "International Conference on '1900: the Boxers, China, and the World'" (London, 2001), but not included in the present volume, also did this. One was Régine Thiriez's survey of the depiction of the 1900 events in the French illustrated press; the other, by Susanne Kuß, analyzed the exterminatory actions of German soldiers in China. Much of the material in Kuß's paper is included in her "Deutsche Soldaten während des Boxeraufstandes in China: Elemente und Ursprünge des Vernichtungskrieges," in *Das Deutsche Reich und der Boxeraufstand*, ed. Susanne Kuß and Bernd Martin (volume 2 in the series titled *Erfurter Reihe zur Geschichte Asiens*) (München: Iudicium Verlag, 2002).

30. This is also an implicit theme in—although it is by no means the main objective of—Hevia's recent book *English Lessons: The Pedagogy of Imperialism in Nineteenth-Century China* (Durham: Duke University Press, 2003); see also Elliott, *Some Did It for Civilisation*, especially chapter 5.

Bibliography

"34-ha no bundori shitsumon." *Yorozu Chōhō*, 25 January 1902.
Acta Ordinis Fratrum Minorum. Quaracchi (Florence). 1898–1910.
Ai Sheng. *Quanfei jilüe* [A brief account of the Boxer bandits]. *Yihetuan* 1:441–64.
Allen, Roland. *The Siege of the Peking Legations.* London: Smith, Elder & Co., 1901.
Ament, William. "A Bishop's Loot." *Independent* 53 (1901): 2217–18.
———. "The Charges against Missionaries." *Independent* 53 (1901): 1051–52.
American Board of Commissioners for Foreign Missions. Alice M. Williams Miscellaneous Papers. Houghton Library, Harvard University, Cambridge, Mass.
———. Shansi Mission. Houghton Library, Harvard University, Cambridge, Mass.
Amery, Julian. *The Life of Joseph Chamberlain.* 4 vols. London: Macmillan, 1932–1951.
Amin, Shahid. *Event, Metaphor, Memory: Chauri Chaura 1922–1992.* Berkeley: University of California Press, 1995.
Annales de la Propagation de la Foi. Lyon: 1880–1903.
Arnold, David. *Famine: Social Crisis and Historical Change.* Oxford: Basil Blackwell, 1988.
"Atrocities by Chinese," *New York Times*, 4 October 1900, 2.
Atwell, Pamela. *British Mandarins and Chinese Reformers: The British Administration of Weihaiwei (1898–1930) and the Territory's Return to Chinese Rule.* Hong Kong: Oxford University Press, 1985.
Australian National University Library. The Giles-Pickford Photographic Collection, album 2 page 1, photograph 1–2, "British Legation—Main Gate," image 2233396.
"Awaya, Hayashi ryūchi." *Yorozu Chōhō*, 15 February 1902.
Balfour Papers. British Library, Add MSS 49706.
Barrow, Edmund George. *The Sepoy Officer's Manual: A Book of Reference for Officers of the Bengal Native Infantry.* Revised and brought up to date by Lt. H. B. Vaughan. Calcutta: Thacker, Spink, 1887.

Bataille, Jules. "Siège de Fan-kia-kata par les Boxeurs (juin–septembre 1900)." *Études* 38e année, tome 87 (20 May 1901): 433–56.

Becker, Emile. *Un demi-siècle d'apostolat en Chine. Le Révérend Père Joseph Gonnet de la Compagnie de Jésus.* 2nd ed. Hejian: Imprimerie de la Mission, 1900.

Bernard, Henri. *La Compagnie de Jésus. L'Ancien vicariat apostolique du Tchéli sud-est-ses filiales, ses annexes.* Tianjin: Procure de la Mission de Sienhsien, 1940.

Bernstein, Lewis. "A History of Tientsin in Early Modern Times, 1800–1911." PhD diss., University of Kansas, 1988.

Bertie Papers, Papers of Francis Leveson Bertie, first Viscount Bertie of Thame, British Library, Add MSS 63013.

Bevans, Charles I. *Treaties and Other International Agreements of the United States of America, 1776–1949.* Washington, D.C.: U.S. Government Printing Office, 1918–1930.

Bickers, Robert. *Britain in China: Community, Culture and Colonialism, 1900–1949.* Manchester: Manchester University Press, 1999.

———. "Boxed Out: How the British Museum Suppressed Discussion of British Looting in China." *The Times Literary Supplement* 5129 (2001): 15.

Bickers, Robert, and Jeffrey N. Wasserstrom. "Shanghai's 'Chinese and Dogs Not Admitted' Sign: History, Legend and Contemporary Symbol." *The China Quarterly* 142 (1995): 444–66.

Biggerstaff, Knight. "Some Notes on the *Tung-hua lu* and the *Shih-lu.*" *Harvard Journal of Asiatic Studies* 4, no. 2 (1939): 101–15.

Bornemann, Fritz. *Johann Baptist Anzer bis zur Ankunft in Shantung 1880.* Rome: Collegium Verbi Divini, 1977.

———. *Der selige P. J. Freinademetz 1852–1909. Ein Steyler China-Missionar. Ein Lebensbild nach zeitgenössischen Quellen.* Bozen: Freinademetz-Haus, 1977.

Boucher, Henri. *Le Père L. Gain S.J. (1852–1930). Apôtre du Siu-tcheou Fou, Vicariat de Nan-king.* Xujiahui, Shanghai: Imprimerie de l'Orphelinat de T'ou-sè-wè, 1931.

Boulger, Demetrius C. *A Short History of China.* London: Allen, 1893.

Bourguignon, Erika. "An Assessment of Some Comparisons and Implications." In *Religion, Altered States of Consciousness, and Social Change,* edited by Erika Bourguignon, 321–39. Columbus: Ohio State University Press, 1973.

Brandt, Nat. *Massacre in Shansi.* Syracuse: Syracuse University Press, 1994.

Brantlinger, Patrick. *Rule of Darkness.* Cornell: Cornell University Press, 1988.

Brett, M. V., ed. *Journals and Letters of Reginald, Viscount Esher.* 2 vols. London: Ivor Nicholson and Watson, 1934.

Brodrick, William St. John. "The Problem of China." *Edinburgh Review* (July 1899): 244–66.

Brody, Jane E. "Lucking Out: Weird Rituals and Strange Beliefs." *New York Times,* 27 January 1991, S11.

Broomhall, Marshall, ed. *Martyred Missionaries of the China Inland Mission with a Record of the Perils & Sufferings of Some Who Escaped.* London: Morgan & Scott, 1901.

Bruce, J. Percy. "Massacre of English Baptist Missionaries and Others in Shansi." *Chinese Recorder* 32 (March 1901): 132–37.

"Bundori jiken no yōryō." *Yorozu Chōhō,* 27 January 1902.

"Bundori jiken no yōryō." *Yorozu Chōhō,* 28 January 1902.

"Bundori mondai semaru." *Yorozu Chōhō,* 26 January 1902.

"Bundori mondai shūgiin ni izu." *Yorozu Chōhō*, 24 January 1902.
"Bundori mondai to gikai." *Yorozu Chōhō*, 3 February 1902.
"Bundori shōkō no muzai to teishoku no riyū." *Jiji Shinpō*, 15 May 1902.
"Bundorigin kokko ni genshutsusu." *Yorozu Chōhō*, 5 February 1902.
Bure, Pierre. "Tientsin." *Bulletin de la Société royale belge de géographie* 23 (1899): 232–68; 24 (1900): 312–39.
Camps, Arnulf, and Pat McCloskey. *The Friars Minor in China (1294–1955): Especially the Years 1925–55*. Rome: General Secretariate for Missionary Evangelization, General Curia, Order of Friars Minor, 1995.
Carnegie Endowment for International Peace. *Signatures, Ratifications, Adhesions, and Reservations to the Conventions and Declarations of the First and Second Hague Peace Conferences*. Washington, D.C.: Carnegie Endowment, 1914.
Celestial Empire, 14 January 1900–22 April 1901.
Chamberlain Papers, Papers of Joseph Chamberlain, Birmingham University Library, JC/11/8/2.
Chamberlain, Wilbur. *Ordered to China*. New York: Frederick A. Stokes Co., 1903.
Chandavarkar, Rajnarayan. "Plague Panic and the Epidemic Politics of India, 1896–1914." In *Imperial Power and Popular Politics: Class, Resistance and the State in India c. 1850–1950*, 234–66. Cambridge: Cambridge University Press, 1998.
Chang Yu-sing [Zhang Youxin]. *L'autonomie locale en Chine*. Thèse de doctorat; droit. Nancy: impr. de Grandville, 1934.
Chang Zanchun. *Changshi jiacheng* [Chang surname family records]. Privately published [1923].
Chatley, Herbert. "The Port of Tientsin: The Shipping Center of North China." *Dock and Harbour Authority* 20, no. 234 (April 1940): 129–34.
Chaturvedi, Vinayak. "Colonial Power and Agrarian Politics in Kheda District (Gujarat), c. 1890–1930." PhD diss., Cambridge University, 2001.
Chaturvedi, Vinayak, ed. *Mapping Subaltern Studies and the Postcolonial*. London: Verso, 2000.
Chen Kyi-ts'ung [Chen Jizhen]. *Le système municipal en Chine*. Gembloux, Belgium: Duculot, 1937.
Ch'en, Jerome. "The Nature and Characteristics of the Boxer Movement: A Morphological Study." *Bulletin of the School of Oriental Studies* 23, no. 2 (1960): 287–308.
———. "The Origin of the Boxers." In *Studies in the Social History of China and South East Asia*, edited by Jerome Chen and Nicholas Tarling, 57–84. Cambridge: Cambridge University Press, 1970.
———. *Yuan Shih-k'ai*. 2nd ed. Stanford: Stanford University Press, 1972.
Chen Xiafei, and Han Rongfang, eds. *Archives of China's Imperial Maritime Customs: Confidential Correspondence between Robert Hart and James Duncan Campbell 1874–1907*. Vol. 1. Beijing: Foreign Languages Press, 1990.
Chilston Papers, Papers of Aretas Akers-Douglas, first Viscount Chilston, Kent Archive Office, Canterbury, C/22/18.
China Inland Mission. *Days of Blessing in Inland China, Being an Account of Meetings Held in the Province of Shan-si*. London: Morgan & Scott, 1887.
China Records Project. Divinity School Library, Yale University, New Haven, Connecticut.
Chirol, Valentine. *Indian Unrest*. A reprint, revised and enlarged, from "The Times," with an introduction by Sir Alfred Lyall. London: Macmillan, 1910.

Chine et Madagascar 8 (September 1901): 427–28, 439.

Chung, Sue Fawn. "The Much Maligned Empress Dowager: A Revisionist Study of the Empress Dowager Tz'u-hsi in the period 1898 to 1900." PhD diss., University of California at Berkeley, 1975.

Coates, P. D. *The China Consuls: British Consular Officials, 1843–1943*. Hong Kong: Oxford University Press, 1988.

Cohen, Paul A. *Discovering History in China: American Historical Writing on the Recent Chinese Past*. New York: Columbia University Press, 1984.

———. *History in Three Keys: The Boxers as Event, Experience, and Myth*. New York: Columbia University Press, 1997.

Cole, H. M. "The Origins of the French Protectorate over Catholic Missions in China." *American Journal of International Law* 34, no. 3 (July 1940): 373–491.

Colombel, Augustin-M. *L'Histoire de la Mission du Kiang-nan*. Three parts in 5 vols. Shanghai: Imprimerie de l'Orphelinat de T'ou-sè-wè, 1899.

Committee of the China Famine Relief Fund. *The Famine in China*. London: C. Kegan Paul, 1878.

Condamy, Capitaine. "Histoire du Gouvernement provisoire de Tien-tsin (1900–1902)." *Revue des Troupes coloniales* 1 (1905): 168–80, 248–64, 414–41, 507–29; 2 (1905): 17–45, 164–85.

Costin, W. C. *Great Britain and China, 1833–1860*. Oxford: Clarendon, 1937.

Curzon Papers, Papers of George Nathaniel Curzon, 1st Marquess Curzon, British Library Oriental Collection, MSS Eur. F111.

Dabringhaus, Sabine. "An Army on Vacation? The German War in China (1900/1901)." In *Anticipating Total War: The German and American Experiences, 1871–1914*, edited by Manfred F. Boemeke, Roger Chickering, and Stig Förster, 459–76. Cambridge: Cambridge University Press, 1999.

"Dai-5 shidanchō no shintai." *Jiji Shinpō*, 15 May 1902.

Darwin, John. "Imperialism and the Victorians: The Dynamics of Territorial Expansion." *English Historical Review* 112, no. 3 (1997): 614–42.

Davis, Oscar King. "The Looting of Tientsin." *Harper's Weekly* 44 (15 September 1900): 863–64.

De Ridder, Koen. "Congo in Gansu (1898–1906): 'Missionary versus Explorer/Exploiter.'" In *Footsteps in Deserted Valleys: Missionary Cases, Strategies and Practice in Qing China*, edited by Koen De Ridder, 111–59. Louvain: Leuven University Press, 2000.

Denby, Charles, Jr. "The Capture and Government of Tientsin." In *China and Her People*, edited by Charles Denby, Jr. 2 vols. Boston: L.C. Page & Co., 1906.

———. "Loot and the Man." *Harper's Weekly* 44 (27 October 1900): 1008–9.

Dickinson, G. Lowes. *Letters from John Chinaman*. London: R. Brimley Johnson, 1901.

"Diguozhuyi esha Shanxi Yihetuan de zuizheng" [Evidence of the smothering of the Shanxi Boxers by Imperialism]. *Shanxi wenshi ziliao* 2–3 (1962).

Dikötter, Frank. *The Discourse of Race in Modern China*. Stanford: Stanford University Press, 1992.

Dilks, David. *Curzon in India*. Vol. 1. London: Rupert Hart-Davis, 1969.

Dillon, E. J. "The Chinese Wolf and the European Lamb." *Contemporary Review* 79 (1901): 1–31.

Doar, Bruce, "The Boxers and Chinese Drama: Questions of Interaction." *Papers on Far Eastern History* 29 (1984): 91–118.

Douglas, Mary. *Purity and Danger: An Analysis of the Concepts of Pollution and Taboo.* New York: Routledge, 1991.

Dreyer, F. C. H. *The Boxer Rising and Missionary Massacres in Central and South Shansi, North China, with an Account of a Missionary Band's Escape to the Coast.* Toronto: China Inland Mission, [1901?].

Duara, Prasenjit. "The Discourse of Civilization and Pan-Asianism." *Journal of World History* 12, no. 1 (2001): 99–130.

Duiker, William J. *Cultures in Collision: The Boxer Rebellion.* San Rafael, Ca.: Presidio Press, 1978.

Dutt, Romesh C. *The Economic History of India under Early British Rule.* New Delhi: Government of India, reprint, 1970.

Edgerton-Tarpley, Kathryn. *Tears from Iron: Cultural Responses to Famine in Nineteenth-Century China.* Berkeley: University of California Press, 2007.

Edgerton, Robert. *Warriors of the Rising Sun: A History of the Japanese Military.* New York: W.W. Norton, 1997.

Edwards, E. H. "More Particulars about the Shansi Murders: Account of Some of the Shansi Massacres as Narrated by Evangelist Chao Who Escaped from the Station of Hsin-cheo, But Subsequently Returned to Ascertain the Fate of the Missionaries." *Peking and Tientsin Times,* 24 November 1900, 114–15.

———. *Fire and Sword in Shansi: The Story of the Martyrdom of Foreigners and Chinese Christians.* New York: Revell, 1903; Edinburgh: Oliphant, Anderson and Ferrier, 1908.

Edwards, E. W. *British Diplomacy and Finance in China, 1895–1914.* Oxford: Clarendon, 1987.

Edwards, Neville P. *The Story of China with a Description of the Events Relating to the Present Struggle.* London: Hutchinson, 1900.

Een blik in Zuid-Chan-Si tijdens de jongste verfolging. Verslag van eenige Missionarissen aan Mgr. J. Hofman, Vic. Ap. Met toelichtingen. Cuyk a. d. Maas: Jos. J. van Lindert, n.d. [Imprimatur 1901].

Elets, Iu. L. "La Mongolie Orientale et les Missions belges pendant la révolte de ce pays en 1900." *Bulletin de la Société royale de géographie d'Anvers* 27 (1903): 335–55.

———. *Smert' idet! (Osvobozhdenie Russkim otradom episkopa, 23 sviashchennikov i 3000 khristian Vostochnoi Mongolii v posledniuiu Kitaiskuiu voinu)* [Death marches! (The liberation by a Russian detachment of a bishop, 23 priests and 3000 Christians of Eastern Mongolia in the recent Chinese war)]. Moscow: Tip. A.S. Zabalueva, 1901.

Elliott, Jane E. *Some Did It for Civilisation, Some Did It for Their Country: A Revised View of the Boxer War.* Hong Kong: Chinese University Press, 2002.

Elvin, Mark, "Mandarins and Millenarians: Reflections on the Boxer Uprising of 1899–1900." *Journal of the Anthropological Society of Oxford* 10, no. 3 (1979): 115–38.

Esherick, Joseph W. *The Origins of the Boxer Uprising.* Berkeley and Los Angeles: University of California Press, 1987.

Fairbank, John K. "The Creation of the Treaty System." In *The Cambridge History of China, Vol. 10: Late Ch'ing, 1800–1911, Part 1,* edited by John K. Fairbank, 213–63. Cambridge: Cambridge University Press, 1978.

Fairbank, John K., Katherine Frost Bruner, and Elizabeth MacLeod Matheson, eds. *The I.G. in Peking: Letters of Robert Hart, Chinese Maritime Customs, 1868–1907.* 2 vols. Cambridge, Mass.: Belknap Press, 1975.

Feis, Herbert. *Europe: The World's Banker, 1870–1914.* New York: W.W. Norton, reprinted 1965.

Felber, Roland, and Horst Rostek. *Der "Hunnenkrieg" Kaiser Wilhelms II.: imperialistische Intervention in China 1900/01.* Berlin: VEB Deutscher Verlag der Wissenschaften, 1987.

Feng xianzhi [Gazetteer of Feng district]. 1894 ed.

Flath, James. *The Cult of Happiness: Nianhua, Art, and History in Rural North China.* Seattle: University of Washington Press, 2004.

Fleming, Peter. *The Siege of Peking.* New York: Harper & Brothers, 1959.

Forsyth, R[obert] C[oventry], comp. and ed. *The China Martyrs of 1900: A Complete Roll of the Christian Heroes Martyred in China in 1900 with Narratives of Survivors.* London: The Religious Tract Society, 1904.

———. "Narrative of Massacre in Shansi, July 1900." *North-China Herald,* 28 November 1900, 1155–57.

Forsyth, W. *In the Shadows of Cairngorm: Chronicles of the United Parishes of Abernethy and Kincardine.* Inverness: The Northern Counties Publishing Company Ltd, 1900. Chapter XXXII, <www.electricscotland.com/history/cairngorm/32.htm> (12 May 2006).

Fox's Book of Martyrs; or, The Acts and Monuments of The Christian Church; Being a Complete History of the Lives, Sufferings, and Deaths of The Christian Martyrs; from the Commencement of Christianity to the Present Period. Revised by the Reverend John Malham. Re-edited by the Reverend T. Pratt. Philadelphia: J. J. Woodward, 1830.

France. Archives Diplomatiques, Nantes, Beijing Legation Archives, Carton 67, Dossier: Correspondances, Missions Tcheli Sud-East 1863–1890.

Franck, Harry A. *Wandering in Northern China.* New York and London: The Century Co., 1923.

Freinademetz, Josef. "Kurzer Überblick über die Missionsverhältnisse in der Praefectur Z'ao-tschou-fu." Received by the German legation on 5 Dec 1897, Bundesarchiv Berlin Lichterfelde, Deutsche Gesandtschaft Peking (R 9208), vol. 326, fol. 200–202.

Freri, Joseph, ed. *The Heart of Pekin: Bishop A. Favier's Diary of the Siege, May–August 1900.* Boston: Marlier, 1901.

Fujimura, Shuntarō. *Aru rōhei no shuki.* (Tokyo: Jinbutsu ōraisha, 1967).

Gamewell, Mary Porter. "History of the Peking Station of the North China Mission of the Woman's Foreign Missionary Society of the Methodist Episcopal Church." In Miscellaneous Personal Papers, Manuscript Group No. 8, Box No. 73, China Records Project.

Giles, Lancelot. *The Siege of the Peking Legations: A Diary,* edited by L[eslie] R. Marchant. Nedlands: University of Western Australia Press, 1970.

Gillard, David. *The Struggle for Asia, 1828–1914.* London: Methuen, 1977.

Gooch, G. P., and H. W. V. Temperley, eds. *British Documents on the Origins of the War, 1898–1914.* 11 vols. London: H.M.S.O., 1926–1932.

Goodrich, Sarah Boardman. "Journal of 1900" and letter. In Miscellaneous Personal Papers, Manuscript Group No. 8, Box No. 88, China Records Project.

Gordon, Andrew. *Labor and Imperial Democracy in Prewar Japan.* Berkeley: University of California Press, 1991.

Graphic (London), August 1900–June 1901.

Great Britain. Admiralty Records. Kew: The National Archives, (1) ADM 116, China, Boxer Rising 1900; (2) ADM 232/32.

——. Cabinet Office Records. Kew: The National Archives, CAB 41/25/45, Siege of Pekin.

——. Foreign Office Archives. Kew: The National Archives, (1) FO 17, General Correspondence, China; (2) FO 64/1496; (3) FO 65/1604; (4) FO 228, Embassy and Consular Archives; FO 800/162 and 800/17.

——. Parliament. *China No. 1 (1901): Correspondence respecting the Disturbances in China.* Cd. 436 (February 1901).

——. Parliament. *China No. 5 (1901): Further Correspondence respecting the Disturbances in China.* Cd. 589 (May 1901).

——. Parliament. *China No. 6 (1901): Further Correspondence respecting the Disturbances in China.* Cd. 675 (August 1901).

——. War Office Records. Kew: The National Archives, WO 32/6144, China Expedition 1900; WO 32/6410.

Guan He. *Quanfei wenjian lu* [A record of things seen and heard concerning the Boxer bandits]. *Yihetuan* 1:465–92.

Gugong bowuyuan Ming Qing dang'anbu, ed. *Yihetuan dang'an shiliao* [Archival sources on the Boxers]. Beijing: Zhonghua shuju, 1959.

Guha, Ranajit. *Elementary Aspects of Peasant Insurgency in Colonial India.* Delhi: Oxford University Press, 1983.

——. *Subaltern Studies I: Writings on South Asian History and Society.* Delhi: Oxford University Press, 1982.

Guo Chongxi. "Taiyuan tianzhujiao shilue" [A history of Catholicism in Taiyuan]. *Taiyuan wenshi ziliao* 17 (1992).

——. "Taiyuan tianzhujiao zhuyao tangkou jianjie" [A brief introduction to the main Catholic churches of Taiyuan]. *Taiyuan wenshi ziliao* 15 (1991).

Guo, Yuanchou, Yunjiang Ma, and Sujie Guo. *Xuncha Taiwan yushi Yang Eryou* [Yang Eryou, the censor sent to inspect Taiwan]. Taiyuan: Shanxi renmin chubanshe, 1993.

Haller, William. *The Elect Nation: The Meaning and Relevance of Foxe's Book of Martyrs.* New York and Evanston: Harper & Row, 1963.

Hamilton Papers, Papers of Lord George Francis Hamilton, British Library Oriental Collection, MSS Eur. C.126/2.

Hao Yen-p'ing, and Wang Erhmin. "Changing Chinese Views of Western Relations, 1840–95." In *The Cambridge History of China, Vol. 11: Late Ch'ing, 1800–1911, Part 2,* edited by John K. Fairbank and Liu Kwang-ching, 142–201. Cambridge: Cambridge University Press, 1980.

Hargreaves, J. D. "Lord Salisbury, British Isolation and the Yangtze Valley, June–September 1900." *Bulletin of the Institute of Historical Research* 30 (1957): 62–75.

Harrison, Henrietta. *The Man Awakened from Dreams: One Man's Life in a North China Village, 1857–1942.* Stanford: Stanford University Press, 2005.

——. "Newspapers and Nationalism in Rural China, 1890–1929." *Past and Present* 166 (2000): 181–204.

Hart, Robert. "China and Non-China." *Fortnightly Review* 75 (1901): 278–93.

———. *"These from the Land of Sinim": Essays on the Chinese Question.* London: Chapman and Hall, 1901.

Hartwich, Richard. *Steyler Missionare in China, vol. 1: Missionarische Erschliessung Südshantungs 1879–1903.* St. Augustin: Steyler Verlag, 1983.

Hatfield House Papers, Hatfield, England, 3M/A/106/30.

Hay, Stephen Northup. *Asian Ideas of East and West: Tagore and His Critics in Japan, China, and India.* Cambridge: Harvard University Press, 1970.

Headrick, Daniel R. *The Tentacles of Progress: Technology Transfer in the Age of Imperialism, 1850–1940.* New York: Oxford University Press, 1998.

Heathcote, T[homas] A[nthony]. *The Indian Army: The Garrison of British Imperial India, 1822–1922.* London: David & Charles, 1974.

Hein, Laura, and Mark Selden, eds. *Censoring History: Citizenship and Memory in Japan, Germany, and the United States.* Armonk, N.Y.: M.E. Sharpe, 2000.

Heissig, Walther. "Some New Information on Peasant Revolts and People's Uprisings in Eastern (Inner) Mongolia in the 19th Century (1861–1901)." In *Analecta Mongolica: Dedicated to the Seventieth Birthday of Professor Owen Lattimore,* edited by Urgunge Onon and John Gombojabe Hangin, 77–99. Bloomington, Indiana: Mongolia Society, 1972.

Henninghaus, Augustin. *P. Joseph Freinademetz SVD. Sein Leben und Wirken. Zugleich Beiträge zur Geschichte des Mission Süd-Schantung.* Yenchow: Verlag der Katholischen Mission, 1920.

Henry, Todd A. "Sanitizing Empire: Japanese Articulations of Korean Otherness and the Construction of Early Colonial Seoul, 1905–1919." *The Journal of Asian Studies* 64, no. 3 (August 2005): 639–75.

Hershatter, Gail. *The Workers of Tianjin, 1900–1950.* Stanford: Stanford University Press, 1986.

Het Missiewerk: tijdschrift voor missiekennis en missieactie 1 ('s-Hertogenbosch, 1919–1920).

Hevia, James L. *English Lessons: The Pedagogy of Imperialism in Nineteenth Century China.* Durham, N. C.: Duke University Press, 2003.

———. "Leaving a Brand on China: Missionary Discourse in the Wake of the Boxer Movement." *Modern China* 18, no. 3 (July 1992): 304–31.

———. "Loot's Fate." *History and Anthropology* 6, no. 4 (1994): 319–45.

———. "Looting Beijing: 1860, 1900." In *Tokens of Exchange: The Problem of Translation in Global Circulation,* edited by Lydia Liu, 192–213. Durham, N.C.: Duke University Press, 1999.

———. "Monument and Memory: The Oberlin College Boxer Memorial as a Contested Site." In *Dong-Ya Jidujiao zaiquanyi* [Reinterpreting the East Asian Christianity] (Studies in Religion and Chinese Society, 9), edited by Tao Feiya and Philip Yuen-Sang Leung, 487–506. Hong Kong: Centre for the Study of Religion and Chinese Society, Chung Chi College, Chinese University of Hong Kong, 2004.

Hewlett, W. Meyrick. *The Siege of the Peking Legations, June to August 1900.* Harrow-on-the-Hill, Mdx: The Harrovian, 1900.

Hicks Beach Papers, Papers of Sir Michael Hicks Beach, Earl of St. Aldwyn, Gloucestershire Record Office, Gloucester. PCC/72/2.

Hicks Beach, Lady Victoria. *Life of Sir Michael Hicks Beach, Earl of St. Aldwyn*. 2 vols, London: Macmillan, 1932.
"Hiroshima daisōsaku zokuhō." *Yorozu Chōhō*, 15 February 1902.
"Hiroshima no gunpō kaigi." *Yorozu Chōhō*, 14 February 1902
Hitch, Margaret A. "The Port of Tientsin and Its Problems." *Geographical Review* 25 (1935): 367–81.
———. The Port of Tientsin. Master's thesis, University of Chicago, 1924.
Hitchcock, R. K. "The Traditional Response to Drought in Botswana." In *Symposium on Drought in Botswana*, edited by Madalon T. Hinchey, 91–97. Gabarone, Botswana: Botswana Society in collaboration with Clark University Press, 1979.
Hoare, J. E. *Embassies of the East*. London: Curzon Press, 1999.
Hoe, Susanna. *Women at the Siege, Peking 1900*. Oxford: Holo Books, 2000.
"Hokushin bundori no kaibun (1)," *Yorozu Chōhō*, 1 December 1901.
Hooker, Mary. *Behind the Scenes in Peking*. 1910. Reprint edition. Hong Kong: Oxford University Press, 1987.
Hoover, Herbert. "History, June, 17th. To 23rd., 1900." In Lou Hoover Papers, Boxer Rebellion: Drafts, Herbert Hoover Presidential Library, West Branch, Iowa.
Horowitz, Richard S. "Central Power and State Making: The Zongli Yamen and Self-Strengthening in China." Unpublished PhD diss., Harvard University, 1998.
Howard, Christopher H. D. *Splendid Isolation: A Study in Ideas Concerning Britain's International Position and Foreign Policy during the Later Years of the Third Marquis of Salisbury*. London: Macmillan, 1967.
Hsü, Immanuel C. Y. "Late Ch'ing Foreign Relations, 1866–1905." In *The Cambridge History of China, Vol. 11: Late Ch'ing, 1800–1911, Part 2*, edited by John K. Fairbank and Liu Kwang-ching, 70–141. Cambridge: Cambridge University Press, 1980.
Hunt, Michael H. "The Forgotten Occupation: Peking, 1900–1901." *Pacific Historical Review*, 45 (1979): 501–29.
Hyam, Ronald. "The British Empire in the Edwardian Era." In *Oxford History of the British Empire, Vol. 4: The Twentieth Century*, edited by Judith M. Brown and William Roger Louis, 47–63. Oxford: Oxford University Press, 2000.
Hyde, Francis E. *Far Eastern Trade, 1860–1914*. London: Adam & Charles Black, 1973.
India Office Records, Department of Asia Pacific and African Collections, British Library, London.
Isoré, Remi. "La chrétienté de Tchao-kia-tchoang sur le pied de guerre (Journal du P. Isoré)." *Chine et Ceylan* 1, no. 2 (April 1899).
Itō Masatoku. "Sōsei kara Meiji-ki." In *Nihon shimbun hyakunen shi*, edited by Nihon shimbun hyakunenshi kankōkai. Tokyo: Nihon shimbun hyakunenshi kankōkai, 1960.
Jahoda, Gustav. *Psychology of Superstition*. Harmondsworth, Middlesex, Eng.: Penguin, 1969.
Jansen, Marius. *The Making of Modern Japan*. Cambridge, Mass.: Harvard University Press, 2000.
Japan Weekly Mail, 14 December 1901.
Jayadhwaja, 2 December 1899–11 August 1900.
Jian Bozan, et al., eds. *Yihetuan* [The Boxers]. 4 vols. Shanghai: Shenzhou guoguang she, 1951.

Jiji Shinpō, 1902.

Jinmen baojia tushuo (Explanation of the Tianjin household census map). Tianjin, 1842.

Joseph, Philip. *Foreign Diplomacy in China, 1894–1900: A Study in Political and Economic Relations with China.* London: George Allen & Unwin, 1928.

Karl, Rebecca E. "Creating Asia: China in the World at the Beginning of the Twentieth Century." *American Historical Review* 103, no. 4 (October 1998): 1096–1118.

Kelly, John S. *A Forgotten Conference: The Negotiations at Peking, 1900–1901* (Travaux de droit, d'économie et de sociologie, No. 5). Geneva: Librairie E. Droz, 1962 [1963].

Kerala Samachar, June 1900.

King, Frank H. H. "The Boxer Indemnity—'Nothing but Bad.'" *Modern Asian Studies* 40, no. 3 (2006): 663–90.

King's Regulations and Orders for the Army. London: His Majesty's Stationary Office, 1901.

Kirke, C. C. A. Papers, diary, private collection.

Kobayashi Kazumi. "Bateigin jiken to Meiji no genronjin." In *Chūgoku genkindaishi ronshū,* edited by Shingai kakumei kenkyūkai. Tokyo: Kyūko shoin, 1985.

———. *Giwadan sensō to Meiji kokka.* Tokyo: Kyūko shoin, 1986.

"Kodama rikushō ni atau." *Yorozu Chōhō,* 21 January 1902.

"Kodama rikushō no danwa," *Yorozu Chōhō,* 20 February 1902.

Kokushi daijiten. Tokyo: Yoshikawa Kōbunkan, 1979–1997.

Kolff, Dirk H. A. *Naukar, Rajput and Sepoy: The Ethnohistory of the Military Labour Market in Hindustan, 1450–1850.* Cambridge: Cambridge University Press, 1990.

Kösters, Josef. "Puoli einst und jetzt." *Stadt Gottes* 46 (1922–1923): 179–82.

Kōtoku Shūsui zenshū henshū iinkai, ed. *Kōtoku Shūsui Zenshū.* Vol. 4. Tokyo: Meiji bunken, 1972.

Kubicek, Robert V. *The Administration of Imperialism: Joseph Chamberlain at the Colonial Office.* Durham, N.C.: Duke University Press, 1969.

Kubota Tatsuhiko. *Nijūichidai senkaku kisha den.* Osaka: Osaka Mainichi Shimbunsha, 1930.

Kuepers, J. J. A. M. *China und die katholische Mission in Süd-Shantung 1882–1900. Die Geschichte einer Konfrontation.* Steyl: Drukkerij van het Missiehuis, 1974.

Kuß, Susanne. "Deutsche Soldaten während des Boxeraufstandes in China: Elemente und Ursprünge des Vernichtungskrieges." In *Das Deutsche Reich und der Boxeraufstand* (vol. 2 in series titled *Erfurter Reihe zur Geschichte Asiens*), edited by Susanne Kuß and Bernd Martin, 165–81. München: Iudicium Verlag, 2002.

Kwan Man Bun. *The Salt Merchants of Tianjin: State-Making and Civil Society in Late Imperial China.* Honolulu: University of Hawaii Press, 2001.

Kwong, Luke S. K. "Oral History in China: A Preliminary Review." *Oral History Review* 20, nos. 1–2 (1992): 23–50.

Lansdowne mss. Papers of Henry Charles Keith Petty-Fitzmaurice, fifth Marquess of Lansdowne, British Library.

Lascelles Papers. Papers of Sir Frank Cavendish Lascelles, Kew: The National Archives, FO 800/6-20.

"La ville actuelle de Tien-tsin et l'Oeuvre de Gouvernement militaire provisoire." *A travers du monde* 10 (1904): 366.

Lazich, Michael C. E. C. *Bridgman (1801–1861), America's First Missionary to China.* Lewiston, Queenstown, Lampeter: Edwin Mellen Press, 2000.

Leboucq, François-Xavier. *Monseigneur Édouard Dubar de la Compagnie de Jésus, évêque de Canathe, et la Mission catholique du Tche-ly-sud-est, en Chine.* Paris: F. Wattelier, 1880.

Lederer, André. *La mission du Commandant A. Wittamer en Chine (1898–1901).* Brussels: Koninklijke Academie voor Overzeese Wetenschapen, 1984.

Lensen, George Alexander. *The Russo-Chinese War.* Tokyo: Sophia University, 1967.

Leonard, Lloyd. *Catalogue of the United States Military Academy Museum.* West Point, N.Y.: United States Military Academy Printing Office, 1944.

Lettres de Jersey. (Bruges, 1882–1901).

Liao Yizhong, et al., eds. *Yihetuan da cidian* [A Boxer dictionary]. Beijing: Zhongguo shehui kexue chubanshe, 1995.

Liao Yizhong, Li Dezheng, and Zhang Zuru. *Yihetuan yundong shi* [A history of the Boxer movement]. Beijing: Renmin chubanshe, 1981.

Li Decheng, Su Weizhi, and Liu Tianlu. *Baguo lianjun qinhua shi* [A history of the Eight Power invasion]. Ji'nan: Shandong University Press, 1990.

Li Di. *Quanhuo ji* [A record of the Boxer calamity]. Shanghai: Tushanwan yin shuguan, 1909.

Lieberthal, Kenneth G. *Revolution and Tradition in Tientsin, 1949–1952.* Stanford: Stanford University Press, 1980.

Literary Digest. New York, 1901.

Liu Dapeng. "Qian yuan suoji" [Sundry information from the Qian Garden]. In *Yihetuan zai Shanxi diqu shiliao* [Historical materials on the Boxers In the Shanxi area], edited by Qiao Zhiqiang. Taiyuan: Shanxi renmin chubanshe, 1980.

———. "Tuixiangzhai riji" [Diary from the study for retreat and contemplation]. *Jindaishi ziliao Yihetuan shiliao* [Materials for modern history: Materials on the Boxers]. Beijing: Zhongguo shehui kexue chubanshe, 1982.

———. *Jinci zhi* [Jinci gazetteer]. Taiyuan: Shanxi renmin chubanshe, 1986.

———. *Tuixiangzhai riji* [Diary of the study for retreat and contemplation]. Taiyuan: Shanxi renmin chubanshe, 1990.

Liu Nai-chen [Liu Naizhen]. "Reform of Chinese City Government based on European Experience." PhD diss., University of London, 1930. 2 vols.

Liu Wenbing. *Xugou xianzhi* [Xugou gazetteer]. Taiyuan: Shanxi renmin chubanshe, 1992.

Liu Xizi. *Jin xi biji* [A cautionary account of the area west of Tianjin]. *Yihetuan* 2:73–138.

Li Zonghuang. *Zhongguo difang zizhi zonglun* [A complete account of local self-government in China]. Taibei: Zhongguo difang zizhi xuehui, 1954.

Lo Hui-min. "Some Notes on Archives on Modern China." In *Essays on the Sources for Chinese History,* edited by Donald D. Leslie, Colin Mackerras, and Wang Gungwu, 203–20. Columbia: University of South Carolina Press, 1973.

Lo, Hui-min, ed. *The Correspondence of G. E. Morrison.* London: Cambridge University Press, 1976.

Loewenberg, Richard D. "Rumors of Mass Poisoning in Times of Crisis." *Journal of Criminal Psychopathology* 5 (July 1943): 131–42.

Lone, Stewart. *Army, Empire and Politics in Meiji Japan.* New York: St. Martin's Press, 2000.

Loo Kou-tung [Li Gantong]. *La vie municipale et l'urbanisme en Chine*. Lyon, 1934.

"The Loot Question." *Japan Weekly Mail*, 14 December 1901, 624.

Lu Yao. *Yihequan yundong qiyuan tansuo* [A search for the origins of the Boxer movement]. Ji'nan: Shandong daxue chubanshe, 1990.

Lu Yao, et al., eds. *Shandong daxue Yihetuan diaocha ziliao huibian* [Collection of Shandong University survey materials on the Boxers]. 2 vols. Ji'nan: Shandong daxue chubanshe, 2000.

Lynch, George. *War of Civilizations*. London: Longmans, Green, and Co., 1901.

MacDonald, Claude M. "The Japanese Detachment during the Defence of the Peking Legations, June-August 1900." *Transactions and Proceedings of the Japan Society* 12, no. 1 (1914): 2–19.

MacDonnell, John. "Looting in China." *Contemporary Review* 79 (1901): 444–52.

MacDonnell, Ranald, and Marcus Macauley, comps. *A History of the 4th Prince of Wales's Own Gurkha Rifles, 1857–1837*. 2 vols. Edinburgh and London: William Blackwood and Sons, 1940.

Mackerras, Colin. *Western Images of China*. Oxford: Oxford University Press, 1989.

MacKinnon, Stephen R. *Power and Politics in Late Imperial China: Yuan Shikai in Beijing and Tianjin, 1901–1908*. Ann Arbor: University of Michigan Press, 1980.

MacMurray, J. V. A., ed. *Treaties and Agreements with and concerning China*. 2 vols. New York: Macmillan, 1921.

Mallon, Florencia E. "The Promise and Dilemmas of Subaltern Studies: Perspectives from Latin American History." *American Historical Review* 99, no. 5 (December 1994): 1491–1515.

"Manabe Akira." *Nihon jinmei daijiten*, vol. 6. Tokyo: Heibonsha, 1979.

Maratha, 17 January–15 July 1900.

Margiotti, Fortunato. *Il cattolicismo nello Shansi dalle origini al 1738*. Roma: Edizioni Sinica Franciscana, 1958.

Martin, W. A. P. *The Siege of Peking*. New York: Fleming H. Revell Co., 1900.

Mateer, Ada Haven. *Siege Days: Personal Experiences of American Women and Children during the Peking Siege*. New York: F. H. Revell Company, 1903.

Matignon, Jean-Jacques. *La défense de la Légation de France (Pékin, du 13 juin au 15 août 1900)*. Conférence de la Croix-Rouge de Bordeaux, le 3 mai 1901. Paris: Libraires Associés; Bordeaux: Feret et Fils, 1902.

Mayers, Sidney Francis. "Report of a Journey from Peking to Shanghai Overland." In *Great Britain, Foreign Office Papers, Diplomatic and Consular Reports. Miscellaneous Series, No. 466*. London: Eyre & Spottiswoode, 1898.

McFarland, Earl. *Catalogue of the Ordnance Museum, United States Military Academy*. West Point, N.Y.: United States Military Academy Printing Office, 1929.

McGinn, Patrick Macartan. "Governance and Resistance in North Indian Towns, c. 1860–1900." PhD diss., Cambridge University, 1993.

Meissner, Hans-Otto, ed. *Denkwürdigkeiten des General-Feldmarschall Alfred Grafen von Waldersee*. 3 vols. Stuttgart: Deutsche Verlagsanstalt, 1923.

Mensaert, Georges. "Les Franciscains au service de la Propagande dans la Province de Pékin, 1705–1785." *Archivum Franciscanum Historicum* 51, nos. 1–2 (January–April 1958): 161–200; 51, no. 3 (July 1958): 273–311.

Mertens, P. X. *The Yellow River Runs Red: A Story of Modern Chinese Martyrs*. St. Louis, Missouri: B. Herder Book Co., 1939.

Middleton, Ben. "Kōtoku Shūsui to teikokushugi e no kongenteki hihan." *Shoki shakaishugi kenkyū* 12 (1999): 134–93.

Midleton Papers: Papers of William St. John Brodrick, later ninth Viscount and first Earl of Midleton. Kew: The National Archives, PRO 30/67.

Midleton, Earl of (William St. John Brodrick). *Record and Reactions, 1856–1939.* London: John Murray, 1939.

Millard, Thomas F. "Punishment and Revenge in China." *Scribner's Magazine* 29 (1901):187–94.

Miller, Stuart Creighton. "Ends and Means: Missionary Justification of Force in Nineteenth Century China." In *The Missionary Enterprise in China and America,* edited by John K. Fairbank, 249–82. Cambridge, Mass.: Harvard University Press, 1974.

Miner, Luella. *China's Book of Martyrs: A Record of Heroic Martyrdom and Marvelous Deliverances of Chinese Christians during the Summer of 1900.* New York, Boston, and Chicago: The Pilgrim Press, 1903.

———. Luella Miner Papers (North China Mission). American Board of Commissioners for Foreign Missions, Papers, Houghton Library, Harvard University.

———. "Ti-to and the Boxers: A True Story of a Young Christian's Almost Miraculous Escape from Death at the Hands of Bold Cut-throats." In Luella Miner Papers. American Board of Commissioners for Foreign Missions, Papers, Houghton Library, Harvard University.

———. *Two Heroes of Cathay.* New York: Fleming H. Revell, 1903.

Ministère des Affaires Étrangères, ed. *Documents Diplomatiques Français (1871–1914).* 1st ser., vol. xiv. Paris: Imprimerie Nationale, 1949.

Missions en Chine et au Congo (Brussels, 1901).

Mitsukawa Kametarō. *Sankoku kanshō igo.* Tokyo: Gendai jānarizumu shuppankai, 1977.

Miyashita Tadao. *Chūgoku kasei no tokushu kenkyū.* Tokyo: Nihon gakujutsu shinkōkai, 1952.

Monger, George W. *The End of Isolation: British Foreign Policy, 1900–1907.* London: Thomas Nelson, 1963.

Mori Etsuko. "Tenshin toto gamon ni tsuite" [On the Tianjin provisional government]. *Toyoshi Kenkyu* 47.2 (September 1988): 86–115.

Mori Yukimasa, ed. *Hyakunenme no kenshū: wakakushitesatta Gihei no shūgai.* Takashima: Kaiyōsha, 2005.

Mori Takehiro. "Shinkoku hahei wo meguru Gihei no ashiato." In *Hyakunenme no kenshū: wakakushitesatta Gihei no shūgai,* edited by Mori Yukimasa, 89–94. Takashima: Kaiyōsha, 2005.

Morse, Hosea Ballou. *The International Relations of the Chinese Empire, Vol. 3: The Period of Subjection, 1894–1911.* London: Longmans, 1918.

Moser, Michael J., and Yeone Wei-chih Moser. *Foreigners within the Gates: The Legations at Peking.* Oxford: Oxford University Press, 1993.

Mulk-o Millat, 25 Aug. 1900.

Naier i -Asifi, 18 October 1900.

Nasson, Bill. *The South African War, 1899–1902.* London: Edward Arnold, 1999.

National Army Museum, London.

National Art Library, London.

Neilson, Keith. *Britain and the Last Tsar: British Policy and Russia*. Oxford: Clarendon, 1995.

Newton, Lord (Thomas Wodehouse Legh). *Lord Lansdowne: A Biography*. London: Macmillan, 1929.

Nicholls, Bob. *Bluejackets and Boxers: Australia Naval Expedition to the Boxer Uprising*. Sidney: Allen & Unwin, 1986.

Nihon Jinmei daijiten. Vol. 6. Tokyo: Heibonsha, 1979.

Nish, Ian H. *The Anglo-Japanese Alliance: The Diplomacy of Two Island Empires, 1894–1907*. Westport, Conn.: Greenwood, reprinted 1976.

———. "Japan and the North China Incident of 1900." Paper presented at the 1900: The Boxers, China and the World conference, London, June 2001.

Nishida Nagahisa. "Tōkyō-to shimbun shi sono II." In *Nihon shimbunshi*, edited by Nihon shimbun kyōkai. Tokyo: Nihon shimbun kyōkai, 1956.

Nkpa, Nwokocha K. U. "Rumors of Mass Poisoning in Biafra." *Public Opinion Quarterly* 41, no. 3 (Fall 1977): 332–46.

North-China Herald and Supreme Court & Consular Gazette. Shanghai, 1900–1901.

O'Conor Papers, Papers of Sir Nicholas Roderick O'Conor, Churchill College Archive Centre, Cambridge, England.

Ohama Tetsuya. *Nogi Maresuke*. Kawade Shobō, 1988.

Oku Takenori. "*Yorozu Chōhō* ni miru shakai genshō no sokumen." *Shakai kagaku tōkyū* 40, no. 3 (1995): 25–52.

"Okura no kainyūhin." *Yorozu Chōhō*, 12 February 1902.

Otte, T. G. *The China Question: Great Power Rivalry and British Isolation, 1894–1905*. Oxford: Oxford University Press, 2007.

———. "'Heaven knows where we shall finally drift': Lord Salisbury, the Cabinet, Isolation, and the Boxer Rebellion." In *Incidents and International Relations: People, Power and Personalities*, edited by Gregory C. Kennedy and Keith Neilson, 25–45. Westport, Conn.: Greenwood, 2002.

———. "'The Winston of Germany': The British Foreign Policy Elite and the Last German Emperor." *Canadian Journal of History* 36, no. 3 (2001): 471–504.

———. "A Question of Leadership: Lord Salisbury, the Unionist Cabinet and Foreign Policy Making, 1895–1900." *Contemporary British History* 14, no. 4 (2000): 1–26.

Oudendyk, William. *Ways and By-ways of Diplomacy*. London: Peter Davies, 1939.

Pan Rushu. "Zuijin ershinian zhi Zhongguo shizheng" [Municipal administration in China during the last twenty years]. *Qinghua zhoukan* 35, no. 8/9 (2 May 1931): 128–69; 35, no. 10 (12 May 1931): 98–125.

Pearl, Cyril. *Morrison of Peking*. Sydney: Angus & Robertson Ltd., 1967.

Peking and Tientsin Times, 1900–1901.

Perry, Elizabeth J. *Rebels and Revolutionaries in North China*. Stanford: Stanford University Press, 1980.

Planchet, Jean-Marie, comp. *Documents sur les martyrs de Pékin pendant la persécution des Boxeurs*. 2 vols. 2nd ed. Beijing: Impr. des Lazaristes, 1922–1923.

Platt, D. C. M. *Finance, Trade, and Politics in British Foreign Policy, 1815–1914*. Oxford: Clarendon, 1968.

Pratt, Mary Louise. *Imperial Eyes: Travel Writing and Transculturation*. London: Routledge, 1992.

Preston, Diana. *The Boxer Rebellion: The Dramatic Story of China's War on Foreigners that Shook the World in the Summer of 1900.* New York: Walker, 2000. British title: *Besieged in Peking: The Story of the 1900 Boxer Rising.* London: Constable, 1999.

Price, Eva Jane. *China Journal, 1889–1900: An American Missionary Family during the Boxer Rebellion.* New York: Scribner's, 1989.

Public Record Office, London, War Office 28 [Records of Military Headquarters, 1746–1926], 302: 28–29.

Purcell, Victor. *Memoirs of a Malayan Official.* London: Cassell, 1965.

———. *The Boxer Uprising: A Background Study.* Cambridge: Cambridge University Press, 1963.

Putnam Weale, B. L. [pseud. Bertram Lenox Simpson]. *Indiscreet Letters from Peking: Being the Notes of an Eye-witness, Which Set Forth in some Detail, from Day to Day, the Real Story of the Siege and Sack of a Distressed Capital in 1900, the Year of Great Tribulation.* London: Hurst and Blackett, 1900.

Qiao Zhiqiang. "Shanxi diqu de yihetuan yundong" [The Boxer movement in the Shanxi area]. In *Yihetuan yundong liushi zhounian jinian lunwenji* [Articles commemorating the sixtieth anniversary of the Boxer movement], 167–83. Beijing: Zhonghua shuju, 1961.

———. *Yihetuan zai Shanxi diqu shiliao* [Historical documents on the Boxers in the Shanxi region]. Taiyuan: Renmin chubanshe, 1980.

Qingxu xian difangzhi bianzuan weiyuanhui, ed. *Qingxu xianzhi* [Qingxu County gazetteer]. Taiyuan: Shanxi guji chubanshe, 1999.

Queen's Regulations and Orders for the Army. London: Her Majesty's Stationary Office, 1868.

Rabinow, Paul. "Representations are Social Facts: Modernity and Post-Modernity in Anthropology." In *Writing Culture: The Poetics and Politics of Ethnography*, edited by James Clifford and George E. Marcus, 234–61. Berkeley: University of California Press, 1986.

Rai, Lajpat. *The Arya Samaj: An Account of Its Aims, Doctrines and Activities.* Lahore: Uttar Chand Kapur, 1932.

Rasmussen, Otto D. *Tientsin: An Illustrated Outline History.* Tianjin: Tientsin Press, 1927.

Rawlinson, H[enry] G[eorge]. *The History of the 3rd Battalion 7th Rajput Regiment (Duke of Connaught's Own).* London: Oxford University Press, 1941.

Read, S. P. "Russia in North China." *Independent* 53 (1901): 486–89.

Reid, Gilbert. "The Ethics of Loot." *Forum* 31 (1901): 581–86.

———. "The Ethics of the Last War." *Forum* 32 (1902): 446–55.

Renaud, Rosario. *Süchow. Diocèse de Chine,* vol. 1: *(1882–1931).* Montreal: Editions Bellarmin, 1955.

Renouvin, Pierre, and Jean-Baptiste Duroselle. *Introduction à l'histoire des relations internationales.* Paris: Librairie Armand Colin, 1964.

Review of Reviews, 1900–1901.

Ricalton, James. *China through the Stereoscope.* New York: Underwood & Underwood, 1901.

Ricci, Giovanni (Jean/Ioannes). *Avec les Boxeurs chinois.* Brive, Corrèze: Éditions Écho des Grottes, 1949.

————. *Barbarie e Trionfi: ossia le vittime illustri del San-si in Cina nella persecuzione del 1900.* 2nd ed. Firenze: Associazioni Nazionale per Soccorrere i missionari Cattolici Italiani, 1910.

————. "Acta Martyrum Sinensium anno 1900 in Provincia San-si occisorum historice collecta ex ore Testium singulis in locis ubi Martyres occubere. Relatio ex parte Ordinis Fratrum Minorum." *Acta Ordinis Fratrum Minorum* 30 (1911); 32 (1913).

————. *Vicariatus Taiyuanfu seu Brevis Historia Antiquae Franciscanae Missionis Shansi et Shensi a sua origine ad dies nostros (1700–1928).* Pekini: Congregationis Missionis, 1929.

Rich, Norman. *Friedrich von Holstein: Politics and Diplomacy in the Era of Bismarck and Wilhelm II.* 2 vols. Cambridge: Cambridge University Press, 1965.

Rich, Norman, and M. H. Fisher, eds. *The Holstein Papers.* 4 vols. Cambridge: Cambridge University Press, 1955.

Richards, Thomas. *The Imperial Archive: Knowledge and the Fantasy of Empire.* London: Verso, 1993.

Rivinius, Karl Josef. *Weltlicher Schutz und Mission: Das deutsche Protektorat über die katholische Mission von Süd-Shantung.* Cologne and Vienna: Böhlau Verlag, 1987.

Robinson, Andrew, and Krishna Datta. *Rabindranath Tagore: The Myriad Minded Man.* London: Bloomsbury, 1995.

Rockhill, William W. "Report of Commissioner to China." In *Papers Relating to the Foreign Relations of the United States, 1901* (Appendix). Washington, D.C.: Government Printing Office, 1902.

Rodgers, Daniel T. *Atlantic Crossings: Social Politics in a Progressive Age.* Cambridge: Belknap Press, 1998.

Rogaski, Ruth. *Hygienic Modernity: Meanings of Health and Disease in Treaty-Port China.* Berkeley: University of California Press, 2004.

Röhl, J. C. G., ed. *Philipp Eulenburgs politische Korrespondenz.* 3 vols. Boppard: Boldt Verlag, 1983.

Romanov, B. A. *Russia in Manchuria, 1892–1906.* Ann Arbor, Mich.: University of Michigan Press, 1952.

Rose, Caroline. *Interpreting History in Sino-Japanese Relations.* London: Routledge, 1998.

Rosenbaum, Arthur Lewis. "The Manchuria Bridgehead: Anglo-Russian Rivalry and the Imperial Railways of North China, 1897–1902." *Modern Asian Studies* 10, no. 1 (1976): 41–64.

Rudolph, Jennifer. "Negotiating Power and Navigating Change in the Qing: The Zongli Yamen, 1861–1901." Unpublished PhD diss., University of Washington, 1999.

Rudolph, Susanne Hoeber, and Lloyd I. Rudolph. *Essays on Rajputana: Reflections on History, Culture and Administration.* New Delhi: Concept Publishing Company, 1984.

Rudolph, Susanne Hoeber, and Lloyd I. Rudolph, with Mohan Singh Kanota, eds. *Reversing the Gaze: Amar Singh's Diary, A Colonial Subject's Narrative of Imperial India.* New Delhi: Oxford University Press, 2000.

Sabatier, Aubin. *La Génie en Chine. Période d'occupation, 1901–1906.* Paris and Nancy: Berger-Levrault & cie., 1910.

Sanbō honbu, ed. *Meiji 33-nen Shinkoku-jihen senshi*. Vol. 4. Tokyo: Senryūdō, 1904.

Sand, Jordan. "Was Meiji Taste in Interiors 'Orientalist'?" *Positions* 8, no. 3 (Winter 2000): 637–74.

Sasaki Hideaki. *Nogi Maresuke: yo wa shokun no shitei o koroshitari*. Kyoto: Minerva Shobō, 2005.

Satow Papers. Papers of Sir Ernest Mason Satow. Kew: The National Archives, PRO 30/33.

Saunders, Alexander R., "An Escape from Shan-si to Han-kau," Letter to the Editor, *Times*, 29 September 1900, 12.

Schimmelpenninck van der Oye, David. "Russia's Ambivalent Response to the Boxers." *Cahiers du Monde russe* 41, no. 1 (January–March 2000): 57–78.

Schofield, A. T., ed. *Memorials of R. Harold A. Schofield M.A., M.B. (Oxon.) (Late of the China Inland Mission), First Medical Missionary to Shan-si, China*. London: Hodder and Stoughton, 1885.

Schrecker, John E. *Imperialism and Chinese Nationalism: Germany in Shantung*. Cambridge, Mass.: Harvard University Press, 1971.

Scott Papers, Papers of Sir Charles Stewart Scott, British Library, Add MSS 52298.

Seagrave, Sterling. *Dragon Lady*. New York: Vintage Books, 1992.

"Seitaikō no isu." *Yorozu Chōhō*, 22 February 1902.

Selborne Papers, Papers of William Waldegrave Palmer, second Earl of Selborne, Bodleian Library, Oxford, Ms. Selborne 2.

Shandong tongzhi [Gazetteer of Shandong Province]. Reprint of 1915 edition. Shanghai: Commercial Press, 1934–1935.

Shandong Yihetuan diaocha ziliao xuanbian [Selected survey materials on the Boxers in Shandong]. Ji'nan: Qi-Lu shushe, 1980.

Shanxi sheng gengzi nian jiaonan qianhou jishi [A complete account of the church difficulties in Shanxi Province in 1900]. *Yihetuan* [The Boxers] 1:295–523.

Shanxi sheng Yuci shizhi bianzuan weiyuanhui, ed. *Yuci shizhi* [Yuci City gazetteer]. Beijing: Zhonghua shuju, 1996.

Sharf, Frederic, and Peter Harrington. *China, 1900*. London: Greenhill Books, 2000.

Sheehan, Brett. *Trust in Troubled Times: Money, Banking and State-Society Relations in Republican Tianjin, 1916-1937*. Cambridge: Harvard University Press, 2003.

Shi, Rongchang. "Gengzi ganshi shi" [Poems in Response to 1900]. *Jindaishi ziliao* [Materials for modern history] 11 (1956).

"Shushō rikushō no sekinin wa ikan." *Yorozu Chōhō*, 9 February 1902.

Singh, Gadhadhar. *Karuna Kahani*. Ajmer: Prakash Book Depot, 1916.

Singh, Thakur Gadhadhar. *Chin meh Terah Mas: (Chin Sangram)*. Lucknow: Thakur Gadhadhar Singh, 1902.

"Sixty Missionaries Killed in Shan-si." *New York Times*, 21 July 1900, 2.

Skidmore, Eliza. *China, the Long-lived Empire*. New York: The Century Co., 1900.

Skinner, G. William. "Social Ecology and the Forces of Repression in North China: A Regional-Systems Framework for Analysis." Paper presented at the ACLS Workshop on Rebellion and Revolution in North China, Harvard University, 27 July–2 August 1979.

Smith, Arthur H. *China in Convulsion*. 2 vols. New York, Chicago, and Toronto: Fleming H. Revell Company, 1901.

———. *Chinese Characteristics*. Shanghai: printed and published at the "North-China Herald" Office, 1890.

———. "The Punishment of Peking." *The Outlook* 66 (1900): 493–501.

Smith, Judson. "The Missionaries and Their Critics." *North American Review* 172 (1901): 724–33.

Smith, Mrs. Arthur. *Mr. Fei's True Story*. Chicago: Woman's Board of Missions of the Interior, [1901?].

Smith, Stanley P. *China from Within: Or the Story of the Chinese Crisis*. London: Marshall Brothers, 1901.

Song Yunpu, ed. *Tianjin zhilue* [A brief account of Tianjin]. Tianjin, 1931. Reprint, Taibei: Chengwen chubanshe, 1969.

Spivak, Gayatri Chakravarty. "Can the Subaltern Speak? Speculations in Widow Sacrifice." *Wedge* 7/8 (1985): 120–30.

St. Michaels Kalender (Steyl, 1879–1901).

Steel, Richard. *Through Peking's Sewer Gate*. Edited by George W. Carrington. New York: Vantage Press, 1985.

Steiger, George Nye. *China and the Occident: The Origin and Development of the Boxer Movement*. New Haven: Yale University Press, 1927.

Steinberg, John W., Bruce W. Menning, David Schimmelpenninck van der Oye, David Wolff, and Shinji Yokote, eds. *The Russo-Japanese War in Global Perspective: World War Zero*. Brill: Leiden, 2005.

Stewart, Norman. *My Service Days: India, Afghanistan, Suakim, '85, China*. London: John Ouseley, 1908.

Storey, William Kelleher. "Big Cats and Imperialism: Lion and Tiger Hunting in Kenya and Northern India, 1898–1930." *Journal of World History* 2, no. 2 (1991): 135–73.

Su Weizhi, and Liu Tianlu, eds. *Yihetuan yanjiu yibai nian* [One hundred years of Boxer studies]. Ji'nan: Qi-Lu shushe, 2000.

Taigu xianzhi bianzuan weiyuanhui. *Taigu xianzhi*. Taiyuan: Shanxi renmin chubanshe, 1993.

Taiyuan shi nanjiaoqu zhi bianzuan weiyuanhui, ed. *Taiyuan shi nanjiaoqu zhi* [Taiyuan City southern suburban district gazetteer]. Beijing: Sanlian shudian, 1994.

Tan, Chester C. *The Boxer Catastrophe*. New York: Columbia University Press, 1955. Reprint, New York: Octagon Books, 1975.

Tanida Isamu. *Jitsuroku: Nihon rikugun no habatsu tōsō*. Tenbōsha, 2002.

Taveirne, Patrick. *Han-Mongol Encounters and Missionary Endeavors: A History of Scheut in Ordos (Hetao) 1874–1911*. Leuven: Leuven University Press, 2004.

Taylor, A. J. P. *The Struggle for Mastery in Europe, 1848–1918*. Oxford: Oxford University Press, 1954.

Thakur, Rabindranath. *Naibedya*. Allahabad, 1902.

Thimme, Friedrich, et al. *Die Grosse Politik der europäischen Kabinette*. 40 vols. Berlin: Deutsche Verlagsanstalt, 1924.

Thiriez, Régine. "Imaging the 1900 China Events." Paper presented at the 1900: The Boxers, China and the World conference, London, June 2001.

Thompson, Andrew S. "The Language of Imperialism and the Meanings of Empire, 1895–1914." *Journal of British Studies* 36, no. 2 (1997): 147–77.

Thompson, Roger R. *China's Local Councils in the Age of Constitutional Reform, 1898–1911*. Cambridge: Harvard University Press, 1995.

Thompson, Roger R., ed. "The Lessons of Defeat: Transforming the Qing State after the Boxer War." *Modern Asian Studies* 37 no. 4 (2003): 769–862.

Thompson, Roger R. "Military Dimensions of the 'Boxer Uprising' in Shanxi, 1898–1901." In *Warfare in Chinese History*, edited by Hans van de Ven, 288–320. Leiden: Brill Academic Publishers, 2000.

——. "Twilight of the Gods in the Chinese Countryside: Christians, Confucians, and the Modernising State, 1861–1911." In *Christianity in China from the Eighteenth Century to the Present*, edited by Daniel H. Bays, 53–72. Stanford: Stanford University Press, 1996.

Thomson, Harry Crauford. *China and the Powers: A Narrative of the Outbreak of 1900*. London: Longmans, Green, and Co., 1902.

Tianjin congkan bianji weiyuanhui, ed., *Tianjin shi zhengfu* (The government of the City of Tianjin). Tianjin: Tianjin shi zhengfu mishichu bianyi shi, 1948.

Tiedemann, R. G. "The Big Sword Society and Its Relations with the Boxer Movement, 1895–1900." Unpublished paper presented at the Symposium Commemorating the Centenary of the Boxer Movement, held in Ji'nan, Shandong, China, October 9–12, 2000.

——. "Boxers, Christians and the Culture of Violence in North China." *The Journal of Peasant Studies* 25, no. 4 (1998): 150–60.

——. "Rural Unrest in North China 1868–1900: With Particular Reference to South Shandong." PhD diss., School of Oriental and African Studies, University of London, 1991.

——. "They Also Served! Missionary Interventions in North China, 1900–1945." In *Dong-Ya Jidujiao zaiquanyi* [Reinterpreting the East Asian Christianity], edited by Tao Feiya and Philip Yuen-Sang Leung, 155–94. Hong Kong: Centre for the Study of Religion and Society, Chung Chi College, Chinese University of Hong Kong, 2004.

Times, London.

Trevor-Roper, Hugh. *Hermit of Peking: The Hidden Life of Sir Edmund Backhouse*. Harmondsworth: Penguin, 1978.

Twain, Mark. "To My Missionary Critics." *North American Review* 172 (1901): 520–34.

——. "To the Person Sitting in Darkness." *North American Review* 172 (1901): 161–76.

Twdry, J. Lüzhou (Anhui), letter dated 16 December 1898. In *Lettres de Jersey* 18, no. 1 (June 1899): 30.

Underdown, Michael. "Banditry and Revolutionary Movements in Late 19th and Early 20th Century Mongolia." *Mongolian Studies* 6 (1980): 109–16.

United States House of Representatives. 57th Congress, 1st Session. "Appendix: Affairs in China: Report of William Rockhill, Late Commissioner to China, with Accompanying Documents." *Papers Relating to the Foreign Relations of the United States, with the Annual Message of the President, Transmitted to Congress, December 3, 1901*. Washington, D.C., 1902.

——. National Archives and Record Administration, Washington, D.C.

United States Military History Institute, Carlisle, Pa. Grove Correspondence.

Van den Borne, Fidentius. "In Memoriam Z. D. H. Mgr. Giesen O.F.M." *Het Missie-werk* 1 (1919–1920): 161–62.

Van Hecken, Joseph Leonard. *Les réductions catholiques du pays des Ordos: une méth-ode d'apostolat des missionnaires de Scheut.* Schöneck/Beckenried: Administration der Neuen Zeitschrift für Missionswissenschaft, 1957.

Van Melckebeke, Carlo. *Service social de l'Église en Mongolie.* Brussels: Éditions de Scheut, 1968.

Vaughan, H[enry] B[athurst]. *St. George and the Chinese Dragon.* London: C. Arthur Pearson, 1902. Reprint, Dartford, Kent: Alexius Press, 2000.

Vereenooghe, Edmond. *Vervolging in China. Belegering van Klein-Brugge, Ortos, Zuid-West Mongolië. Van 1 Oogst (vooravond van St. Pieter in de banden) tot 29 September 1900.* Brugge: Karel Beyart, 1901.

Vinchon, Albert, S.J. "La culte de la Sainte Vierge du Tche-li sud-est: Rapport présenté au Congrès marial de 1904." *Chine, Ceylan, Madagascar: Lettres mission-naires français de la Compagnie de Jésus (Province de Champagne)* 18 (March 1905): 125-33.

Vrittanta Chintamani, 21 June-11 July 1900.

Waite, Carleton Frederick. *Some Elements of International Co-operation in the Suppres-sion of the 1900 Antiforeign Rising in China with Special Reference to the Forces of the United States.* Los Angeles: University of Southern California Press, 1935.

Waldersee, Alfred. *A Field Marshal's Memoirs.* Translated by Frederic White. London: Hutcheson & Co., 1924.

Waley, Arthur. *The Opium War through Chinese Eyes.* Stanford: Stanford University Press, 1958.

Wang Jiajian. *Qingmo minchu woguo jingcha zhidu xiandaihua de licheng* (1901-1928) (The progress and modernization of Chinese police organization in the late Qing and early Republican eras, 1901-1928). Taibei: Commercial Press, 1984.

War Department. *Reports on Military Operations in South Africa and China.* Washing-ton: U.S. Government Printing Office, 1901.

War Office. *Manual of Military Law.* London: Her Majesty's Stationary Office, 1887.

Weale, B. L. Putnam [pseud. Bertram Lenox Simpson]. *Indiscreet Letters from Peking: Being the Notes of an Eye-witness, Which Set Forth in some Detail, from Day to Day, the Real Story of the Siege and Sack of a Distressed Capital in 1900, the Year of Great Tribulation.* London: Hurst and Blackett, 1907. Reprinted: New York: Arno Press & The New York Times, 1970.

Wen, Henry Leonidas (Wen Lingxiong). "Comparative Study of Municipal Structure and Activities in the United States and China." PhD diss., Indiana University, 1942.

Wetterwald, Albert. "Une armée chrétienne improvisée. Défense de Wei-tsuen. (Ex-traits du journal du P. A. Wetterwald)." *Études* 38e année, tome 86 (5 March 1901): 663-93; also published in Chine et Ceylan 2 (March 1901): 275-314.

Wheaton, Henry. *Elements of International Law.* Boston: Little, Brown and Co., 1863.

Wiest, Jean-Paul. "Catholic Images of the Boxers." *The American Asian Review* 9, no. 3 (1991): 41-66.

Wilgus, Mary H. *Sir Claude MacDonald, the Open Door, and British Informal Empire in China, 1895-1900.* New York: Garland Publishing, 1987.

Wilkinson, Endymion. *Chinese History: A Manual.* 2nd. ed. Cambridge: Harvard University Asia Center, 2000.

Willeke, Bernward H. *Imperial Government and Catholic Missions in China during the Years 1784-1785.* St. Bonaventure, N.Y.: Franciscan Institute, 1948.

Wilson, James H. *China.* 3rd ed. New York: D. Appleton and Co, 1901.

Wolseley, Garnet. *Narrative of the War With China in 1860.* 1862. Reprint edition, Wilmington, Del.: Scholarly Resources Inc., 1972.

Wood, Frances. *No Dogs and Not Many Chinese: Treaty Port Life, 1843-1943.* London: John Murray, 1998.

Wright, Mary Clabaugh, ed. *China in Revolution: The First Phase 1900-1913.* New Haven: Yale University Press, 1968.

Wu Huayuan, et al., comps. *Xu Tianjin xianzhi* [Renewed gazetteer of Tianjin County]. Tianjin, 1870.

Wu Tinghua, and Cheng Fengwen, comps. *Tianjin fuzhi* [Tianjin prefecture gazetteer]. Tianjin, 1739. Reprint, Taibei, 1971.

Wu Tingluan. "Yuci yihetuan yundong shimo" [The full story of the Yuci Boxers]. *Jinzhong shizhi ziliao* 12, no. 1 (1989).

Wu Xiangxiang. "Qing Dezong Shilu benji de zhengben" (On the original version of the *Veritable Records* of the Guangxu Period). *Dalu zazhi* (Taibei) 2, no. 12 (30 June 1951): 7-10.

——. "Gugong cang juanluan shiliao zhushi" [Notes on the archives concerning the Boxer Uprising kept in the Palace Museum]. *Guoli Zhongyang yanjiuyuan Lishi yuyan yanjiusuo jikan* 23 (1951): 161-98.

Xiang Lanxin. *The Origins of the Boxer War: A Multinational Study.* London and New York: RoutledgeCurzon, 2003.

Xuxiu Juye xianzhi [Continuation of the Juye gazetteer]. Facsimile of the 1921 ed. Taibei: Chengwen chubanshe, 1967.

Yadav, K[ripal] C[handra], and K[rishan] S[ingh] Arya. *Arya Samaj and the Freedom Movement, Volume One: 1875-1918.* New Delhi: Manohar, 1988.

"Yamaguchi Motoomi." *Nihon jinmei daijiten,* vol. 6. Tokyo: Heibonsha, 1979.

"Yamaguchi Soshin no jihyō." *Yorozu Chōhō,* 21 February 1902.

Yamaizumi Susumu. "Ikioi to shinkaron." In *Seijigaku,* edited by Kataoka Hiromitsu. Tokyo: Seibundō, 1980.

Yamamoto Taketoshi. *Shimbun to minshū.* Tokyo: Kinokuniya shoten, 1978.

Yang Mushi. *Gengzi jiaoban quanfei dianwen lu* [Selected telegrams concerning the suppression of the Boxer bandits in 1900]. In *Yihetuan* 4:329-62.

Yang Tianhong. "Yihetuan 'shenshu' lunlüe" [A summary discussion of the "magical powers" of the Boxers]. *Jindaishi yanjiu* [Studies in modern Chinese history] 5 (1993): 189-204.

Yee, Frank Y. C. "Police in Modern China." PhD. diss., University of California, Berkeley, 1942.

Yihetuan yanjiuhui tongxun [The Boxer Study Association newsletter]. No. 25 (March 2001).

Yong Zheng [Yung Cheng]. "The Martyrdom at T'aiyuanfu on the 9th of July, 1900. By an Eye-witness." *North China Herald,* 3 April 1901, 637.

Yoshinami Takashi. "Shinshishi yorimita Shinsui shi kyo no suiri kangai" [Water utilization and irrigation through the four channels of the Jin river from reading the Jincizhi]. *Shigaku kenkyu* 170 (1986).

Yoshizawa Seiichiro. Kosho matsu Tenshin ni okeru junkei sosetsu to minshi (The establishment of police and the people in late Guangxu Tianjin). Master's thesis, Tokyo University, 1990.

Young, Ernest P. *The Presidency of Yuan Shih-k'ai: Liberalism and Dictatorship in Early Republican China.* Ann Arbor: University of Michigan Press, 1977.

Young, L. K. *British Policy in China, 1895-1902.* Oxford: Oxford University Press, 1970.

Young, Marilyn. *The Rhetoric of Empire: American China Policy, 1895-1901.* Cambridge, Mass.: Harvard University Press, 1968.

Young, Robert. *Colonial Desire.* London: Routledge, 1995.

Yuan Weishi. "Modernization and History Textbooks." *Bingdian* supplement, *Qingnian bao*, 11 January 2006.

Yuki Tanaka. *Hidden Horrors: Japanese War Crimes in World War II.* Oxford: Westview Press, 1998.

Yule, Henry, and A. C. Burnell. *Hobson Jobson.* 2nd. ed. Delhi: Munshiram Manoharlal, 1968.

Zhang Haipeng. "The Main Theme in Modern Chinese History Is Anti-Imperialism/Anti-Feudalism." *Bingdian* supplement, *Qingnian bao*, 1 March 2006.

Zhang Tao. *Jinmen zaji* [Notes on Tianjin]. Tianjin, 1884. Reprint, Taibei: Wenhai chubanshe, 1969.

Zhang Xiaobo, Merchant Associational Activism in Early Twentieth Century China: The Tianjin General Chamber of Commerce, 1904-1928. PhD diss., Columbia University, 1995.

Zhao Zhencheng. *Qingdai dili yange biao* [Successive geographic changes of the Qing period]. Beijing: Zhonghua shuju, 1955.

Zhongguo di yi lishi dang'anguan, and Fujian shifan daxue lishi xi, eds. *Qingmo jiao'an* [Late Qing religious cases]. Beijing: Zhonghua shuju, 1998.

Zhongyang yanjiuyuan jindaishi yanjiusuo, ed. *Jiaowu jiaoan dang* [Archives of religious affairs and cases], Series 4-6. Taibei: Zhongyang yanjiuyuan jindaishi yanjiusuo, 1976–1980.

Index

About the Contributors

C. A. Bayly is Vere Harmsworth Professor of Imperial History at the University of Cambridge and a Fellow of St. Catharine's College. He has specialized in Indian and British imperial history and has published *Rulers, Townsmen and Bazaars* (1983, Indian ed. 1992) and *Empire and Information* (1996). Most recently he has published *The Birth of the Modern World: 1780–1914* (2003) and, with Tim Harper, *Forgotten Armies: The Fall of British Asia* (2004) and *Forgotten Wars: The End of Britain's Asian Empire* (2007).

Lewis Bernstein has a Ph.D. from the University of Kansas. At present he is the United Nations Command/U.S.–Republic of Korea Combined Forces Command/U.S. Forces–Korea Command Historian in Seoul, Korea. He has published book reviews and articles in various journals, and is currently working on a manuscript about the effects of the Boxer rising and its aftermath on Tianjin.

Robert Bickers is professor of history, University of Bristol, and the author of *Britain in China: Community, Culture and Colonialism* (1999) and *Empire Made Me: An Englishman Adrift in Shanghai* (2003), and coeditor of *Missionary Encounters: Sources and Issues* (1996), with Rosemary Seton, and *New Frontiers: Imperialism's New Communities in East Asia, 1842–1957* (2000), with Christian Henriot. Current work includes a study of the Chinese treaty ports, a project exploring archives of pre-1949 photographs of China in Britain, and research on the history of the Chinese Maritime Customs Service.

Paul A. Cohen is Edith Stix Wasserman Professor of Asian Studies and History, emeritus, Wellesley College, and an associate at the Fairbank Center for

East Asian Research, Harvard University. His books include *Discovering History in China: American Historical Writing on the Recent Chinese Past* (1984), *History in Three Keys: The Boxers as Event, Experience, and Myth* (1997), and most recently *China Unbound: Evolving Perspectives on the Chinese Past* (2003). *History in Three Keys* was the winner of the 1997 New England Historical Association Book Award and the American Historical Association's 1997 John K. Fairbank Prize in East Asian History. Cohen is currently completing a book on the impact of the story of King Goujian of Yue (late Zhou) on twentieth-century China.

Henrietta Harrison, professor of history, Harvard University, works on Shanxi local history in the nineteenth and twentieth centuries and is the author of *The Making of the Republican Citizen: Ceremonies and Symbols in China, 1911–1929* (2000) and *The Man Awakened from Dreams: One Man's Life in a North China Village, 1857–1942* (2005).

James L. Hevia is director of the international studies program at the University of Chicago. His most recent work is *English Lessons: The Pedagogy of Imperialism in Nineteenth-Century China* (2005).

Ben Middleton is associate professor in the faculty of global studies at Ferris University, Yokohama. He is currently working on a manuscript analyzing the emergence of sociology as a discipline in Japan. He has published articles in Japanese on Meiji-era liberalism, socialism, and anti-imperialism, and has translated the first major Japanese anti-imperialist statement, Kōtoku Shūsui's *Imperialism: The Spectre of the Twentieth Century* (1901).

T. G. Otte teaches international history at the University of East Anglia. He is currently working on a major long-term study of British foreign policy, 1874–1914, which aims at offering a fresh, comprehensive analysis of the subject. His most recent book is *The China Question: Great Power Rivalry and British Isolation, 1894–1905* (2007).

Roger R. Thompson is associate professor and chair in the department of history at Western Washington University. His work on war and imperialism in China includes "Military Dimensions of the 'Boxer Uprising' in Shanxi, 1898–1901," which appeared in Hans van de Ven (ed.), *Warfare in Chinese History* (2000), and "Twilight of the Gods in the Chinese Countryside: Christians, Confucians, and the Modernizing State, 1861–1911," which appeared in Daniel H. Bays (ed.), *Christianity in China: From the Eighteenth Century to the Present* (1996).

R. G. Tiedemann is a senior research fellow at the Centre for the Study of Christianity in China (Oxford). His publications include "Christianity and

Chinese 'Heterodox Sects': Mass Conversion and Syncretism in Shandong Province in the Early Eighteenth Century," *Monumenta Serica* 44 (1996), 339–82. He is currently editing the *Handbook of Christianity in China, Volume Two: 1800 to the Present*, to be published by E. J. Brill, Leiden. In addition, he is a collaborator in "The Ricci 21st Century On-line Roundtable on the History of Christianity in China" at the Ricci Institute for Chinese-Western Cultural History, University of San Francisco (http://ricci.rt.usfca.edu).

Anand A. Yang is Golub Chair (professor) of International Studies and the director of the Jackson School of International Studies, University of Washington. His most recent book, *Bazaar India*, appeared in 1998. He is currently working on a book manuscript, *Empire of Convicts*, that relates the history of South Asian convicts who were banished to Southeast Asia in the eighteenth and nineteenth centuries. His forthcoming studies include an account of Chinese and Indian indentured laborers in various regions of the world and a translation/biography of an Indian soldier in China during the Boxer War.

The Boxers, China, and the World